Gregg
College

Keyboarding

ELECTRONIC

&Document
Processing

7th Edition

(formerly Gregg College Typing)

Intensive Course

Scot Ober, Ph.D.
Professor, Department of Business
Education and Office Administration
Ball State University
Muncie, Indiana

Robert P. Poland, Ph.D.
Professor Emeritus, Business and
Distributive Education
Michigan State University
East Lansing, Michigan

Robert N. Hanson, Ed.D.
Professor Emeritus, Department of
Office Systems and Business Education
Northern Michigan University
Marquette, Michigan

Albert D. Rossetti, Ed.D.
Dean, School of Business
Administration
Montclair State College
Montclair, New Jersey

Jack E. Johnson, Ph.D.
Professor, Department of
Administrative Systems and Business
Education, School of Business
West Georgia College
Carrollton, Georgia

GLENCOE

Macmillan/McGraw-Hill

New York, New York   Columbus, Ohio   Mission Hills, California   Peoria, Illinois

Gregg college keyboarding & electronic document processing. Intensive
course / Scot Ober . . . [et al.].—7th ed.
   p.   cm.—(Gregg college typing, series six)
"Formerly Gregg college typing."
Includes index.
ISBN 0-02-801740-4
   1. Word processing.   I. Ober, Scot, date.   II. Gregg college
typing.   III. Title: Gregg college keyboarding and electronic
document processing.   IV. Series.
Z52.4.G735 1994
652.5—dc20
                                                                93-44426
                                                                CIP

**Gregg College Keyboarding & Electronic Document Processing,
Intensive Course, 7th Edition**

Send all inquiries to:

GLENCOE DIVISION
Macmillan/McGraw-Hill
936 Eastwind Drive
Westerville, OH 43081

Contents

PART 1

PART 2

PRODUCTION ASSIGNMENTS

CORRESPONDENCE	TABLES/ FORMS	REPORTS
Letters 1–2		
Letters 3–4		
Letters 5–6		
Letters 7–9		
Letters 10–12		
		Report 1
		Reports 2–3
		Reports 4–5
		Reports 6–7
		Reports 8–9
	Tables 1–3	
	Tables 4–6	

PRODUCTION ASSIGNMENTS

INDEX

1-MINUTE TIMED WRITINGS

WAM	Page
8	3
10	5
12	6
13	8
14	9
15	11
16	12
17	14
18	16
19	18

2-MINUTE TIMED WRITINGS

WAM	Page
19	20
20	22
21	24
22	26
23	27
24	30
25	31
26	33
27	35
28	37

3-MINUTE TIMED WRITINGS

WAM	Page
30	42
30	46
32	49
32	55
32	60
33	65
34	70
35	74

35	79
36	83
36	85
38	90
38	95
39	102
39	107
39	112

5-MINUTE TIMED WRITINGS

WAM	Page
39	119
39	124
40	128
40	132
40	136
40	138
40	144
41	154
42	165
43	176
43	184
44	190
45	201
46	212
47	223
47	232
48	238
49	248
50	260
50	272
50	281
60	SB-19–
	SB-26

12-Second Sprints, 44, 54, 72, 80, 99, 109,
    120, 127, 142, 154, 164, 174, 189, 200,
    211, 223, 237, 247, 260, 271

Preface

Gregg College Keyboarding & Electronic Document Processing, 7th Edition, is a multicomponent instructional program designed to give the student and the instructor a high degree of flexibility and a high degree of success in meeting their respective goals. To facilitate the choice and use of materials, the core components of this teaching-learning program are available in either a kit format or a book format.

THE KIT FORMAT

Gregg College Keyboarding & Electronic Document Processing, 7th Edition, provides a complete kit of materials for each of the three courses in the keyboarding curriculum generally offered by colleges. Each kit, which is briefly described below, contains a softcover textbook with an easel back, working papers, and supplementary instructional materials.

The text in each kit contains 60 lessons, with each lesson requiring approximately 45–50 minutes of class time. The working papers provide a technique evaluation form, progress record sheets, stationery for use in completing the production jobs, and additional language arts and proofreading activities.

Kit 1: Basic. This kit provides the text and working papers for Lessons 1–60. Since this kit is designed for the beginning student, its major objectives are to develop touch control of the keyboard and proper keyboarding techniques; build basic speed and accuracy skill; and provide practice in applying those basic skills to the formatting of letters, reports, tables, memos, and other kinds of personal, personal-business, and business communication.

Kit 2: Intermediate. This kit includes the textbook and working papers for Lessons 61–120. This second course continues the development of basic keyboarding skills and empha-sizes the formatting of various kinds of business correspon-dence, reports, tables, and forms from unarranged and rough-draft sources.

Kit 3: Advanced. This kit, containing the text and working papers, which covers Lessons 121–180, is designed for the third semester. After a brief review of basic document process-ing techniques and an integrated office project in Part 7, stu-dents are placed in different office situations that emphasize such modern office skills as editing, decision making, abstract-ing information, setting priorities, maintaining a smooth work flow, following directions, and working under pressure and with interruptions.

Format Guides. A pad of self-check keys is available for each of the three kits to enable students to check the correct format of all documents processed.

THE BOOK FORMAT

For the convenience of those who wish to obtain the core in-structional materials in separate volumes, the *Gregg College Keyboarding & Electronic Document Processing, 7th Edition,* program offers the following textbooks, working papers, and self-check keys. In each instance, the content of these compo-nents is identical with that of the corresponding part or parts in the kit format.

Textbooks. *Gregg College Keyboarding & Electronic Docu-ment Processing, Intensive Course, 7th Edition,* contains Les-sons 1–120. The content and objectives of this two-semester hardcover text exactly match the content and objectives of the softcover textbooks in the *Basic* and *Intermediate* kits.

Working Papers. The *Working Papers* for each semester's work are available separately for use with the *Intensive* and *Complete* hardcover texts. These three components are identi-cal in content and purpose with those in the kits.

Format Guides. These self-check keys of formatted docu-ments are also available for use with the *Intensive* and *Com-plete* hardcover texts.

SUPPORTING MATERIALS

The *Gregg College Keyboarding & Electronic Document Process-ing, 7th Edition,* program includes these additional compo-nents. The special materials provided for the instructor can be used with either the *Gregg College Keyboarding & Electronic Document Processing, 7th Edition,* kits or the hardcover text-books. These special materials include the following:

Instructor's Editions. A separate *Instructor's Edition* is available for each of the three courses. Each *Instructor's Edi-tion* contains annotated student pages and solution keys for all of the formatting exercises.

Instructor's Manual. This separate *Instructor's Manual* contains teaching and grading suggestions.

ACKNOWLEDGMENTS

We wish to express our appreciation to all the instructors and students who have used the previous editions and who have contributed much to this 7th Edition.

The Authors

Reference Section

MICROCOMPUTER SYSTEM

CORRESPONDENCE

REPORTS

EMPLOYMENT DOCUMENTS

TABLES AND FORMS

MISCELLANEOUS

LANGUAGE ARTS

THE COMPUTER KEYBOARD

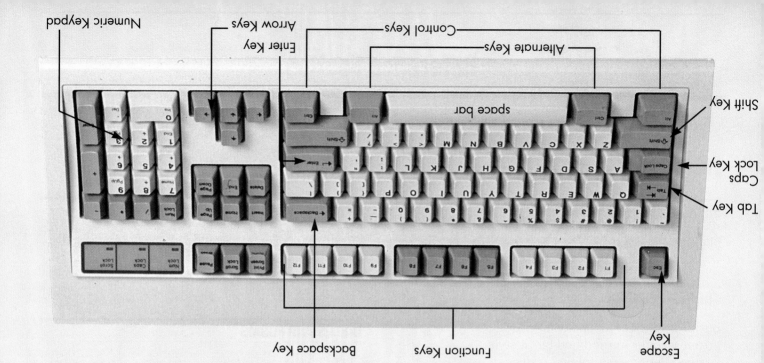

Numeric Keypad

Arrow Keys

Enter Key

Control Keys

Alternate Keys

space bar

Shift Key

Caps Lock Key

Tab Key

Escape Key

Function Keys

Backspace Key

MAJOR PARTS OF A MICROCOMPUTER SYSTEM

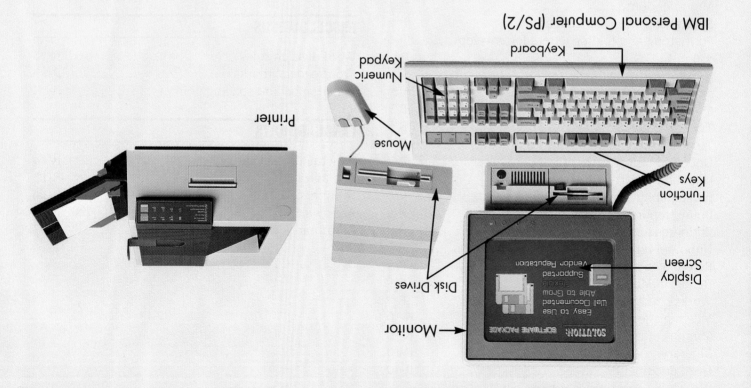

IBM Personal Computer (PS/2)

Keyboard

Numeric Keypad

Mouse

Printer

Function Keys

Disk Drives

Monitor

Display Screen

SOLUTION!
SOFTWARE PACKAGE
Easy to Use
Well Documented
Able to Grow
Flexible
Supported
vendor Reputation

AMERICAN HOMES, INC.

One Southeast Financial Center, Miami, FL 33131-3213   Phone: 305-555-7500 • FAX 305-555-7600

↓ 2 inches
September 5, 19--   ↓ 1 inch

Ms. Joan R. Hunter
Bolwater Associates
One Parklands Drive
Darien, CT 06820-3214   ↓ 2

Dear Ms. Hunter   ↓ 2

I am returning a signed contract to have your organization conduct a one-day workshop for our employees on eliminating repetitive-motion injuries in the workplace. I understand that this workshop will be applicable for both our office and construction workers.

To enhance the quality and relevance of the workshop, we have made the following changes to the contract:

0.4 →   1. We revised Paragraph 4-b to require that the instructor for this workshop be a full-time employee of Bolwater Associates.
inch   2. We added Paragraph 10-c to require our prior approval of the syllabus for the workshop.

If these revisions are satisfactory, please sign and return one copy of the contract for our files. We look forward to this opportunity to enhance the health and well-being of our employees.   ↓ 2

Sincerely   ↓ 4

John R. Merritt
John R. Merritt, Director
Human Resources Department   ↓ 2

jem
Enclosure
c: Legal Department

BUSINESS LETTER IN BLOCK STYLE
(open punctuation)

AMERICAN HOMES, INC.

One Southeast Financial Center, Miami, FL 33131-3213   Phone: 305-555-7500 • FAX 305-555-7600

↓ 2 inches
Center →   September 5, 19--   ↓ 1 inch

Ms. Joan R. Hunter
Bolwater Associates
One Parklands Drive
Darien, CT 06820-3214   ↓ 2

Dear Ms. Hunter: ↓ 2

0.5 →   I am returning a signed contract to have your organization
inch   conduct a one-day workshop for our employees on eliminating repet-itive-motion injuries in the workplace. I understand that this workshop will be applicable for both our office and construction workers.

To enhance the quality and relevance of the workshop, we have made the following changes to the contract:

1. We revised Paragraph 4-b to require that the instructor for this workshop be a full-time employee of Bolwater
0.9 →   Associates.
inch   2. We added Paragraph 10-c to require our prior approval of the syllabus for the workshop.

If these revisions are satisfactory, please sign and return one copy of the contract for our files. We look forward to this opportunity to enhance the health and well-being of our employees.   ↓ 2

Center →   Sincerely,   ↓ 4
John R. Merritt
John R. Merritt, Director
Human Resources Department   ↓ 2

jem
Enclosure
c: Legal Department

BUSINESS LETTER IN MODIFIED-BLOCK STYLE
(standard punctuation; indented paragraphs)

[handwritten notes: "Mixed", "not indented", "Left Blocked Common"]

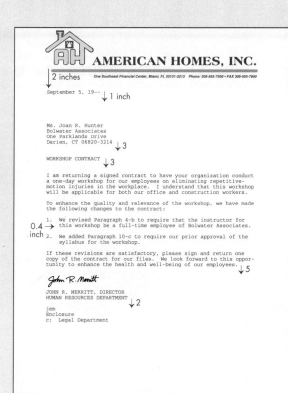

AMERICAN HOMES, INC.

One Southeast Financial Center, Miami, FL 33131-3213   Phone: 305-555-7500 • FAX 305-555-7600

↓ 2 inches
September 5, 19--   ↓ 1 inch

Ms. Joan R. Hunter
Bolwater Associates
One Parklands Drive
Darien, CT 06820-3214   ↓ 3

WORKSHOP CONTRACT   ↓ 3

I am returning a signed contract to have your organization conduct a one-day workshop for our employees on eliminating repetitive-motion injuries in the workplace. I understand that this workshop will be applicable for both our office and construction workers.

To enhance the quality and relevance of the workshop, we have made the following changes to the contract:

1. We revised Paragraph 4-b to require that the instructor for this workshop be a full-time employee of Bolwater Associates.
0.4 →   2. We added Paragraph 10-c to require our prior approval of the
inch   syllabus for the workshop.

If these revisions are satisfactory, please sign and return one copy of the contract for our files. We look forward to this opportunity to enhance the health and well-being of our employees.   ↓ 5

John R. Merritt
JOHN R. MERRITT, DIRECTOR
HUMAN RESOURCES DEPARTMENT   ↓ 2

jem
Enclosure
c: Legal Department

BUSINESS LETTER IN SIMPLIFIED STYLE

↓ 2 inches
Center →   January 3, 19--   ↓ 1 inch

Mr. Luis Fernandez, Manager
Customer Relations Department
Arvon Industries, Inc.
1000 Ashland Drive
Russell, KY 41169   ↓ 2

Dear Mr. Fernandez: ↓ 2

As a former employee and present stockholder of Arvon Industries, I wish to protest the planned sale of the Consumer Products Division to Browning Manufacturing Company.

According to published reports, consumer products accounted for 19 percent of last year's corporate profits, and they are expected to account for at least as much this year. In addition, Dun & Brad-street predicts that consumer products nationwide will outpace the general economy for the next five years.

I am concerned about the effect the planned sale of this division will have on overall corporate profits, on cash dividends for investors, and on the economics of Louisville and Paducah, where the two consumer-products plants are located.

Please ask your board of directors to reconsider this matter.   ↓ 2

Center →   Sincerely,   ↓ 4
Roger J. Michaelson
Roger J. Michaelson
901 East Benson, Apt. 3
Ft. Lauderdale, FL 33301

PERSONAL-BUSINESS LETTER
(modified-block style; standard punctuation)

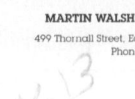

MARTIN WALSH & MEREDITH
499 Thornall Street, Edison, NJ 08818
Phone: 201-555-8000

↓ 2 inches
July 18, 19--   ↓ 1 inch   *line 13*

Mr. Rodney Eastwood
BBL Resources
52A Northern Ridge
Mt. Stuart, Tasmania 7000
AUSTRALIA ↓ 2

Dear Rodney: ↓ 2

I see no reason why we should continue to consider the
locality around Geraldton for our new refinery. Even
though the desirability of this site from an economic
point of view is undeniable, there is insufficient
housing readily available for those workers whom we
would have to transfer.

In trying to control urban growth, the city has either
been turning down building permits for new housing or
placing so many restrictions on foreign investment as
to make it too expensive to build.

Please continue to seek out other areas of exploration
where we might form a joint partnership.

Sincerely,
↓ 4

Arlyn J. Bunch
Vice President of Operations ↓ 2

lem
By Fax

Petroleum Exploration and Refining

BUSINESS LETTER ON MONARCH STATIONERY
(1-inch side margins; 7¼" × 10½")

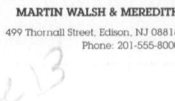

MARTIN WALSH & MEREDITH
499 Thornall Street, Edison, NJ 08818
Phone: 201-555-8000

↓ 2 inches
July 18, 19-- ↓ 4

Mr. Rodney Eastwood
BBL Resources
52A Northern Ridge
Mt. Stuart, Tasmania 7000
AUSTRALIA ↓ 2

Dear Rodney: ↓ 2

I do not believe we should continue to
consider Geraldton for our new refinery.
There is insufficient housing for those
workers whom we would have to transfer;
and in trying to control urban growth,
the city has placed so many restrictions
on foreign investment as to make it too
expensive to build.

Please continue to seek out other areas
of exploration where we might form a
joint partnership.

Sincerely, ↓ 4

Arlyn J. Bunch
Vice President of Operations ↓ 2

lem

Petroleum Exploration and Refining

BUSINESS LETTER ON BARONIAL STATIONERY
(0.75-inch side margins; 5½" × 8½")

MARTIN WALSH & MEREDITH
499 Thornall Street, Edison, NJ 08818
Phone: 201-555-8000

↓ 2 inches
July 18, 19-- ↓ 3

Mr. Rodney Eastwood
BBL Resources
52A Northern Ridge
Mt. Stuart, Tasmania 7000
AUSTRALIA ↓ 3

Dear Rodney: ↓ 2

I see no reason why we should continue to consider the locality
around Geraldton for our new refinery. Even though the desirability of this site from an economic point of view is undeniable,
there is insufficient housing readily available for those workers
whom we would have to transfer.

In trying to control urban growth, the city has either been turning down building permits for new housing or placing so many restrictions on foreign investment as to make it too expensive to
build.

Please continue to seek out other areas of exploration where we
might form a joint partnership.

Sincerely, ↓ 4

Arlyn J. Bunch
Vice President of Operations ↓ 2

lem
Enclosure ↓ 2

PS: I thought you might enjoy the enclosed article from a recent
Forbes magazine on the latest misfortunes of one of your major competitors.

Petroleum Exploration and Refining

**BUSINESS LETTER FORMATTED FOR A WINDOW
ENVELOPE**

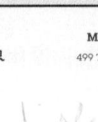

MARTIN WALSH & MEREDITH
499 Thornall Street, Edison, NJ 08818
Phone: 201-555-8000

↓ 2 inches   *line 13*

MEMO TO: Nancy Price, Executive Vice President

FROM: Arlyn J. Bunch, Operations *AJB*

DATE: July 18, 19--

SUBJECT: New Refinery Site ↓ 3

As you can see from the attached letter, I've informed BBL Resources that I see no reason why we should continue to consider the
locality around Geraldton, Australia, for our new refinery. Even
though the desirability of this site from an economic standpoint is
undeniable, there is insufficient housing readily available for
those workers whom we would have to transfer. As of July 3, the
number of appropriate single-family homes listed for sale by real-
estate agents within a 25-mile radius of Geraldton was as follows: ↓ 2

Agency	No.
Castleton Homes	123
Belle Real Estate	5
Red Carpet	11
Geraldton Sales	9
	148

↓ 2

In addition, in trying to control urban growth, Geraldton has either been turning down building permits for new housing or placing
so many restrictions on foreign investment as to make it too expensive for us to consider building housing ourselves.

Because of this deficiency of housing for our employees, we have no
choice but to look elsewhere. ↓ 2

lem
Attachment

Petroleum Exploration and Refining

MEMORANDUM

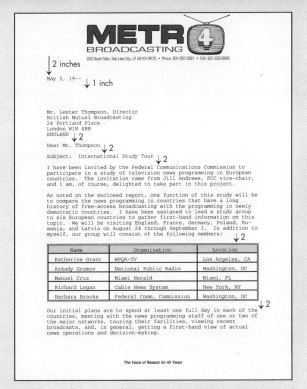

METRO 4 BROADCASTING
200 South Main, Salt Lake City, UT 84101-8675 • Phone: 801-555-3997 • FAX: 801-555-3998

↓ 2 inches

May 5, 19-- ↓ 1 inch

Mr. Lester Thompson, Director
British Mutual Broadcasting
24 Portland Place
London W1N 4BB
ENGLAND ↓ 2

Dear Mr. Thompson ↓ 2

Subject: International Study Tour ↓ 2

I have been invited by the Federal Communications Commission to participate in a study of television news programming in European countries. The invitation came from Jill Andrews, FCC vice-chair, and I am, of course, delighted to take part in this project.

As noted on the enclosed report, one function of this study will be to compare the news programming in countries that have a long history of free-access broadcasting with the programming in newly democratic countries. I have been assigned to lead a study group to six European countries to gather first-hand information on this topic. We will be visiting England, France, Germany, Poland, Rumania, and Latvia on August 24 through September 3. In addition to myself, our group will consist of the following members: ↓ 2

Name	Organization	Location
Katherine Grant	WPQR-TV	Los Angeles, CA
Arkady Gromov	National Public Radio	Washington, DC
Manuel Cruz	Miami Herald	Miami, FL
Richard Logan	Cable News System	New York, NY
Barbara Brooks	Federal Comm. Commission	Washington, DC

↓ 2

Our initial plans are to spend at least one full day in each of the countries, meeting with the news programming staff of one or two of the major networks, touring their facilities, viewing recent broadcasts, and, in general, getting a first-hand view of actual news operations and decision-making.

The Voice of Reason for 45 Years

↓ 1 inch
Mr. Lester Thompson
Page 2
May 5, 19--

Our tentative itinerary calls for us to arrive at Heathrow Airport at 7:10 p.m. on Tuesday evening, August 27. Would it be possible for us to do the following: ↓ 2

1. Meet with various members of your staff on August 28. We would be available from 8:30 a.m. until 1:30 p.m. ↓ 2

0.4 inch → 2. Receive a copy of your programming log for the week of August 26-30 and especially a minute-by-minute listing of the programming segments for your national news reporting. ↓ 2

I would appreciate your contacting Barbara Brooks, our liaison at the Federal Communications Commission (1919 M Street, NW, Washington, DC 20554; phone: 202-555-3894), to let us know whether we may study your operations on August 28.

So that we can finalize our plans and make the necessary arrangements, may we please hear from you by May 15. If your decision is positive, I will work directly with you in coordinating the details of our visit.

Sincerely ↓ 2

METRO BROADCASTING ↓ 4

Denise J. Watterson

Denise J. Watterson
General Manager ↓ 2

urs
Enclosure: FCC Report
By International Express Mail
c: Barbara Brooks ↓ 2

PS: The Federal Communication Commission will reimburse your organization for any expenses associated with our visit, including phone calls, duplicating, and the like.

SPECIAL CORRESPONDENCE FEATURES

FOREIGN ADDRESS. Key the name of a foreign country in all capital letters on a line by itself.

SUBJECT LINE. If used, key a subject line in upper- and lowercase letters below the salutation, with 1 blank line above and below; the terms *Re:* or *In re:* may also be used.

TABLE. Leave 1 blank line above and below a table without a title (regardless of whether the table has column headings) and 3 blank lines above and below a table with a title.

MULTI-PAGE LETTERS. Key the first page on letterhead stationery and the second page on matching plain stationery. On the second page, key the addressee's name, page number, and date beginning 1 inch from the top, blocked at the left margin. Leave 1 blank line between the page-2 heading and the first line of the body.

ENUMERATION. Key the number followed by a period at the point where paragraphs begin (the left margin for blocked paragraphs or indented 0.5 inch for indented paragraphs). Leave 2 spaces after the number and period and indent turnover lines 0.4 inch. Single-space the items within an enumeration and double-space between items.

COMPANY NAME IN CLOSING LINES. If included, key the company name in all capital letters below the complimentary closing, with 1 blank line above and 3 blank lines below it.

REFERENCE INITIALS. Key only the keyboarder's initials (not the signer's) in lowercase letters a double space below the writer's name and/or title. (Optional: You may also include the computer filename; for example: *urs/SMITH.LET*).

ENCLOSURE NOTATION. Key an enclosure notation a single space below the reference initials if an item is enclosed with a letter. Use the term "Attachment" if an item is attached to a memo instead of enclosed in an envelope. Examples: *3 Enclosures, Enclosure: Contract, Attachment.*

DELIVERY NOTATION. Key a delivery notation a single space below the enclosure notation. Examples: *By Certified Mail, By Fax, By Federal Express.*

COPY NOTATION. Key a copy notation *(c:)* a single space below the delivery notation if someone other than the addressee is to receive a copy of the message.

POSTSCRIPT NOTATION. Key a postscript notation as the last item, preceded by 1 blank line. Indent the first line of the postscript if the paragraphs in the body are indented.

FORMATTING ENVELOPES

A standard large (No. 10) envelope is 9¹/₂ by 4¹/₈ inches. A standard small (No. 6³/₄) envelope is 6¹/₂ by 3⁵/₈ inches. Although either address format shown below is acceptable, the format shown for the large envelope (all capital letters and no punctuation) is recommended by the U.S. Postal Service for mail that will be sorted by an electronic scanning device.

Window envelopes are often used in a word processing environment because of the difficulty of aligning envelopes correctly in some printers. A window envelope requires no formatting, since the letter is formatted and folded so that the inside address is visible through the window.

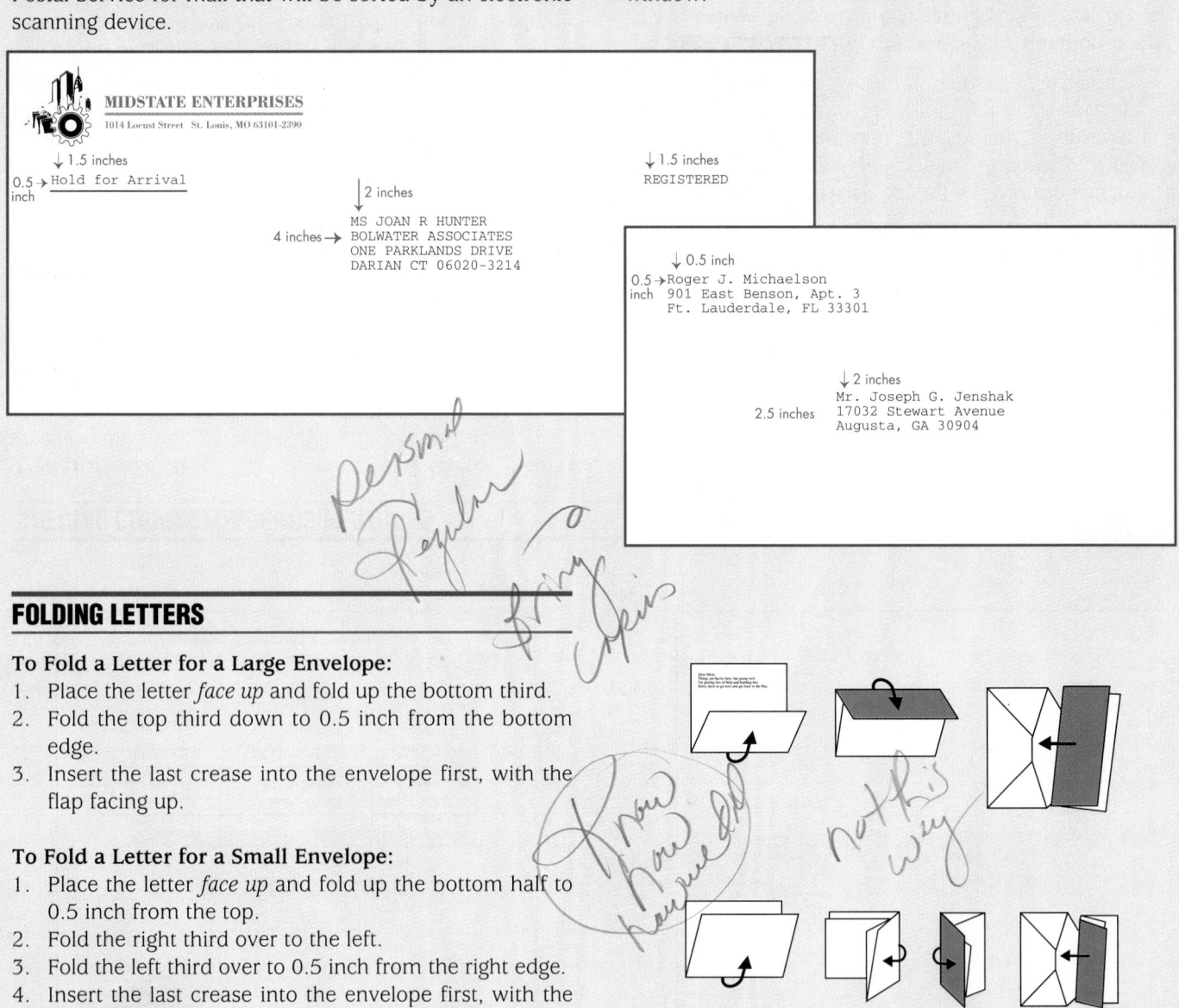

FOLDING LETTERS

To Fold a Letter for a Large Envelope:
1. Place the letter *face up* and fold up the bottom third.
2. Fold the top third down to 0.5 inch from the bottom edge.
3. Insert the last crease into the envelope first, with the flap facing up.

To Fold a Letter for a Small Envelope:
1. Place the letter *face up* and fold up the bottom half to 0.5 inch from the top.
2. Fold the right third over to the left.
3. Fold the left third over to 0.5 inch from the right edge.
4. Insert the last crease into the envelope first, with the flap facing up.

To Fold a Letter for a Window Envelope:
1. Place the letter *face down* with the letterhead at the top and fold the bottom third of the letter up.
2. Fold the top third down so that the address shows.
3. Insert the letter into the envelope so that the address shows through the window.

OUTLINE

↓ 2 inches

THE FEASIBILITY OF IN-HOUSE MANUFACTURING

OF NAIL-POLISH LACQUERS ↓3

   I.   INTRODUCTION ↓2

0.6 →   A.   Statement of the Problem
inch   B.   Scope
        C.   Procedures
        D.   Organization of the Report ↓3

  II.   FINDINGS ↓2

        A.   Current Manufacturing Processes
1.0 →   1.   Contract Manufacturing
inch   2.   In-House Manufacturing
        B.   Market Differentiation
           1.   Image Advertising
           2.   Product Characteristics
           3.   Manufacturing Control
        C.   Advantages and Disadvantages ↓3

 III.   CONCLUSIONS ↓2

        A.   Summary of Findings
        B.   Conclusions and Recommendations

OUTLINE

TITLE PAGE

(Equal top and bottom margins)

CONSOLIDATION OF THE PARTS WAREHOUSES AT ↓2

SIOUX CITY AND CEDAR FALLS ↓2

Maintaining Profitability in a Declining Market ↓15

Prepared by ↓2

Catherine Rogers-Busch
Chief Product Engineer
Helene Ponds and Associates ↓15

December 3, 19--

(Equal top and bottom margins)

TITLE PAGE

TABLE OF CONTENTS

↓ 2 inches

CONTENTS ↓3

TABLE OF CONTENTS

UNBOUND REPORT (first page)

↓ 2 inches

PREPARING FORMAL REPORTS ↓2

Formatting Guidelines for Writers ↓2

By Keith Stallings ↓3

    Formatting formal reports is not a difficult task if you just take the time to study the technical aspects involved. This report discusses report headings, page numbers, margins, reference citations, and the bibliography.

Headings

    The major heading in a report is the title. It should be centered in all capital letters 2 inches from the top. A subtitle or byline, if used, is keyed in initial capital letters a double space below the title. The body of the report begins on the third line below the title or byline.

    Side Headings. A side heading (such as "Page Numbering" shown below) is keyed at the left margin in initial capital letters and in bold, with double-spacing before and after it.

    Paragraph Headings. A paragraph heading is indented and keyed in initial capital letters and in bold a double space below the preceding paragraph. The paragraph heading is followed by a period and two spaces, with the text beginning on the same line.

Page Numbering

    The first page of the body of a report is counted as page 1 but is not numbered. All other pages are numbered flush right at the top margin, with the first line of the text beginning a double

UNBOUND REPORT (first page)

↓ 1 inch
₂ ↓2

a real-estate agent from Central Michigan/Tucker Realty, provided a
copy of selected reports that are available only to real estate
agents.[1] The relevant statistics for the Mt. Rainey school district for those homes selling for $60,000 or more during the past
year are shown in Table 2. ↓4

TABLE 2. MT. RAINEY HOME SALES FOR $60,000 OR MORE

Jan-Dec 19--

Selling Price	No. of Homes	Days Listed	Average Sq. Ft.
$60,000-$79,999	55	145	1,571
$80,000-$99,999	29	81	1,917
$100,000-$149,999	7	105	2,094
$120,000-$149,999	8	85	2,291
$150,000 or more	6	109	2,659

↓4

The data reflected in Table 2 are based on used homes, so
comparisons to newly constructed homes are not always appropriate.
According to one source, the typical residential community offers
fewer new homes than resales, new homes sell faster, and they
average about 20 percent larger than resales.[2] ↓2

Young Family ↓2

The young family submarket is moving from rental or otherwise
limited accommodations into their first new home. The mobile-home ↓1

[1]Jacqueline Miller, *Residential Real Estate: Central Michigan
Edition*, Michigan Real Estate Association, Lansing, Michigan, 1994,
pp. 216-224. ↓2

[2]Benjamin J. Ashley, "New Sales Versus Resales: Apples to
Oranges?" *Real Estate Quarterly*, September 1993, p.143.

UNBOUND REPORT WITH FOOTNOTES (second page)

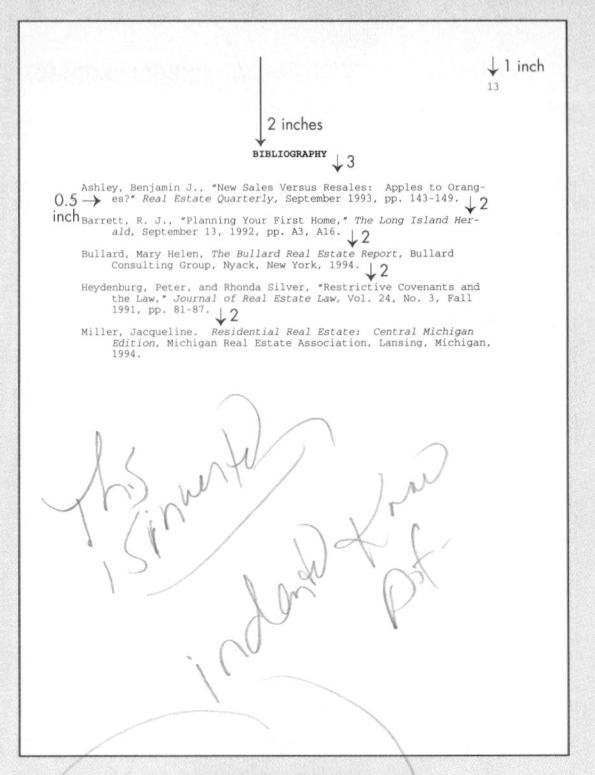

↓ 1 inch
₁₃

2 inches

BIBLIOGRAPHY ↓3

0.5 inch → Ashley, Benjamin J., "New Sales Versus Resales: Apples to Oranges?" *Real Estate Quarterly*, September 1993, pp. 143-149. ↓2

Barrett, R. J., "Planning Your First Home," *The Long Island Herald*, September 13, 1992, pp. A3, A16. ↓2

Bullard, Mary Helen, *The Bullard Real Estate Report*, Bullard
Consulting Group, Nyack, New York, 1994. ↓2

Heydenburg, Peter, and Rhonda Silver, "Restrictive Covenants and
the Law," *Journal of Real Estate Law*, Vol. 24, No. 3, Fall
1991, pp. 81-87. ↓2

Miller, Jacqueline. *Residential Real Estate: Central Michigan
Edition*, Michigan Real Estate Association, Lansing, Michigan,
1994.

BIBLIOGRAPHY FOR UNBOUND REPORT

↓ 1 inch
₃ ↓2

1.5 inches → product was eliminated as an option for this submarket because of the numerous developments of this type that already
exist or are under construction in the area.[1]

Modular homes, which have been partially constructed
before being brought to the building site, were likewise rejected because: ↓2

0.5 inch → Contrary to popular belief, modular homes are generally not less expensive than conventionally con- ← 0.5 inch
structed homes. Their advantage, instead, is the
speed with which they can be constructed. Their
major disadvantage relates to the restrictions often placed on them by municipal zoning ordinances.[2] ↓2

Since the River Road development is not subject to time
pressures, conventional construction methods were evaluated as
the most appropriate for this submarket.

Most of the homes sold in Mt. Rainey contain at least
three bedrooms, but in the lowest price bracket most contain
less than 1,600 square feet, as shown below. ↓2

Selling Price	No. of Homes	Days Listed	Average Sq. Ft.
$60,000-$79,999	55	145	1,571
$80,000-$99,999	29	81	1,917
$100,000-$119,999	7	105	2,094
$120,000-$149,999	8	85	2,291
$150,000 or more	6	109	2,659

↓2

Because several planning experts have noted the importance of overall outside dimensions for first-time home
buyers,[3] the home plan selected for this submarket is only 37
feet wide, allowing it to be placed on a 67-foot-wide lot,
with ample setback from the lot lines both from a zoning
standpoint and from an aesthetic point of view.

BOUND REPORT WITH ENDNOTES (third page)

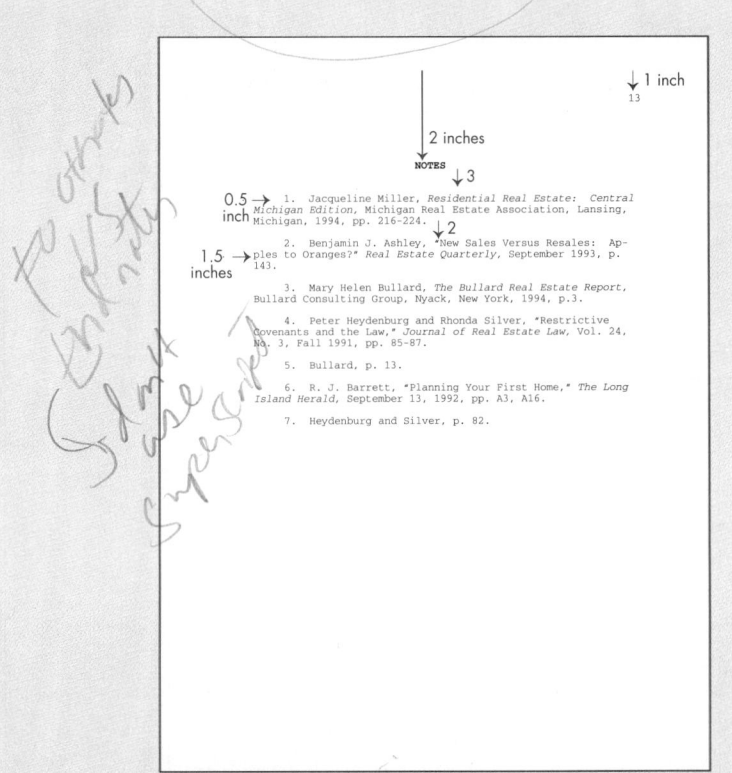

↓ 1 inch
₁₃

2 inches

NOTES ↓3

0.5 inch → 1. Jacqueline Miller, *Residential Real Estate: Central
Michigan Edition*, Michigan Real Estate Association, Lansing,
Michigan, 1994, pp. 216-224. ↓2

1.5 inches → 2. Benjamin J. Ashley, "New Sales Versus Resales: Apples to Oranges?" *Real Estate Quarterly*, September 1993, p.
143.

3. Mary Helen Bullard, *The Bullard Real Estate Report*,
Bullard Consulting Group, Nyack, New York, 1994, p.3.

4. Peter Heydenburg and Rhonda Silver, "Restrictive
Covenants and the Law," *Journal of Real Estate Law*, Vol. 24,
No. 3, Fall 1991, pp. 85-87.

5. Bullard, p. 13.

6. R. J. Barrett, "Planning Your First Home," *The Long
Island Herald*, September 13, 1992, pp. A3, A16.

7. Heydenburg and Silver, p. 82.

ENDNOTES FOR BOUND REPORT

UNBOUND REPORT WITH AUTHOR/DATE CITATIONS

↓ 1 inch
3
↓ 2

product was eliminated as an option for this submarket because, as Bullard (1994) has noted, numerous developments of this type already exist or are under construction in the area.

Modular homes, which have been partially constructed before being brought to the building site, were likewise rejected for the following reasons (Modlin, 1994, p. 232): ↓ 2

0.9 inch → 1. Contrary to popular belief, modular homes are generally not less expensive than conventionally constructed homes. ↓ 2

2. Zoning regulations and restrictive covenants often forbid the construction of modular homes, especially in upscale areas. ↓ 2

The big advantage of modular homes is the speed with which they can be constructed. However, since the River Road development is not subject to time pressures, conventional construction methods were evaluated as the most appropriate for this submarket.

Home Requirements. Based on current mortgage criteria in the Mount Rainey area, a buyer in this submarket cannot afford more than $70,000 for a home. Since family size is still small (fewer than four family members), a 1,250-square-foot model with one full bath on each level was selected for planning purposes.

Lot Requirements. Because several planning experts have noted the importance of overall outside dimensions for first-time home buyers (see, for example, Barrett, 1992; Heydenburg and Silver, 1994), the home plan selected for this submarket is only 37 feet wide, which allows it to be located on a 67-foot-wide lot with ample setback from the lot lines.

(handwritten note: "how spaces etc.")

REFERENCES PAGE IN APA FORMAT

↓ 1 inch
13

↓ 2 inches

REFERENCES ↓ 3

0.5 inch →
Connor, E. (1994, June). Body Language Cues. *Management Today*, pp. 250-261. ↓ 2

LePoole, A. (1988). *Your Tour of Duty Overseas* (2nd ed.). Oklahoma City: American Press.

LePoole, A. (1990). *What American Business Can (and Must) Learn From the Japanese*. New York: Management Press.

Newby, C. J. (1994). Global Implications for American Business: The Numbers Don't Lie. *Marketing Research Quarterly*, 50, 90-215.

Roncaro, P. L. & Lance, G. D. (1992, June 2). Losing Something in the Translation. *Winston-Salem Herald*, pp. 4A, 12A.

Tell It Like It Is: Making Yourself Understood in the New Russia. (1993, October 19). *International Times*, p. 38.

REPORT IN MLA FORMAT

↓ 0.5 inch
Jenson 1

↓ 1 inch
Sherlon Jenson ↓ 2
Professor Zhao
Comm 201
8 October 19-- ↓ 2

Communication Skills Needed in International Business

International business plays an increasingly important role in the U.S. economy, and U.S. companies recognize that to be competitive nationally, they must be competitive internationally. Reflecting this trend, direct investment by U.S. private enterprises in foreign countries increased from $309 billion in 1987 to $415 billion in 1991, an increase of 34 percent in four years (Connor 253). Today, more than 3,000 U.S. corporations have over 25,000 subsidiaries and affiliates in 125 foreign countries, and more than 25,000 American firms are engaged in international marketing (Newby 193, 205).

International business is highly dependent on communication. According to Arnold LePoole, chief executive officer of Armstrand Industries, an international supplier of automotive parts:

1.0 inch → If a company cannot communicate with its foreign subsidiaries, customers, suppliers, and governments, it cannot achieve success. And the sad fact is that most American managers are ill-equipped to communicate with their international counterparts. (143-144).

Because competent business communication skills are one of the most important components for success in international business affairs, a survey was designed to explore the importance of, level of competence in, and methods of developing four types of

WORKS-CITED PAGE IN MLA FORMAT

↓ 0.5 inch
Jenson 13

↓ 1 inch
Works Cited ↓ 2

0.5 inch →
Connor, Earl. "Body Language Cues." *Management Today* June 1994: 250-261. ↓ 2

LePoole, Arnold. *What American Business Can (and Must) Learn From the Japanese*. New York: Management Press, 1990.

---. *Your Tour of Duty Overseas*. 2nd ed. Oklahoma City: American Press, 1988.

Newby, Corrine J. "Global Implications for American Business: The Numbers Don't Lie." *Marketing Research Quarterly* 50 (1994): 190-215.

Roncaro, Paul L., and Glenn D. Lance. "Losing Something in the Translation," *Winston-Salem Herald* 2 June 1992: 4A+.

"Tell It Like It Is: Making Yourself Understood in the New Russia." *International Times* 19 October 1993: 38.

ITINERARY

PORTLAND SALES MEETING
Itinerary for Arlene Gladsdorf
March 12-15, 19—

Thursday, March 12

Detroit/Minneapolis   Northwest 83
Leave 5:10 p.m.; arrive 5:55 p.m.
Seat 8D; nonstop

Minneapolis/Portland   Northwest 2363
Leave 6:30 p.m.; arrive 8:06 p.m.
Seat 15C; nonstop; dinner

Sunday, March 15

Portland/Minneapolis   Northwest 360
Leave 7:30 a.m.; arrive 12:26 p.m.
Seat 15H; one stop; breakfast

Minneapolis/Detroit   Northwest 748
Leave 1 p.m.; arrive 3:32 p.m.
Seat 10D; nonstop; snack

NOTES

1. Jack Weatherford, assistant western regional manager, will meet your flight on Thursday and return you to the airport on Sunday.
2. All seat assignments are aisle seats; smoking is not allowed on any of the flights.
3. A single-room reservation (Reservation 36812-0), guaranteed for late arrival, has been made at the Airport Sheraton for March 12-14.
4. Important phone numbers:
   Jack Weatherford   503-555-8029, Ext. 87
   Airport Sheraton   503-555-4032
   Northwest Reservations   800-555-1289

LEGAL DOCUMENT

POWER OF ATTORNEY

KNOW ALL MEN BY THESE PRESENTS that I, ANTHONY LEE FERNANDEZ, of the City of Tulia, County of Swisher, State of Texas, do hereby appoint my son, Robert Fernandez, of this City, County, and State as my attorney-in-fact to act in my name, place, and stead as my agent in the management of my real estate transactions, chattel, and goods transactions, banking and securities transactions, and business operating transactions.

I give and grant unto my said attorney full power and authority to do and perform all and every act and thing whatsoever requisite and necessary to be done in the said management as fully, to all intents and purposes, as I might or could do if personally present, with full power of revocation, hereby ratifying and confirming all that my said attorney lawfully do or shall cause to be done in my behalf by virtue hereof.

IN WITNESS WHEREOF, I have hereunto set my hand and seal this thirteenth day of April, 1994.

————————————— (L.S.)

SIGNED and affirmed in the presence of:

—————————————

—————————————

Page 1 of 1

MEETING AGENDA

BUCK HARDWARE EXECUTIVE COMMITTEE
Meeting Agenda
June 7, 19—, 3 p.m.

1. Call to order
2. Approval of minutes of May 5 meeting
3. Progress report on building addition and parking lot (Norman Hedges)
4. Unfinished business:
   a. May 15 draft of Five-Year Plan
   b. Review of National Hardware Association annual convention
5. New business:
   a. Employee grievance filed by Ellen Burrows (John Lennon)
   b. New expense-report forms (Anne Richards)
   c. Home office visit by Jay Nelson
6. Announcements
7. Program: "The One-Second Manager" (30-minute videotape)
8. Adjournment

MINUTES OF MEETING

RESOURCE COMMITTEE
Minutes of the Meeting
March 13, 19—

ATTENDANCE

The Resource Committee met on March 13, 19—, at the Airport Sheraton in Portland, Oregon, in conjunction with the western regional meeting. Members present were Michael Davis, Cynthia Giovanni, Don Madsen, and Edna Pitner. Michael Davis, chairperson, called the meeting to order at 2:30 p.m.

OLD BUSINESS

The members of the committee reviewed the sales brochure on electronic copyboards. They agreed to purchase an electronic copyboard for the conference room. Cynthia Giovanni will secure quotations from at least two suppliers.

NEW BUSINESS

The committee reviewed a request from the Purchasing Department for three new electronic typewriters. After extensive discussion regarding the appropriate uses of electronic typewriters versus microcomputers, the committee approved the request.

A request from the Marketing Department for a new photocopier was sent back to the department for more justification.

ADJOURNMENT

The meeting was adjourned at 4:45 p.m. The next meeting has been scheduled for May 4 in the headquarters conference room. Members are asked to bring with them copies of the latest resource planning document.

Respectfully submitted,

D. S. Madsen, Secretary

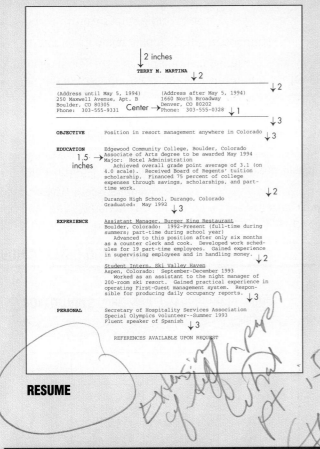

RESUME

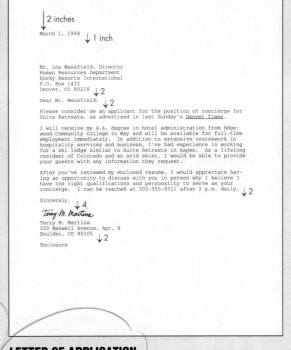

LETTER OF APPLICATION

PLACING INFORMATION ON PRINTED LINES

Because of the difficulty of aligning copy on a printed line with a computer and printer, lined forms such as job-application forms are most efficiently completed on a typewriter.

When keying on a lined form, use the typewriter's variable spacer to adjust the paper so that the line is in the position that a row of underlines would occupy. (On many machines, this is accomplished by pressing in the left platen knob.)

Do not leave any requested information blank; use "N/A" (not applicable) if necessary. Because of space limitations, it may be necessary to abbreviate some words.

Because first impressions are important, ensure that all your employment documents are in correct format, are neat in appearance, and are free from errors.

JOB-APPLICATION FORM (first page)

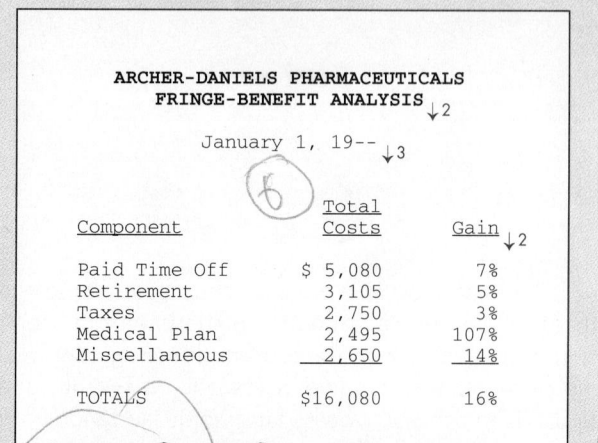

ARCHER-DANIELS PHARMACEUTICALS
FRINGE-BENEFIT ANALYSIS ↓2

January 1, 19-- ↓3

Component	Total Costs	Gain ↓2
Paid Time Off	$ 5,080	7%
Retirement	3,105	5%
Taxes	2,750	3%
Medical Plan	2,495	107%
Miscellaneous	2,650	14%
TOTALS	$16,080	16%

OPEN TABLE (with blocked column headings)

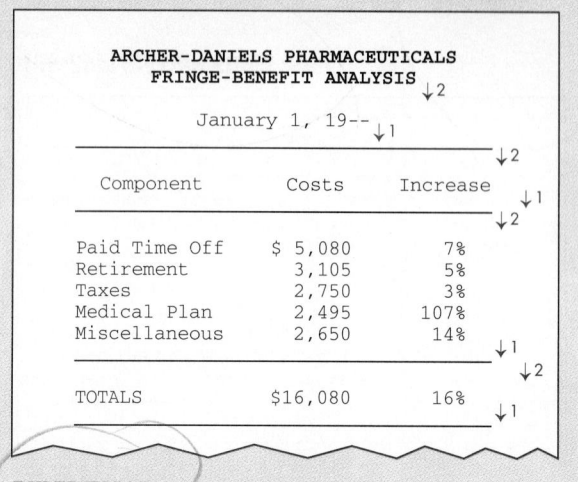

ARCHER-DANIELS PHARMACEUTICALS
FRINGE-BENEFIT ANALYSIS ↓2

January 1, 19-- ↓1
↓2

Component	Costs	Increase	↓1
			↓2
Paid Time Off	$ 5,080	7%	
Retirement	3,105	5%	
Taxes	2,750	3%	
Medical Plan	2,495	107%	
Miscellaneous	2,650	14%	↓1
			↓2
TOTALS	$16,080	16%	↓1

RULED TABLE (with centered column headings)

Table 14 ↓2

COMPOUND INTEREST ↓1

	Rate of 9%[a] ↓1		↓2
Year	Beginning Amount	Interest	Ending Amount ↓1
1	$50.00	$ 4.50	$54.50
2	54.50	4.91	59.41
3	59.41	5.35	64.76
4	64.76	5.83	70.59
5	70.59	6.35	76.94 ↓1
TOTAL	. . . . . .	$26.94	↓1

[a]Accrued annually.

BOXED TABLE (with centered column headings)

CHIEF EXECUTIVE ALMA MATERS

As of January 1992

Company	Chief Executive	Education	
		Undergraduate	Graduate
Apple	John Sculley	Brown	Princeton
Compaq	Joseph R. Canion	Houston	Houston
IBM	John F. Akers	Yale	
Unisys	James A. Unruh	Jamestown	Denver
Zenith	Jerry Pearlman	Princeton	Harvard

BOXED TABLE (prepared in WordPerfect)

FORMATTING BUSINESS FORMS

Most business forms can be formatted most efficiently on a typewriter. Whether formatted on a typewriter or computer, follow these guidelines:

- Align number columns at the right, centered visually within each ruled area.

- Align word columns (or combination word and number columns) at the left, 2 or 3 spaces after the vertical rule.

- Set the left margin for the first column and set left or decimal tabs for each additional column.

- Do not key a dollar sign for amount columns.

- Indent turnover lines 2 or 3 spaces.

MASCO SHIPPING LINES
1336 Dublin Road, Columbus, OH 43215 Phone: 614-555-9971

Purchase Order No. 1074

Please ship and bill us for the goods listed below. If for any reason you cannot deliver within 30 days, let us know at once. Please refer to our Purchase Order number in all communications. Your bill to us should indicate all your usual discounts. Payment will be made upon receipt of bill with goods.

To:

Reliable Office Supply
Great Lakes Distribution Center
1001 West Van Buren St.
Chicago, IL 60607

QTY.	CAT. NO.	DESCRIPTION	UNIT PRICE	AMOUNT
120	H02048	Perforated ruled pads	.48	57.60
20	564LQ4	Correction fluid	1.09	21.80
2	22z398	Paper punch	58.67	117.34
1	B48560	Hi-style tackboard, 24" x 36", burgundy frame/blue fabric	31.98	31.98
20	J22502	Fax rolls	11.33	226.60
500	NS2315	Kraft catalog envelopes, 10" x 13", clasp with gummed flap	104.86	104.86
36	AC7861	Recyclable storage boxes, legal size	3.69	132.84
		Subtotal		693.02
		Shipping and handling (10%)		69.30
		TOTAL AMOUNT DUE		762.32

Date: November 12, 19--   Purchasing Agent

BUSINESS FORM

(thoughts, planned), contractions (shouldn't, haven't), or abbreviations (UNICEF, assoc.).

2. Divide words only between syllables. Whenever you are unsure of where a syllable ends, consult a dictionary.

3. Leave at least three characters (the last will be a characters (the last may be a punctuation mark) to the next line. Thus de- lay and af- ter, but not a- maze or trick- y.

4. Divide compound words either at the hyphen (self-confidence) or where the two words join to make a solid compound. Thus master- piece, not mas- terpiece.

PROOFREADERS' MARKS

Proofreaders' Mark	Draft	Final Copy
SS Single-space	ss [first line / second line]	first line / second line
ds Double-space	ds [first line / second line]	first line / second line
V or ∧ Insert punctuation	if he's not↑	if he's not,
old/new Change word	and if you (when)	and when you
⌋ Delete and close up	co⌿operation	cooperation
/ Use lowercase letter	our President	our president
○ Spell out	the only ①	the only one
⌐ Move right	Please send	Please send
⌐ Move left	May I	May I

Proofreaders' Mark	Draft	Final Copy
⌒ Omit space	data base	database
∽ Transpose	they all see	they see all
∧ Insert	she may go (not)	she may not go
≡ Capitalize	Maple street	Maple Street
ℓ Delete	a final draft	a draft copy
♂ Move as shown	no copy machine	no machine
# Paragraph	Most of the	Most of the
# Insert space	allready to	all ready to
⊙ Make a period	one way ⊙	one way.
⋯ Don't delete	a true story	a true story

PUNCTUATION AND SPACING POINTERS

AMPERSAND. One space before and after.

CLOSING QUOTATION MARK. (a) Keyed *after* a period or comma and *before* a colon or semicolon. *Always.* (b) Keyed *after* a question mark or exclamation point if the quoted material is a question or an exclamation; otherwise, it is keyed *before* the question mark or exclamation point.

COLON. Two spaces after.

COMMA. One space after.

EQUALS SIGN. One space before and after.

EXCLAMATION POINT. Two spaces after.

PERIOD. (a) Two spaces after a period at the end of a sentence; (b) one space after the period following some-

one's initials or the abbreviation of a single word (e.g., *Mrs. Jones*); (c) no space after each internal period in an abbreviation (e.g., *a.m.*).

QUESTION MARK. Two spaces after.

SEMICOLON. One space after.

TABLE COLUMNS. Six spaces between.

UNDERLINE. (a) To key a magazine or book title, underline the entire title, including internal spaces and punctuation. (b) To stress individual words, underline them separately; do not underline the punctuation or the spaces between the words.

ZIP CODE. One space before.

COMMAS

1. Use a comma to separate two independent clauses in a compound sentence when they are joined by *and, but, or,* or *nor.*

I want to attend, but Dee has tickets to the game.

Ellen left her job in May, and she and her sister went to Paris.

But: Ellen left her job and went to Paris with her sister.

2. Use commas to separate three or more items in a series when the last item is preceded by *and, or,* or *nor.*
   They saved their work, exited the program, and turned their computers off.
   Patsy, Kris, or Bill will be elected.

3. When a dependent clause *precedes* the independent clause, separate the clauses with a comma.
   Before we can make a decision, we need the facts.

4. Use commas to set off a nonessential expression (a word, phrase, or clause that may be omitted without changing the basic meaning of the sentence). When an expression is essential to the completeness of a sentence, do not set it off with commas.
   Our present projections, you must admit, are inadequate.
   But: You must admit the projections are inadequate.

5. Use commas to set off the year when it follows the month and day.
   It was mailed on Tuesday, the day your order was received.
   But: It was mailed the day your order was received.
   The reunion will be held on May 2, 1995, in Chicago.
   But: The reunion will be held on May 2 in Chicago.
   But: In March 1988 the firm was incorporated.

6. When two adjectives modify the same noun, use a comma to separate the adjectives if they are not joined by *and.* (Note: If the first adjective modifies the combined idea of the second adjective plus the noun, do not separate the adjectives with a comma.)
   Rue is an intelligent, understanding counselor.
   But: Rue is an intelligent and understanding counselor.

7. Use commas to set off a transitional expression (such as *therefore*) or an independent comment (such as *of course*).
   Thomas told her, however, that the new printers would arrive today.
   In the first place, the members have not yet reached an agreement.

8. Use commas to set off an expression in apposition (that is, a word, phrase, or clause that identifies or explains other terms).
   The projectionist, Kelsey Auland, will show the film tonight.

OTHER PUNCTUATION MARKS

1. Use a semicolon to separate two independent clauses that are not joined by *and, but,* or *nor.*
   Leslie worked on Labor Day; Jean did not.
   But: Leslie worked on Labor Day but Jean did not.

2. If either of the independent clauses in a compound sentence contains a comma, separate the clauses with a semicolon rather than a comma.

3. Use a semicolon to separate items in a series if any of the items already contain commas.
   Staff meetings were held on Thursday, May 7; Monday, June 7; and Friday, June 12.

4. Hyphenate a compound adjective (two or more words that function as a unit to describe a noun) that comes *before* a noun. Exception: If the first word is an adverb ending in *ly,* do not hyphenate such adjectives.
   The determination of production goals for each of the plants is a high-level decision.
   But: Decisions about production goals are made at a high level.

5. Underline titles of complete published works, and use the quotation marks around titles that represent only a part of a complete published work.
   The chapter entitled "IRAs and Personal Financial Planning" will be discussed tomorrow.
   The sales director reported that excellent results had been

6. Use a period to end a sentence that is a polite request, suggestion, or command if you expect the reader to respond by acting rather than by giving a yes-or-no answer.
   Will you please send the report by overnight express.
   May I have a copy of your report before you leave.

7. To make a singular noun possessive, add the apostrophe before the s.
   a customer's request   the company's profits

8. To make a possessive from a singular noun that ends in an s sound, be guided by the way the word is pronounced. If a new syllable is formed by making the noun possessive, add an apostrophe and an s (my boss's office, the witness's testimony). If the addition of an extra syllable to a singular noun would make a word that is hard to pronounce, add only an apostrophe (Mr. Phillips' career, Mrs. Hodges' friend).

9. To make a plural noun not ending in s possessive, place the apostrophe before the s.
   the women's offices   the children's school

10. To make a possessive from a plural noun ending in s, place the apostrophe after the s.
    the secretaries' computers   the Halls' reception

11. Do not use an apostrophe with possessive pronouns.
    The new house is ours.   The team won its first three debates.

1. Capitalize the first word of all sentences and the first word of expressions used as a sentence.

   How may I help you?

   Enough said about that!

2. Capitalize every proper noun. A proper noun is the official name of a particular person, place, or thing.

   Ohio State University   Memorial Day

3. Capitalize common organization terms such as *advertising department* and *finance committee* when they are the actual names of units within the writer's own organization and are modified by the word *the*.

   The Board of Trustees of our college meets on Thursday.

   The advertising department of A & G will reorganize.

4. Capitalize adjectives derived from proper nouns.

   America (n.)   American (adj.)

5. Capitalize the names of places such as *streets, buildings, parks, monuments, rivers, oceans,* and *mountains.* Do not capitalize short forms used in place of the full name.

   Northland Mall   Front Street

   Pacific Ocean   Washington Monument

6. Capitalize *north, south, east, west,* and derivative words when they designate definite regions or are an integral part of a proper name.

   She lives in the Southwest.

   Go north for two blocks, then head west.

   He is a southern gentleman.

7. Capitalize the names of the days of the week, months, holidays, and religious days.

   Veterans Day   Tuesday, October 8

8. Do not capitalize the names of the seasons.

   We will publish the book in the fall.

   During the spring, my allergies bother me.

9. Capitalize the names of specific course titles. Do not, however, capitalize the names of subjects or areas of study (except for any proper nouns or adjectives in such names).

   I'm enrolled in American History 201.

   She's studying modern art.

10. Capitalize a noun followed by a number or letter that indicates sequence. Exceptions: Do not capitalize the nouns *line, note, page, paragraph, size.*

    The Section 2 class was assigned Chapter 5.

    Many read only pages 15–27.

NUMBERS

1. Spell out numbers 1 though 10, and use figures for numbers above 10. Exception: If two or more *related* numbers both below and above 10 are used in the same sentence, use figures for all numbers.

   She invited seven managers to the meeting.

   There were 20 people at the seminar.

2. To express even millions or billions, use the following style: 35 million; 7 billion.

   20 million (**not** 20,000,000)

   $45 billion (**not** 45,000,000,000)

3. When two numbers come together in a sentence and one is part of a compound adjective, spell out the first number unless the second number would make a much shorter word.

   three 9-room suites   175 six-page reports

4. When expressing numbers in words, hyphenate all compound numbers between 21 and 99 (or *21st* and *99th*), whether they stand alone or are part of a number over 100.

   They sent forty-six invitations.

5. Spell out (and hyphenate) fractions that stand alone, and use figures for mixed numbers.

   four-fifths of the market   7 3/8 yards

6. To form the plural of figures, add *s* (without the apostrophe).

   the 1990s

7. Spell out a number at the beginning of a sentence.

   Seven students missed the class.

8. Use commas to separate thousands, millions, and billions.

   $12,752,099   10,000   199,999

9. Use figures for house numbers.

   They live at 10 Eastland Drive.

10. Do not use a decimal with even amounts of money.

    $550 (**Not:** $550.00)

11. Use the word *cents* for amounts under $1.

    75 cents (**Not:** $.75 or 75¢)

12. Use *st, d,* or *th* only if the day precedes the month.

    Start the work on the 3rd of June.

    But: Start work on June 1.

GRAMMAR

1. A verb must agree with its subject in number and person.

   They are looking for the dog.
   He is looking for them.

2. The following pronouns are always singular and take singular verbs: *each, either, neither, much,* and pronouns ending in *body, thing,* and *one.*

   Neither of the assistants is busy.
   Everybody has to participate.

3. When establishing agreement between subject and verb, disregard intervening phrases and clauses.

   The doctor, not the interns, is working there.
   Only one of the students finished the test.

4. Verbs in the subjunctive mood (those that talk of conditions which are improbable, doubtful, or contrary to fact) require the plural form.

   I wish I were on that harbor cruise.
   If I were she, I would use a different format.

5. Use a singular pronoun with a singular antecedent and a plural pronoun with a plural antecedent.

   Neither Karla nor Marie must change her coat.
   Neither Mr. Brown nor his aides finished their work.

6. Use nominative pronouns (*I, he, she, we, they,* and so on) as subjects of a sentence or clause.

   The programmer and he are reviewing that.
   It is she who likes this software program.

7. Use objective pronouns (*me, him, her, us, them,* and so on) as objects in a sentence or clause.

   The folders are for Susan and him.
   She went out with him and me.

8. Use comparative adjectives and adverbs (*er, more,* and *less*) in referring to two persons, places, or things; use superlative adjectives and adverbs (*est, most,* and *least*) in referring to more than two.

   He is the quicker of the two ball players.
   He is the quickest of the two ball players.
   This computer is faster than the other.
   This computer is the fastest of all.

ABBREVIATIONS

1. In lowercase abbreviations made up of single initials, use a period after each initial but no space after each internal period.

   p.m.   i.e.   f.o.b.

2. Always abbreviate *Mr., Mrs.,* and *Dr.,* when they are used with personal names. In general, spell out all other titles used with personal names.

   Ms. Joan Brandt   Dr. James Rich

3. Always abbreviate *Jr., Sr.,* and *Esq.* when they follow personal names.

   Mr. Harold A. Smith, Jr.   George Barr, Esq.

4. Spell out compass points used as ordinary nouns and adjectives or when included in street names. Exception: Abbreviate compass points without periods when they are used *following* a street name.

   He bought a lot on the southeast corner.
   18 Front Street, NW
   12 North Adams Street

5. In nontechnical writing, spell out units of measure.

   a 5-quart bottle   12 yards of material
   3½ by 5 inches   a 110-acre development

6. Abbreviate units of measure when they occur frequently, as in technical or scientific works, on forms, and in tables. Do not use periods.

   14 oz   6 qts   5 ft 10 in   55 mph

13. Use figures to express time with *o'clock* or with *a.m.* and *p.m.* (The abbreviations *a.m.* and *p.m.* should be keyed in small letters without spaces.)

   9 o'clock (**Not:** nine o'clock)
   I left at 8:30 a.m. and returned at 5 p.m.

14. Express percentages in figures and spell out the word *percent.* Note: The percent sign (%) may be used in tables.

   7 percent   15.6 percent

15. When ages are used as significant statistics, express them in figures. Otherwise, spell them out.

   You may drive at the age of 16.
   My father is seventy-five years old.

Orientation Lesson

MAJOR PARTS OF AN ELECTRONIC TYPEWRITER

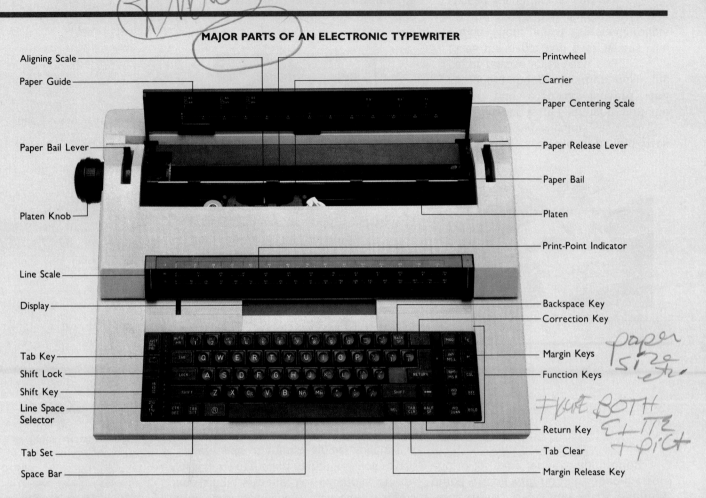

Aligning Scale
Paper Guide
Paper Bail Lever
Platen Knob
Line Scale
Display
Tab Key
Shift Lock
Shift Key
Line Space Selector
Tab Set
Space Bar

Printwheel
Carrier
Paper Centering Scale
Paper Release Lever
Paper Bail
Platen
Print-Point Indicator
Backspace Key
Correction Key
Margin Keys
Function Keys
Return Key
Tab Clear
Margin Release Key

ALIGNING SCALE. Aids in positioning the carrier on a line of text for inserting or deleting characters.

BACKSPACE KEY. Moves the carrier to the left 1 space at a time.

CARRIER. Moves from left to right, carrying the printwheel across the paper.

CORRECTION KEY. Engages correction tape and lifts off an error.

DISPLAY. Displays text as it is keyed into memory and before it is printed on the paper.

FUNCTION KEYS. Perform special functions, such as automatic centering and moving to the beginning or end of the document.

LINE SCALE. Indicates horizontal spaces across the length of the platen, carrier position, and margin stops.

LINE SPACE SELECTOR. Controls the space between keyed lines.

MARGIN KEYS. Used to set left and right margins.

MARGIN RELEASE KEY. Temporarily unlocks the left or right margin.

PAPER BAIL. Holds the paper against the platen.

PAPER-BAIL LEVER. Controls the paper bail.

PAPER CENTERING SCALE. Used to center any size of paper in the machine.

PAPER GUIDE. Guides and aligns the paper as it is in-

serted into the machine.

PAPER RELEASE LEVER. Loosens the paper for straightening or removing.

PLATEN. Large cylinder around which the paper is rolled.

PLATEN KNOB. Used to turn the platen by hand. The *variable platen* in the left platen knob can be pushed in to turn the platen freely for slight vertical adjustments.

PRINT-POINT INDICATOR. Shows the exact point on the line at which the next character will be printed.

PRINTWHEEL. A printing element that has each character engraved at the end of a spoke. When a key is struck, the

printwheel spins and prints the corresponding character.

RETURN KEY. Returns the carrier to the start of a new line.

SHIFT KEY. Used to key individual capital letters.

SHIFT LOCK. Locks the shift key so that the machine prints in all capitals.

SPACE BAR. Moves the carrier to the right 1 space at a time.

TAB CLEAR. Removes tabs.

TAB KEY. Moves the carrier to a point where a tab has been set.

TAB SET. Sets tabs at desired points.

This Orientation Lesson provides an overview of the basic procedures you will need to know to complete the first several lessons. This lesson also is designed to help you understand the terms, procedures, and directions used throughout this book. Read the lesson and refer to it whenever you have a question or a problem.

A. STARTING A LESSON

Margins: 1 inch
Spacing: single
Tab: 5 spaces
Drills: 2 times
Format Guide: 3–4
Working Papers: 11–14

Goals:
To key 39 wam/5'/5e; to format a letter of application.

Each lesson heading (each unit heading beginning with Unit 13) includes a display to tell you what settings to use to format your documents and what supplementary materials you may need. Unless you are told otherwise, use 1-inch side margins and single spacing. For example, the instructions in the left margin tell you to use 1-inch side margins, single spacing, a 5-space tab, and to key each drill line 2 times. The instructions also tell you to use Format Guide pages 3–4 and Working Papers pages 11–14.

The goals for the lesson are to key 39 wam (words a minute) on a 5-minute timed writing with no more than 5 errors and to format a letter of application.

B. INSERTING PAPER

To insert paper into the machine:

1. Adjust the paper guide so that paper will be inserted in the correct position (usually at zero on the margin scale).
2. Pull the paper bail forward.
3. Place the paper behind the platen with the left edge against the paper guide.

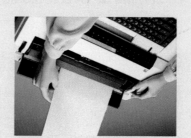

4. Feed the paper into the machine using the paper insert key or by turning the platen knob.
5. Check that the paper is straight by turning it up a few inches and aligning

the left edges of the front and back against the paper guide.

6. If the paper is not straight, pull the paper release lever forward and straighten the paper; then push the paper release lever back.
7. Place the paper bail back against the paper. Then, adjust the small rollers on the paper bail so that they are spaced evenly across the paper.
8. Unless directed otherwise, adjust your paper to leave an appropriate 1-inch top margin.

C. REMOVING PAPER

To remove paper from the machine:
1. Pull the paper bail forward.
2. Use the correct key to eject the paper or pull the paper release lever forward and slide the paper out of the machine.
3. Return the paper release lever and the paper bail back to their normal positions.

D. LEARNING ABOUT PAPER SIZE

A standard sheet of paper is 8½ inches wide by 11 inches long. With 10-pitch type (10 characters = 1 inch), there are 85 characters across the page (8½ × 10 = 85). With 12-pitch type (12 characters = 1 inch), there are 102 characters across the page (8½ × 12 = 102).

To determine the center of the page, divide the number of horizontal spaces across the page by 2. With 10-pitch type, the center point is 42 (85 ÷ 2 = 42—drop the ½). With 12-pitch type, the center point is 51 (102 ÷ 2 = 51).

With standard vertical line spacing there are 6 lines to 1 vertical inch. Therefore, a sheet of paper 11 inches long has 66 lines.

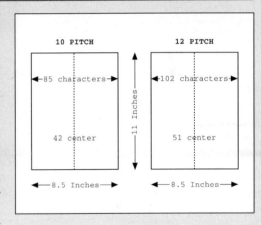

E. LEARNING ABOUT PITCH (TYPE SIZE)

Many electronic typewriters can print either 10 characters per inch (10 pitch) or 12 characters per inch (12 pitch). Some electronic typewriters can also print 15 characters per inch (15 pitch) or proportional spacing, in which the width of each character varies. The jobs in this text have been planned for using 10-pitch type.

Determine which size type your machine has by keying the numbers 1 through 0 and comparing your keyed copy with the illustration below.

```
1234567890  10 pitch
123456789012  12 pitch
```

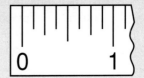

F. LEARNING ABOUT LINE SPACING

The line-space selector controls the amount of space between lines of type. Set the line-space selector at 1 for single spacing (no blank lines between keyed lines) and 2 for double spacing (1 blank line between keyed lines).

On some typewriters you can also set the line-space selector at 1.5 for half-line spacing (½ blank line between keyed lines) and 3 for triple spacing (2 blank lines between keyed lines).

LINE SPACING

single	1.5	double	triple
	1.5		
single		double	
single	1.5	double	triple

G. LEARNING ABOUT MARGINS

Margins are the white (empty) space around all sides of a keyed document. For most documents you will use 1-inch side margins. Follow these instructions to determine where to set the left and right margins.

To determine the left margin setting, multiply the number of characters per inch by the number of inches in the margin (10 pitch: 10 characters × 1 inch = 10; 12 pitch: 12 characters × 1 inch = 12).

To determine the right margin, multiply the number of characters per inch by the number of inches in the margin; then subtract that number from the number of spaces across the page (10 pitch: 85 − 10 = 75; 12 pitch: 102 − 12 = 90).

To set the margins, move the carrier to the correct points on the margin scale and follow the instructions for setting margins on your machine.

> When a key or the space bar is tapped, the cursor advances 1 space. The default font (that is, the preset style of the printed characters for most printers is a monospaced font, where each character occupies the same amount of space.
>
> Font sizes are measured in points; 1 point = 1/72 of an inch. The most common font size for business documents is either 10 points or 12 points, measured vertically. A 10-point monospaced font prints 12 characters per inch, corresponding to elite type on a typewriter. A 12-point monospaced font prints 10 characters per inch, corresponding to pica type.
>
> Although fonts and font sizes can be changed, a 12-point monospaced font (pica-size) is the default setting for most printers and is the font used for all jobs in this text. A 12-point font prints 6 lines per inch (72 points per inch ÷ 12). The default setting is single-spacing, which contains no blank space between printed lines.
>
> Margins are the white (empty) space around each side of your document. Most word processing software programs have default margins of 1 inch, meaning that a full printed page will have 1 inch of blank space at the top, bottom, left, and right.
>
> When you open a new document in WordPerfect, the status line indicates that your cursor is on Ln 1" (top margin) and Pos 1" (left margin). Even though no margins show on the computer screen, the printed page will have the appropriate margins.
>
> In order for your printer to print with the appropriate margins, you must insert the paper correctly into the printer. Learn how to operate the printer you will be using in class so

H. SETTING TABS

Tab settings enable you to indent paragraphs and to format columns of data efficiently. Some electronic typewriters have default tabs (which can be changed) set every 5 spaces.

To set a new tab, clear the existing tabs. Then, position the carrier where you want the new tab to be and set the tab. Check the tab setting by returning the carrier to the left margin and pressing the tab key. The carrier should move directly to the point where you set the tab.

I. DAILY ROUTINE

Perform these steps at the start of each class:

1. Arrange your work area: typewriter even with the front edge of the desk; textbook on one side of the machine, tilted for ease of reading; and paper on the other side of the machine.
2. Open your textbook to the correct lesson, and read the directions in the heading.
3. Set margins, tabs, and line spacing as directed.
4. Insert a sheet of paper and straighten it if necessary.
5. Sit in correct position, and begin the Warmup drill for the lesson.

J. KEYBOARDING TECHNIQUE

Assuming the correct position at the typewriter enables you to key with greater speed and accuracy and less fatigue. When keying for long periods of time, rest your eyes periodically by looking away from the copy, shifting your position, or moving about.

To the extent possible, adjust your work station as follows:

Chair. Adjust the chair height so that your upper and lower legs form a 90 degree angle and your lower back is supported by the back of the chair.

Keyboard. Center your body opposite the J key, leaning forward slightly. Keep your forearms horizontal and raise your hands slightly when keying so that your wrists do not touch the keyboard or desk.

Text. Position your textbook (or other copy) on either side of the typewriter. Elevate the book to a comfortable reading angle to minimize head and eye movements and to avoid neck strain.

K. BUILDING STRAIGHT-COPY SKILL

Warmups. Beginning with Lesson 15, each lesson or unit starts with a 3-line warmup paragraph. All alphabet and number keys are included, as well as several common symbols. Key the Warmup twice or take three 1-minute timed writings on the paragraph.

Back-of-Book Drills. In addition to the specially constructed drills contained within the lessons, you will frequently be asked to turn to a specific drill in the back of the book for individualized practice on the passage most appropriate for your skill level. Always start at the point where you left off the previous time.

Pretest/Practice/Posttest Routines. When practicing P/P/P drills, your practice routine depends on whether you reached your accuracy goal on the Pretest. If you did, emphasize speed by keying each *individual* drill the specified number of times. If you did not reach your speed goal, emphasize accuracy by keying each *group* of lines (as though it were a paragraph) the specified number of times. These two practice routines are illustrated in the left margin.

L. MEASURING STRAIGHT-COPY SKILL

number of words you keyed divided by the number of minutes you keyed. Round off a fraction to the nearest whole number.

All timed writings in this book contain small numbers, called speed markers, above the copy. When you take a 5-minute timed writing, the highest number that you pass is your *wam* (words-a-minute) speed.

In addition to the timed writings in the lessons and units, the back of the book contains eight additional timed writings that may be used at any time for additional skill measurement.

All timed writings in the text are the exact length needed to reach the speed goal that is set for each lesson or unit. Thus, if you finish the timed writing, you know you have reached your speed goal.

All timed writings in the same course (that is, in the Basic, Intermediate, and Advanced courses) are of equivalent difficulty as measured by syllabic intensity (the average number of syllables per word). Thus, you can be sure that any change in your speed is due to a change in your skill rather than a change in the difficulty level of the timed writing.

Your speed on a timed writing is the

M. BUILDING FORMATTING SKILL

Horizontal arrows (→) indicate the point at which to begin keying. For example, → 4 inches means to begin keying 4 inches from the left edge of the page. Down arrows (↑) indicate how far down the page a line should be keyed. For example, ↑ 2 inches means to begin keying 2 inches from the top edge of the page. Likewise, ↑ 4 means to press Return 4 times before keying the next line.

Marginal notes and arrows are sometimes used to remind you of margins, spacing, and so on. These aids are gradually reduced as you gain experience in formatting each kind of job.

Some jobs have special explanations which are positioned as close to the point of use as possible. Always look for and read any marginal notes before you begin to key.

↑ 2 inches

→4 inches Mr. Edward Whitman
Smith & Whitman Inc.
1047 Fifth Avenue
New York, NY 10028

Leave 1 space between state and ZIP Code.

```
20  Ethical people sh
                    24
21  they say and what they
                       28
22  are in the best intere
                       32
23  should always try to a
                    35  36
24  in an ethical manner.
20                    21
```

Speed

aw awaken while
se severe seized
rd ordeal burden

aw awaken while
se severe seized
rd ordeal burden

Accuracy

aw awaken while
se severe seized
rd ordeal burden

aw awaken while
se severe seized
rd ordeal burden

1

OBJECTIVES

KEYBOARDING

To operate the letter, number, and symbol keys by touch.

To make all machine adjustments needed: set margins, tabs, and line spacing.

To compute keyboarding speed.

To key 28 words a minute on a 2-minute timed writing with no more than 5 errors.

LANGUAGE ARTS

To divide words correctly.

To proofread documents and correct errors.

To use quotation marks correctly.

FORMATTING

To format paragraph copy.

To set tabs for columns of information.

To underline text.

© David Ximeno Tejada/Tony Stone Worldwide

Spacing: Double

Working Papers: 273

End page 1 at an appropriate
point.

CRITERIA TO USE IN DETERMINING OFFICE SALARIES
By Kathy McCormack

As the need for office workers increased over the past two decades, the need to determine appropriate office salaries was evident. There are three criteria that companies consider when establishing the salaries for their office workers. Each of the three criteria will now be discussed.

Company Philosophy Toward Office Salaries

Companies, influenced by the quality of workers they hope to attract and retain, may adopt a policy of paying office salaries that are the same as, more than, or less than the average salaries paid by surrounding firms. Some managers consider the theories of behaviorists like Maslow and Herzberg in setting office salaries.[1] Of course, a basic factor to consider in setting salaries for office workers is that the salaries cannot exceed the ability of the firm to pay and still earn a profit.

Expectations of Office Employees

Like other employees at every level in an organization, office workers bring to their jobs their own expectations. Salary is one such area. These employees consider the supply of and demand for office workers. They evaluate the amount of education and training that is necessary for them to perform their jobs satisfactorily.

Office Salaries Paid by Other Companies

The local going rates for office salaries are extremely strong determinants and guides in establishing office salaries. Information from salary surveys that have been conducted on a local, regional, or national level can be useful. For example, the AMS publishes the results of a salary survey once a year.[2] It is important that a business firm have someone in the personnel department who is given major responsibility for keeping abreast of changing salary rates for office workers.

NOTES

1. John F. DeVries, Office Administration, Crane Publishing Company, Chicago, 1988, p. 87.

2. Patricia B. Wilcox, "Office Salaries," Management World, September/October 1988, p. 34.

LESSON 1

Home Keys

Margins: 1 inch • Spacing: Single • Drills: 2 times

Goals:
To control the home keys (A S D F J K L ;), the return key, and the space bar.

A. THE HOME KEYS

The A S D F J K L ; keys are known as the home keys. Place your fingers on the home keys as follows. **Left hand:** first finger on F; second finger on D; third finger on S; fourth finger on A. **Right hand:** first finger on J; second finger on K; third finger on L; and fourth finger on ;. Keep your fingers curved.

B. THE [SPACE BAR]

The space bar is used to space between words and after marks of punctuation.

With fingers held motionless on the home keys, poise your right thumb about 1/4 inch above the space bar. Tap the space bar in the center, and bounce your thumb off.

Space once (*tap the space bar once*) . . . twice (*tap the space bar twice*) . . . once . . . once . . . twice . . . once . . . twice . . . once . . . twice . . . twice

---

NEW KEYS

C. THE [RETURN] KEY

Tap the return key twice to leave a blank line between drills.

Reach to the return key with the fourth finger of your right hand. Keep your J finger at home. Lightly tap the return key to move the carrier to the beginning of a new line.

Practice using the return key until you can do so with confidence and without looking at your hands.

RETURN

Space once . . . twice . . . once . . . twice . . . Return! Home! (*return fingers to home-key position*) . . . Repeat.

D. THE [F] AND [J] KEYS

Use first fingers on F and J keys. Tap the space bar with your right thumb.

```
1 fff fff jjj jjj fff jjj ff jj ff jj f j
2 fff fff jjj jjj fff jjj ff jj ff jj f j
```

TEST 6-C
LETTER 72
MODIFIED-BLOCK STYLE
WITH INDENTED
PARAGRAPHS

Working Papers: 271

Current Date / Mr. Donald Hart, President / Welco Aluminum / 178 Washington Street / Henderson, NC 27536 / Dear Mr. Hart:

Thank you for your recent inquiry concerning the benefits package that we provide for business firms like yours. We have just recently begun working with some organizations in the Henderson area. I am glad to hear that you received a favorable reference about us from Thomas Glass in Oxford.

The enclosed brochure will give you a broad overview of the benefits that we could provide for your employees. You can get more information in one of the following ways:

1. Call us at 1-800-555-1840 to ask one of our representatives to visit you at your site.

2. Attend an open house that we are holding at the Stonehedge Inn in Raleigh on Friday, May 15, from 1 to 4 p.m.

3. If you will be attending a trade show or conference in the near future, let us know where and when it will be held. We will have one of our agents meet you there.

Thank you again for your interest in the benefits package that Liberty can provide for you. I will look forward to meeting you at some future time.

Sincerely yours, / Martha Browning / Industrial Account Agent / u r s / Enclosure

LEFT HAND
Forefinger   F
Second Finger   D
Third Finger   S
Fourth Finger   A

RIGHT HAND
J   Forefinger
K   Second Finger
L   Third Finger
;   Fourth Finger
Space Bar   Thumb

Leave 1 blank line (strike the return key twice) between drills.

E. THE D AND K KEYS

3 ddd ddd kkk kkk ddd kkk dd kk dd kk d k
4 ddd ddd kkk kkk ddd kkk dd kk dd kk d k

Use second fingers on D and K. A and Sem fingers remain in home position.

F. THE S AND L KEYS

5 sss sss lll lll sss lll ss ll ss ll s l
6 sss sss lll lll sss lll ss ll ss ll s l

Use third fingers on S and L. A and Sem fingers remain on home keys.

G. THE A AND ; KEYS

7 aaa aaa ;;; ;;; aaa ;;; aa ;; aa ;; a ;
8 aaa aaa ;;; ;;; aaa ;;; aa ;; aa ;; a ;

Use fourth fingers on A and Sem. F and J fingers remain on home keys.

SKILLBUILDING

H. WORD BUILDING

H. Key lines 9–15 twice, leaving a blank line after each pair. Note the word patterns.

Space once after a semicolon.

9 aaa ddd ddd add aaa lll lll all add all
10 aaa sss kkk ask ddd aaa ddd dad ask dad
11 lll aaa ddd lad fff aaa ddd fad lad fad
12 aaa ddd ;;; ad; aaa sss ;;; ad; as; ad;
13 f fa fad fads; a as ask asks; d da dad;
14 l la las lass; f fa fal fall; s sa sad;
15 a ad add adds; l la lad lads; a ad ads;

I. PHRASES

I. Key lines 16–17 twice, leaving a blank line after each pair. Note the phrase patterns.

16 dad ask; ask a lad; dad ask a lad; as a
17 a fall; a lass; ask a lass; a lad asks;

J. 1-MINUTE TIMED WRITING

J. Take three 1-minute timed writings. Try to complete the line each time.

18 ask a sad lad; a fall fad; add a salad;

Progress Test on Part 6

Spacing: Double

Working Papers: 267

Business firms are deeply involved with a lot of   11
different groups in our society. These groups include the   23
workers of the firm, the stockholders, the consumers or the   35
public at large, all the firms that compete with one   45
another, the tax collectors for the city and state and   56
federal governments, and quite a few others, ranging from   68
health bureaus to welfare offices. It's hard to fully   79
realize just how many persons and agencies are affected by   91
each success and failure on the business scene.   100

Those who work for a firm are involved in its welfare   112
for two reasons. First, the effects which they exert will   124
be factors in determining how much success the business   135
does or does not enjoy; and second, if a firm does badly,   147
not only the employees' incomes but also their chances of   158
advancement may be jeopardized. Thus a company has a right   170
to employee loyalty; employees have the right to expect a   182
fair wage, good working conditions, and a future.   192

Each business firm matters to the whole community. It   204
provides jobs for citizens, revenue for the stores and for   216
all kinds of supply vendors, more market value for property   228
and housing, and its fair share of taxes. It is absolutely   240
essential that business succeed in every community.   250

| 1 | 2 | 3 | 4 | 5 | 6 | 7 | 8 | 9 | 10 | 11 | 12 |

Working Papers: 269

INVOICE 9123. On November 26, 19—, Midwest Contracting Supplies invoices Richard Moose, Builder, 1335 Dublin Road, Columbus, OH 43215, for its Purchase Order 4862 for the following items:

1 fiberglass 28-foot ladder @ $149.99 = $149.99; 8 interior luan bifold doors @ $39.00 = $312.00; 4 clear-view storm doors @ $199.99 = $799.96; 3 double-glazed contemporary doors @ $219.99 = $659.97; Total = $1,921.92; Less 10% trade discount = $192.19; Plus tax and shipping = $108.65; TOTAL AMOUNT DUE = $1,838.38.

LESSON 2

New Keys

Margins: 1 inch • Spacing: Single • Drills: 2 times

Goal:
To control the H, E, O, and R keys.

Fingers are named for home keys. (Example: second finger of the left hand is the D finger.)

A. WARMUP

1 fff jjj ddd kkk sss lll aaa ;;; fff jjj
2 a salad; a lad; alas a fad; ask a lass;

NEW KEYS

B. THE **H** KEY

Use the J finger.

Space once after a semicolon.

3 jjj jhj jhj hjh jjj jhj jhj hjh jjj jhj
4 has has hah hah had had aha aha ash ash
5 hash half sash lash dash hall shad shah
6 as dad had; a lass has half; add a dash

C. THE **E** KEY

Use the D finger.

Keep your eyes on the copy as you key.

7 ddd ded ded ede ddd ded ded ede ddd ded
8 lea led see he; she eke fed sea lee fee
9 keel fake head feed seal ease lead held
10 she held a lease; he fed a seal; a keel

D. THE **O** KEY

Use the L finger.

Keep fingers curved.

11 lll lol lol olo lll lol lol olo lll lol
12 doe off foe hod oh; oak odd ode old sod
13 shoe look kook joke odes does solo oleo
14 he held a hook; a lass solos; old foes;

E. THE **R** KEY

Use the F finger.

Keep A finger at home.

15 fff frf frf rfr fff frf frf rfr fff frf
16 red ark ore err rah era rod oar her are
17 oars soar dear fare read role rare door
18 he read a rare reader; a dark red door;

Educational institutions are a source we have often used to fill some of our middle-management and newly developed positions.

I am not sure how we have we used public employment agencies? I do know that the United States Employment service has assisted firms in hiring new employees and with out cost.

Have we used private employment agencies? Their are fees for their services depending on the nature of the position and the reputation of the agency, fees may be charged

Temporary agencies are often a last resort. I know that we have used a local temporary agency to fill some part-time positions in the office systems area. There is much to be said about this form of recruitment because a firm does not have the responsibility for payroll taxes, social security, unemployment taxes, insurance, and other fringe benefits.

Please let me know if I would like you to review the data in the table below. As you look at the information, does it clearly reflects the best sources so that we may have of employees in light of our current demand for all new employees to have with top-notch basic skills?

SOURCES AND NUMBER OF EMPLOYEES HIRED, 1992-1994

Sources	1992	1993	1994
Advertising	12	11	8
Data Banks	--	--	--
Educational Institutions	3	4	6
Employee Referral	4	5	3
Private Agencies	--	--	--
Promoting from Within	10	12	9
Public Agencies	--	--	--
Temporary agencies	16	20	21
Unsolicited Applications	8	9	6
TOTAL	53	61	53

urs

F. WORD FAMILIES

Do not pause at the vertical lines that mark off the word families.

19 hale sale kale dale | sold fold hold old;
20 seed heed deed feed | sash dash lash ash;
21 rake sake fake lake | rear sear dear ear;

G. Take three 1-minute timed writings. Try to complete both lines each time. Use word wrap.

G. 1-MINUTE TIMED WRITING

22 he asked for a rare old deed; she had a
23 door ajar;

LESSON 3 · New Keys

Margins: 1 inch • Spacing: Single • Drills: 2 times

Goal:
To control the M, T, I, and C keys.

A. WARMUP

1 aa ;; ss ll dd kk ff jj hh ee oo rr aa;
2 he held a sale for her as she had asked

NEW KEYS

Use the J finger.

B. THE **M** KEY

3 jjj jmj jmj mjm jjj jmj jmj mjm jjj jmj
4 mad mom me; am jam; ram dam ham ma; mar
5 same lame room fame make roam loam arms
6 she made more room for some of her ham;

Use the F finger.

C. THE **T** KEY

7 fff ftf ftf tft fff ftf ftf tft fff ftf
8 hot jot rat eat tam mat lot sat art tar
9 mate tool fate mart date late told take
10 he told her to set a later date to eat;

Format the heading for page 2 of the memo the same as you would for a two-page letter. (See Unit 18, page 203, or page R-5 in the Reference Section.)

MEMO

TO: Lucy White

FROM: Martin Beck, Personnel

DATE: (current)

SUBJECT: Sources of Recruitment

In attending various personnel management meetings, ~~association~~ *various journal articles* *talking* with other ~~personnel~~ managers, and readings, I have become aware of how important it is ~~for the future of our firm~~ to have the best-qualified employees in ~~lieu~~ *light* of the current economy and our desire to be the ~~leader~~ *premier firm* in our product field. Therefore, I think that we ~~should~~ *must* review our sources of recruiting.

In the past, we have used internal and external sources for recrutment. Listed below are my ~~ideas~~ *thoughts* about each of these sources.

Internal

Our employees have for the most part referred excellent individuals to us. The only major problem we have had with employee referral is that once in a while an individual may not succeed, and the individual employee is often embarassed.

Promoting our own employees is a ~~place~~ *source* that we have utilized. As you ~~are aware, we have been able to~~ *know this source* save time and money ~~with this source~~ because we have not had the expense of recruiting or lengthy training. *Additionally, it* ~~Promoting employees from within does~~ boosts morale and loyalty to the firm. A draw back often occurs from our not being able to bring fresh ideas to the firm.

transpose

Some firms are now using *data* banks. These *data* banks are computer files on the qualifications of current employees. One can quickly scan a file to see if an employee is qualified for a vacant or new ~~job~~ *position*.

External

One source we have used in the past is unsolicted applications. This source has provided us with employees who have had outstanding qualifications. If we have not installed a data bank on this source, I think we ~~should~~ *must*.

We have been very successful in recruiting employees though our advertizing in the local papers, on radio and television, and in trade magazines. This method does result in our obtaining a large number of responses; however, the pool is larger.

(Continued on next page.)

NOTE: Do not be concerned if you make errors in these early lessons. Making errors is expected at this stage of your learning.

If you forget where a key is located, look at the keyboard chart, not at your fingers.

D. THE I KEY

Use the K finger.

11 kkk kik kik iki kkk kik kik iki kkk kik
12 air fir dim sir him rim kit sit did lid
13 iris tide site item fire idea tile tire
14 this time he left his tie at the store;

E. THE C KEY

Use the D finger.

15 ddd dcd dcd cdc ddd dcd dcd cdc ddd dcd
16 cot sac cod act car coo cat arc ice ace
17 rich tack chat face aces itch coat deck
18 he liked to race cars at the old track;

SKILLBUILDING

Sit in the correct position as you key these drills. Refer to the illustration on page OL-5.

F. WORD FAMILIES

19 sail tail rail fail | mace face lace ace;
20 dots tots jots lots | mire tire fire ire;
21 jade fade made ade; | seed deed feed heed
22 hale tale sale dale | cads lads fads ads;

G. SHORT PHRASES

23 as so | do as | if it | she is | he did | she had
24 so as | as if | it is | did it | it had | has met
25 to it | do it | if he | for it | as she | let her
26 he is | as do | of it | far as | of her | had his

H. Take three 1-minute timed writings. Try to complete both lines each time.

H. 1-MINUTE TIMED WRITING

27 their old store had lots of deck chairs
28 for his leased home;

TABLE 57
BOXED TABLE WITH
BRACED COLUMN
HEADINGS

Center the column headings.

BARKER-FOWLER ELECTRICAL REPAIR
COMPARISON OF ACTUAL AND PROJECTED OPERATIONS

For the Month Ended October 31, 19--

Category	Actual		Projected	
	Amount	% of Sales	Amount	% of Sales
Sales	22,845	100.0	22,900	100.0
Cost of Goods	3,200	14.0	4,800	20.9
Profit	19,645	86.0	19,000	83.0
Expenses	15,438	67.6	15,000	65.5
Net Income	4,207	18.4	4,000	17.5

Leave the appropriate spacing
before and after the date line.

September 22, 19--

Mr. Clark Roberts, Sales
The Highsmith Co., Inc.
W5527 Highway 106
P.O. Box 800
Fort Atkinson, WI 53538-0800

Dear Mr. Roberts:

I recently received your fall catalog and would like to order
the following:

 2   Brown Plastic Files, D41-28288
10   Green 3-Ring Binders, D41-52263
30   One-Step Binder Index Systems, D41-52451
 3   Suspension Frames, D41-59838

I am interested in your Sirco Computer Console. Do you have
a console in a walnut finish rather than oak? If so, would
you please send me a brochure and the price of the console.

Sincerely yours,

Margaret L. Conklin
202 Locust Street
Weston, OH 43416

New Keys

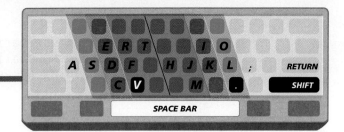

Margins: 1 inch • Spacing: Single • Drills: 2 times

Goals:
To control the right shift, V, and period keys; to count errors.

A. WARMUP

1 the farmer hired her to feed the mares;
2 the first callers came to see the iris;

NEW KEYS

To capitalize letters on the left half of the keyboard:
1. With the J finger at home, press and hold down the right shift key with the Sem finger.
2. Strike the letter key.
3. Release the shift key and return fingers to home position.

B. THE RIGHT **SHIFT** KEY

3 ;;; ;A; ;A; ;;; ;S; ;S; ;;; ;D; ;D; ;;;
4 Art Alf Sal Tom Sam Dee Ted Rae Sam Ada
5 Chet Edie Elsa Carl Amos Todd Sara Dick
6 Sara Edie Carter married Carl Sam Amos;

Use the F finger.

C. THE **V** KEY

7 fff fvf fvf vfv fff fvf fvf vfv fff fvf
8 Val eve Eva via vim vis Viv vet Ava vie
9 live have Vida ever vast Vera move vote
10 Victor Vida moved to Vassar to see Val;

Use the L finger.

Space once after a period following an abbreviation; none after a period within an abbreviation; twice after a period ending a sentence.

D. THE **.** KEY

11 lll l.l l.l .l. lll l.l l.l .l. lll l.l
12 sr. sr. dr. dr. ea. ea. Dr. Dr. Sr. Sr.
13 misc. D.C. jr. A.D. loc. cit. i.e. a.m.
14 Eva left. David came. Elsa came home.

SKILLBUILDING

E. PHRASES

15 as some | let him | are so | has had | ask them
16 to move | see her | for it | had the | did some
17 do have | her old | did he | jot the | had this
18 so ever | let her | she is | see him | for them

LETTER 70
(Continued)

Insert an appropriate Page 2 heading.

Leave 3 blank lines before and after a table with a title.

We plan to use various instructional strategies; for example, case studies, small-group discussions, and role playing. The best training takes place when the learner is ~~directly~~ involved in the process.

Listed below are the session topics, ~~the~~ director(s), special events, and dates for the training program.

APPRAISING AND EVALUATING EMPLOYEES ⌐ center and bold

Topics	Directors	Special Events	Dates
Appraising Performance	l'Huillier		May 6
Analyzing Jobs	Kopaca	Consultant	May 13
Evaluating Jobs	l'Huillier	Film	May 20
Administering Salaries	Kopaca		May 27
Measuring Ouput	L'Huillier	Field trip	June 3
Improving Productivity	L'Huillier and Kopaca		June 10

I will be glad to discuss the ~~fees~~ cost of this programs with you. As you know, we have always provided an ~~good~~ excellent program at a minimal cost. Please write or call me at your convenience so that we may develop your program as soon as possible. earliest

Sincerely yours

Wendy Humphries
training director

urs

Key the postscript as the last item in the letter, preceded by 1 blank line.

PS: I will be out of twon next week.

F. COUNTING ERRORS

Count an error when:

1. Any stroke is incorrect.
2. Any punctuation after a word is incorrect or omitted. Count the word before the punctuation.
3. The spacing after a word or after its punctuation is incorrect. Count the word as incorrect.
4. A letter or word is omitted.
5. A letter or word is repeated.
6. A direction about spacing, indenting, and so on, is violated.
7. Words are transposed.

Note: Only one error is counted for each word, no matter how many errors it may contain.

Compare the copy with lines 19–21 below.

Ada (mailwd) a letter; Dee mailed a card.
Ada mailed a (letter.) Dee mailed a card.
Dell (soldsome) of the food to a market.
Dell sold some the food to (to) a market.
(Alma) asked for (Dick) three more tickets.
Alma asked Dick for three more (tockits).

G. After keying each line 2 times, count your errors.

G. SENTENCES

19 Ada mailed a letter; Dee mailed a card.
20 Dell sold some of the food to a market.
21 Alma asked Dick for three more tickets.

H. Take three 1-minute timed writings. Try to complete both lines each time.

H. 1-MINUTE TIMED WRITING

22 Vic asked them to tell the major to see
23 Carla at the local firm.

LESSON 5

Review

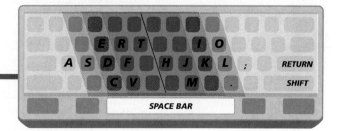

Margins: 1 inch • Spacing: Single • Drills: 2 times

Goals:
To reinforce new-key reaches; to compute speed.

A. WARMUP

1 Val called Dale to ask for a ride home.
2 Edie took three old jars to her mother.

Working Papers: 263

Refer to the Reference Section (page R-5) for formatting a two-page letter.

Read the letter before keying. Refer to the Reference Section (page R-13) for a review of proofreaders' marks.

Change the style to modified block with open punctuation. Do not indent paragraphs.

(Current Date)

Mr. Larry Dwyer
Personnel Department
Erickson and Lee Company, 3735 Booth Street
Kansas City, ~~KS~~ MO 66103-1304

Dear Mr. Dwyer

It has been a pleasure to ~~aid~~ assist you and your ~~company~~ firm with the various ~~educational~~ training programs you have implemented over the past few years. ~~i~~ I hope that we can continue this excellent relationship.

We are announcing a new ~~personnel~~ training program for next ~~year~~ spring. This program will include two-week sessions on the following personnel areas: appraising performance, analyzing jobs, evaluating ~~work~~ jobs, administering ~~wages~~ salaries, measuring output, and improving productivity. I am sure that your ~~company~~ firm will want to ~~give~~ provide this program for your supervisors, and middle-management employees

The ~~rpogram~~ program will be under the direction of Dr. Alice l'Huillier, professor, ~~Personnel Management~~ Human Resources, Tufts University. Dr. L'Huillier, as you know, is one of the leading authorities in personnel management today. He has conducted many training programs for all of the major firms in the United States and is the ~~writer~~ author of many articles and text books in the areas of personnel management and management.

Each of the ~~five~~ six sessions will be conducted in your firm's corporate headquarters. The program is tailor-made so that sessions can be offered in any sequence you wish; however, we think the order in which we schedule them may be the best for most firms. Each session will last one and a half hours and will be conducted by Dr. L'Huillier and/or her assistant, Mr. Timothy Kopaca.

Instructional materials will be provided for each student and are covered by the fee charged for the program. As it has in the past, I am sure your firm will provide times for your employees to attend the sessions. We expect each participant to be an integral part of these training sessions.

(Continued on next page.)

B. WORD FAMILIES

3 lace face mace race | fame tame lame same
4 mail tail sail rail | fold cold mold told
5 mate late date fate | feed seed deed heed

C. PHRASES

6 or there | did he | for the | some mail | is he
7 is after | has it | ask the | come home | if it
8 he liked | she is | did she | late date | he is
9 it faces | had he | her hat | same mail | as if

D. COMPUTING SPEED

Compare with line 12.

Carl asked him to deed the farm to Ted.
Carl asked him to deed the farm to Ted.
Carl asked
| 1 | 2 | 3 | 4 | 5 | 6 | 7 | 8 |

Keyboarding speed is measured in words a minute (wam). To compute wam, count every 5 strokes, including spaces, as 1 "word." Horizontal word scales (see E) divide lines into 5-stroke words. In paragraph copy, words are cumulatively totaled at the end of each line (see F).

In Example 1, speed is 18 wam (8 +

Compare with lines 13–15.

Della asked David to take her to school for a short time. She had to meet Fred or Sarah at the school office at three. Della asked David to
| 1 | 2 | 3 | 4 | 5 | 6 | 7 | 8 |

8 + 2). In Example 2, speed is 28 wam (24 + 4). For timed writings other than a minute, divide the number of words keyed by the number of minutes in the timed writing. For example, if you key 28 words in 2 minutes, your speed is 14 wam (28 ÷ 2); in 1 minute, 28 wam (28 ÷ 1); or in 1/2 minute, 56 wam (28 ÷ 1/2).

E. Take a 1-minute timed writing on each line. Compute your speed and count errors.

E. SENTENCES

10 Vickie loved the fame she had achieved.
11 Art dashed to take the jet to his home.
12 Carl asked him to deed the farm to Ted.
| 1 | 2 | 3 | 4 | 5 | 6 | 7 | 8 | = 5-stroke words

F. Take two 1-minute timed writings on the paragraph. Compute your speed and count errors.

F. PARAGRAPH

CUMULATIVE WORDS

13 Della asked David to take her to school   8
14 for a short time. She had to meet Fred   16
15 or Sarah at the school office at three.   24
| 1 | 2 | 3 | 4 | 5 | 6 | 7 | 8 |

G. Take three 1-minute timed writings. Compute your speed and count errors.

G. 1-MINUTE TIMED WRITING

16 Cass said she asked Al Rice to meet her   8
17 at five to look for a jacket.   14
| 1 | 2 | 3 | 4 | 5 | 6 | 7 | 8 |

REPORT 57
TWO-PAGE UNBOUND
REPORT WITH HEADERS,
FOOTERS, AND
ENDNOTES

Spacing: Double

ARE WE ON TRACK FOR THE '90s?
By Malcolm Lund

The personal computer will affect our company in many ways over the next decade. It will impact on how we process information, produce our goods and services, hire employees, network throughout our organization, and purchase computers and related equipment. Just think what has happened in only one decade. Schlender states it well: "The PC rendered the typewriter nearly extinct, turned secretaries into word processing experts, pulled small businesses into the information age, and inspired man-machine love affairs every bit as passionate as automobiles have."[1]

What are the predictions for firms such as ours for the future?

Predictions

Many predictions are being made about the computer industry for the remainder of the '90s. Some of these predictions are discussed below:

Pioneers' Predictions. Two early pioneers of the personal computer industry—Steven P. Jobs, Apple Computer cofounder, and William G. Gates III, Microsoft cofounder—in a face-to-face interview predicted the following:

1. Razzle-dazzle technology will emerge faster than ever.
2. Data networks will come of age.
3. Users could confront a bewildering array of choices.
4. Japan's electronics companies will become more of a force.
5. Computers will finally change the nature of organizations and office work.[2]

Predictions by Others. Writers for <u>Business Week</u> indicated that the bulk of the computer market will be standards-based desktop computers.[3]

Recommendations

If these predictions occur, then we should establish a committee to determine what changes we should make with regard to our firm's organization, the continued use of PCs, and our networking throughout the company.

NOTES

1. Brenton R. Schlender, "The Future of the PC," <u>Fortune</u>, August 26, 1991, p. 40.
2. Ibid., pp. 40–41.
3. John W. Verity, with Gary McWilliams, Joseph Weber, and Alice Cuneo, "The Computer Slump Becomes a Sea of Change," <u>Business Week</u>, August 19, 1991, p. 106.

New Keys

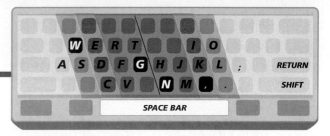

Margins: 1 inch • Spacing: Single • Drills: 2 times

Goals:
To control the N, W, comma, and G keys; to key 15 wam/ 1'/3e.

"15 wam/1'/3e" means to key at the rate of 15 words a minute for 1 minute with no more than 3 errors.

A. WARMUP

1 A major firm sold office items at cost.
2 Viola had her office clerks assist her.

NEW KEYS

Use the J finger.

Keep other fingers at home as you reach to N.

B. THE **N** KEY

3 jjj jnj jnj njn jjj jnj jnj njn jjj jnj
4 man fan ran sin den kin tin tan and not
5 sane rain even cent find seen then none
6 Dan and Al can enter the main entrance.

Use the S finger.

C. THE **W** KEY

7 sss sws sws wsw sss sws sws wsw sss sws
8 now two tow how wow row who law few saw
9 want will when wine warm wait saws wave
10 Walt Shaw will want to walk with Wanda.

Use the K finger.

Space once after a comma.

D. THE **,** KEY

11 kkk k,k k,k ,k, kkk k,k k,k ,k, kkk k,k
12 or, of, to, oh, it, no, if, is, so, do,
13 too, if it is, as soon as, if so, what,
14 Dale, Annie, Sadie, and Edith left too.

Use the F finger.

Keep wrists low, but not resting on the keyboard.

E. THE **G** KEY

15 fff fgf fgf gfg fff fgf fgf gfg fff fgf
16 log rag egg age nag tag sag get leg got
17 sage grow rage wing grew gown wage gain
18 Gail greeted the Garden Town Gardeners.

LETTERS 68–69
FORM LETTER IN BLOCK STYLE WITH STANDARD PUNCTUATION

Working Papers: 259–262

First key one copy of the form letter showing the variable names in all-capital letters and in parentheses. Then key a letter to Ms. Elsie Stonehouse, who is listed on the mailing list in Memo 32.

(Current Date) / (FULL NAME) / (COMPANY NAME) / (STREET ADDRESS) / (CITY), (STATE) (ZIP) / Dear (NAME): / Subject: Renewal Notice for Software News

Your firm's subscription to Software News will expire in approximately eight weeks. If (COMPANY NAME) is to keep abreast of current and future software developments, you will want to extend your subscription to the magazine.

Over the past 12 months we have published a variety of articles on new software and its uses in firms such as (COMPANY NAME), on the future development of and research on desktop computers as they relate to employee usage and satisfaction, and on how users in firms are accepting and implementing new software packages.

Whatever you do, don't delay. Act now to be sure that Software News keeps arriving without interruption at your firm. Just complete the enclosed renewal form, and return it in the enclosed addressed envelope.

Sincerely yours, / SOFTWARE NEWS / Arnold Smythe / Circulation Manager / Enclosures 2

TABLE 56
RULED TABLE

Spacing: Double

STARR-HARRISON, INC.
Year-to-Date Sales of Selected Mason Products

Model	First Quarter	Second Quarter	Third Quarter	Total for Year
11-1075	$42,084	$48,650	$43,791	$134,525
11-1079	1,379	1,465	1,821	4,665
12-1003	15,367	15,894	16,253	47,514
12-1025	4,549	5,412	5,880	15,841
13-1650	10,002	8,876	11,453	30,331
13-1655	8,392	9,416	9,832	27,640
13-1771	10,456	9,781	9,890	30,127
TOTAL	$92,229	$99,494	$98,920	$290,643

F. TECHNIQUE PRACTICE: SPACE BAR

19 Al is here. Ed is fine. Cal can meet.
20 Do it. See them. Rae did. Del is it.
21 Dora is home. Fred went. Cal is here.
22 Take the tram. Ed is in. Art is home.
23 Walt is there. Edith lost it. She is.

G. Take two 1-minute timed writings. Compute your speed and count errors.

G. 1-MINUTE TIMED WRITING

WORDS

24 Ted joined the firm one month ago. Ted   8
25 will see Valerie for a review too.   15

| 1 | 2 | 3 | 4 | 5 | 6 | 7 | 8 |

New Keys

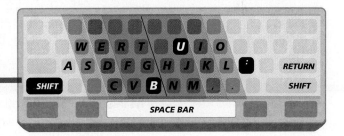

Margins: 1 inch • Spacing: Single • Drills: 2 times

Goals:
To control the left shift, U, B, and colon keys; to key 16 wam/1'/3e.

A. WARMUP

1 Evie jogged more than a mile with Walt.
2 Will Shea joined the Georgia Five team.

NEW KEYS

To capitalize letters on the right half of the keyboard:
1. With the F finger at home, press and hold down the left shift key with the A finger.
2. Strike the letter key.
3. Release the shift key and return fingers to home position.

B. THE LEFT **SHIFT** KEY

3 aaa Jaa Jaa aaa Kaa Kaa aaa Laa Laa aaa
4 Lee Joe Kim Ira Hal Ned Kit Mel Ken Jed
5 John Hans Mark Nita Iris Kate Hank Lian
6 Kate Mace went with Ned Hall to Kenton.

Use the J finger.

Keep other fingers at home as you reach to U.

C. THE **U** KEY

7 jjj juj juj uju jjj juj juj uju jjj juj
8 dug cue rut run due jug sue lug sun urn
9 just hulk nuns dunk sulk hums must junk
10 Hugh Unger urged that Hugo must unload.

MEMO 32

Key the memorandum, making the necessary corrections.

Indent the two-line subject line.

Be sure the first line of each address in Column 2 aligns with the first line of each address in Column 1.

The name of a publishing company can be the same as the name of the publication; for example, *Toledo Daily News*. Underline the name when it refers to the publication but not when it refers to the company, as in an inside address.

MEMO

TO: Alice Carlson

FROM: Arnold Smythe

DATE: (Current Date)

SUBJECT: Mailing List for Selected Firms Whose Subscriptions to
Software News Expires in Eight Weeks

Listed below is a selected list of firms whose subscription
to Software News expires in eight weeks. We want to be sure that
they renew their subscriptions because of their influence on
adoptions and their prestige.
Please send the enclosed form letter with the appropriate names and
addresses, to the designated individuals as soon as possible.

Mr. Alex Whitmore
Allison & Sons
1801 Investment Plaza
Cleveland, OH 43213-2305

Mrs. Susan Meiske-Rose
Arts and Crafts, Inc.
121 East Seventh Street
St. Paul, MN 55101-1332

Mr. Mark Riordion
Vice President
Riordion Software, Inc.
23030 Peachtree Road, NW
Atlanta, GA 31709-2317

Ms. Zenalda Diaz
A-One Markets
423 Commercial Square
Cincinnati, OH 45202-1006

Ms. Elsie Stonehouse
Diamond Foods, Inc.
Commonwealth Building
719 Griswold
Detroit, MI 48226-1785

Ms. Mary V. Moore
First National Bank
11 North Pennsylvania
Indianapolis, IN 46204-1321

Ms. Sandy Ramos
Toledo Daily News
606 Madison Street
Toledo, OH 43604-2376

Mr. Albert Chan
Montrose Associates
705 Hamilton
Peru, IN 46970

Enclosure

D. THE B KEY

Use the F finger.

11 fff fbf fbf bfb fff fbf fbf bfb fff fbf
12 big orb cab bun bow bid bit bin bag job
13 bush back bask bulb bent bunt blew bend
14 Bob backed Bill in a bid for a big job.

E. THE : KEY

The colon is the shift of the semicolon key.

Use the Sem finger.

Space once after a period following an abbreviation; twice after a colon.

15 ;;; ;:; ;:; :;: ;;; ;:; ;:; :;: ;;; ;:;
16 Mr. Uhl: Mrs. Low: Dr. Roe: Ms. See:
17 Dear Mrs. Mills: Dear John: Dear Lee:
18 Date: To: From: Subject: as listed:

SKILLBUILDING

F. KEYBOARD PRACTICE

Top row

19 We were told to take our truck to Hugo.
20 There were two tired men waiting there.
21 Write to their hometown to inform them.

Home row

22 Jake asked his dad for small red flags.
23 Sara added a dash of salt to the salad.
24 Dale said she had a fall sale in Elson.

Bottom row

25 He can come at five for nine old canes.
26 Burton came to vote with vim and vigor.
27 Bob had nerve to come via a Boston bus.

G. 1-MINUTE TIMED WRITING

G. Take two 1-minute timed writings. Compute your speed and count errors.

Goal: 16 wam/1'/3e

WORDS

28 Dear Jack: Fred would like to take Ben   8
29 and us to a home game at five tomorrow.   16

| 1 | 2 | 3 | 4 | 5 | 6 | 7 | 8

O. NUMBER AND SYMBOL PRACTICE

O. Key this paragraph twice as you concentrate on some of the commonly used symbols.

74 What high prices! The tag shows 50# @ $2.49 and 10# @ 78¢.
75 But the new ad* for Frost & Coyne shows prices that are 36%
76 lower. Let's build an inventory (an up-to-date one) now by
77 buying at these "summer discount prices." Don't you agree?

P. DIAGNOSTIC PRACTICE: ALPHABET

Turn to the Diagnostic Practice: Alphabet routine at the back of this book. Take the Pretest and record your performance. Then practice the drill lines for those reaches on which you made errors. Finally, repeat the Pretest and compare your performance.

Q. 5-MINUTE TIMED WRITING

Q. Spacing: double. Take two 5-minute timed writings. Compute your speed and count errors.

Goals: 50 wam/5'/5e

78   Major businesses across the land have found a unique   12
79 means to assist nonprofit organizations by using a new type   24
80 of marketing designed to do well by doing good. Advocates   35
81 call it a great idea because each player wins: the company   47
82 promotes its product, while the charity gains funding.   58
83   Unsure what this new pitch is all about? Chances are   70
84 good that you see some examples of this means of corporate   82
85 sponsorship each time you shop in a grocery store or read a   94
86 magazine circular. It occurs whenever you, the consumer,   105
87 purchase something and the company that makes the product   117
88 agrees to donate a portion of the proceeds to the nonprofit 129
89 agency of its choice. So if you buy a box of soap flakes,   141
90 you may be helping the Special Olympics. And if you pay   152
91 for that box by credit card, you may be helping to fight   164
92 cancer or Alzheimer's disease.   170
93   The trend for giving gifts with strings attached is   181
94 likely to stretch into the next few decades as budgets get   193
95 smaller and tighter. For companies, the link to a cause   205
96 can help make a product stand out. And for charities that   216
97 are facing reduced government dollars and fewer corporate   228
98 contributions, having their names linked to a product can   239
99 make the difference between their continuing or folding.   250

| 1 | 2 | 3 | 4 | 5 | 6 | 7 | 8 | 9 | 10 | 11 | 12 |

LESSON 8

New Keys

Margins: 1 inch • Spacing: Single • Drills: 2 times

Goals:
To control the P, Q, slash, and X keys; to key 17 wam/1'/3e.

A. WARMUP

1 Jack asked Morgan if Charlie came home.
2 Keith went to lunch with Vic and Baker.

NEW KEYS

B. THE P KEY

Use the Sem finger.

3 ;;; ;p; ;p; p;p ;;; ;p; ;p; p;p ;;; ;p;
4 pan sap rap pad pen sip lip dip pat rip
5 page pale stop trip pace peep palm park
6 Pat Page kept him in step with Pauline.

C. THE Q KEY

Use the A finger.

7 aaa aqa aqa qaq aaa aqa aqa qaq aaa aqa
8 quip aqua quick quiet equip quack quite
9 quell quark quotas quarts quills quests
10 The quiet quints quilted an aqua quilt.

D. THE / KEY

Use the Sem finger.

Do not space before or after a slash.

11 ;;; ;/; ;/; /;/ ;;; ;/; ;/; /;/ ;;; ;/;
12 his/her him/her he/she either/or ad/add
13 do/due/dew hale/hail fir/fur heard/herd
14 Ask him/her if he/she and/or Al can go.

E. THE X KEY

Use the S finger.

15 sss sxs sxs xsx sss sxs sxs xsx sss sxs
16 vex box tax nix mix wax lux lax hex fox
17 axle next taxi flux text flax flex apex
18 Max coaxed six men to fix a sixth taxi.

J. NUMBER PRACTICE

43 6601 5902 1103 3904 4005 5606 9007 3408 3609 8810 5611 2112
44 3213 4714 5615 8916 7017 1318 4419 2820 5921 6022 9223 4424
45 7325 5026 2227 9428 1929 3930 4431 2132 8933 6234 3835 2036
46 8937 2738 5839 6040 3241 5742 1843 2444 9345 9146 8847 4848

J. Take three 1-minute timed writings. The last two digits of each number provide a cumulative word count to help you determine your wam speed.

K. 12-SECOND SPRINTS

47 Flight #97 to Tulsa cost $543; Flight #34 to Reno was $561.
48 One-sixth or 1/6 equals 16.7%; 80% is equal to four-fifths.
49 Trace these policies: (1) #2428, (2) #1894, and (3) #1627.
50 On 10/28 he (Bart) paid $97, which is 36% less than I paid.

| | | | |5| | | |10| | |15| | |20| | |25| | |30| | |35| | |40| | |45| | |50| | |55| | |60

K. Take three 12-second timed writings on each line. The scale gives wam for a 12-second timed writing.

L. TECHNIQUE PRACTICE: TAB KEY

51 prize   pizza   amaze   sizes   zebra
52 mixed   extra   sixth   boxes   fixed
53 quick   quiet   quite   quart   quilt
54 judge   jumps   jokes   enjoy   banjo

L. Clear all tabs. Then set four new tabs every 10 spaces. Key lines 51–54, using the tab key to go across from column to column.

M. TECHNIQUE PRACTICE: CONCENTRATION

55   Ti ringrazio per la foto che mi hai mandato, anche per   12
56 tutti auguri che hai mandato. Noi siamo tutti bene e spero   24
57 che la tua famiglias anche si trovano tutti en bene salute.   36

| 1 | 2 | 3 | 4 | 5 | 6 | 7 | 8 | 9 | 10 | 11 | 12

M. Key this Italian paragraph once, concentrating on each letter keyed. Then take three 1-minute timed writings, trying to increase your speed each time.

N. SUSTAINED PRACTICE: ALTERNATE-HAND WORDS

58   The city planners appointed a panel of eight people to   12
59 handle the work. The chair of the panel will keep a formal   24
60 record of meetings. The chair will also sign any form that   36
61 panel members may wish to send to any visitor to a meeting.   48

62   When the chair called the first meeting for that panel   12
63 to order, all five members were available. The chair asked   24
64 each member to sign a form for reimbursement of expenses to   36
65 all panel meetings. The work for the panel was determined.   48

66   After that initial meeting, the chair was planning for   12
67 another meeting during the following week. Since all panel   24
68 members were available, the chair set an agenda. The chair   36
69 plans to give out assignments for all of the panel members.   48

70   The planners were anxious to have the group submit its   12
71 plans by the end of the first quarter of the year. This is   24
72 in keeping with the objective of having each section within   36
73 the governing board prepared for the final budget hearings.   48

| 1 | 2 | 3 | 4 | 5 | 6 | 7 | 8 | 9 | 10 | 11 | 12

N. Take a 1-minute timed writing on the first paragraph to establish your base speed. Then take four 1-minute timed writings on the remaining paragraphs. As soon as you equal or exceed your base speed on one paragraph, advance to the next one.

F. PHRASES

19 and it is|she can do|will he come|he is
20 she said so|who left them|can she drive
21 after all|he voted|just wait to|ask her
22 some needed it|for the firm|did he seem

G. TECHNIQUE PRACTICE: SHIFT KEY

23 Ada, Idaho; Sitka, Alaska; Eaton, Ohio;
24 Mr. and Mrs. Lee; Miss Sabin; Mr. Neal;
25 Mr. Don King; Ms. Sue Bell; Ames, Iowa;
26 Dr. Jo Smith; Mr. Ault; Mrs. Dean Bell;

H. Take two 1-minute timed writings. Compute your speed and count errors.

Goal: 17 wam/1'/3e

H. 1-MINUTE TIMED WRITING

27 George planned that Lu should have five   8
28 boxed lunches. Quint was to pack seven   16
29 mugs.   17

| 1 | 2 | 3 | 4 | 5 | 6 | 7 | 8

New Keys

LESSON

Margins: 1 inch • Spacing: Single • Drills: 2 times

Goals:
To control the hyphen, Z, Y, and ? keys; to key 18 wam/1'/3e.

A. WARMUP
1 I have quit the marketing job in Idaho.
2 Alice packed two boxes of silver disks.

NEW KEYS

Use the Sem finger.

Do not space before or after a hyphen.

Keep the J finger in home position.

B. THE - KEY

3 ;;; ;p; ;-; ;-; -;- ;;; ;-; -;- ;;; ;-;
4 one-sixth one-fifth one-third self-made
5 tie-in ha-ha show-off has-been ice-cold
6 Mr. Ward-Hughes is a well-to-do patron.

D. PACED PRACTICE

Turn to the Paced Practice routine at the back of the book. Take three 2-minute timed writings, starting at the speed at which you left off the last time.

Turn to the Paced Practice routine at the back of the book.

PRETEST.
Take a 1-minute timed writing; compute your speed and count errors.

E. PRETEST: VERTICAL REACHES

15 The third skier knelt on the knoll and secured a loose 12
16 ski as the race was about to begin. Each of the rival team 24
17 members awaited the starting signal way above the crowd. A 36
18 variety of trophies and awards would go to all the winners. 48

| 1 | 2 | 3 | 4 | 5 | 6 | 7 | 8 | 9 | 10 | 11 | 12

PRACTICE.
Speed Emphasis: If you made no more than 1 error on the Pretest, key each line twice.
Accuracy Emphasis: If you made 2 or more errors on the Pretest, key each group of lines (as though it were a paragraph) twice.

F. PRACTICE: UP REACHES

19 aw away award crawl straw drawn sawed drawl await flaw lawn
20 se self sense raise these prose abuse users serve send seem
21 ki kind kites skill skier skims skips skits kilts king skid
22 rd lard third beard horde gourd board guard sword cord curd

G. PRACTICE: DOWN REACHES

23 ac ache track paced brace races facts crack acute back aces
24 kn knob knife kneel knows knack knelt known knoll knot knew
25 ab drab about label table above abide gable abbey able abet
26 va vain vague value valve evade naval rival avail vats vase

POSTTEST.
Repeat the Pretest (E) and compare performance.

H. POSTTEST: VERTICAL REACHES

I. Take a 1-minute timed writing on the first paragraph to establish your base speed. Then take four 1-minute timed writings on the remaining paragraphs. As soon as you equal or exceed your base speed on one paragraph, advance to the next one.

I. SUSTAINED PRACTICE: NUMBERS

27 The membership director for a national association was 12
28 compiling a report on membership statistics for each region 24
29 in the association. This would be presented to the leaders 36
30 of the organization at an upcoming meeting of the officers. 48

31 Membership was organized into five regions. The total 12
32 number of members for the past year was 12,562. This was a 24
33 decline of 2,420 from the previous year. This decrease has 36
34 created a great deal of discussion on the part of officers. 48

35 The southern region had a membership of 3,640 for this 12
36 past year. It had 3,120 members in the previous year; this 24
37 meant it had an increase of 16.7 percent. Its goal for the 36
38 new year was 4,100 members. This goal would be attainable. 48

39 The other four regions had membership totals of 3,172, 12
40 2,289, 1,950, and 1,511. In one of the regions, a decrease 24
41 of 244 members took place; in another, there was a decrease 36
42 of 226 members. The other two regions had small decreases. 48

| 1 | 2 | 3 | 4 | 5 | 6 | 7 | 8 | 9 | 10 | 11 | 12

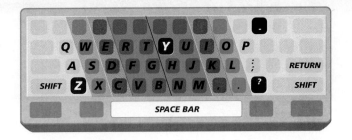

Elbow Control. Keep your elbows in close, hanging loosely by your sides. Do not let elbows swing out. Keep your shoulders relaxed, fingers curved, and wrists level.

C. THE Z KEY

Use the A finger.

Keep the F finger at home as you reach to Z.

7 aaa aza aza zaz aaa aza aza zaz aaa aza
8 zoo zap zig zip fez daze buzz jazz fizz
9 zing gaze zoom zone zinc quiz zest doze
10 The size of the prized pizza amazed us.

D. THE Y KEY

Use the J finger.

11 jjj jyj jyj yjy jjj jyj jyj yjy jjj jyj
12 ray say way may you joy yam yet yes eye
13 yarn year yawn yard holy fray eyed duty
14 Lucy, Nancy, and Peggy may try to stay.

E. THE ? KEY

The question mark is the shift of the slash.

Use the Sem finger.

Space twice after a question mark at the end of a sentence.

15 ;;; ;/? ;/? ?;? ;;; ;/? ;/? ?;? ;;; ;?;
16 Can Ken go? If not him, who? Can Joe?
17 Is that you? Can it be? Who will see?
18 Did he ask? Can they go? Why not her?

SKILLBUILDING

Hyphens are used:
1. To show that a word is divided (line 19).
2. To make a dash (two hyphens with no space before or after, see lines 20 and 23).
3. To join words in a compound (lines 21, 22, and 24).

F. TECHNIQUE PRACTICE: HYPHEN

19 Can Larry go to the next tennis tourna-
20 ment? I am positive he--like you--will
21 find it a first-class sports event. If
22 he can go, I will get first-rate seats.
23 Zane--like Ellen--liked to write texts.
24 Tony took Liza to a drive-in for lunch.

G. PHRASES

25 and the|for the|car is able|can they go
26 did they fly|ask her|for him|they still
27 of what|with us|ought to be|can he send
28 has been able|they need it|he will call

Unit 2   **Lesson 9**   **15**

LESSONS 116-120

Margins: 1 inch • Spacing: Single • Drills: 2 times • Format Guide: 85–89 • Working Papers: 259–266

Goals for Unit 24

Begin each day with approximately 15 minutes of skill-building, selecting activities from pages 269–272. In the remaining class time, complete as many production jobs from pages 273–280 as you can.

1. To improve accuracy and speed on alphabet and number keys.
2. To key 50 wam for 5 minutes with no more than 5 errors.
3. To improve proofreading skills.
4. To format various letters—personal-business, business, two-page—and memorandums from typeset and rough-draft input.
5. To format tables in a variety of styles.
6. To format a report with a variety of features—side headings, paragraph headings, endnotes, and enumerations.

A. WARMUP

```
1    Flight #1120 to Phoenix on August 19 was quoted at the    12
2  rate of $464.  Flight #357 to Las Vegas on July 7 was given  24
3  as $385.  Becky Zinn confirmed the rates with Bill Walmach.  36
```
| | 1 | 2 | 3 | 4 | 5 | 6 | 7 | 8 | 9 | 10 | 11 | 12 |

LANGUAGE ARTS

B. Study the rules at the right. Then key lines 4–7, making necessary changes.

B. NUMBERS

Rule: When two numbers come together in a sentence and one is part of a compound adjective, spell the first number unless the second number would make a much shorter word.

They have begun constructing three 16-story condominiums.

Rule: In high-level executive writing, hyphenate all compound numbers between 21 and 99 (or *21st* and *99th*), whether they stand alone or are part of a number over 100.

He has already received twenty-two congratulatory letters.

```
4  The real estate agent showed them 3 4-bedroom houses.
5  The package contained one hundred fifty 10-dollar bills.
6  A dividend will be paid for thirty-four years in a row.
7  My company plans to have a big 25th anniversary party.
```

C. Compare this paragraph with the last paragraph of the 5-minute timed writing on page 272. Key a list of the words that contain errors, correcting the errors as you key.

C. PROOFREADING

```
 8      The trend for give gifts with strings attached is
 9  liekly to stretch in to the next few decades as bugets get
10  smaller and tighter.  For companys, the link to a cause
11  can help make a product standout.  And for chairties that
12  are facing reduced goverment dollars and fewer corporate
13  contributions, having their names linked to a produce can
14  make the difference between continuing or folding.
```

H. Space once after a semi-colon and comma, twice after a period and question mark at the end of a sentence, twice after a colon.

H. PUNCTUATION PRACTICE

29 John sings; Paul writes. Is she there?
30 Can Morgan drive? I will drive; hurry.
31 Pat, Janice, and May left. I will fly.

I. Take two 1-minute timed writings. Compute your speed and count errors.

Goal: 18 wam/1'/3e

I. 1-MINUTE TIMED WRITING

32 Zelig judged six keying contests that a   8
33 local firm held in Piqua. Vic Bass was   16
34 a winner.   18

| 1 | 2 | 3 | 4 | 5 | 6 | 7 | 8

LESSON 10

Review

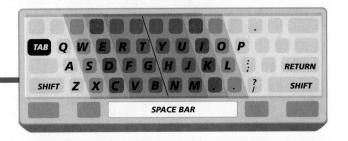

Margins: 1 inch • Spacing: Single • Drills: 2 times

Goals:
To strengthen controls; to format paragraph copy; to key 19 wam/1'/3e.

A. WARMUP

1 Gwen Dunne expects too much from a job.
2 Keith had a very quiet, lazy afternoon.

FORMATTING

The word counts in this book credit you with 1 word (5 strokes) for each paragraph indention in a timed writing. Press the tab key after the timing starts.

B. PARAGRAPH INDENT

When paragraphs are double spaced, the first line of each paragraph should be indented 5 spaces or ½ inch (the default setting on some equipment).

To set a tab for a 5-space paragraph indention, clear existing tabs. then position the carrier 5 spaces from the left margin and set a tab. Press the tab key with the A finger to indent.

When paragraphs are single spaced, leave 1 blank line between them. The first line may be either indented 5 spaces or blocked at the left margin. (See the illustrations below.)

        I would like to visit you
next month. What plans do you
have during June?

        We could go to Avon for a
trip down the river. We had a
good time last year.

Double-spaced, indented.

        I would like to visit you
next month. What plans do you
have during June?

        We could go to Avon for a
trip down the river. We had a
good time last year.

        Can you let me know how a
trip like this sounds? A raft
is a lot of fun, as you know.

Single-spaced, indented.

I would like to visit you next
month. What plans do you have
during June?

We could go to Avon for a trip
down the river. We had a good
time last year.

Can you let me know how a trip
like this sounds? A raft is a
lot of fun, as you know.

Single-spaced, blocked.

Get this in the mail by July 19. As usual, please check for additional errors!

Mr. Leland G. Paulin
Krevitz and Paulin, Attorneys-at-Law
52 Laurentian St.
Sault Sainte Marie, Ontario
CANADA P6B4G

Subject: Schneidermann Arbitration Case

Dear Mr. Paulin:

I have been informed that your firm is now representing Lanmoore Engineering Designs, Ltd. with respect to our joint arbitration hearing. As you likely are now aware, the case will be heard before the London Court of International Arbitration in in London, England on November 15. Rockford International has had a good relationship with Lanmoore that dates back to our first years of partnership. This is the first time that our marketing efforts have resulted in an arbitration setting. As we have been selling sub-assembly components to Schneidermann Engineering in Germany for several years, we are surprised that this situation has developed.

Jim Watters of our legal video department has informed me that the two of you have scheduled a conference with members of your staffs in early August. I shall look forward to recieving a summary of these discussions.

Sincerely yours

Carter B. Phillips
Vise President for Marketing

c : Jim Waters

C. LINE SPACING

Line spacing sets the amount of space between keyed lines. Single spacing (1) leaves no blank lines; double spacing (2) leaves 1 blank line; triple spacing (3) leaves 2 blank lines, and so forth. Some equipment also has half-line spacing.

To change the line spacing within a document, position the carrier where you want the new spacing to begin. Set the line-space selector at "1" for single spacing, "2" for double spacing, and so forth.

SKILLBUILDING

D. SHORT PARAGRAPHS

D. Spacing: double; tab: 5 spaces. Take a 1-minute timed writing on each paragraph, or key lines 3–8 once. Compute your speed and count errors. Use the tab key to indent the first line of each paragraph.

3   You can now use your keying skills   8
4 to do many jobs. Quite a few will have   16
5 to be printed.   19

6   It will amaze you to find how easy   8
7 and exact keying is used to rough out a   16
8 good thought.   19

```
|  1  |  2  |  3  |  4  |  5  |  6  |  7  |  8
```

E. TECHNIQUE PRACTICE: RETURN AND TAB KEYS

E. Spacing: double; tab: 5 spaces. Key each sentence on a separate line. Tab to indent each line.

Technique hint: Keep your eyes on the copy as you make the reach to the tab key.

9 Edna asked Quincy to order some stamps.
10 Joseph left for New York at noon today.
11 Mary was amazed to find Robert at home.
12 When is Mary or Lucy to be interviewed?
13 Oscar ordered some pizza for the class.
14 The manager was explicit in directions.
15 Kyle was on time for the short meeting.
16 Who left their worksheets on the table?

Format the heading for page 2 of the memo the same as you would for a two-page letter. (See page R-5 in the Reference Section.)

This is Carter Phillips. Please transcribe this dictation of a memo report right away. I would like you to look up some information in reference works to fill in various parts of the report.

This report is being sent to Sheryl Alvarez, Director of South American Operations. Please remember to enter an appropriate subject line. Here is the body of the memo:

The enclosed materials will provide useful background information as you prepare for our next meeting to review our South American operations.

(Put a side heading here labeled "Background.") Deliberate decisions were made during the 1980s by Rockford International not to market our products to domestic companies in Brazil. this was true even though the market potential is significant in a country with a population of . . . .

(Would you please look up the population of Brazil and insert it here.)

Our position began to change when Brazil developed a comprehensive environmental program for the Amazon region in 1989. The subsequent move toward an increasingly diversified economic climate has altered our views. We are now ready to move forward.

(Let's put a side heading here labeled "Present Concerns."

Brazil's government land policies combined with a high inflation rate have led to a severe economic recession. The people suffer from a severe mal-distribution of income, and the country's foreign debt is among the largest in the world.

The literacy rate for the population of Brazil is . . . *(please look this up for me)* compared with . . . *(please look this up also)* in the United States.

(Let's put another side heading here labeled "Reasons for Optimism.")

Brazil is fortunate to have extensive mineral reserves. Of particular importance are iron, coal, tin, and oil. But the country also has rich fields of diamonds, gold, nickel, and gemstones.

The present form of government is a . . . . *(Please check to see what the exact wording should be.)*

Efforts are being made to more equitably distribute income throughout the country. The present numbers of such items as television sets, radios, and telephones would seem to indicate that there is a tremendous potential in the consumer market.

Sheryl, I look forward to seeing you on August 23 in Sao Paulo.

F. Spacing: single. Key each line twice.

Keep fingers curved and wrists low but not resting on the keyboard as you practice these lines.

F. ALPHABET REVIEW

17 Alma Adams asked Alda to fly to Alaska.
18 Both Bill and Barbara liked basketball.
19 Can Cass accept a classic car in Clare?
20 David did dine in the diner in Drayton.
21 Earl says Elmer edited the entire text.
22 Four fables focused on the five friars.
23 Gina gave a bag of green grapes to Gil.
24 Hal hoped Seth had helped haughty Hugh.
25 Irene liked to pickle pickles in brine.
26 Jody Judd joined a junior jogging team.
27 Keith kept a kayak for a trip to Koyuk.
28 Lance played a razzle-dazzle ball game.
29 Martha made more money on many markups.
30 Nan knew ten men in a main dining room.
31 Opal Olah opened four boxes of oranges.
32 Pat paid to park the plane on the ramp.
33 Quincy quickly quit his quarterly quiz.
34 Robin read rare books in their library.
35 Sal signed, sealed, and sent the lease.
36 Todd caught trout in the little stream.
37 Uncle Marty urged Julie to go to Utica.
38 Viva Vista vetoed the five voice votes.
39 Walt waited while Wilma went to Weston.
40 Xu mixed extra extract exactly as told.
41 Yes, your young sister played a cymbal.
42 Zesty zebras zigzagged in the Ohio zoo.

G. Take two 1-minute timed writings. Compute your speed and count errors.

Goal: 19 wam/1'/3e

G. 1-MINUTE TIMED WRITING

43   Zoe expected a quiet morning to do   8
44 her work. Joy was to bring five of the   16
45 ruled tablets.   19

| 1 | 2 | 3 | 4 | 5 | 6 | 7 | 8 |

No rush with these minutes. Next week will be fine.

Rockford International
Minutes of Executive Committee Meeting
July 17, 19--

Introduction	Barbara J. Rosemont, President of Rockford International, reported that ~~early~~ preliminary sales figures for the second quarter of the calendar year show a 17% increase over projected figures. She indicated that she plans to send a communication to all employees expressing her personal appreciation for their performance.
Kangas-Rockford	Josh Bransen reported that Bob Wilson will go to Finland on September 4 to finalize arrangements for the Kangas-Rockford endeavor.
Annual Meeting	Joe Rosemount reviewed ~~arrangements~~ plans for the annual meeting, scheduled for December 3. Earlier rumors of demonstrations by anti-military groups appear to be unfounded.
Contract for Rockford-China	Jim Watters reported on progress with the Rockford-China project, ~~indicating that it appears that there will be~~ no roadblocks ~~set up~~ are expected by the government of the people's Republic of China.
North Atlantic Oil Fields	Bobbi Kjome provided the following information relating to the proposed purchase of either Jovaag Enterprises in Norway or Emerson Electronics, Ltd., in England.

	Square Footage	Number of Employees	Year Built
Jovaag	42,000	178	1983
Emerson	35,000	164	1977

Foreign Visitor Program	Valerie Thomas reported on the dramatic growth of our ~~visitor~~ foreign program. The results are directly tied to increases in foreign sales, licensing, training, and consulting.
CONCLUDING REMARKS	*Carter Phillips thanked everyone for their work and then adjourned the meeting.*

Number Keys

Margins: 1 inch • Tab: 5 spaces • Spacing: Single •
Drills: 2 times

Goals:
To control the 4, 7, 3, and 8 keys; to key 19 wam/2'/5e.

Key the paragraph twice from now on.

A. WARMUP

1   Robert Vaughn wrote a good article in one of 10
2 our new magazines. He quotes Paul Jones, William 20
3 Paley, and Xenia May. Read it--you will like it. 30

  | 1 | 2 | 3 | 4 | 5 | 6 | 7 | 8 | 9 | 10

NEW KEYS

Use the F finger.

Do not space after a colon used with figures to express time.

B. THE 4 KEY

4 fr4f fr4f f44f f44f f4f4 f4f4 4 44 444 4,444 4:44
5 44 fins 44 fish 44 feet 44 figs 44 fans 44 flakes
6 The 44 boys had 44 tickets for the games at 4:44.
7 Fred Lyons had read 44 articles and 44 magazines.

Use the J finger.

C. THE 7 KEY

8 ju7j ju7j j77j j77j j7j7 j7j7 7 77 777 7,777 7:77
9 77 jigs 77 jobs 77 jugs 77 jets 77 jars 77 jewels
10 The 77 men bought Items 77 and 777 for their job.
11 Joe had 47 books and 77 tablets for a 7:47 class.

Use the D finger.

D. THE 3 KEY

12 de3d de3d d33d d33d d3d3 d3d3 3 33 333 3,333 3:33
13 33 doze 33 died 33 dine 33 days 33 dogs 33 drains
14 The 33 vans moved 73 cases in less than 33 hours.
15 If Charles adds 43, 44, and 347, he will get 434.

Use the K finger.

E. THE 8 KEY

16 ki8k ki8k k88k k88k k8k8 k8k8 8 88 888 8,888 8:88
17 88 inks 88 inns 88 keys 88 kits 88 kids 88 knives
18 Bus 38 left at 3:38 and arrived here at 8:37 p.m.
19 Kenny called Joe at 8:38 at 883-7878 or 484-3878.

SKILLBUILDING

F. NUMBER PRACTICE: 4, 7, 3, AND 8

20 The 47 tickets were for the April 3 show at 8:48.
21 Mary was to read pages 33, 47, 84, and 87 to him.
22 Kate planted 43 tulips, 38 mums, and 87 petunias.
23 Only 387 of the 473 coeds could register at 4:38.

MEMO 29

Please date and send this on the 19th.

MEMO TO: Della Stenerud, Director
Rockford Scandinavian Office
FROM: CBP
DATE: July 19, 19——
SUBJECT: Considered Purchase of Jovaag Enterprises

I have studied your report on the considered purchase of Jovaag Enterprises in Porsgrunn, Norway. As we move into the North Atlantic oil market, the production of control systems in the area likely will result in significantly reduced manufacturing costs.

There is one other manufacturing site near the North Atlantic oil fields that is also being considered. In order to expedite a decision on the selection, a team of three people headed by Bobbi Kjome will be visiting Norway in about two weeks.

Della, would you please have information relating to the questions on the enclosure ready for the team members' review when they arrive.

Enclosure

MEMO 30

The manufacturing site referred to in the first paragraph of the Jovaag Enterprises memo is Emerson Electronics, Ltd., located in Manchester, England. Please revise the Jovaag memo, and address it to Margaret Milford, director of the Rockford British office. Steve Keane has been appointed to serve as head of the team for the visit to England.

G. SUSTAINED PRACTICE: NUMBERS

G. Take a 1-minute timed writing on the first paragraph to establish your base speed. Then take four 1-minute timed writings on the remaining paragraphs. As soon as you equal or exceed your base speed on one paragraph, advance to the next one.

24   In the past 34 months, we constructed stores 10
25 in 38 states. We hope to build 47 stores in some 20
26 of the 48 states in which we are currently found. 30

27   Of the 37 stores built, many will have 73 to 10
28 84 employees. In 33 stores, most of the managers 20
29 supervise 34 to 48 employees in all of the units. 30

30   In Ohio, 38 stores serve 43 counties. In 37 10
31 stores, we have over 483 varieties of products to 20
32 sell. All 38 stores sell the Bates 877 products. 30

33   The top 447 stores meet the needs of 874,374 10
34 people in 38 cities in 34 states. Our 43 leading 20
35 stores are found in 33 major cities in Louisiana. 30

| 1 | 2 | 3 | 4 | 5 | 6 | 7 | 8 | 9 | 10 |

H. TECHNIQUE PRACTICE: SHIFT KEY

H. Keep other fingers at home as you reach to the shift keys.

36 Joe Sal Ann Yuk Sue Pat Jae Tab Fay Vera Rosa Tao
37 Dick Fern Juan Mike Andre Fidel Pedro Chong Alice
38 Karen Ojars Marta Scott Carlos Maria Julie Caesar
39 Al Ken Bob Ray Joan Marge Mary Ted Bill Jerry Mel

I. PUNCTUATION PRACTICE

I. Keep other fingers and elbow still as you reach to the hyphen.

40 Jan Brooks-Smith was a go-between for the author.
41 The off-the-record comment led to a free-for-all.
42 Louis was a jack-of-all-trades as a clerk-typist.
43 Ask Barbara--who is in Central Data--to find out.
44 Joanne is too old-fashioned to be that outspoken.

J. PROGRESSIVE PRACTICE: ALPHABET

Turn to the Progressive Practice: Alphabet routine at the back of the book. Take six 30-second timed writings.

Follow the directions at the top of the page for beginning the activity.

K. 2-MINUTE TIMED WRITING

K. Spacing: double. Take two 2-minute timed writings. Compute your speed and count errors.

Goal: 19 wam/2'/5e

45   If you are seeking a job, do you possess the 10
46 expected skills? Quite often just a list of them 20
47 will let you size up those which you already have 30
48 or may be acquired in your new position. 38

| 1 | 2 | 3 | 4 | 5 | 6 | 7 | 8 | 9 | 10 |

TABLE 53

QUOTATION FOR PROPOSED INITIAL ORDER

Leave 4 spaces between columns.

Kangas-Rockford
Effective ~~on~~ August 1, 19--

Number	Item	Item Price*	Total
1,000	XLB Transformer	$ 19.60	
1,000	103 Wiring board	4.20	
1,000	4B Resistor network	3.12	
4,000	MPN Transistor	.07	
2,000	4CD Capacitor, Ceramic	56 .63	
4,000	6D Resistor	.12	
2,000	2CD Diode	.89	
ds 1	Temperature Test Station	184,000.00	
1	Diagnostic Test Fixture	3,600.00	
1	Test Strength Fixture	12,047.00	
1	Swaging Press	3,200.00	
1	Oscilloscope	7,355.00	

Increase item prices 10% (round to nearest cent); then enter the totals.

TOTAL

*All prices are in U. S. dollars and are subject to change on 60 days' written notice. All prices are f.o.b. Jacksonville, Florida, USA, and do not include any applicable ~~added~~ taxes.

TABLE 54

Kangas-Rockford may wish to delay ordering the testing equipment until January 1. Please prepare a separate table for these items (the last five entries). The prices should reflect a 15 percent increase rather than 10 percent. These prices are effective January 1, 19--. Change the title to Quotation for Testing Equipment Order.

TABLE 55

We'll also have to prepare an August 1 quotation for just the other items (first seven entries). Please use the prices that were increased 10 percent.

---

12 LESSON

Review

Margins: 1 inch • Tab: 5 spaces • Spacing: Single •
Drills: 2 times

Goal:
To key 20 wam/2'/5e.

A. WARMUP

1   Alex said 37 men quit unexpectedly. The men 10
2 worked in 48 firms. At least 34 have found a job 20
3 in 33 firms. Amazingly, the men like their jobs. 30

  | 1 | 2 | 3 | 4 | 5 | 6 | 7 | 8 | 9 | 10

SKILLBUILDING

B. Take a 1-minute timed writing on the first paragraph to establish your base speed. Then take four 1-minute timed writings on the remaining paragraphs. As soon as you equal or exceed your base speed on one paragraph, advance to the next one.

B. SUSTAINED PRACTICE: SYLLABIC INTENSITY

4   There is no question that we have entered an 10
5 age of information. Many new processes and smart 20
6 equipment can now provide more data in less time. 30

7   The entire telecommunications industry has a 10
8 very bright future. With the use of the computer 20
9 and the phone, much stored data is now available. 30

10   The ease with which financial records can be 10
11 updated and revised is truly phenomenal. Visit a 20
12 nearby financial institution for a demonstration. 30

13   Inventory control has become simpler with an 10
14 emphasis on technology. Optical scanning devices 20
15 can help businesses with their inventory records. 30

  | 1 | 2 | 3 | 4 | 5 | 6 | 7 | 8 | 9 | 10

C. ALPHABET PRACTICE

16 Packing jam for the dozen boxes was quite lively.
17 Fay quickly jumped over the two dozen huge boxes.
18 We vexed Jack by quietly helping a dozen farmers.
19 The quick lynx from the zoo just waved a big paw.
20 Lazy brown dogs do not jump over the quick foxes.

D. NUMBER PRACTICE

21 Mary was to read pages 37, 48, 74, and 83 to Zoe.
22 He invited 43 boys and 48 girls to the 7:34 show.
23 The 8:37 bus did not come to our stop until 8:44.
24 Purchase Order 43 listed Items 34, 77, 83, and 8.
25 Flight 374 will be departing Gate 37 at 8:48 p.m.

Please date this letter July 28. As usual, correct any errors I may have made. Leave the inside address blank. Key the salutation 3 inches from the top.

ds To Share Holders of Rockford International:
It is with a great deal of pleasure that we send you this ~~second~~
report on our entry in to the Scandinavian market.

Our early discussions with firms in Norway are progressing about
on schedule. Our big news is that we will soon likely enter
into a relationship with Kangas Automation, Inc. in Finland.
They will purchase selected Rockford components to be resold
with their equipment under the tradename Kangas-Rockford. They
are confident that the western ~~soviet~~ states will become large
users of their products. We look forward to seeing most of you
at our annual meeting. If you are not planing to attend, the
enclosed proxy must be returned to our office by September 1
19--.

in the former Soviet Union

Sincerely Yours,

CarterB. Phillips
Vice-President for Marketing

MEMO 28

MEMO TO: Jim Watters
Legal Department
From: CBP
Date:
Subject: Contract for Rockford-China

Please correct any errors.

There are still several unresolved issues relating to our establishment
of a wholly foreign-owned enterprise in the Peoples Republic of
China (PRC).

1. ~~Our first concern is that~~ Rockford-China must be able to accept
orders from ~~any~~ customers within the PRC in either local or
foreign currency without Government interference.

2. ~~Also,~~ Rockford-China must be able to pay duties in local
chinese currency for imported components, sub-assemblies, and
complete products in order to utilize locally generated revenues.

We must be able to hire local chinese people through out the PRC.

3. Rockford-China must have the freedom to set sales prices in any
currency and to pay dividends without Government interference.

4.
Please incorporate these provisions in the draft agreement,
which, it is hoped, will be ready for signing within a month.

Please initial this for me and get it over to the Legal Department right away.

E. TECHNIQUE PRACTICE: RETURN KEY

26 Can he go? If so, what? I am lost. Joe is ill.
27 Did he key the memo? Tina is going. Susan lost.
28 Max will drive. Xenia is in Ohio. He is taller.
29 Nate is fine; Ty is not. Who won? Where is Nan?
30 No, he cannot go. Is he here? Where is Roberta?

F. TECHNIQUE PRACTICE: SPACE BAR

31 a b c d e f g h i j k l m n o p q r s t u v w x y
32 to an is of we no it in as go by me be or but for
33 Do you go to Ada or Ida for work every day or so?
34 I am sure he can go with you if he has some time.
35 He is to be at the car by the time you get there.

G. Spacing: double.
Take two 2-minute timed writings. Compute your speed and count errors.

Goal: 20 wam/2'/5e

G. 2-MINUTE TIMED WRITING

36   Skills in expressing our thoughts are needed 10
37 more than ever. One who can write and speak well 20
38 quite often does well on the job. You really can 30
39 learn these amazing skills if you will take time. 40

    | 1 | 2 | 3 | 4 | 5 | 6 | 7 | 8 | 9 | 10

LESSON 13

Number Keys

Margins: 1 inch • Tab: 5 spaces • Spacing: Single •
Drills: 2 times

Goals:
To control the 2, 9, 1, and 0 keys; to key 21 wam/2'/5e.

A. WARMUP

1   Quincy Loven took the 3:34 jet to Chicago to 10
2 attend an 8:37 meeting tomorrow. He expects Fran 20
3 Ladda will have a short buzz session before 7:34. 30

    | 1 | 2 | 3 | 4 | 5 | 6 | 7 | 8 | 9 | 10

NEW KEYS

Use the S finger.

B. THE 2 KEY

4 sw2s sw2s s22s s22s s2s2 s2s2 2 22 222 2,222 2:22
5 22 subs 22 suns 22 seas 22 sons 22 sets 22 sports
6 The 22 seats sold at 2:22 to 22 coeds in Room 22.
7 He added Items 22, 23, 24, 27, and 28 on Order 2.

Please prepare the following letter to be sent to Mr. Uno Kukkonen, President of Kangas Automation, Inc., at 2728 Maki Street in Helsinki, Finland.

Ms. Della Stenerud of our Scandinavian office in Stockholm has been keeping me informed of developments with your firm. It is my understanding that Kangas Automation, Inc., wishes to enter into a relationship with Rockford International to purchase selected electronics components. These would then be resold with certain Kangas equipment under the trade name Kangas-Rockford.

Some provisions are not discussed in the proposed contract. Conditions for payment, remedies for damage, and term length for the agreement must also be addressed. Mr. Robert W. Wilson, our chief financial officer, will be flying to Finland on September 4 to discuss these items with members of your staff.

We at Rockford look forward to this new association.

CBP

PS: Thank you, Mr. Kukkonen, for the invitation to visit your plant in Helsinki. I look forward to doing this when I go there for the formal signing of the agreement.

REPORT 55
AGENDA

For tomorrow's meeting! ds

ROCKFORD INTERNATIONAL ← Bold
Executive Committee Meeting
Wednesday, July 17, 19-- (4)

Opening Remarks	Barbara J. Rosemont
Kangas Automation, Inc.	Josh Bransen
Annual Meeting	Joseph E. Rosemont, Jr.
Contract for Rockford-China	Jim Watters
North Atlantic Oil Market	Bobbi Kjome
Foreign Visitor Program	Valerie Thomas
Concluding Remarks	Carter B. Phillips

C. THE 9 KEY

Use the L finger.

8 lo9l lo9l 1991 1991 1919 1919 9 99 999 9,999 9:99
9 99 lads 99 lights 99 labs 99 legs 99 lips 99 logs
10 Their 99 cans of No. 99 were sold to 99 managers.
11 He had 29 pens, 39 pads, 93 pencils, and 9 clips.

D. THE 1 KEY

Use the A finger.

12 aq1a aq1a a11a a11a a1a1 a1a1 1 11 111 1,111 1:11
13 11 adds 11 arts 11 aims 11 axes 11 aces 11 arenas
14 Sam left here at 1:11; Sue at 11:11; Don at 9:11.
15 Eric moved from 1992 Main Street to 1994 in 1991.

E. THE 0 KEY

Use the Sem finger.

16 ;p0; ;p0; ;00; ;00; ;0;0 ;0;0 0 00 000 0,000 0:00
17 10 pads 10 pegs 10 pits 10 pins 10 pens 100 parks
18 You will get 220 when you add 30, 40, 70, and 80.
19 The 20 men met at 2:02 with 10 agents in Room 20.

SKILLBUILDING

F. NUMBER PRACTICE

20 Jill bought 44 tickets for the 7:30 or 8:30 show.
21 When you add 44, 30, 40, 80, and 90, you get 284.
22 Maxine called from 829-7430 or 829-7431 for Mary.
23 Sally had 12 cats, 20 dogs, and 30 birds at home.

24 Items 37, 38, 39, and 40 were sent on October 18.
25 Did Flight 1478 leave from Gate 19 at 2:30 today?
26 Sue went from 380 29th Street to 471 27th Street.
27 He sold 43 tires, 28 air filters, and 139 wipers.

G. Indent and key each sentence on a separate line.

G. TECHNIQUE PRACTICE: RETURN AND TAB KEYS

28 Casey left.   Susan asked for Tom.   Where is John?
29 How fast do you key?   Is Maxine faster?   I drive.
30 She lived at 1991 Main Street.   He sold old cars.
31 Do you have the software?   If not you, who could?

Situation: Today is July 16, 19—, and you are the administrative assistant to Mr. Carter B. Phillips, vice president for marketing of Rockford International in Jacksonville, Florida. Rockford International was founded by Rockford Electronics, Inc., in 1983 to handle its exports and to coordinate other marketing functions in foreign countries. As 53 percent of its stock is currently owned by Rockford Electronics, the parent company continues to be a strong force in all management decisions.

Rockford International is responsible for the sales of all Rockford Electronics products outside the United States and Canada. Additionally, the firm acts as the licenser to foreign enterprises for the manufacture of Rockford products as well as the distribution of Rockford products. At times these goods are distributed under a different brand name and may even have a localized logo.

The primary products are transmitters, which are designed to relay electrical impulses of mechanical movements. Many other electronic instruments and components are manufactured by Rockford, however.

Mr. Phillips has a number of jobs ready for you to complete. Read through the materials first so that you can ask for clarification right away.

You are expected to format documents properly, capitalize correctly, and review all jobs for errors that Mr. Phillips may have missed. Use the modified-block letter style with standard punctuation for all outgoing correspondence, and include this closing:

```
Sincerely yours,



Carter B. Phillips
Vice President for Marketing
```

Once you have looked over your work assignments and have cleared up any questions, you will need to prioritize the jobs. Determine the priority levels (1, 2, and 3) of the jobs according to these guidelines:

1. Those items which have been identified by Mr. Phillips as having high priority or which, in your judgment, should be in this category.
2. Those items which are timely but, on the basis of their content, do not warrant a high-priority label.
3. Those items which may be delayed until after you have completed the jobs in Levels 1 and 2.

TABLE 52
JOB PRIORITY LIST

Create the table shown below. List the job names and numbers in Column 1. In Column 2, show their priority (according to the directions above). Next, complete the jobs in order of priority. Check off each job (in Column 3), as you complete it.

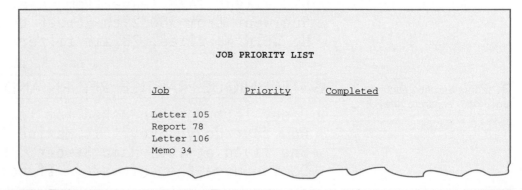

```
                    JOB PRIORITY LIST


        Job              Priority      Completed

        Letter 105
        Report 78
        Letter 106
        Memo 34
```

H. Take a 1-minute timed writing on the first paragraph to establish your base speed. Then take four 1-minute timed writings on the remaining paragraphs. As soon as you equal or exceed your base speed on one paragraph, advance to the next one.

H. SUSTAINED PRACTICE: NUMBERS

32   In the past quarter, we have added the names 10
33 of 178 clients to our database. This gives us an 20
34 exciting total of 249 clients in this first year. 30

35   Of the 249 clients, 92 were being handled by 10
36 Charles Thompson; 84 were controlled by Charlotte 20
37 Baines; and 73 were being serviced by Gail Banks. 30

38   We got 24 clients in July from 108 contacts; 10
39 August brought us 20 clients from 138 contacts; a 20
40 record of 34 clients was gained during September. 30

41   We were able to get 249 clients in our first 10
42 year; our aim is 470, 733, and 880 clients in the 20
43 next three years--or 2,332 clients in four years. 30

| 1 | 2 | 3 | 4 | 5 | 6 | 7 | 8 | 9 | 10 |

I. Spacing: double. Take two 2-minute timed writings. Compute your speed and count errors.

Goal: 21 wam/2'/5e

I. 2-MINUTE TIMED WRITING

44   We can expect quite a few changes in our job 10
45 market in the next few years. There will be jobs 20
46 that have new skills due to the many uses of the 30
47 computer. The labor market will increase in its 40
48 size, too. 42

| 1 | 2 | 3 | 4 | 5 | 6 | 7 | 8 | 9 | 10 |

LESSON 14

Number Keys

Margins: 1 inch • Tab: 5 spaces • Spacing: Single • Drills: 2 times

Goals:
To control the 5 and 6 keys; to key 22 wam/2'/5e.

A. WARMUP

1   Liza Quigley moved to 4397 South Main Street 10
2 on July 20. She expected Frank would spend a few 20
3 extra hours helping her move 18 chairs and books. 30

| 1 | 2 | 3 | 4 | 5 | 6 | 7 | 8 | 9 | 10 |

N. TECHNIQUE PRACTICE: TAB KEY

N. Clear all tabs. Then set four new tabs every 10 spaces. Key lines 64–67, using the tab key to go across from column to column.

64 165	343	298	126	618
65 304	981	762	493	804
66 235	976	890	558	129
67 841	982	563	204	975

O. 12-SECOND SPRINTS

O. Take three 12-second timed writings on each line. The scale gives wam for a 12-second timed writing.

68 Mr. James J. Baylorth lives at 15 Kent Street, Parma, Ohio.
69 Dr. Marcia Bates and Dr. Robert Gorem will be in Las Vegas.
70 The National Association of Realtors could meet in El Paso.
71 Morris County includes Budd Lake, Dover, and Morris Plains.

| | | | 5 | | | |10| | | |15| | |20| | |25| | |30| | | |35| | |40| | | |45| | |50| | | |55| | |60

P. 5-MINUTE TIMED WRITING

P. Spacing: double.
Take two 5-minute timed writings. Compute your speed and count errors.

Goal: 50 wam/5'/5e

72   Do you like the idea of helping run a food bank for   11
73 the homeless? How about tutoring grammar school children   23
74 in math? Or teaching adults to read? In the coming years,   35
75 you may not have to work for a nonprofit organization in   46
76 order to be able to help out in this way. Your job may   58
77 give you some time to volunteer in your community.   68
78   More and more employers are recognizing their role   79
79 in keeping charities running. Many companies do this by   90
80 asking their employees to help out both on and off company   102
81 time. What kind of return on investment does this type of   114
82 help bring to the company? Unlike direct cash donations,   126
83 the gift of people power brings little in the way of tax   137
84 relief. However, there are many who call this a win-win   148
85 situation for all three groups: employers, employees, and   160
86 nonprofits alike.   164
87   With mergers giving companies a bad name and a growing   176
88 shortage of employees, many are discovering that volunteer   188
89 programs are an effective way to quell an upset public.   199
90 There are over a thousand companies that send some workers   211
91 into the community each year. For employees, such efforts   223
92 offer the chance to brush up on old skills or learn new   234
93 ones. For companies, this gives a chance to provide some   245
94 service for less cost.   250

| | 1 | 2 | 3 | 4 | 5 | 6 | 7 | 8 | 9 | 10 | 11 | 12

NEW KEYS	**B.** THE **5** KEY
Use the F finger.	4 fr5f fr5f f55f f55f f5f5 f5f5 5 55 555 5,555 5:55 5 55 fury 55 foes 55 fibs 55 fads 55 furs 55 favors 6 The 55 students read the 555 pages in 55 minutes. 7 She found Items 5, 10, and 29; I found 47 and 38.
	C. THE **6** KEY
Use the J finger.	8 jy6j jy6j j66j j66j j6j6 j6j6 6 66 666 6,666 6:66 9 66 jots 66 jams 66 jump 66 jabs 66 join 66 jewels 10 Tom Lux left at 6:16 on Train 66 to go 600 miles. 11 There were 53,640 people in Bath; 28,179 in Hale.
SKILLBUILDING	**D.** NUMBER PRACTICE: 5 AND 6
	12 The 65 adults went to 5566 Wooster Avenue on 6/5. 13 On 5/6 at the age of 6, Andrew weighed 55 pounds. 14 If Gail takes 10 percent of 650, she will get 65. 15 Call Jeffrey at 555-8407 or 555-5143 by 8:30 p.m.
	E. NUMBER PRACTICE
NOTE: Focus on accuracy rather than speed as you practice the number drills.	16 Adding 10 and 20 and 30 and 40 and 70 totals 170. 17 On July 25, 1994, 130 girls ran in a 4-mile race. 18 Al selected Nos. 16, 17, 18, 19, and 20 to study. 19 The test took 10 hours and 8 minutes to complete. 20 Alice took 14 men and 23 women to the 128 events. 21 Did the 33 men drive 567 miles on Route 23 or 27? 22 On 10/29/94, she keyed lines 16-47 in 35 minutes. 23 In 1993 there were 2,934 people in the 239 camps. 24 The 18 shows were sold out by 8:37 on October 18. 25 On April 29-30 we will be open from 7:45 to 9:30.
	F. PROGRESSIVE PRACTICE: NUMBERS

Turn to the Progressive Practice: Numbers routine at the back of the book. Take six 30-second timed writings.

Follow the directions at the top of the page for beginning the activity.

I. TECHNIQUE PRACTICE: SPACE BAR

I. This paragraph is made up of very short words, requiring frequent use of the space bar. Take three 1-minute timed writings. Do not pause before or after striking the space bar.

```
36      In just a few days, we will be taking a long trip to a      12
37 small town in the woods.  This will give us some time to be     24
38 quiet and take a good, long rest.  There is no way to reach     36
39 us in that town, and we shall not plan to call at any time.     48
```
| 1 | 2 | 3 | 4 | 5 | 6 | 7 | 8 | 9 | 10 | 11 | 12

J. NUMBER PRACTICE

J. Key lines 40–43 twice each as you concentrate on number reaches. Notice that each number uses the same reaches as the preceding word.

```
40 we 23 it 85 ore 943 the 563 top 590 yet 635 out 975 two 529
41 et 35 or 94 tie 583 you 697 yet 635 pup 070 rip 480 tip 580
42 up 70 to 59 rot 495 pie 083 owe 923 wit 285 pet 035 wet 235
43 re 43 ie 83 toy 596 pot 095 owl 929 pit 085 yet 635 put 075
```

K. TECHNIQUE PRACTICE: CONCENTRATION

K. Each of these sentences contains two words that are not used properly. Correct those words as you key each sentence twice.

```
44 The assistance were board with the jobs they were assigned.
45 The advise from the personal department will help the man.
46 Please seize righting about the failures of our new workers.
47 An access amount of desert was being offered after dinner.
```

L. PROGRESSIVE PRACTICE: ALPHABET

Turn to the Progressive Practice: Alphabet routine at the back of the book. Take six 30-second timed writings, starting at the point where you left off the last time.

M. SUSTAINED PRACTICE: SYLLABIC INTENSITY

M. Take a 1-minute timed writing on the first paragraph to establish your base speed. Then take four 1-minute timed writings on the remaining paragraphs. As soon as you equal or exceed your base speed on one paragraph, advance to the next one.

```
48      Do you want a safe, fast, and easy way to improve your     12
49 health?  Try walking; it may be the best thing you could do     24
50 for yourself.  Although people have been walking for years,    36
51 it is but in recent times that it has been seen as a sport.    48

52      The new approach towards walking began about ten years     12
53 ago when one shoe company produced the first shoe made just    24
54 for walking.  Currently, there are many companies that make   36
55 hundreds of models all geared to make walking safe and fun.   48

56      Podiatrists believe that walking improves skeletal and    12
57 muscular development by exercising and toning all the bones    24
58 and muscles in the body.  Walking with excellent posture is   36
59 a good way to strengthen the back, stomach, and upper legs.   48

60      Whether you call it aerobic walking, power walking, or     12
61 exercise walking, it has fast become a favorite workout and   24
62 participation sport in America.  There are easily a million   36
63 Americans maximizing their health by striding for exercise.   48
```
| 1 | 2 | 3 | 4 | 5 | 6 | 7 | 8 | 9 | 10 | 11 | 12

G. HANDWRITTEN PARAGRAPH

G. Spacing: double. Take two 1-minute timed writings. Compute your speed and count errors.

26   *Jobs in business require good skills in oral*   10
27 *and written communications. Confirmation of this*   20
28 *fact can be found in various magazines and books.*   30

H. 2-MINUTE TIMED WRITING

H. Spacing: double. Take two 2-minute timed writings. Compute your speed and count errors.

Goal: 22 wam/2'/5e

```
29      New equipment is letting us share more and    10
30 more data in less time than ever.  Experts tell    20
31 us if we link phones and computers, we could have  30
32 data that will quickly zoom from site to site to    40
33 help all jobholders.                                44
   |  1  |  2  |  3  |  4  |  5  |  6  |  7  |  8  |  9  |  10
```

LESSON 15

Review

Margins: 1 inch • Tab: 5 spaces • Spacing: Single • Drills: 2 times

Goals:
To key 23 wam/2'/5e; to set tabs; to align text right and left; to align decimals.

A. WARMUP

```
1      Hazel Jacobson asked the attendant what time   10
2 Flight 948 was expected to arrive in Quincy.  She   20
3 said probably at 2:30 or 2:35 at Gate 16A or 17B.   30
  |  1  |  2  |  3  |  4  |  5  |  6  |  7  |  8  |  9  |  10
```

FORMATTING

B. DECIMAL AND RIGHT TABS

A left tab is used to indent paragraphs or to align columns of words. To set a left tab, position the carrier where you want the text to align and set a tab.

A right tab can be used to align text or numbers at the right. To set a right tab, position the carrier at the point you want the text or numbers to align and set a right tab.

A decimal (dec) tab can be used to align numbers with decimals at the decimal point. To set a decimal tab, position the carrier where you want the decimal points to align and set a decimal (dec) tab.

PRACTICE.
Speed Emphasis: If you made no more than 1 error on the Pretest, key each line twice.
Accuracy Emphasis: If you made 2 or more errors on the Pretest, key each group of lines (as though it were a paragraph) twice.

POSTTEST.
Repeat the Pretest (D) and compare performance.

H. Take a 1-minute timed writing on the first paragraph to establish your base speed. Then take four 1-minute timed writings on the remaining paragraphs. As soon as you equal or exceed your base speed on one paragraph, advance to the next one.

D. PRETEST: DISCRIMINATION PRACTICE

```
 8        Lois said the rear of the long train was right next to   12
 9  the column of poplar trees.  A robber had entered a red car   24
10  and stolen a case of grapefruit juice and ten cases of soda   36
11  pop.  The officer quickly arrested him; the train moved on.   48
     |  1  |  2  |  3  |  4  |  5  |  6  |  7  |  8  |  9  |  10  |  11  |  12
```

E. PRACTICE: LEFT HAND

```
12  rtr art part trip sort trot start train skirt depart strobe
13  asa ash mass sand cash salt grass salad trash splash salmon
14  sds sad used suds said pods based drips curds stride guards
15  rer red rear fear rest pier tread lower press rental flower
```

F. PRACTICE: RIGHT HAND

```
16  mnm menu mine numb meant named melon column mention mansion
17  pop post poor coop point troop poise police popular operate
18  olo tool yolk loon spoil lodge color stroll lottery rolling
19  iui unit suit quit quiet unite juice sluice biscuit uniform
```

G. POSTTEST: DISCRIMINATION PRACTICE

H. SUSTAINED PRACTICE: ROUGH DRAFT

```
20        In one way or another, the great majority of women who   12
21  were born in the Baby Boom generation, and their daughters,   24
22  will probably be deeply involved in the work force from now   36
23  on.  These women will greatly change the future job market.   48
24        Woman will account for two-thirds of the net growth in   12
25  the work force in the years to come, even through their rate  24
26  of entry in to the job market may slow.  By the next century  36
27  it will most liely level to a bit below the male job rate.    48
28        The portion of adult women at work will rise faster     12
29  then their total numbers, reaching three out of five in the   24
30  near future.  Women's number will grow in managerial ranks    36
31  and in many entrepreneurial business which will open.         48
32        Additionally, the disparity not found between male and   12
33  female earnings will narow.  This will be do to increased     24
34  legal presure and, more significantly, the growing business   36
35  experince and educational background that women will have.    48
     |  1  |  2  |  3  |  4  |  5  |  6  |  7  |  8  |  9  |  10  |  11  |  12
```

C. TECHNIQUE PRACTICE: ALIGN WORDS LEFT

4 dear   business   loan   office
5 computer   disk   yours   sincerely
6 keying   budget   our   employees

C. Spacing: double. Set multiple left tabs every 12 spaces. Press tab to begin the first column.

D. TECHNIQUE PRACTICE: ALIGN NUMBERS RIGHT

7   109   780,331   10,456   1
8 9,456   67   273   8,780
9   33   1,489   410,345   105

D. Spacing: double. Set multiple right tabs every 15 spaces. Clear existing tabs before setting new right tabs.

E. TECHNIQUE PRACTICE: ALIGN DECIMALS

10   .05   10.33   100.25   1.6
11   9.25   133.66   1,345.66   100.67
12 106.09   1.333   .025   56.89

E. Spacing: double. Decimal tabs every 15 spaces. Clear existing tabs before setting new decimal tabs.

SKILLBUILDING

PRETEST.
Take a 1-minute timed writing; compute your speed and count errors.

F. PRETEST: VERTICAL REACHES

13   A few of our business managers attribute the 10
14 success of the bank to a judicious and scientific 20
15 reserve program. The bank cannot drop its guard. 30

| 1 | 2 | 3 | 4 | 5 | 6 | 7 | 8 | 9 | 10

G. PRACTICE: UP REACHES

PRACTICE.
Speed Emphasis: If you made 2 or fewer errors on the Pretest, key each line twice.
Accuracy Emphasis: If you made 3 or more errors, key each group of lines (as though it were a paragraph) twice.

16 at atlas plate water later batch fatal match late
17 dr draft drift drums drawn drain drama dress drab
18 ju jumpy juror junky jumbo julep judge juice just
19 es essay press bless crest quest fresh rises less

H. PRACTICE: DOWN REACHES

20 ca cable cabin cadet camel cameo candy carve cash
21 nk trunk drink prank rinks brink drank crank sink
22 ba batch badge bagel baked banjo barge basis bank
23 sc scale scald scrub scalp scare scout scarf scan

POSTTEST.
Repeat the Pretest (F) and compare performance.

I. POSTTEST: VERTICAL REACHES

J. 2-MINUTE TIMED WRITING

J. Spacing: double. Take two 2-minute timed writings. Compute your speed and count errors.

Goal: 23 wam/2'/5e

24   One of the reasons for all the technology is 10
25 to help us become more productive. If this does 20
26 happen, we would have an amazing amount of extra 30
27 time off. Quite a few of our job skills would be 40
28 changed to meet new standards. 46

| 1 | 2 | 3 | 4 | 5 | 6 | 7 | 8 | 9 | 10

LESSONS 111-115

Margins: 1 inch • Spacing: Single • Drills: 2 times • Format Guide: 81–85 • Working Papers: 247–252

Goals for Unit 23

Begin each day with approximately 15 minutes of skill-building, selecting activities from pages 257–260. In the remaining class time, complete as many production jobs from pages 261–268 as you can.

1. To improve accuracy and speed on alphabet and number keys.
2. To key 50 wam for 5 minutes with no more than 5 errors.
3. To improve proficiency in composing at the keyboard.
4. To format a variety of documents for an international company—letters, memos, tables, an agenda, and minutes.
5. To transcribe copy from simulated dictation.

A. WARMUP

1   A requisition has been completed to purchase 8 items @   12
2 $71 and 30 items @ $59. Just add a 6% sales tax for a cost   24
3 of $2,478.28. Analyze, check, and verify the gross weight.   36

| 1 | 2 | 3 | 4 | 5 | 6 | 7 | 8 | 9 | 10 | 11 | 12

LANGUAGE ARTS

B. Study the rules at the right. Then key lines 4–7, making necessary changes.

B. NUMBERS

Rule: Spell out fractions that stand alone, and use figures for mixed numbers.

The gauge shows that the tank is over one-third full.
Expenses are nearly 2 1/2 times higher than last year.

Rule: To form the plurals of figures, add *s.*

That particular stock is now priced in the high 30s.

4 They now control about 2/3 of the market in that region.
5 The recipe called for two and one-half cups of flour.
6 That form of technology was introduced in the 1970's.
7 The temperatures were in the 90s every day of the month.

C. COMPOSING

Compose the body of a letter to respond to Letter 52, Unit 18, page 203. Use the following suggestions for each paragraph:

Paragraph 1. Tell Mr. Fabereisen that you are pleased with his thorough inspection of the Larch Street building and that his information was clear and to the point.

Paragraph 2. Tell Mr. Fabereisen that you are still interested in purchasing the building but would like to have a soils engineer review the available compaction reports. Ask if he can provide you with a list of people he would recommend to do this for you.

Paragraph 3. Thank Mr. Fabereisen for his prompt response in this matter.

LESSON 16

Symbols and Word Division

Margins: 1 inch • Tab: 5 spaces • Spacing: Single •
Drills: 2 times

Goals:
To control the #, (, and)
keys; to make correct word-
division decisions; to key
24 wam/2'/5e.

A. WARMUP

1   Fay Jacobs drove 1,568 miles last week. She 10
2 met 39 aides in Arizona and Oregon. She expected 20
3 and required a 4:20 meeting with 17 new managers. 30

| 1 | 2 | 3 | 4 | 5 | 6 | 7 | 8 | 9 | 10

NEW KEYS

NUMBER (if before a
figure) or POUNDS (if
after a figure) is the
shift of 3. Use the D finger.

Do not space between the figure and symbol.

PARENTHESES
are the shifts of
9 and 0. Use
the L finger on (and the Sem
finger on).

Do not space between the
parentheses and the text
within them.

B. THE # KEY

4 de3d de3#d d3#d d3#d d##d d##d #3 #33 #333 #3,333
5 Al wants 33# of #200 and 38# of #400 by Saturday.
6 My favorite seats are #2, #34, #56, #65, and #66.
7 Please order 45# of #245 and 13# of #24 tomorrow.

C. THE (AND) KEYS

8 lo9l lo9l lo(l lo(l l((l ;p0; ;p0; ;p); ;p); ;));
9 Please ask (1) Al, (2) Pat, (3) Ted, and (4) Dee.
10 Sue has some (1) skis, (2) sleds, and (3) skates.
11 Mary is (1) prompt, (2) speedy, and (3) accurate.

12 Our workers (Lewis, Jerry, and Ty) were rewarded.
13 The owner (Ms. Parks) went on Friday (August 18).
14 The Roxie (a cafe) had fish (salmon) on the menu.
15 The clerk (Ms. Fay Green) will vote yes (not no).

LANGUAGE ARTS

Whenever you key material
and you don't have word
wrap, you must decide where
each line should end.

If it is necessary to divide a
word, follow the rules given
here.

Some word pro-
cessing programs auto-
matically hyphenate words
at the ends of lines.

D. WORD DIVISION

1. Do not divide (*a*) words pronounced as
one syllable (*thought, planned*), (*b*)
contractions (*isn't, shouldn't*), or (*c*)
abbreviations (*ILGWU, Inc.*).
2. Divide words only between syllables.
Whenever you are unsure of where a
syllable ends, consult a dictionary.
3. Leave at least three characters (the last
will be a hyphen) on the upper line,

and carry at least three characters (the
last may be a punctuation mark) to the
next line. Thus, *al-ways* and *mat-ter*,
but not *a-round* or *trick-y*.

4. Divide compound words either at the
hyphen (*self-control*) or where the two
words join to make a solid compound.
Thus *master-mind*, not *mas-termind*.

LETTER 64
TWO-PAGE LETTER IN
BLOCK STYLE WITH
OPEN PUNCTUATION,
DISPLAY PARAGRAPH,
AND BOXED TABLE

Working Papers: 239

Please key this letter for Tom Panian.

April 27, 19--

Ms. Charlene Jo Helbert   2307 Reeves Avenue
Ogden, Ut 84401

Thank you for your letter in which you inquired about the air traffic control program here at the Chandler Air Traffic Control School. Your first question was an inquiry as to what an air traffic controller does. I am confident that these statements from our new bulletin will provide a good answer for you:

> Air traffic controllers are responsible for the safe, methodical, and expeditious movement of air traffic. They are men and women with special skills who can handle complex and precise tasks and yet remain alert in pressure situations.

You also inquired about job opportunities. Qualified graduates from CATCS continue to be in high demand. Almost all of our graduates obtained positions with the Federal Aviation Administration (FAA), which is in the Dept. of Transportation. Most of them work at en route centers, where air traffic is controlled along established air ways in the geographic area served by each center. Others work at FAA airport traffic control towers. The table below details the placement of our December 19-- graduates:

Center the braced heading and the column headings.

Sex	FAA INSTALLATIONS	
	En Route Center	Airport Tower
Male	8	6
Female	9	3

Our instructors are particularly well qualified. All have at least five years of experience in air traffic control positions. Our instructional facilities are excellent, equipped with the latest in instructional media and technology.

A packet of materials, including an application form, is enclosed being sent to you today. If you have any other questions, please do let me know.

Yours truly

CHANDLER AIR TRAFFIC CONTROL SCHOOL
                ← 3 blank lines
Thomas V. Panian
Admissions Director

E. Select the words in each line that can be divided, and key them with a hyphen to show where the division should be (Example: *con-sult*).

E. WORD-DIVISION PRACTICE

16 dragged   weren't   today
17 safety   moment   USMC
18 grandmother   teenagers   trailing
19 expect   reproach   couldn't

F. Compare this paragraph with the timed writing in Section I on page 30. Key a list of the words that contain errors, correcting the errors as you key.

F. PROOFREADING PRACTICE

20   The personnel computer has changed all our
21 lives in just a few year. Since we have quiet a
22 variety of software programs for your use, we can
23 expect to find that a computer well let use do an
24 amasing amount of work in less time then before.

SKILLBUILDING

G. Take a 1-minute timed writing on the first paragraph to establish your base speed. Then take four 1-minute timed writings on the remaining paragraphs. As soon as you equal or exceed your base speed on one paragraph, advance to the next one.

G. SUSTAINED PRACTICE: SYLLABIC INTENSITY

25   One should always try to keep in good shape. 10
26 As the first step in keeping in good shape, avoid 20
27 starting or being tempted with the smoking habit. 30

28   A second step that helps in maintaining good 10
29 health for years is drinking the proper amount of 20
30 water. Most doctors suggest eight glasses a day. 30

31   Making exercise a step is another method for 10
32 staying in good health. Many experts suggest one 20
33 spend a few minutes each day in regular exercise. 30

34   A final step of importance is maintaining an 10
35 appropriate body weight. The clue to maintaining 20
36 weight is developing the positive eating pattern. 30

| 1 | 2 | 3 | 4 | 5 | 6 | 7 | 8 | 9 | 10

H. Spacing: double. Take two 1-minute timed writings. Compute your speed and count errors.

H. HANDWRITTEN PARAGRAPH WITH NUMBERS

37   The membership in our credit union is 1,850. 10
38 We need 200 new members if we are to reach 2,050. 20
39 There were 46 new members in May, 33 in June, and 30
40 24 in July for a total of 103. If we are to have 40
41 93 new members, it means we must get started now. 50

MEMO TO: Jane Pfeiffer
FROM: Warren D. Ebert, Director
DATE: April 26, 19--
SUBJECT: Case Study for Orientation Course

I know that you are always on the lookout for ideas for the Orientation to Air Traffic Control course. The enclosed case might be of interest.

The case involves the accident that occurred on January 18, 1990, when Eastern Airlines Flight 111, a Boeing 727, struck a Beech 100 at the Atlanta Hartsfield International Airport.

Let's get together to discuss the ways in which this case might relate to course objectives.

TABLE 51
BOXED TABLE WITH
BRACED COLUMN
HEADING

COMPENSATION EXPENDITURES

Group	First Quarter, 19--			Totals
	January	February	March	
Administration	$ 42,833	$ 42,833	$ 51,834	$137,500
Instructional	106,250	106,250	106,250	318,750
Staff	14,779	16,542	18,179	49,500
TOTAL	$163,862	$165,625	$176,263	$505,750

I. Spacing: double. Take two 2-minute timed writings. Compute your speed and count errors.

Goal: 24 wam/2'/5e

I. 2-MINUTE TIMED WRITING

42   The personal computer has changed all of our 10
43 lives in just a few years. Since we have quite a 20
44 variety of software programs for our use, we can 30
45 expect to find that a computer will let us do an 40
46 amazing amount of work in less time than before. 48

| 1 | 2 | 3 | 4 | 5 | 6 | 7 | 8 | 9 | 10

LESSON 17

Symbols

Margins: 1 inch • Tab: 5 spaces • Spacing: Single •
Drills: 2 times

Goals:
To control the %, ', and " keys; to key 25 wam/2'/5e.

A. WARMUP

1   Jack Xua quizzed the men about 345# of grain 10
2 (wheat) found by 26 boys on Lot #98. Two men had 20
3 paid 17 students to place the wheat in 20# units. 30

| 1 | 2 | 3 | 4 | 5 | 6 | 7 | 8 | 9 | 10

NEW KEYS

%
5

PERCENT is the shift of 5. Use the F finger.

Do not space between the number and the percent sign.

B. THE % KEY

4 ft5f ft5%f f5%f f5%f f%%f f%%f 5% 55% 555% 5,555%
5 Robert quoted rates of 8%, 9%, 10%, 11%, and 12%.
6 Pat scored 82%, Jan 89%, and Ken 90% on the test.
7 Only 55% of the students passed 75% of the exams.

APOSTROPHE is to the right of the semicolon. Use the Sem finger.

C. THE , KEY

8 ;'; ''' ;'; ''' Can't we go in Sue's or Al's car?
9 It's Bob's job to cover Ted's work when he's out.
10 What's in Mike's lunch box for Stanley's dessert?
11 He's left for Ty's banquet which is held at Al's.

QUOTATION is the shift of the apostrophe. Use the Sem finger.

Do not space between the quotation marks and the text they enclose.

D. THE " KEY

12 ;'; """ ;"; """ "That's a super job," said Mabel.
13 The theme of the meeting is "Improving Your Job."
14 Jill liked "Grand Hotel"; Sharon liked "Fiddler."
15 Allison said, "I'll take Janice and Jo to Flint."

THE 1940$

The (U.) (S.) and Great Britain continued to work togheter on the improvement of radar into the 1940s. The two countries agreed in late 1940 to share information on their techno-logical advancements.

Radar equipment has now been installed at major air traffic control facilities around the world. While radar is not the cure-all for air traffic control, it greatly assists in the safe and orderly movement of aircraft.

Please send this letter to the following people, who have applied for our two vacant faculty positions.

Roy A. Rossback	Carol E. Tarmann
2414 Bush Lake Road	4467 14th Avenue East
Gwinn, MI 49841	Denver, CO 80220
team lab instructor	basic radar instructor
eight	five
Air Force control tower	airport control tower

Dear _____ :

We are pleased to have received your application for a position as a _____ at the Chandler Air Traffic Control school. Even though you provided a copy of your resume, would you please also complete the enclosed Application Form and return it to our office in the envelope that is also enclosed.
The _____ years of experience you have had at an _____ are appropriate for this position. We shall look forward to receiving your completed application form. Our plan is to choose select candidates for interviews after June 1. We shall inform you of the status of your application at that time.

W. Ebert
Enclosures 2

E. PLACEMENT OF QUOTATION MARKS

Read these rules about the placement of quotation marks. Then key lines 16–19 twice.

1. The closing quotation mark is always keyed *after* a period or comma but *before* a colon or semicolon.

2. The closing quotation mark is keyed *after* a question mark or exclamation point if the quoted material is a question or an exclamation; otherwise, the quotation mark is keyed *before* the question mark or exclamation point.

16 "Hello," I said. "My name is Al; I am new here."
17 Zack read the article "Can She Succeed Tomorrow?"
18 John said, "I'll mail the check"; but, he didn't.
19 Did he say, "We lost"? She said, "I don't know."

F. ALPHABET AND SYMBOL PRACTICE

20 Gaze at views of my jonquil or red phlox in back.
21 Jan quickly moved the six dozen big pink flowers.
22 Joe quietly picked six razors from the woven bag.
23 Packing jam for the dozen boxes was quite lively.

24 Mail these "Rush": #38, #89, and #99 (software).
25 Joe's note carried a rate of 6%; Ann's only 5.5%.
26 Lee read "The Computer Today." It's here Monday.
27 Ask (1) Tom, (2) Dick, and (3) Harry (Feigleson).

G. Spacing: double. Set tabs every 15 spaces. Press tab to begin the first column. Key lines 28–31 using the tab key to move from column to column.

G. TECHNIQUE PRACTICE: TAB KEY

28 perfect	agency	office	disc
29 security	company	employer	firm
30 Monday	workers	vacation	employee
31 also	wouldn't	it's	computer

H. Spacing: double. Take two 1-minute timed writings. Compute your speed and count errors.

H. HANDWRITTEN PARAGRAPHS

32 You have now completed the first sequence of   10
33 your class and have learned how to make the right   20
34 reaches to the alpha, numeric, and symbol keys.   30
35   In the next sequence, you will be taught how   40
36 to center and to develop your keyboarding skills.   50

I. Spacing: double. Take two 2-minute timed writings. Compute your speed and count errors.

Goal: 25 wam/2'/5e

I. 2-MINUTE TIMED WRITING

37   We can expect quite a few changes in our job   10
38 market in the next few decades. People will have   20
39 jobs that will require new tasks due to the many   30
40 uses of the computer. We will have a gain in the   40
41 size of the labor force which processes our data.   50

| 1 | 2 | 3 | 4 | 5 | 6 | 7 | 8 | 9 | 10

Please make these changes to pages 8 and 9 of my draft manuscript.

sophisticated equipment is being used at all large air traffic control centers throughout the world.

the 1920s

The work of two German scientists, Heinrich Hertz and Christian Hulsmeyer, led to the development of what we now call Radar. Their work attracted the attention of Guglielmo Marconi, who recommended to the Institute of Radio Engineers in 1922 that their experiments be investigated for any practical applications. The resulting system was used successfully for the first time at the Carnegie Institute in Washington in 1925 by Gregory Breit and Merle A. Tune.

THE 1930s

In late 1930, Dr. A. Hoyt Taylor of the U. S. naval Research Laboratory began investigating the use of radar to detect the presence of other ships and aircraft. These experiments were conducted in full cooperation with scientists in England. By 1931 it was possible to detect both ships and planes under favorable conditions. Dr. Taylor indicated that the next step was to develop instruments that would automatically collect, record, and analyze data to show the exact position, angle, and speed of approaching ships and planes.

Both the army and the navy continued the further development of radar devices through the 1930s. The first demonstration of radar equipment to Army officials took place in 1938, when a device designed for control of anti-aircraft guns and search lights was used. The SCR-286 was the first radar set actually used by the Army.

The Signal Corps Laboratory developed a radar instrument in 1939 for detecting airplanes at much greater distances. After a successful demonstration for the Secretary of War, it was adopted for military use.

(Continued on next page.)

18 LESSON

Symbols and Line-Ending Decisions

Margins: 1 inch • Tab: 5 spaces • Spacing: Single •
Drills: 2 times

Goals:
To control the &, $, and ___ keys; to underline; to key 26 wam/2'/5e.

A. WARMUP

1   Of the 345 votes cast, 279 were for Jo. She 10
2 won by 81%. Jo's quick win amazed 60 of her pals 20
3 from home. The crowd exalted their huge victory. 30

  | 1 | 2 | 3 | 4 | 5 | 6 | 7 | 8 | 9 | 10

NEW KEYS

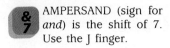 AMPERSAND (sign for *and*) is the shift of 7. Use the J finger.

Space before and after the ampersand.

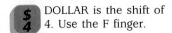 DOLLAR is the shift of 4. Use the F finger.

Do not space between the dollar sign and the number.

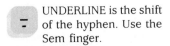 UNDERLINE is the shift of the hyphen. Use the Sem finger.

Blank lines within sentences are 5 characters long.

B. THE & KEY

4 juj ju7j j7j j7&j j&&j j&&j Max & Dee & Sue & Ken
5 Brown & Sons shipped goods to Crum & Lee Company.
6 Johnson & Loo brought a case against May & Green.
7 Ball & Trump vs. Vens & See is being decided now.

C. THE $ KEY

8 frf fr4f f4f f4$f f$$f f$$f $44 $444 $4,444 $4.44
9 I quoted $48, $64, and $94 for the set of chairs.
10 His insurance paid $150; our insurance paid $175.
11 First-floor seats were $25, $30, and $55 in June.

D. THE – KEY

12 ;p; ;p-; ;p-; ;p_; ;___; ;___; Use a date of ___.
13 My new hours are from ___ a.m. until ___ p.m.
14 My sales goal of $___ is an increase of ___%.
15 There are ___ graduating; only ___ will stay.

E. UNDERLINING

Many electronic typewriters have an automatic underline feature that enables you to underline text while you key the text. Determine the appropriate procedure for your equipment to underline text as you key it.

SKILLBUILDING

F. Underline individual words separately; for titles, underline the entire title, including the spaces.

F. TECHNIQUE PRACTICE: UNDERLINING

16 The <u>Sindbad Voyages</u> is an excellent book for all.
17 Are the words <u>for</u>, <u>fore</u>, and <u>four</u> used correctly?
18 We had an ad in <u>The Wall Street Journal</u> in March.
19 Max <u>will not</u> or <u>should not</u> attend the conference.

Mr. Orlyn R. Glatzer
1706 Belasco Avenue
Sacramento, CA 95815

Subject: June Seminar at CATCS

The Chandler Air Traffic Control School is only three years old, but our program continues to be going very well. Among our varied efforts to bring enrichment to our program, we are continuing with our monthly seminar series.

We would like you to conduct a one-hour seminar again for our students on a date convenient for you during the first half of June. We would prefer that your topic be a current, relevant issue in the state of California.

I shall call you on Thursday to finalize plans.

W. Ebert
By Fax

REPORT 53
ITINERARY

WARREN D. EBERT
Nevada Itinerary
May 18-19, 19--

Monday, May 18

San Jose / Las Vegas . . . . Southwest 64
    Leave 7:10 a.m.; arrive 8:50 a.m.
    Seat 7E; nonstop; breakfast

Las Vegas / Reno . . . . Nevada-Utah 1824
    Leave 4:20 p.m.; arrive 6:35 p.m.
    Seat 5A; 1 stop

Tuesday, May 19

Reno / San Jose . . . . CalCoastal 372
    Leave 2:00 p.m.; arrive 2:50 p.m.
    Seat 4C; nonstop

G. Keep your eyes on the copy so that you do not lose your place as you key these longer words.

G. TECHNIQUE PRACTICE: CONCENTRATION

20 The provocative statement caused an insurrection.
21 A congregation in Connecticut intervened quickly.
22 A lackadaisical traveler crisscrossed continents.
23 All resignations were interpreted as irrevocable.

H. Spacing: double. Take two 1-minute timed writings. Compute your speed and count errors.

H. HANDWRITTEN PARAGRAPH

24 You will discover when you begin working in   10
25 industry that there are other skills you need to   20
26 possess beyond the basic business skills. Skills   30
27 in human relations are desirable for every worker.   40

I. Spacing: double. Take two 2-minute timed writings. Compute your speed and count errors.

Goal: 26 wam/2'/5e

I. 2-MINUTE TIMED WRITING

28   Van Clark was amazed at how quickly he could 10
29 key on a new computer. It took him just a little 20
30 time to learn the functions it can perform. He 30
31 expected he would surely forget how to use it his 40
32 first time alone, but he did not. He had learned 50
33 the skill. 52

| 1 | 2 | 3 | 4 | 5 | 6 | 7 | 8 | 9 | 10

FORMATTING

Equipment or software with automatic word wrap eliminates the need for a manual return at the end of a line.

J. LINE-ENDING DECISIONS

When keying text that is not line for line on equipment without word wrap, you must decide where each line should end. As you near the end of a line, a margin signal will sound (either a beep or a bell) anywhere from 8 to 10 spaces before the right margin. When you hear the signal, you need to decide how much more copy you can key before pressing Return. Once you hear the signal, try to end the line as near to the margin as you can (without dividing a word, if possible).

    For example, if your typewriter gives an 8-space warning, here are some typical line-ending decisions you might encounter:

DESIRED ENDING		RETURN AFTER KEYING
SIGNAL	MARGIN	
Winter isn't pleasant		isn't
With pleasant hopes		pleasant
The calamity struck		calamity
Members maintained		main-

(bold) — CHANDLER AIR TRAFFIC CONTROL SCHOOL

ds [Minutes of Faculty Meeting
April 15, 19--
2 blank lines

(bold) REVIEW OF MINUTES

ds [The minutes of the CATSC faculty meeting held on April 1 were reviewed and approved. There was one correction; the faculty and staff family picnic will be held at Hodges Park on Sunday, May 22 (not on Saturday, May 21), at 3 p.m.

ds [TEXT AND REFERENCES (bold)
Brad Danielson and Fran Hybbert reported that they are reviewing five text books and about a dozen published documents that which could be considered for adoption for the Advanced Radar course.

ds [COURSE OBJECTIVES FOR ADVANCED RADAR COURSE (bold)
course
There was agreement that all basic radar program objectives relating to interpreting and performing radar procedures should be achieved by all enrollees in the advanced radar course at the 85% level. In addition to other topics previously identified, there was agreement that the following topics should be added: instrument approaches, traffic advisories, merging target procedures, aircraft safety alerts, and aircraft emergency procedures.

ds [ADJOURNMENT (bold)
The faculty meeting was adjourned at 9:35 a.m.; the next faculty meeting will be held in two weeks.

Respectfully Submitted,

your name ___
Administrative Assistant

MEMO TO: All Faculty

FROM: Warren D. Ebert, Director

DATE: April 42, 19--

SUBJECT: Faculty Meeting on April 29

A meeting for all instructional faculty has been scheduled for 8 a.m. on April 29, 19-- to continue a review of the following as they relate to the new course entitled advanced radar, which will begin in January.

Course course
1. Program Description: A program description that reflects course objectives will be developed.

X
2.3 Text and References: Brad Danielson and Fran Hybert will submit their recommendations at the meeting.

3.2 Course Objectives: The committee will distribute a revised list on Apr. 26; please review this list before the meeting.

LESSON 19

Symbols and Error Correction

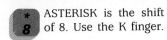

Margins: 1 inch • Tab: 5 spaces • Spacing: Single •
Drills: 2 times

Goals:
To control the *, @, and = keys; to edit text; to key 27 wam/2'/5e.

A. WARMUP

1　　　　The owner (Mr. Judd) quoted a sales price of 10
2 $3.86 for the items. He expects Grove & Baker to 20
3 buy nearly 129,457 units of these sizzling items. 30

　| 1　| 2　| 3　| 4　| 5　| 6　| 7　| 8　| 9　| 10

NEW KEYS

* **8** ASTERISK is the shift of 8. Use the K finger.

B. THE * KEY

4 kik ki8k k8*k k8*k k**k k**k Al's book* is great.
5 Use the * to show book/table footnote references.
6 Asterisks keyed in a row (*******) make a border.
7 Harry's* article quoted Hanson* and Pyle* in May.

@ **2** AT is the shift of 2. Use the S finger.

Space before and after @.

C. THE @ KEY

8 sws sw2s s2@s s2@s s@@s s@@s Buy 15 @ $5 in June.
9 Order 12 items @ $14 and another 185 items @ $16.
10 He bought 12 units @ $14.50 and 6 units @ $12.30.
11 Buy 10 shares @ $75 and another 15 shares @ $125.

+ **=** EQUAL is to the right of the hyphen. Use the Sem finger.

Space before and after =.

D. THE = KEY

12 ;=; ;=; ;==; ;==; A = 40, B = 160, C = 18, D = 1.
13 If x = 4 and y = 6 and z = 8, what is the answer?
14 He learned that A = B and was able to solve that.
15 The = sign, equal, is used by our mathematicians.

SKILLBUILDING

E. Keep your eyes on the copy while keying.

E. SYMBOL PRACTICE

16 Invoice #356 to Rice & Sons required May's reply.
17 My total bill was $450.65, including a tax of $7.
18 She (May) read How to Save Money; it costs $9.50.
19 Luke said, "I'll buy 1 share @ $6 and 2 @ $7.55."

Ms. Brenda J. Boettcher
Office for Compliance Review
State of California
3902 Bacchini Avenue
Sacramento, CA 95828

Dear Ms. Boettcher:

A table summarizing the ethnic composition of our January 19-- entering class is enclosed.

You will note that exactly half of our students are female. Also, 12 of the 28 students are in the nonwhite categories.

Please let me know if further information is needed.

W. Ebert

PS: Our detailed report, which analyzes the ethnic composition for all applicants for the July 19-- class, will be forwarded by August 1.

TABLE 50
RULED

ETHNIC COMPOSITION
January 19 -- Entering Class

Category	Male	Female
American Indian or Alaskan Native	2	0
Asian or Pacific Islander	1	2
Black	2	1
Hispanic	2	2
White	7	9

F. Take a 1-minute timed writing on the first paragraph to establish your base speed. Then take four 1-minute timed writings on the remaining paragraphs. As soon as you equal or exceed your base speed on one paragraph, advance to the next one.

F. SUSTAINED PRACTICE: NUMBERS AND SYMBOLS

20   Our new store enjoyed an unexpected increase 10
21 in sales. We were quite astonished and amazed by 20
22 the gain in numbers of customers served and kept. 30

23   We opened 18 new outlets in 14 centers and a 10
24 catalog outlet in 29 counties. We were then able 20
25 to serve 150,670 possible customers in 10 states. 30

26   Our gross sales were $4,560,871 (an increase 10
27 of 9%). Knox & Sons paid $46/share and said, "It 20
28 was a great year." These figures are confirmed.* 30

| 1 | 2 | 3 | 4 | 5 | 6 | 7 | 8 | 9 | 10 |

G. Spacing: double. Take two 2-minute timed writings. Compute your speed and count errors.

Goal: 27 wam/2'/5e

G. 2-MINUTE TIMED WRITING

29   If you have plans to be an expert on a job, 10
30 you must first have the skills; you must possess 20
31 good English skills as a second requirement; and 30
32 a third criterion is knowing how to proofread all 40
33 work. Start to analyze your work with care and 50
34 find all errors. 54

| 1 | 2 | 3 | 4 | 5 | 6 | 7 | 8 | 9 | 10 |

H. ERROR CORRECTION

Errors should be corrected as soon as they are made. Since you may not know when you make an error, however, always proofread your work carefully and correct any errors that you find before removing the paper from your typewriter.

To correct an error on equipment with correction memory, follow these steps.

1. Position the carrier one character to the right of the error.

2. Press the backspace key or the correction key as many times as necessary to delete the incorrect characters.

3. Key the correct characters.

If the error is outside the correction memory, follow these steps:

1. Position the carrier one character to the right of the error.

2. Press the backspace or correction key and rekey the incorrect characters to delete them.

3. Once the errors are deleted, key the correct characters.

I. Key lines 35–38; then make the following corrections:
Lines 35 and 36: Change *Kim* to *Jim*
Lines 37 and 38: Change *four* to *five*

I. TECHNIQUE PRACTICE: CORRECTING ERRORS

35 Kim's brother showed Kim how to repair the damage.
36 While Kim visited Linda, Kim found the old photos.
37 Four of the students took four trips in two years.
38 Four errors may be allowed in four-minute timings.

IN-BASKET EXERCISE

CHANDLER AIR TRAFFIC CONTROL SCHOOL

Situation: Today is April 23, 19—. You are working as an administrative assistant for Mr. Warren D. Ebert, director of the Chandler Air Traffic Control School, located in San Jose, California. Mr. Ebert is on a business trip to Washington, D.C., and has left the following jobs in your in-basket for you to complete during his absence.

Add headers and footers as needed.

Mr. Ebert prefers his letters in block style with standard punctuation and this closing:

Sincerely yours,

Warren D. Ebert
Director

REPORT 51
DIRECTORY

Please prepare a two-column directory of CATCS advisory board members. Use ADVISORY BOARD MEMBERS as the title, and alphabetize by last name.

Hernandez, Enrique J.
Pilot   Coastal
California Airlines
2489 Redondo Street
San Francisco, CA 94124
415-555-3673

Pham, Hoan Khai
Air Traffic Controller
South California Center
2608 43d Street West
Los Angeles, CA 90008
213-555-1768
Malzachar, M. C.
Manager
San Diego Midway Airport
1457 Vista De La Orilla
San Diego, CA 92117
619-555-2038

Margaret M. O'Connor
Instructional Dean
Arizona Aviation Center
10026 Black Canyon Drive N.
Phoenix, AZ 85051
602-555-4379

April 23, 19--

Marquez-Shroyer, Carmen
Air traffic controller
Central California Center
4306 Laurite Ave. East
Fresno, CA 93725
209-555-8175
Jackson, Kathryn M.
Pilot
Nevada-Utah Commuter Airline
803 Natasha Way
Reno, NV 89512

702-555-4693

Johnson, Thomas A.
Vice President for Operations
California Coastal Airlines
22 Oakmont Circle
Cupertino, CA 95014
408-555-3276
Seidler, Naomi V.
Assistant Secretary
U.S. Department of Transportation
6025 Lee Highway
Arlington, VA 22205
703-555-8149

Symbols

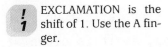

Margins: 1 inch • Tab: 5 spaces • Spacing: Single •
Drills: 2 times

Goals:
To control the ! and + keys; to improve speed and accuracy; to key 28 wam/2'/5e.

A. WARMUP

1   Ken bought 11 prized lots @ $975. The sizes 10
2 varied but there were 3,482* (*square feet). Joe 20
3 was amazed that Ken expected to buy 12 more lots. 30

  | 1 | 2 | 3 | 4 | 5 | 6 | 7 | 8 | 9 | 10

NEW KEYS

! / 1 EXCLAMATION is the shift of 1. Use the A finger.

Space twice after an exclamation point at the end of a sentence.

B. THE ! KEY

4 aqa aqla aq!a a!!a a!!a Where! Why! How! When!
5 It's his! Don't do that! Stop! No! Exit Only!
6 He did say that! Jill can't take a vacation now!
7 What he said was startling! She does believe it!

+ / = PLUS is the shift of EQUAL. Use the Sem finger.

Space before and after plus.

C. THE + KEY

8 ;=; ;=+; ;=+; ;++; ;++; 10 + 20 + 3 + 4 + 5 = 42.
9 When you add 13 + 40 + 50 + 60 + 90, you get 253.
10 The + sign, plus, was used in an arithmetic task.
11 Do you ever use the plus (+) sign in your office?

SKILLBUILDING

D. SYMBOL PRACTICE

12 Al said, "Stop it at once!" He's selling 5 @ $6.
13 Brown & Daughters held their annual Dollar Sales.
14 Julie's article* was reprinted in Newsweek today.
15 "Can't I read Catcher in the Rye?" asked Rob Lee.

E. PROGRESSIVE PRACTICE: NUMBERS

Turn to the Progressive Practice: Numbers routine at the back of the book. Take six 30-second timed writings, starting at the point where you left off the last time.

N. ALPHABET REVIEW: INFREQUENT-LETTER PRACTICE

N. Take two 1-minute timed writings on each line as you concentrate on infrequently used letters.

J 72 Jolly jugglers joined the judge, jury, and jealous jailers.   12
Q 73 I quickly acquired an eloquent quartet for the quiet queen.   12
X 74 Dexter expects extra excise taxes in excess of six percent.   12
Z 75 A dozen puzzled zebras were seized by a dozen dizzy guards.   12

| 1 | 2 | 3 | 4 | 5 | 6 | 7 | 8 | 9 | 10 | 11 | 12

O. DIAGNOSTIC PRACTICE: NUMBERS

Turn to the Diagnostic Practice: Numbers routine at the back of this book. Take the Pretest and record your performance. Then practice the drill lines for those reaches on which you made errors. Finally, repeat the Pretest and compare your performance.

P. 5-MINUTE TIMED WRITING

P. Spacing: double.
Take two 5-minute timed writings. Compute your speed and count errors.

Goal: 49 wam/5'/5e

76   Frequent business travelers know quite well what the   12
77 annoying side effects of long-distance plane trips include.   24
78 That tired, dizzy feeling may stay with a traveler for up   35
79 to two or three days after a trip. Jet lag, as it is often   47
80 called, is really the physical disorientation of all bodily   59
81 and mental functions that occurs when a flight crosses a   71
82 number of time zones.   75

83   Our bodies operate by some internal time clock, which   87
84 tells us when to eat, sleep, and awake. When you change   98
85 time zones, a watch may be set to that new time, but your   110
86 body is still operating in the old one. How can you avoid   122
87 the stress that comes with jet lag? Stay away from such   133
88 common temptations as late-night movies, free alcoholic   144
89 drinks, and loads of food served at unusual hours. The   156
90 main causes of that tired feeling are lack of sleep and,   167
91 unexpectedly, dehydration.   172

92   In a pressurized aircraft, it is essential that the   184
93 humidity be kept at a very low level. Every breath gives   195
94 up more water, making your skin and mouth feel dry. If you   207
95 replace this loss of fluid with alcohol, you are worsening   219
96 the dehydration process. Your best bet for a stress-free   231
97 trip is to drink all the bottled water you can and take   242
98 a few power naps.   245

| 1 | 2 | 3 | 4 | 5 | 6 | 7 | 8 | 9 | 10 | 11 | 12

F. KEYING IN ALL CAPS

Use the A finger.

To key in all-capital letters:
1. Depress the shift lock key.
2. Key the word or words.

3. Release the shift lock by pressing the shift lock key.

F. Key each sentence on a separate line.

Remember to shift for ?, !, and :.

16 Is MABEL going? Attend the MINNESOTA STATE FAIR.
17 NO SMOKING! STOP IT! Post the sign, NO HUNTING.
18 Are there EXIT and ENTRANCE signs? DO NOT ENTER.
19 An ad read: SPEND YOUR VACATION IN NORTH DAKOTA.

PRETEST.
Take a 1-minute timed writing; compute your speed and count errors.

G. PRETEST: ALTERNATE- AND ONE-HAND WORDS

20   The chairman should handle their tax problem 10
21 downtown. If they are reversed, pressure tactics 20
22 might have changed the case as it was being held. 30

| 1 | 2 | 3 | 4 | 5 | 6 | 7 | 8 | 9 | 10 |

PRACTICE.
Speed Emphasis: If you made 2 or fewer errors on the Pretest, key each line twice.
Accuracy Emphasis: If you made 3 or more errors, key each group of lines (as though it were a paragraph) twice.

H. PRACTICE: ALTERNATE-HAND WORDS

23 the with girl right blame handle antique chairman
24 for wish town their panel formal problem downtown
25 sit work make tight amend profit element neighbor
26 pan busy they flair signs thrown signals problems

I. PRACTICE: ONE-HAND WORDS

27 lip fact yolk poplin yummy affect reverse pumpkin
28 you cast kill uphill jumpy grease wagered opinion
29 tea cage lump limply hilly served bravest minimum
30 fat tree only unhook jolly garage reserve million

POSTTEST.
Repeat the Pretest (G) and compare performance.

J. POSTTEST: ALTERNATE- AND ONE-HAND WORDS

K. Spacing: double. Take two 2-minute timed writings. Compute your speed and count errors.

Goal: 28 wam/2′/5e

K. 2-MINUTE TIMED WRITING

31   The purpose for all the new technology is to 10
32 make workers more productive. If this happens, a 20
33 decrease in the number of hours on the job may be 30
34 noticed. This could mean that workers would have 40
35 extra time off. This could be quite a benefit to 50
36 a large number of those workers. 56

| 1 | 2 | 3 | 4 | 5 | 6 | 7 | 8 | 9 | 10 |

J. TECHNIQUE PRACTICE: RETURN KEY

J. Key each sentence on a separate line.

41 Who should go? Can you attend? Why not? Will Ann attend?
42 Someone should go. They asked us. It shouldn't take long.
43 Ask Lynn to go. She may like it. I could go. He will go.
44 When can you go? Can I ride with you? Will you stay long?
45 Thanks for the offer. I'll pay the toll. Let's eat lunch.

K. TECHNIQUE PRACTICE: CONCENTRATION

K. Insert the necessary capitalization as you key these sentences twice.

46 Erik hall is attending notre dame university in south bend.
47 The statue of liberty and the hudson river are in new york.
48 The cities of dallas, austin, and san antonio are in texas.
49 The alexander graham bell museum is located in cape breton.
50 The boston red sox play their games at home in fenway park.

L. 12-SECOND SPRINTS

L. Take three 12-second timed writings on each line. The scale gives wam for a 12-second timed writing.

51 They were 65 or 70 miles south of Freeway #429 at 8:31 a.m.
52 I shipped 20 crates each of items #485 and #697 on July 31.
53 Our city's population grew from 39,612 to 40,587 in a year.
54 She will be on Route 67 for 1,308 of the 2,495 total miles.
55 The 45 teachers and 761 students arrived at 8:30 on May 29.

| | | | | 5 | | | |10| | | |15| | | |20| | | |25| | | |30| | | |35| | | |40| | | |45| | | |50| | | |55| | | |60

M. SUSTAINED PRACTICE: SYLLABIC INTENSITY

M. Take a 1-minute timed writing on the first paragraph to establish your base speed. Then take four 1-minute timed writings on the remaining paragraphs. As soon as you equal or exceed your base speed on one paragraph, advance to the next one.

56 If you would like to be a success as a spouse, parent, 12
57 friend, or worker, you should think about the words you use 24
58 on a daily basis. These words can enable you to go through 36
59 life being pleased with things that must be done every day. 48

60 Through the use of certain words and by regulating the 12
61 tone of voice, one can help to build the self-esteem of any 24
62 person spoken to. This may encourage these others to react 36
63 in a positive way to any type of order that will be issued. 48

64 For example, you might improve your relationships with 12
65 others by trying to show a sympathetic understanding. This 24
66 can be done by giving others a feeling of worthiness. Make 36
67 an effort to find something to admire and praise in others. 48

68 In summary, there are words which achieve miracles. A 12
69 person who masters the art of praising discovers that it is 24
70 possible to have receivers react in a very favorable way to 36
71 the giver. Strive to provide reassurance and appreciation. 48

| 1 | 2 | 3 | 4 | 5 | 6 | 7 | 8 | 9 | 10 | 11 | 12

2

OBJECTIVES

KEYBOARDING

To operate the entire keyboard by touch.

To key 36 words a minute on a 3-minute timed writing with no more than 4 errors.

LANGUAGE ARTS

To improve language arts skills, including correct grammar, spelling, use of punctuation marks, capitalization, numbers, titles in business correspondence, and abbreviations.

To proofread documents and correct errors.

To develop keyboard composing skill.

DOCUMENT PROCESSING

To center text horizontally and vertically.

To format business letters and personal-business letters in block style.

To format one-page unbound reports, enumerations, outlines, and bibliographies.

To format tables with column headings.

© Maria Paraskevas

D. PACED PRACTICE

Turn to the Paced Practice routine at the back of the book. Take three 2-minute timed writings, starting at the speed at which you left off the last time.

E. PRETEST: ALTERNATE- AND ONE-HAND WORDS

13   Banks must not be carefree with their minimum reserves 12
14 or they might encounter a problem with the auditor. Such a 24
15 case might find a penalty being assessed. The opinion that 36
16 most eager bankers have is to exceed the required reserves. 48

| 1 | 2 | 3 | 4 | 5 | 6 | 7 | 8 | 9 | 10 | 11 | 12

F. PRACTICE: ALTERNATE-HAND WORDS

17 also amend maps island blame city problem panel formal down
18 snap rigid lens social visit with penalty right height half
19 chap burnt such enrich shape dish auditor spend eighty lamb
20 girl usual tick thrown laugh then suspend slept mantle kept

G. PRACTICE: ONE-HAND WORDS

21 fad only craft pupil regret uphill drafter homonym carefree
22 bed join water nylon target pompon savages minimum exceeded
23 was hook great knoll teased kimono scatter pumpkin attracts
24 age milk eager union bazaar limply reserve opinion cassette

H. POSTTEST: ALTERNATE- AND ONE-HAND WORDS

I. SUSTAINED PRACTICE: NUMBERS AND SYMBOLS

25   The number of people who are completing their shopping 12
26 through the use of a catalog has increased significantly in 24
27 the past few years. The following examples will serve as a 36
28 sample of the types of activities being processed this way. 48

29   Fox & Day included 20 new items in the newest catalog. 12
30 Item #19 was being imported from Finland and was priced for 24
31 $99. This item was handmade by a group of individuals in a 36
32 distant village in the southwestern region of that country. 48

33   A catalog for sports enthusiasts distributed by Gall & 12
34 Spenillo included items for about 25 different sports. The 24
35 items ranged from a low of $18 to a high of $199. A few of 36
36 the items (#140 and #221) were imported from other nations. 48

37   The catalog from Shafer & Wilson listed new electronic 12
38 equipment at big savings. For example, Item #89 was listed 24
39 at $99, a discount of 60%. Some items (#41, #97, and #121) 36
40 were discounted 50%. There were 433 items in this catalog. 48

| 1 | 2 | 3 | 4 | 5 | 6 | 7 | 8 | 9 | 10 | 11 | 12

Horizontal Centering

Margins: 1 inch • Tab: 5 spaces • Spacing: Single • Drills: 2 times • Format Guide: 1

Goals:
To improve speed and accuracy; to center material horizontally.

A. WARMUP

1   Jill gave an expert a quick breakdown of all the sizes   12
2 made. She may ask clients to call 642-3598 to get a better   24
3 understanding of the shipping charge of $10.75 on Item #22.   36

| 1 | 2 | 3 | 4 | 5 | 6 | 7 | 8 | 9 | 10 | 11 | 12

LANGUAGE ARTS

B. COMPOSING

Composing at the keyboard can save you considerable time when you create first drafts of documents. When composing at the keyboard, keep the following points in mind:

1. Key at a comfortable pace as your thoughts come to you. Do not stop to correct errors.

2. Keep your eyes on your keyed copy as you key.

3. Do not be overly concerned with correct grammar. It is more important that you get your thoughts recorded. Any errors you make can be corrected later.

B. Answer each question with a single word.

4 Do you have a computer?
5 What is your favorite sport?
6 What is your favorite color?
7 When is your favorite time of day?
8 Do you read a daily newspaper?
9 What is your favorite hobby?
10 Where would you like to spend your next vacation?
11 What is the name of the happiest person you know?

SKILLBUILDING

PRETEST.
Take a 1-minute timed writing; compute your speed and count errors.

PRACTICE.
Speed Emphasis: If you made 2 or fewer errors on the Pretest, key each line twice.
Accuracy Emphasis: If you made 3 or more errors, key each group of lines (as though it were a paragraph) twice.

C. PRETEST: COMMON LETTER COMBINATIONS

12   The manager tried to react with total control. He was   12
13 indeed annoyed and devoted all his efforts to being fair to   24
14 the entire staff. His daily schedule was rampant with ways   36
15 in which to confront the situation and to apply good sense.   48

| 1 | 2 | 3 | 4 | 5 | 6 | 7 | 8 | 9 | 10 | 11 | 12

D. PRACTICE: WORD BEGINNINGS

16 re relay react reply reuse reason record return results red
17 in index inept incur inset inning indeed insure interns ink
18 be beast berry being beeps berate belong became beavers bet
19 de dealt death decay devil detest devote derive depicts den

---

106-110 LESSONS

Margins: 1 inch • Spacing: Single • Drills: 2 times • Format Guide: 75–81 • Working Papers: 231–239

Goals for Unit 22

Begin each day with approximately 15 minutes of skill-building, selecting activities from pages 245–248. In the remaining class time, complete as many production jobs from pages 249–256 as you can.

1. To improve accuracy and speed on alphabet and number keys.
2. To key 49 wam for 5 minutes with no more than 5 errors.
3. To develop proficiency in spelling commonly misspelled words.
4. To gain an understanding of an orientation to an in-basket exercise.
5. To format a variety of reports—directory, minutes of a meeting, itinerary, and magazine article.
6. To format letters and memorandums with various features.
7. To format boxed tables with braced column headings.

A. WARMUP

```
1      Three accounting firms (Braxx & Jackson, Zack & Villa,    12
2  and Powl & Yale) placed requests with the collection agency   24
3  to collect the following amounts:  $612.50, $489, and $370.   36
```
```
   |  1  |  2 . |  3  |  4  |  5  |  6  |  7  |  8  |  9  |  10  |  11  |  12
```

LANGUAGE ARTS

B. Study the rules at the right. Then key lines 4–7, making necessary changes.

B. CAPITAL LETTERS

Rule: Capitalize all official titles of honor and respect when they precede personal names.

One of the new Golden Wildcats members is Dr. Chi Pang Yu.

Rule: Capitalize words such as *mother, father, aunt,* and *uncle* when they stand alone or they are followed by a personal name.

The letter from Aunt Mary was extremely encouraging.

```
4  Mr. Tim Swendsen and Ms. Sara Terrell were both elected.
5  The student debate was coordinated by professor Coleman.
6  The ladies and mother plan to form a string quartet.
7  Many of the regulations had been written by uncle Roger.
```

C. These words are among the 500 most frequently misspelled words in business correspondence.

C. SPELLING

```
8  labor station quarter conditions modifications applications
9  companies questionnaire certainly except pertinent previous
10 agreement brochure ability claimants responsible curriculum
11 liability phase consumer treasurer's coordinator counseling
12 orientation institution enrollment reasonable signed growth
```

E. PRACTICE: WORD ENDINGS

20 ly dimly daily apply lowly barely deeply unruly finally sly
21 ed cured moved tamed tried amused billed busted creamed fed
22 nt mount blunt front stunt absent rodent splint rampant ant
23 al canal total local equal plural rental verbal logical pal

POSTTEST.
Repeat the Pretest (C) and compare performance.

F. POSTTEST: COMMON LETTER COMBINATIONS

G. PROGRESSIVE PRACTICE: NUMBERS

Turn to the Progressive Practice: Numbers routine at the back of the book. Take six 30-second timed writings, starting at the point where you left off the last time.

H. Take two 1-minute timed writings. The last two digits of each number provide a cumulative word count for determining wam.

H. NUMBER PRACTICE

24 2201 2202 2203 2204 2205 2206 2207 2208 2209 2210 2211 2212
25 8813 8814 8815 8816 8817 8818 8819 8820 8821 8822 8823 8824
26 4725 4726 4727 4728 4729 4730 4731 4732 4733 4734 4735 4736
27 9237 9238 9239 9240 9241 9242 9243 9244 9245 9246 9247 9248

FORMATTING

I. HORIZONTAL CENTERING

Horizontally centered text has equal white space to the left and the right of it.

To center text using automatic centering, use the appropriate code or command keys to move the carrier to the center of the line (42 for 10-pitch type; 51 for 12-pitch type). Then key the text to be centered and press Return.

DOCUMENT PROCESSING

Correct your errors.

Practice 1. Horizontally center each line.

Tennessee
North Carolina
Ohio
California
Florida
Rhode Island

Practice 2. Horizontally center each line.

Nashville
Raleigh
Columbus
Sacramento
Tallahassee
Providence

Practice 3. Horizontally center each line.

Phi Chi Beta
Is Sponsoring a Career Fair
Friday, April 17, 19--
Room 419
Student Center Building

Practice 4. Horizontally center each line.

COMMUNITY BLOOD DRIVE
Saturday, April 18
Sponsored by the Rotary Club
Municipal Building
Denville, New Jersey

paper so that the underline is in the correct position; then key your name. Check the relation of the letters to the underline and the underline to the aligning scale, and adjust your paper as necessary. Repeat the procedure one more time to be sure you can align correctly.

Correct

Steven Desmarais

Incorrect

Steven Desmarais

Steven Desmarais

DOCUMENT
PROCESSING

FORM 9
CREDIT APPLICATION

Working Papers: 225

Format a credit application from the handwritten information on the form to the right.

FORM 10
CREDIT APPLICATION

Working Papers: 227

Format a credit application for yourself, using actual data that applies to your own situation.

APPLICATION FOR CREDIT

NAME _Zverov_____ _Nikolai_____ _V._____
      Last   First   Middle Initial

SOCIAL SECURITY NO. _187-05-0246_ TELEPHONE _404-555-2168_

ADDRESS _2170 Piedmont Road, NE_____
              Street Address

_Atlanta, GA 30324_____
          City, State, ZIP

HOW LONG AT ABOVE ADDRESS? _3_ YRS. OWN OR RENT? _own_

PREVIOUS ADDRESS _2999 Circle 75 Parkway_
                 Street Address

_Atlanta, GA 30339_____
          City, State, ZIP

CURRENT EMPLOYER _Turner Broadcasting_

One CNN Center, Atlanta, GA 30348
                Address

HOW LONG EMPLOYED HERE? _5_ YRS. JOB TITLE _Records Manager_

SUPERVISOR NAME _Lynn Bryant_ PHONE NO. _404-555-1500_

ANNUAL SALARY $_32,500_ TOTAL FAMILY INCOME $_39,300_

CHECKING ACCOUNT NO. _218-7456-B_ NAME OF BANK _City National_

SAVINGS ACCOUNT NO. _19635-738_ NAME OF BANK _CNN Credit Union_

CREDIT CARDS

NAME	ACCOUNT NO.	CURRENT BALANCE
Mastercard	550 172 463 099	173
Visa	5012 76 1839	280
American Express	145 99637 041	0

OTHER CURRENT OBLIGATIONS

NAME	ACCOUNT NO.	CURRENT BALANCE
Federal Mortgage	7321659	68,500
Ford Credit Corp.	187-59263	4,600

_____   _August 5, 19--_
    Applicant Signature   Date

Vertical Centering

Margins: 1 inch • Tab: 5 spaces • Spacing: Single • Drills: 2 times • Format Guide: 1

Goals:
To key 30 wam/3'/5e; to center text vertically.

A. WARMUP

1   Liza bought two very exquisite jackets from a downtown   12
2 shop. The prices were $739 and $681, which included a nice   24
3 discount of 20%. Her total savings amounted to about $145.   36

| 1 | 2 | 3 | 4 | 5 | 6 | 7 | 8 | 9 | 10 | 11 | 12

LANGUAGE ARTS

B. Study the rules at the right. Then key lines 4–7, making any necessary changes.

B. NUMBERS

Rule: Spell out numbers from 1 through 10; use figures for numbers above 10.
Exception: If two or more *related* numbers both below and above 10 are used in the same sentence, use figures for all numbers.

He bought two horses. He now has 12 horses and 2 dogs.

Rule: To express even millions or billions, use the following style: 10 million (not 10,000,000) and 3.6 billion (not 3,600,000,000).

The state's population was slightly over 7 million.

4 Our dealers sold thirty-four cars during the weekend sale.
                        34
5 The order was for seven desks, 12 tables, and 55 chairs.
          7
6 The county's wheat production was about 2,000,000 bushels.
                      2 million
7 There were 3.4 billion shares traded during the period.

SKILLBUILDING

C. Take two 1-minute timed writings. Try not to slow down for the capital letters.

C. TECHNIQUE PRACTICE: SHIFT KEY

8   D. M. Mays from Clark, Ohio, and Dr. C. H. Miller from   12
9 Aurora, Utah, attended the Miss America Pageant in Atlantic   24
10 City, New Jersey. They met Veronica B. Baxter from Georgia   36
11 and Pat D. Parr from Connecticut, who is Miss Congeniality.   48

| 1 | 2 | 3 | 4 | 5 | 6 | 7 | 8 | 9 | 10 | 11 | 12

D. Take two 1-minute timed writings. Focus on correct techniques and accuracy rather than speed.

D. SYMBOL PRACTICE

12   Order #2310 was sent to Van & Blake for the following: 12
13 (1) 12 ribbons @ 9.75 each; (2) 8 boxes of envelopes @ 2.25   24
14 each; (3) 24 computer disks @ 1.75 each. The amount of the   36
15 invoice came to $187.62, which included 6% for a sales tax.   48

| 1 | 2 | 3 | 4 | 5 | 6 | 7 | 8 | 9 | 10 | 11 | 12

FORM 6
INVOICE

Working Papers: 217

An invoice (or a bill) is an itemized list of the charges for providing the goods.

INVOICE 6452. On November 28, 19—, Universal Outlet invoices Richard Moose, Builder, for its Purchase Order 4863 for the following items:

4 ctns. of light-oak trim kits for tub enclosure @ $12.80 = $51.20; 1 drop-in self-rimming thermoplastic sink @ $28.50 = $28.50; 3 twin-panel tub enclosures @ $129.95 = $389.85; and 2 doz. caulk and adhesive kits @ $26.50 = $53.00; Total = $522.55; Plus tax = $28.30; TOTAL AMOUNT DUE = $550.85.

FORM 7
INVOICE

Working Papers: 219

INVOICE 1895. On November 30, 19—, Midwest Contracting Supplies bills Empire Manufacturing, 113 Liston Avenue, Rocky Mount, NC 27801, for its Purchase Order 442 for the following items:

12 ctns. of Arrow staples, ½", T-50 @ $4.25 a carton = $51.00; 6 boxes of round-head bolts, 1½" @ $3.25 a box = $19.50; and 15 ctns. of nails unlimited, 2", 6D @ $8.00 a carton = $120.00. Invoice total = $190.50, Plus 6% sales tax of $11.43. TOTAL AMOUNT DUE = $201.93.

FORM 8
INVOICE

Working Papers: 221

INVOICE 56101. On December 5, 19—, Continental Office Wholesalers invoices Cameron Office Equipment, 1100 Canyon Boulevard, Salt Lake City, UT 84401, for its Purchase Order 7290 for the following items:

2 facsimile copiers, J412 @ $250.00 each = $500.00; 14 stackable paper trays, L104 @ $3.98 each = $55.72; 18 file-folder labels, green, S17 @ $5.75 each = $103.50; 18 file-folder labels, yellow, S17 @ $5.75 each = $103.50; 17 ctns. copier paper, white, S71 @ $6.30 a carton = $107.10. Invoice total = $869.82, Plus 5.75% sales tax of $50.01. TOTAL AMOUNT DUE = $919.83.

FORMATTING

R. KEYING TEXT ON PRINTED LINES

To position text on a printed form, use the paper release lever to position the form horizontally and the variable line space or micro-line space key to position the form vertically so that the printed line is in the same position that an underline would be. If you are unsure of how keyed text appears when it is underlined, key the alphabet, then underline it. Note the exact relation of the bottom of the letters to the underline. Also note the position of the underline and the letters in relation to the aligning scale.

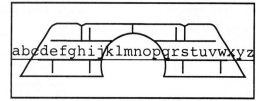

To practice positioning text on a printed line, key a line 2 inches long. Remove your paper and reinsert it. Adjust the

(Continued on next page.)

E. PROGRESSIVE PRACTICE: NUMBERS

Turn to the Progressive Practice: Numbers routine at the back of the book. Take six 30-second timed writings, starting at the point where you left off the last time.

F. 3-MINUTE TIMED WRITING

F. Spacing: double. Take two 3-minute timed writings. Compute your speed and count errors.

Goal: 30 wam/3'/5e

Interlinear numbers in the paragraph show wam for a 3-minute timed writing.

16   Getting a job is something that you are quite likely   12
17 thinking about as you look to your future. It is vital for   24
18 you to learn some appropriate skills to assist you in that   35
19 venture. Keyboarding is an extremely important skill in   47
20 preparing for that first job.   53
21   Of course, you must realize that your future boss is   64
22 looking for more than skills. He or she wants you to have   76
23 the right kind of attitude and work ethic as you begin that   88
24 first job.   90

| 1 | 2 | 3 | 4 | 5 | 6 | 7 | 8 | 9 | 10 | 11 | 12 |

FORMATTING

G. VERTICAL CENTERING

The concept of vertical centering is similar to that of horizontal centering. Vertically centered text has equal space above and below it. Text should appear to be framed on a sheet of paper with equal side margins and equal top and bottom margins.

To center text vertically:

1. Count the number of lines (including blank ones) that the text will fill.
2. Subtract that number from the number of lines on the page. Standard paper is 11 inches long; standard line spacing is 6 lines per inch. Therefore, there are 66 lines on a page (11 × 6 = 66).
3. Divide the remainder by 2 and drop any fraction and add 1 to find the line number on which to begin keying.

Example: To center 12 double-spaced lines on a full sheet, you will need 23 lines (12 keyed + 11 blank = 23; 66 − 23 = 43 ÷ 2 = 21.5). Begin keying on line 22.

Many word processing programs enable you to vertically center a page with one command.

DOCUMENT PROCESSING

Spacing: Double

Practice 5. Center lines horizontally and vertically.

THE ELECTION RESULTS ARE:
Sharon Coleman, President
Victor Puglio, Vice President
Thomas Parciak, Treasurer
Megan Cull, Secretary
Joseph Browning, Historian
Karen Labadie, Public Relations

Practice 6. Center lines horizontally and vertically.

INTERNATIONAL ART SOCIETY
cordially invites you to attend
The Premier Showing of
ART FROM AROUND THE WORLD
Friday and Saturday, March 6–7
from 10 a.m. until 10 p.m.
CIVIC AUDITORIUM BUILDING

FORM 2	PURCHASE ORDER 4862. On November 6, 19—, the Purchasing Depart-

FORM 2
PURCHASE ORDER

Working Papers: 207

PURCHASE ORDER 4862. On November 6, 19—, the Purchasing Department orders the following items from Midwest Contracting Supplies, 2622 West Central, Wichita, KS 67203.

1 heavy-duty 20-foot extension ladder (Catalog No. 634-8B) @ $88.99 = $88.99; 4 full-view exterior doors with kickplate (No. 251-6C) @ $219.99 = $879.96; 3 raised-panel exterior doors (No. 604-7B) @ $179.99 = $539.97; and 3 double-glazed colonial doors (No. 629-9H) @ $199.99 = $599.97; TOTAL = $2,108.89.

FORM 3
PURCHASE ORDER

Working Papers: 209

PURCHASE ORDER 4863. On November 6, 19—, the Purchasing Department orders the following items from Universal Outlet, 1472 Florida Avenue, Hagerstown, MD 21740.

4 ctns. of light-oak trim kits for tub enclosure (Catalog No. 171) @ $12.80 = $51.20; 1 drop-in self-rimming thermoplastic sink (for 4-inch center faucet) (No. 876) @ $28.50 = $28.50; 3 twin-panel tub enclosures with mirror panel, gold tone (No. 355) @ $129.95 = $389.85; and 2 doz. caulk and adhesive kits (No. 201) @ $26.50 = $53.00; TOTAL = $522.55.

FORM 4
PURCHASE ORDER

Working Papers: 211

PURCHASE ORDER 1077. On April 18, 19—, the Purchasing Department orders the following items from Quality-First Computer Supplies, 1045 South Service Road, Plainview, NY 11803.

18 data cartridges, 1/4 inch (Cat. No. 1980) @ $22.35 = $402.30; 8 PC keyboard templates—MicroWord 3.2 (No. 8212) @ $12.95 = $103.60; 9 front-loading cartridges (No. 1840) @ $77.00 = $693.00; 12 space-saving copyholders (No. 6239) @ $34.95 = $419.40; Total = $1,618.30; Shipping/Handling = $243.00; TOTAL AMOUNT DUE = $1,861.30

FORM 5
INVOICE

Working Papers: 215

INVOICE 9076. On November 13, 19—, Midwest Contracting Supplies invoices Richard Moose, Builder, 1335 Dublin Road, Columbus, OH 43215, for its Purchase Order 4862 for the following items:

1 heavy-duty 20-foot extension ladder @ $88.99 = $88.99; 4 full-view exterior doors with kickplate @ $219.99 = $879.96; 3 raised-panel exterior doors @ $179.99 = $539.97; and 3 double-glazed colonial doors @ $199.99 = $599.97; Total = $2,108.89; Less 10% trade discount = $210.89; Plus tax and shipping = $164.36; TOTAL AMOUNT DUE = $2,062.36.

Horizontal Centering

Margins: 1 inch • Tab: 5 spaces • Spacing: Single • Drills: 2 times • Format Guide: 3

Goals:
To improve speed and accuracy; to review vertical and horizontal centering.

A. WARMUP

```
1        Invoice #1436-78 for $2,590 was billed incorrectly for   12
2 five (5) new quartz watches.  It was sent to Maxwell Jacobs     24
3 on Buckingham Boulevard in Parma, Ohio.  He was very upset.     36
   |  1  |  2  |  3  |  4  |  5  |  6  |  7  |  8  |  9  | 10  | 11  | 12
```

LANGUAGE ARTS

B. Compare this paragraph with the Pretest (E) on page 42. Key a list of the errors, correcting the errors as you key.

B. PROOFREADING

```
4        We were hopping to agree on the need to check the valu
5 of our assets.  No one should be opposed to finding ansers
6 that would give us our worth.  Old records and legers will
7 be sorted, and we will unit in our effort to get the data.
```

SKILLBUILDING

C. DIAGNOSTIC PRACTICE: ALPHABET

Turn to the Diagnostic Practice: Alphabet routine at the back of this book. Take the Pretest and record your performance. Then, practice the drill lines for those reaches on which you made errors. Finally, repeat the Pretest and compare your performance.

D. Take a 1-minute timed writing on the first paragraph to establish your base speed. Then take four 1-minute timed writings on the remaining paragraphs. As soon as you equal or exceed your base speed on one paragraph, advance to the next one.

D. SUSTAINED PRACTICE: SYLLABIC INTENSITY

```
8        One should always attempt to maintain good health.  As   12
9 the first step in keeping good health, one should avoid the      24
10 habit of smoking.  Volumes have been written on this topic.     36

11       A second habit that will help maintain your health for    12
12 decades is consuming an appropriate amount of water, day in     24
13 and day out; most physicians recommend eight glasses a day.     36

14       Making exercise a habit is another important trait for    12
15 staying in good health.  Most experts agree that spending a     24
16 few minutes a day in regular, vigorous exercise is helpful.     36

17       A final habit of importance is maintaining appropriate    12
18 body weight.  The key to maintaining weight is developing a     24
19 positive eating pattern.  Calculating calorie intake helps.     36
   |  1  |  2  |  3  |  4  |  5  |  6  |  7  |  8  |  9  | 10  | 11  | 12
```

Please send the following memo to Mr. R. N. Halsten, President. It is from James F. Demings, Employee Services. Use the current date and an appropriate subject line.

This is a progress report on plans for the annual Hi-Teck Winter Ball, to be held on February 11. As usual, the event will be held in the Regis-Biltmore Hotel. Invitations have been sent to all home-office employees. (Similar events have been scheduled for other employees at various sites throughout the country.)

The menu has been planned, the orchestra has been selected, and the Performance Awards recipients have been identified.

Let's hope that the weather will be more favorable than it was last year, when we had a snowstorm on the night of the party!

FORMATTING

Q. PURCHASE ORDERS AND INVOICES

To fill in a printed form such as an invoice or a purchase order, follow these general directions:

1. Key any heading information 2 spaces after any printed guide words or vertical lines.
2. Set the left margin for the first column. Set tabs for remaining columns.
3. Visually center number columns between the vertical lines. Set decimal tabs to align the number columns at the right.
4. Align word columns at the left, 2 spaces after the vertical line. Indent turnover lines 3 spaces.
5. Begin the total information a double space below the last line in the *Description* column.

DOCUMENT PROCESSING

FORM 1
PURCHASE ORDER

Working Papers: 205

A purchase order is used by a company to order goods or services from another company.

<table>
<tr><td colspan="6">(**CONTINENTAL OFFICE**)
Wholesalers
1335 Dublin-Granville Road, Columbus, OH 43215, Phone: 614-555-3991</td></tr>
<tr><td colspan="6">*Purchase Order No.* 1076</td></tr>
<tr><td colspan="3">**TO:** Industrial Furniture Company
P.O. Box 2152
High Point, NC 27261</td><td colspan="3">**DATE:** April 17, 19--</td></tr>
<tr><td colspan="6">PLEASE SHIP AND BILL US FOR THE GOODS LISTED BELOW. IF FOR ANY REASON YOU CANNOT DELIVER WITHIN 30 DAYS, LET US KNOW AT ONCE. PLEASE REFER TO OUR PURCHASE ORDER NUMBER (ABOVE) IN ALL COMMUNICATIONS.</td></tr>
<tr><th>QUANTITY</th><th>DESCRIPTION</th><th>CAT. NO.</th><th>UNIT PRICE</th><th>AMOUNT</th></tr>
<tr><td>3</td><td>Printer stands</td><td>3907</td><td>209.95</td><td>629.85</td></tr>
<tr><td>3</td><td>Paper baskets</td><td>3911</td><td>39.95</td><td>119.85</td></tr>
<tr><td>3</td><td>Paperfeed racks</td><td>3945</td><td>19.95</td><td>59.85</td></tr>
<tr><td>6</td><td>Workstation modules, light oak, extra wide</td><td>3147</td><td>279.00</td><td>1,674.00</td></tr>
<tr><td>9</td><td>Locking casters (set of 4)</td><td>4096</td><td>18.75</td><td>168.75</td></tr>
<tr><td></td><td>Total</td><td></td><td></td><td>2,652.30</td></tr>
<tr><td></td><td>Shipping (10%)</td><td></td><td></td><td>265.23</td></tr>
<tr><td></td><td>TOTAL AMOUNT DUE</td><td></td><td></td><td>2,917.53</td></tr>
</table>

E. 12-SECOND SPRINTS

E. Take three 12-second timed writings on each line. The scale shows your wam speed for a 12-second timed writing.

20 Sixty equals only five dozen, but we promised Jackie eight.
21 Vic quickly mixed frozen strawberries into the grape juice.
22 Jeff amazed the audience by quickly giving six new reports.
23 Five big jet planes zoomed quickly by the six steel towers.

| | | | 5 | | | |10| | | |15| | | |20| | | |25| | | |30| | | |35| | | |40| | | |45| | | |50| | | |55| | | |60

F. PRETEST: CLOSE REACHES

PRETEST. Take a 1-minute timed writing; compute your speed and count errors.

24   We were hoping to agree on the need to check the value   12
25 of our assets. No one should be opposed to finding answers   24
26 that would give us our worth. Old records and ledgers will   36
27 be sorted, and we will unite in our effort to get the data.   48

| | 1 | 2 | 3 | 4 | 5 | 6 | 7 | 8 | 9 | 10 | 11 | 12

G. PRACTICE: ADJACENT KEYS

PRACTICE.
Speed Emphasis: If you made 2 or fewer errors on the Pretest, key each line twice.
Accuracy Emphasis: If you made 3 or more errors, key each group of lines (as though it were a paragraph) twice.

28 as ashes cases class asset astute passes chased creased ask
29 op optic ropes grope snoop oppose copied proper trooper top
30 we weave tweed towed weigh wealth twenty fewest answers wet
31 rt worth alert party smart artist sorted charts turtles art

H. PRACTICE: CONSECUTIVE FINGERS

32 sw sweet swarm swing swift switch answer swampy swims swirl
33 un undue bunch stung begun united punish outrun untie funny
34 gr grand agree angry grade growth egress hungry group graph
35 ol older solid tools spool volume evolve uphold olive scold

I. POSTTEST: CLOSE REACHES

POSTTEST. Repeat the Pretest (F) and compare performance.

FORMATTING

J. BOLD

Bold text prints darker than normal text. Use bold to highlight or display text. Determine the appropriate procedure for your equipment to key bold type.

DOCUMENT PROCESSING

Practice 7. Center lines horizontally and vertically.

WHAT: Hear Anne Crane speak
TOPIC: CHANGING DEMOGRAPHICS
WHEN: 6 p.m., March 24, 19--
BY: Glendale CC
WHERE: Civic Auditorium

Practice 8. Center lines horizontally and vertically.

INVENTORY CONTROL ANALYSIS
A Report by Josephine Baker
Harrison Supply Company
Saturday, April 18, 19--
FALL RIVER, MASSACHUSETTS

To: Patricia Hewson   From: George M. Dow
    Media Relations   General Manager
Subject: Press Release   Date: April 11, 19--

                an impressive
You have done ~~a masterful~~ job on the press release, Pat. I have
                                               legal counsel
no changes to suggest at all. As soon as you have our ~~attorney~~
review it, you may send it out.

Perhaps you should set up a press conference for me on Wednesday
afternoon--early enough to make the evening news. My office has
also recieved several calls from the News Media, and I've
refered all inquiries to your office. Please let me have a list
of likely questions by Tuesday afternoon.
                                    —and suggested responses
pcb

MEMO 24
ON PRINTED FORM

Working Papers: 201

The abbreviation *RE* is sometimes used in place of the
word *SUBJECT* in a memo or
letter.

ENUMERATION. Treat each
item as a separate paragraph
with numbers at the left margin and turnover lines indented 4 spaces.

(TO:)   All Members of ASB Local 407   *(FROM:)*   Evelyn Cunningham,
Human Resources Director   *(DATE:)*   October 19, 19—   *(RE:)*   Annual
Performance Appraisal

As called for in our recent agreement, an annual performance appraisal
will be conducted for all covered employees. Basically, the agreement requires each supervisor to compare each employee's job performance with
established job standards.

The purpose of the annual appraisal is to:

1. Document present job performance to provide management with information needed to make decisions regarding salary, promotion, transfer, and
termination.

2. Aid in developing plans for improvement based on agreed-on goals,
strengths, and weaknesses.

3. Identify growth opportunities.

4. Provide feedback on the success of previous training and disclose the
need for additional training.

5. Provide the opportunity for formal feedback.

A joint labor-management committee is now developing an evaluation form
that will be submitted to management for approval. If you have any questions or concerns about this new personnel policy, please call me at
Extension 1040. / *(Your initials)*

Block Centering

Margins: 1 inch • Tab: 5 spaces • Spacing: Single • Drills: 2 times • Format Guide: 3

Goals:
To key 30 wam/3'/5e; to block-center material.

A. WARMUP

1 Order 14 items @ $95 and another 10 items @ $86. When 12
2 you add the 7% sales tax, the total will be $2,343.30. The 24
3 boxes should be sent to P. J. Quigley of Vanzant, Kentucky. 36

 | 1 | 2 | 3 | 4 | 5 | 6 | 7 | 8 | 9 | 10 | 11 | 12

LANGUAGE ARTS

B. These words are among the 500 most frequently misspelled words in business correspondence.

B. SPELLING

4 personnel information its procedures their committee system
5 receive employees which education services opportunity area
6 financial appropriate interest received production contract
7 important through necessary customer employee further there
8 property account approximately general control division our

---

SKILLBUILDING

C. Take two 1-minute timed writings. The last two digits of each number provide a cumulative word count for determining wam.

C. NUMBER PRACTICE

9 5601 3802 8203 1104 1505 2806 9207 4408 5009 6110 2811 4912
10 7813 4814 2915 9016 8317 5618 4419 1520 3321 8722 5623 4124
11 3925 2426 9627 5528 6829 1930 2831 4332 6633 7834 2135 9036
12 3337 5638 7439 8340 3941 2742 1043 6444 5945 1946 3447 6248

D. Take a 1-minute timed writing on the first paragraph to establish your base speed. Then take four 1-minute timed writings on the remaining paragraphs. As soon as you equal or exceed your base speed on one paragraph, advance to the next one.

D. SUSTAINED PRACTICE: NUMBERS

13 In the past quarter, we have added the names of 78 new 12
14 clients to our list of customers. This brings our total of 24
15 new clients for this entire past year to 249, a new record. 36

16 Of the 249 new clients, 91 were being serviced by Pete 12
17 Thompson; 85 were being helped by Charlotte Anne Baine; and 24
18 73 of the new clients were being handled by Melanie Murphy. 36

19 We got 24 clients in October from 107 contacts; during 12
20 November we gained 29 new clients through our 168 contacts; 24
21 in December we earned 35 new clients through some contacts. 36

22 It was exciting to get 249 new clients this past year. 12
23 Next year we want 350 more; then, gains of 425 and 475 will 24
24 give us a total of 1,499 new clients in a four-year period. 36

 | 1 | 2 | 3 | 4 | 5 | 6 | 7 | 8 | 9 | 10 | 11 | 12

P. MEMORANDUMS ON PRINTED FORMS

Although interoffice memorandums can be keyed on plain paper or letterhead stationery, they are often keyed on forms on which the guide words *To, From, Date,* and *Subject* are printed.

To format a memorandum on a printed form:

1. Set the left margin 2 spaces after the guide words; set the right margin to equal the left.
2. Set a tab stop 2 spaces after the guide words in the second column (if there is a second column).
3. Key the heading information at the margin or the tab, aligning the type with the bottom of the printed guide words.
4. Separate the heading and the body with 2 blank lines.
5. Use reference initials and other notations as appropriate.

DOCUMENT PROCESSING

MEMO 22
ON PRINTED FORM

Working Papers: 197

To: George M. Dow, General Manager

From: Patricia Hewson, Media Relations

Date: April 10, 19--

Subject: Accident at Site 5

I have reveiwed the technical reports from the chemical and engineering (depts.) and have also interviewed the operator who was on duty the night of the accident. Based on the basis of the information I have on hand, I've drafted the enclosed attached press release.

¶ Would you please review this release and make any changes you feel are necessary. Station KXAR-TV and the Morning Herald have already called to asking for our side of the story. Therefore, Thus I would like to issue this press release as soon as possible.

wpr

Enclosure Attachment

E. PACED PRACTICE

Turn to the Paced Practice routine at the back of the book. Take four 2-minute timed writings, following the directions at the top of the page.

Turn to the Paced Practice routine at the back of the book.

F. Spacing: double.
Take two 3-minute timed writings. Compute your speed and count errors.

Goal: 30 wam/3'/5e

F. 3-MINUTE TIMED WRITING

```
25      The first day on a new job can be quite exciting. You    12
26  are looking forward to meeting the different people you may   24
27  be working with, as well as to finding out about the daily    36
28  tasks and duties you will handle.                             43
29      It is very important that you approach that first day     54
30  in the right frame of mind. Think carefully about the way     66
31  you dress. Be friendly to all people you meet. Show some      78
32  enthusiasm and zest for the tasks and duties you will have.   90
```

| 1 | 2 | 3 | 4 | 5 | 6 | 7 | 8 | 9 | 10 | 11 | 12 |

FORMATTING

G. BLOCK CENTERING

To horizontally center several lines of text as a group (or block) rather than individually:

1. Determine the correct starting line to vertically center the job.
2. Insert a sheet of scrap paper and center the longest line.
3. Position the carrier under the first character of the centered line and note its position on the margin scale.
4. Clear existing tabs and set a new tab at this position.
5. Insert a clean sheet, space down to the correct starting line, and center and key the title in bold and all-capital letters; then triple-space.
6. Key the remaining group of lines, beginning each one at the tab stop.

DOCUMENT PROCESSING

Spacing: Double

Center titles horizontally and key them in bold; then triple-space. Block-center the items.

Practice 9. Center vertically.

SKILLS NEEDED FOR WORK SUCCESS ↓3

Communications
Interpersonal
Setting Priorities
Organization
Technical
Managing Time
Critical Thinking

Practice 10. Center vertically.

BUSIEST U.S. AIRPORTS ↓3

Chicago O'Hare International
Dallas/Ft. Worth International
Los Angeles International
Atlanta International
New York (JFK) International
San Francisco International

M. TECHNIQUE PRACTICE: SHIFT KEY

62 Pat left for Boise, Idaho, in May to see Ms. Ann A. French.   12
63 Diane, Lynn, Dave, Vicki, and Frank left for Bangor, Maine.   12
64 Megan was to go to Cape Cod, Boston, Fall River, and Dover.   12
65 Peter and Gina left for Niagara Falls on Saturday, June 22.   12

| 1 | 2 | 3 | 4 | 5 | 6 | 7 | 8 | 9 | 10 | 11 | 12

N. Change every singular noun to a plural noun.

N. TECHNIQUE PRACTICE: CONCENTRATION

66   The employee read the letter from the annoyed customer
67 and gave the letter to the manager in charge of the section
68 to handle. The manager will respond to the question raised
69 by the customer. Hopefully, the answer will be acceptable.

O. Spacing: double.
Take two 5-minute timed writings. Compute your speed and count errors.

Goal: 48 wam/5'/5e

O. 5-MINUTE TIMED WRITING

70   Can you relax when you are under pressure? If not,   11
71 you may want to discover the benefits of taking a power   23
72 nap. Most people are able to relax when they take a two-   34
73 week vacation. Other people find that the weekends leave   46
74 them feeling refreshed. And some people can even unwind   57
75 every evening after work. But the power nap is designed   68
76 to relax your body and brain completely anytime, anywhere,   80
77 in a few quick minutes.   85
78   The advantage of taking a snooze is not to fall sound   97
79 asleep in the middle of each day but simply to slow your   108
80 pulse and breathing rate and reverse many of the natural   120
81 stress responses in your body. For example, if you enjoy   131
82 the ocean, slowly count to ten and picture yourself on a   143
83 beautiful, deserted beach lying in warm sand and listening   154
84 to waves crashing on the shore. Then count back down to   166
85 zero and awake rejuvenated and ready to tackle anything.   177
86   This type of self-hypnosis may be difficult for some   189
87 folks to learn, but with practice the power nap may become   201
88 a terrific technique for recharging your batteries in only   212
89 a few minutes each day. Spare yourself the burnout that   224
90 comes from constant use of the same mind and body circuits; 236
91 take a nap instead.   240

| 1 | 2 | 3 | 4 | 5 | 6 | 7 | 8 | 9 | 10 | 11 | 12

Centering Review

Margins: 1 inch • Tab: 5 spaces • Spacing: Single • Drills: 2 times • Format Guide: 3–5

Goals:
To improve speed and accuracy; to review horizontal, vertical, and block centering.

A. WARMUP

1   There were 567 people watching Joseph's performance as   12
2 Keith in "Always Heavy."   Zwigg's role as Baxter in "Unsung   24
3 Hero" was seen by 1,284.   There were 390 tickets requested.   36

| 1 | 2 | 3 | 4 | 5 | 6 | 7 | 8 | 9 | 10 | 11 | 12

SKILLBUILDING

B. Use the shift lock to key a word or series of words in all-capital letters. Reach to the shift lock with the A finger.

B. TECHNIQUE PRACTICE: SHIFT LOCK

4 The new company, RINALDI SERVICES, is located in AKRON, OH.
5 MS. MARIDEL CUEVAS, 921 POTTERDAM AVENUE, won the election.
6 Did the WANT AD section of the STAR-LEDGER help her at all?
7 On the way home I saw both the YIELD and the CAUTION signs.

C. Key each sentence on a separate line.

C. TECHNIQUE PRACTICE: RETURN KEY

8 Who will be attending?   How many will sing?   Who is taller?
9 The file was black.   The desk was brown.   The rug was gray.
10 Jim ate.   Jan joked.   Joe danced.   Vin laughed.   Pat cried.
11 Jan ran two miles.   Jill ran three miles.   Sue did not run.

D. Take a 1-minute timed writing on the first paragraph to establish your base speed. Then take four 1-minute timed writings on the remaining paragraphs. As soon as you equal or exceed your base speed on one paragraph, advance to the next one.

D. SUSTAINED PRACTICE: NUMBERS AND SYMBOLS

12   Our sales to Johnson & Clark showed an increase of 30%   12
13 over the same month last year.   Last year we sold them $650   24
14 worth of merchandise in May; sales for this year were $845.   36

15   Shipment of items on Invoice #478 (radios, tape decks,   12
16 & stereos) was to be postponed to June 12.   The delay would   24
17 mean that our cash flow for May would be reduced by $3,605.   36

18   Errors were found on some invoices.   The errors (#336,   12
19 #391, and #402) resulted in a shortfall of revenue.   Errors   24
20 this year have increased by 25%.   We must correct this now!   36

21   The amount of $6,840 (owed by Ashe & Cull) covered all   12
22 these invoices: #242, #284, #311, & #385.   Bentley & Sklar   24
23 made the last payment on the amount that was still owed us.   36

24   Two invoices had 24% discounts (#561 & #582).   We gave   12
25 22% discounts on four invoices (#248, #283, #302, #347).   A   24
26 total savings of $425 was realized from these six invoices.   36

| 1 | 2 | 3 | 4 | 5 | 6 | 7 | 8 | 9 | 10 | 11 | 12

I. PROGRESSIVE PRACTICE: ALPHABET

Turn to the Progressive Practice: Alphabet routine at the back of the book. Take six 30-second timed writings, starting at the point where you left off the last time.

J. Take three 12-second timed writings on each line. The scale gives wam for a 12-second timed writing.

J. 12-SECOND SPRINTS

42 Jack required an extra big size of shade for his new lamps.
43 The juniors who excelled did not find the quiz very taxing.
44 Chocolate-flavored pie is amazingly unique and costs extra.
45 Six of the women quietly gave the prizes back to the judge.

| | | | |5| | | |10| | | |15| | |20| | | |25| | | |30| | | |35| | | |40| | | |45| | | |50| | | |55| | | |60

K. Tab: center.
The opening lines of a letter require the quick operation of the Return key. Key these opening lines 3 times as quickly as possible.

K. TECHNIQUE PRACTICE: LETTER OPENING

2 inches ↓ *(Current Date)*

1 inch ↓

Mr. Armando Sabatini
Vice President of Administration
Bentley Technology, Inc.
189 Henderson Street
Norristown, PA 19402-1520

Dear Mr. Sabatini:

L. Take a 1-minute timed writing on the first paragraph to establish your base speed. Then take four 1-minute timed writings on the remaining paragraphs. As soon as you equal or exceed your base speed on one paragraph, advance to the next one.

L. SUSTAINED PRACTICE: CAPITALIZATION

46   Taking a cruise has become a very popular way to spend   12
47 a vacation these days. The growth in the numbers of people   24
48 who have made arrangements to set sail on a cruise ship for   36
49 a week or more has been phenomenal in these past few years.   48

50   One of the most popular companies for providing such a   12
51 vacation is the Norwegian Cruise Line. There are currently   24
52 seven ships that are sailing on a regular basis out of four   36
53 different ports. All of these ships take an exotic voyage.   48

54   As an example, the Norway departs Miami every Saturday   12
55 afternoon. It alternates its destination every other week.   24
56 It always stops at St. John and St. Thomas, but it plans to   36
57 make a stop at some other islands in the alternating weeks.   48

58   Another ship in this firm always departs from San Juan   12
59 and follows the same route each week. It departs on Sunday   24
60 and stops at Barbados, Martinique, St. Thomas, Antigua, and   36
61 St. Maarten before it returns to its home port of San Juan.   48

| | 1 | 2 | 3 | 4 | 5 | 6 | 7 | 8 | 9 | 10 | 11 | 12

Center each activity vertically on a new page.

Practice 11. Double-space. Center each line horizontally.

TRAINEES FOR CUSTOMER SERVICES ↓3

Armando Lorenzini
Maria Rodriquez
Jane Mangiamelli
Matthew Wyble
Sharon Ostrowski
Paul Madison

Practice 12. Block-center and double-space the paragraph. Double-space after the paragraph, then block-center and key the list with single spacing.

The Smithville Community Club will be holding its annual Rummage Sale on Saturday, April 21, from 10 a.m. to 4 p.m. The sale will be on Route 206. Items for sale include:

Furniture
Toys
Household Appliances
Children's Clothing
Sporting Equipment
Garden Tools

Practice 13. Double-space. Center each line horizontally.

You are cordially invited to attend the
COMPUTER SOFTWARE DISPLAY
Sponsored by ASTD
Thursday, May 15, 19--, 4-7 p.m.
FAIRFIELD MOTOR INN
Fairfield, CT

Practice 14. Double-space. Block-center the list.

PROGRAMMING LANGUAGES
BASIC
Pascal
Fortran
COBOL
Logo
RPG

D. PRETEST: CLOSE REACHES

14   Avoiding gloomy sales figures is a point of concern in 12
15 many firms. The same will be said for the need to trim any 24
16 losses in daily operations. Many firms look at simple ways 36
17 to obtain thrift and savings by trying to motivate workers. 48

| 1 | 2 | 3 | 4 | 5 | 6 | 7 | 8 | 9 | 10 | 11 | 12 |

PRACTICE.
Speed Emphasis. If you made no more than 1 error on the Pretest, key each line twice.
Accuracy Emphasis: If you made 2 or more errors on the Pretest, key each group of lines (as though it were a paragraph) twice.

E. PRACTICE: ADJACENT KEYS

18 tr trim tree trait strap truce stripe pantry tremor truants
19 po post spot pours vapor poker powder oppose weapon pockets
20 sa sash same usage essay sadly safety dosage sample sailing
21 oi oily coin point voice doing choice boiled egoist loiters

F. PRACTICE: CONSECUTIVE FINGERS

22 my myth army foamy yummy myrrh stormy mystic gloomy mystery
23 ft left soft often after shift gifted crafts thrift uplifts
24 ny onyx deny nylon vinyl phony anyway skinny felony canyons
25 lo loss solo loser flood color locate floral ballot loaders

POSTTEST.
Repeat the Pretest (D) and compare performance.

G. POSTTEST: CLOSE REACHES

H. Take a 1-minute timed writing on the first paragraph to establish your base speed. Then take four 1-minute timed writings on the remaining paragraphs. As soon as you equal or exceed your base speed on one paragraph, advance to the next one.

H. SUSTAINED PRACTICE: ROUGH DRAFT

26   The thought of a tax audit is bound to make one just a 12
27 bit nervous. At the present time, the IRS audits about one 24
28 of every 100 returns. The amount of income earned is a big 36
29 factor in determining whether or not an audit will be done. 48
30   In some cases, tax returns might be audited owing to a 12
31 math*e*matical formula on some portion of the *tax* return. In 24
32 other cases, there ~~may~~ *might* be some questions about deductions 36
33 taken. What ever the reason, an audit should not be feared. 48
34   Keep *ing* good records and saving them is a major factor 12
35 if one is called for a *n* audit. Three years can pass from a 24
36 filing of a tax return until the IRS may call for ~~the~~ *an* audit. 36
37 During ~~this~~ *that* time, it is e*s*sential that all records be kept. 48
38   If one is call*ed* for an audit, the meeting that *will* ~~to~~ be 12
39 held ~~could~~ *might* prove to be stressful. A review of the rights of 24
40 one being audited ~~might~~ *should* be conducted. Also, it is crit*i*cal 36
41 that a thorough review of the completed return be conducted. 48

| 1 | 2 | 3 | 4 | 5 | 6 | 7 | 8 | 9 | 10 | 11 | 12 |

Business Letters

Margins: 1 inch • Tab: 5 spaces • Spacing: Single • Drills: 2 times • Format Guide: 5 • Working Papers: 25—28

Goals:
To key 32 wam/3'/5e; to format business letters.

A. WARMUP

1 A 13 percent adjustment resulted in an invoice balance   12
2 of $568.49. In addition, two equal checks for $270 will be   24
3 needed as payment for six medium-sized gates for the court.   36

| 1 | 2 | 3 | 4 | 5 | 6 | 7 | 8 | 9 | 10 | 11 | 12 |

LANGUAGE ARTS

B. Compare this paragraph with the second paragraph of the letter on page 51. Key a list of the errors, correcting them as you key.

B. PROOFREADING

4 Please come to my office at our address, which is show in
5 the letter head above. It will be helpful if you have
6 figures relating to your volumn of copying as well as
7 information about size and color needs. After determining
8 your needs we can then visit our ajoining showroom so that
9 you can select the model that will be best for your.

SKILLBUILDING

C. Key line 10. Then key lines 11–13, reading the words from right to left.

C. TECHNIQUE PRACTICE: CONCENTRATION

10 When keying copy, always strive for complete concentration.
11 concentration. complete for strive always copy, keying When
12 errors. your on down cut may rate keying your in decrease A
13 errors. of number the reduce to rate reading your down Slow

D. Spacing: double.
Take two 3-minute timed writings. Compute your speed and count errors.

Goal: 32 wam/3'/5e

D. 3-MINUTE TIMED WRITING

14   Our legal system defines to a sizable degree what we   12
15 who work at a business can and cannot do. But it is also   23
16 true that the customs, mores, and values of our culture   34
17 play a part. The joining of these factors in the business   46
18 world can be thought of as business ethics.   55
19   Questions of ethical behaviors might be raised in this   67
20 example: A receptionist accepts gifts from a new client,   79
21 one whom she knows would like to have privileged access   90
22 to the manager.   92

| 1 | 2 | 3 | 4 | 5 | 6 | 7 | 8 | 9 | 10 | 11 | 12 |

101-105
LESSONS

Margins: 1 inch • Spacing: Single • Drills: 2 times • Format Guide: 71–75 • Working Papers: 197–228

Goals for Unit 21

Begin each day with approximately 15 minutes of skill-building, selecting activities from pages 235–238. In the remaining class time, complete as many production jobs from pages 239–244 as you can.

1. To improve accuracy and speed on alphabet and number keys.
2. To key 48 wam for 5 minutes with no more than 5 errors.
3. To improve proofreading skills.
4. To gain proficiency in completing forms.
5. To format and key purchase orders and invoices.
6. To format and key memorandums on printed forms.
7. To format and key credit applications.

A. WARMUP

1   Zeke was anxious to plan his vacation. He had several   12
2 options. Ten days to Italy was $2,340; ten days to Jamaica   24
3 was $1,965; or he could go to Quebec for a total of $1,087.   36

| 1 | 2 | 3 | 4 | 5 | 6 | 7 | 8 | 9 | 10 | 11 | 12

LANGUAGE ARTS

B. Study the rules at the right. Then key lines 4–7, making necessary changes.

B. CAPITAL LETTERS

Rule: Capitalize common organizational terms such as *advertising department* and *finance committee* when they are the actual names of units within the writer's own organization and are modified by the word *the*.

Send the new collection plan to the Accounting Department.

Rule: Capitalize adjectives derived from proper nouns. **Exceptions:** congressional, senatorial, constitutional

Almost all of the European countries endorse the plan.

4 Our purchasing department has advertised for sealed bids.
5 One result was the formation of a Security Department.
6 The airport was located 60 miles from the Canadian border.
7 Each witness testified before the Congressional committee.

C. Compare this paragraph with the last paragraph of the 5-minute timed writing on page 238. Key a list of the words that contain errors, correcting the errors as you key.

C. PROOFREADING

8   This type of self-hypnosis may be dificult for some
9 folks to learn, but with practise the power map may become
10 a terific technique for recharging your bateries in only
11 a few minets each day. Spare your self the burnout that
12 comes from constant use of the same mind and body circuits;
13 take a nap insted.

E. BASIC PARTS OF A BUSINESS LETTER

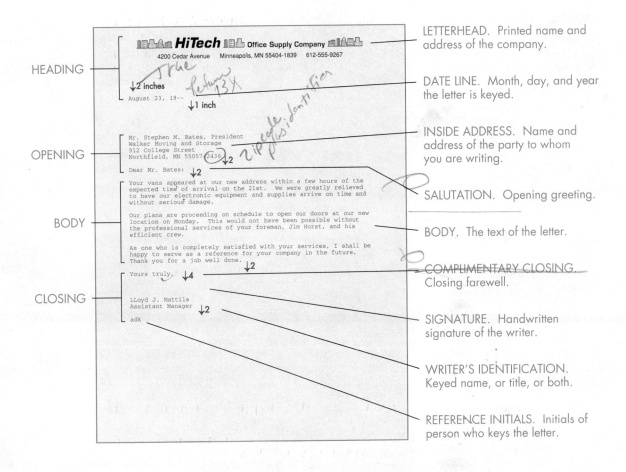

HEADING

OPENING

BODY

CLOSING

LETTERHEAD. Printed name and address of the company.

DATE LINE. Month, day, and year the letter is keyed.

INSIDE ADDRESS. Name and address of the party to whom you are writing.

SALUTATION. Opening greeting.

BODY. The text of the letter.

COMPLIMENTARY CLOSING. Closing farewell.

SIGNATURE. Handwritten signature of the writer.

WRITER'S IDENTIFICATION. Keyed name, or title, or both.

REFERENCE INITIALS. Initials of person who keys the letter.

F. BUSINESS LETTERS IN BLOCK STYLE

Some software enables you to store frequently used text (such as the closing and writer's identification) in a macro. The macro eliminates re-keying repetitive information.

1. Use 1-inch side margins for all letters.
2. Key all lines beginning at the left margin.
3. Key the date 2 inches from the top of the page (line 13).
4. Key the inside address 1 inch (6 lines) below the date.
5. Key the salutation a double space below the inside address. Double-space after the salutation.
6. Single-space the body of the letter, but double-space between paragraphs. Do not indent paragraphs.
7. Key the complimentary closing a double space below the body.
8. Key the writer's identification 4 lines below the complimentary closing.
9. Key your reference initials in lowercase letters with no periods a double space below the writer's identification.

6

OBJECTIVES

KEYBOARDING

To key 50 words a minute
on a 5-minute timed writing
with no more than 5 errors.

LANGUAGE ARTS

To improve language arts
skills, including the correct
use of capitalization, numbers, and spelling.

To develop composing skill.

To proofread and correct
errors.

DOCUMENT PROCESSING

To fill in forms.

To apply formatting skills in
a simulated office environment.

Highlander Photographics/
Mark MacLeod

LETTER 1
BLOCK STYLE

Margins: 1 inch
Date: 2 inches

Working Papers: 25

The date should begin at least ½ inch below the last line of the letterhead.

Standard punctuation: Colon after the salutation and comma after the complimentary closing.

Leave 1 space between the state and the ZIP Code.

Your lines may end differently from those shown here.

HiTech Office Supply Company

4200 Cedar Avenue   Minneapolis, MN 55404-1839   612-555-9267

↓ 2 inches
August 24, 19--
↓ 1 inch

Ms. Kathryn M. Amsbury
Home Care Nursing, P.C.
6807 Crestridge Drive
Hopkins, MN 55343-1921 ↓2

Dear Ms. Amsbury: ↓2

As you requested, I shall be happy to meet with you on August 30 at 10 a.m. to review your copy needs. I am confident that we have just the right copier for you.

Please come to my office at our new address, which is shown in the letterhead above. It will be helpful if you have some figures relating to your volume of copying as well as information about size and color needs. After determining your needs, we can then visit our adjoining showroom so that you can select the model that will be best for you.

HiTech is dedicated to providing up-to-date office services in the greater Twin Cities area. Our new, expanded facilities will help us achieve that goal. ↓2

Sincerely yours, ↓4

David G. Kramer
Customer Relations Associate ↓2

Key your own initials for the reference initials.

hsg

Business letter in block style with (a) all lines beginning at left margin and (b) standard punctuation.

Working Papers: 193

Supply an appropriate salutation, the closing lines, and any necessary notations.

On March 15, 19—, Mr. Raymond Miramontes, Vice President for Sales, Midstate Enterprises, sends a letter to Ancona Marble, Via II Strada, No. 40, Cesano Di Senigallia, Ancona, ITALY. The subject is "May Visit." Mr. Miramontes uses the company name, his name, and his title in the closing lines. Send a copy of the letter to Mr. Paul Sirocco, CEO.

This is to inform you that I will be taking a business trip to Europe during the last two weeks of May in order to purchase items for our decreasing inventory.

I would like to visit Ancona during either May 24–25 or May 28–29. Please let me know which of those dates is better for you, and I will plan on visiting with you at that time.

Please send me your most recent catalog so that I can anticipate any new items that you have available for exporting.

PS: Your last shipment of marble products caused a great deal of enthusiasm with our customers.

Working Papers: 195

Spacing: Double

RESPONSIBILITIES OF AN OFFICE SUPERVISOR
By Jean Auriemma

As more and more workers are employed in office environments, it is beneficial to review some of the responsibilities of an office supervisor.

Upward Responsibilities

It is essential that an office supervisor be aware of the expectations of top management. Keeping superiors informed of what is being done in the department and passing along ideas for improvement are musts. At the same time, the office supervisor should interpret employees' needs to management and vice versa (Cohen, 1991, p. 87).

Horizontal Responsibilities

The supervisor must keep a good communications link with other supervisors. There should be cooperation in coordinating the work of the department with that of other supervisors for the good of the firm (Taubald, 1992, p. 15).

Downward Responsibilities

Motivating workers to become more productive is a major goal for an office supervisor. Selecting, orienting, training, and evaluating employees are additional critical tasks (Berkowitz, 1990, p. 16). Scheduling the work for the department and developing harmony, cooperation, and teamwork among the workers are essential.

LETTER 2
BLOCK STYLE

Working Papers: 27

The slash marks in the inside address and closing lines indicate line breaks and should not be keyed.

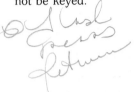

(Current Date) / Ms. Judith A. Ghiardi / G & G Electrical, Inc. / 4614 12th Avenue, NW / Minneapolis, MN 55901-3281 / Dear Ms. Ghiardi:

Thank you for doing the electrical work at our new location as scheduled. A check for 80 percent of the contract amount is being sent to you by our Accounts Payable Department. The balance will be paid within 90 days if all of the work has been completed to our satisfaction.

The light intensity and quality are excellent throughout the building. However, there is one problem: Only half of the electrical outlets in the showroom have been installed.

Please arrange to have this work completed as soon as possible.

Yours truly, / Lloyd J. Mattila / Assistant Manager / *Your initials*

27 LESSON

Business Letters

Margins: 1 inch • Tab: 5 spaces • Spacing: Single • Drills: 2 times • Format Guide: 5 • Working Papers: 29—32

Goals:
To improve speed and accuracy; to format business letters.

A. WARMUP

1   Jan can't believe it! The quick Wildcats won 29 of 34   12
2 games. The loyal puck fans were excited and amazed as they   24
3 had scores of 6 to 1, 8 to 5, and 7 to 0 in the last games.   36

| 1 | 2 | 3 | 4 | 5 | 6 | 7 | 8 | 9 | 10 | 11 | 12 |

SKILLBUILDING

PRETEST.
Take a 1-minute timed writing; compute your speed and count errors.

B. PRETEST: DISCRIMINATION PRACTICE

4   Few of you were as lucky as Bev was when she joined us   12
5 for golf. She just dreaded the looks of the work crew when   24
6 she goofed. But she neatly swung a club and aced the hole.   36
7 The team made her wait while they tried to match her score.   48

| 1 | 2 | 3 | 4 | 5 | 6 | 7 | 8 | 9 | 10 | 11 | 12 |

PRACTICE.
Speed Emphasis: If you made 2 or fewer errors on the Pretest, key each line twice.
Accuracy Emphasis: If you made 3 or more errors, key each group of lines (as though it were a paragraph) twice.

C. PRACTICE: LEFT HAND

8 vbv verb bevy vibes bevel brave above verbal bovine behaves
9 wew west weep threw wedge weave fewer weight sewing dewdrop
10 ded deed seed bride guide dealt cried secede parted precede
11 fgf gulf gift fight fudge fugue flags flight golfer feigned

D. PRACTICE: RIGHT HAND

12 klk kiln lake knoll lanky locks liken kettle kindle knuckle
13 uyu buys your usury unity youth buoys unruly untidy younger
14 oio coin lion oiled foils foist prior oilcan iodine iodized
15 jhj jury huge enjoy three judge habit adjust slight jasmine

POSTTEST.
Repeat the Pretest (B) and compare performance.

E. POSTTEST: DISCRIMINATION PRACTICE

Any person who returns to visit his or her birth site   12
is almost sure to be amazed by changes that have occurred.   24
Some of the oldest buildings will have been replaced by new   36
and modern structures. Other buildings will have been made   48
over in line with some theme for that part of the city. If   60
you look for old stores or other businesses that you   70
recall, it is likely to be vexing, for they aren't there   82
anymore. The fact that no one recognizes you is equally   93
frustrating. You may feel like an outsider, because you   104
truly are one. You get a sense of being a part of history.   116

After you linger for a while in your old neighborhood,   128
you may get back in your car and drive around to look over   140
the town. This likely will be just as shocking. Where   151
there were deluxe houses, apartment towers now exist. Park   163
meadows are shopping malls, and the old swimming hole is in   175
the middle of a tract of look-alike homes. Slowly it will   187
dawn on you that you don't really like that place anymore.   199

Of course, any visitor coming to where you live now is   211
just as likely to have pangs of regret when he or she views   223
all those changes which have happened in that old hometown.   235

| 1 | 2 | 3 | 4 | 5 | 6 | 7 | 8 | 9 | 10 | 11 | 12

EMPIRE MANUFACTURING, INC.

Salesperson	Budgeted Sales	Actual Sales
Mary Ann Stanek	$148,000	$146,750
Lester Boyd	131,000	133,250
James Green	114,000	108,000
Stanley Barusiwicz	103,000	107,500
Linda Lanzi	98,000	99,300

F. Take two 1-minute timed writings. The last two digits of each number provide a cumulative word count to help you determine your wam speed.

F. NUMBER PRACTICE

16 4701 5802 6303 2704 1005 8406 3807 4408 9309 5610 7511 2412
17 6513 4414 1815 2116 3017 5818 3219 1920 6621 3822 7223 5624
18 8025 5626 7427 3828 1729 9130 4431 9832 4233 5734 4035 9636
19 7137 6438 3939 1540 3041 8342 5643 9144 7145 4446 9547 6648

G. Take three 1-minute timed writings. Key these opening lines as many times as you can. Triple-space between each group.

G. TECHNIQUE PRACTICE: OPENING LINES

(Current Date) ↓1 inch

Mr. Peter J. Phillips
Anoka Abstract & Title Co.
3104 137th Avenue, NW
Anoka, MN 55303 ↓2

Dear Mr. Phillips:

FORMATTING

H. ENCLOSURE NOTATION

To indicate that an item is enclosed with a letter, key the word *Enclosure* a single space below the reference initials.

Example: mcs
               Enclosure

DOCUMENT PROCESSING

LETTER 3
BLOCK STYLE

Date: 2 inches

Working Papers: 29

(Current Date) / Mr. Chad P. Treml / Vice President / Treml & Associates, Inc. / 12438 Lake Street East / St. Paul, MN 55117 / Dear Mr. Treml:

Miss Sue Mills has informed me that you called yesterday concerning your office needs. Three lines of modular furniture components are described in the enclosed brochure.

May I suggest an alternative to your visiting our showroom at this time. I would first like to visit the fourth-floor office areas that your firm occupies in order to discuss requirements with both you and your staff.

It is my understanding that you will be out of the office until next Thursday. I shall call on Friday of next week after you return from your trip to arrange for my visit.

Sincerely yours, / David G. Kramer / Customer Relations Associate / *(Your Initials)* / Enclosure

LETTER 4
BLOCK STYLE

Date: 2 inches

Working Papers: 31

(Current Date) / Mrs. Jennifer Ann Yu / Branch Manager / Oriental Imports / 3960 Lyndale Avenue North / Minneapolis, MN 55412-6745 / Dear Mrs. Yu:

We at HiTech wish to thank you for your letter of appreciation for the recent furniture installation. We make every effort to complete projects on schedule and with full customer satisfaction.

We look forward to continuing to provide you with your office supplies. Also, if you have other furniture or equipment needs, please let us know.

Our long business relationship with you is valued very much.

Yours truly, / Lloyd J. Mattila / Assistant Manager / *(Your Initials)*

TABLE 48
RULED TABLE

Center the column headings.

Use periods across the width of a column to indicate no entry.

Repeat the % sign with each number unless the word *Percent* appears in the column heading.

SALARY INCREASES
Effective March 1, 19--

Name	Old Salary	New Salary	Increase
Arndt, Daniel R.	$ 38,480	$ 48,000	24.74%
Lavine, Rhonda	16,210	19,700	21.53%
Weber, Kathy M.	14,890	16,500	10.81%
Rogers, Kristin	31,567	34,500	9.29%
King, Jon J.	29,420	31,000	5.37%
AVERAGE	....	....	14.35%

LETTER 58
MODIFIED-BLOCK STYLE LETTER WITH RULED TABLE

Working Papers: 187

Use the current date.

Horizontally center the table on the page. Leave 1 blank line before and after the table. Center the column headings.

Mr. Fritz Dietsche, Director
Bureau of Employment
Ministry of the Interior
Pascalstrasse 51
5300 Bonn 1
Germany

Dear Mr. Dietsche:

We are happy to provide the information your nationality of the office requested regarding the work force at our production facility in Berlin (Ohmstrasse 4-6, 1000 Berlin 13). On December 31 of this past year, we had 435 full-time employees in the following groups:

Classification	German	American
Managerial	5	10
Clerical	51	47
Production	274	13
Miscellaneous	21	14
TOTAL	351	84

Please telephone Mr. Rudi Georg, plant manager, at (30) 41.060 if you have questions or if you desire additional information. Since its opening, our Berlin plant has become an very integral part of our international production network, and we look forward to expanding our operation within the next few years.

Sincerely,

David C. Perkins, Director
International Operations

Business Letters

Margins: 1 inch • Tab: 5 spaces • Spacing: Single • Drills: 2 times • Format Guide: 7 • Working Papers: 33—36

Goals:
To key 32 wam/3'/5e; to format business letters.

A. WARMUP

```
1      Gravitz & Jacoby, Inc., has equipped 26 trucks with my    12
2 safety devices.  They plan to equip the remainder (15) next    24
3 week at their new warehouse located at 3970 East 48 Street.    36
   |  1  |  2  |  3  |  4  |  5  |  6  |  7  |  8  |  9  |  10  |  11  |  12
```

LANGUAGE ARTS

B. TITLES IN BUSINESS CORRESPONDENCE

Courtesy titles always precede a person's name in the inside address of a letter; for example, *Mr., Mrs., Ms.,* or *Dr.* In the closing lines, however, a man's name is not preceded by a courtesy title; a woman should include a courtesy title in either her keyed name or her signature.

A person's title may be keyed on the line with the name (preceded by a comma) or on a separate line.

INSIDE ADDRESS	CLOSING LINES
Ms. Rose E. Nebel, Owner Nebel Financial Services	Sincerely yours, *Mildred D. King* Miss Mildred D. King Adjunct Instructor
Dr. Prayad Chayapruks Executive Director Toye Memorial Hospital	
Mr. Craig R. Weiger Manager, Dahlke Oil Co.	Cordially, *(Mrs.) Evelyn Marketto* Evelyn Marketto Senior Programmer Analyst

SKILLBUILDING

C. PROGRESSIVE PRACTICE: ALPHABET

Turn to the Progressive Practice: Alphabet routine at the back of the book. Take six 30-second timed writings, starting at the point where you left off the last time.

D. Take three 12-second timed writings on each line. The scale shows your wam speed for a 12-second timed writing.

D. 12-SECOND SPRINTS

```
J 4 Judy joined a jolly group and ate jelly with Jan and Jamie.
Q 5 Queens quietly acquired quite large quails near the quarry.
Z 6 Zeke zigzagged past four dozen dozing zebras near Zanzibar.
   | | | |5| | | |10| | |15| | |20| | |25| | |30| | |35| | |40| | |45| | |50| | |55| | |60
```

E. Clear all tabs. Set new tabs every 10 spaces. Tab to begin the first column. Key lines 7—10 using the tab key to move from column to column.

E. TECHNIQUE PRACTICE: TAB KEY

```
7 trade    badge    under    fancy    elect    leads
8 candy    amend    fined    decay    weeps    bench
9 check    yield    agent    joked    after    older
10 saves    dodge    clone    stage    weave    cargo
```

TABLE 47
BOXED TABLE
FORMATTED SIDEWAYS

Margins: ½ inch

Center the table on one sheet of paper turned sideways.

Use blocked column headings.

Accounting reports often omit the $ sign.

PAYROLL REGISTER
Week Ending May 23

Employee	Total Hours	Rate	Overtime Hours	Overtime Rate	Gross Pay	Net Pay
Adamiec, Steven J.	40.00	10.50	6.00	15.75	514.50	370.44
Bills, Lori A.	40.00	10.50		15.75	420.00	302.40
Clark, Randall S.	40.00	8.00		12.00	320.00	230.40
Cooper, Karen L.	20.00	17.35		26.00	347.00	249.84
Cusick, Rebecca D.	40.00	6.50		9.75	260.00	187.20
Eytcheson, Vanessa L.	40.00	10.50	3.00	15.75	467.25	336.42
George, Kelly M.	35.00	6.50		9.75	227.50	163.80
Hall, Lola D.	35.00	8.00		12.00	280.00	201.60
Jarnecke, Deborah K.	40.00	12.00		18.00	480.00	345.60
Kuhlman, Frank W.	20.00	10.00	2.50	15.00	237.50	171.00
Sarrazine, Marie A.	20.00	10.50		15.75	210.00	151.20
Tellezgarcia, Mario P.	32.00	14.00		21.00	448.00	322.56
Watson, Lana M.	40.00	12.50	1.75	18.75	532.81	383.63
Wilson, Jason C.	25.00	10.00		15.00	250.00	180.00
TOTALS	467.00	.....	13.25	.....	4,994.56	3,596.09

F. Take three 1-minute timed writings. Key these closing lines as many times as you can. Triple-space between groups.

F. TECHNIQUE PRACTICE: CLOSING LINES

Sincerely yours, ↓4

Ms. Adeline G. Tate-Winters
Executive Director ↓2

(Your Initials)
Enclosure

G. Spacing: double.
Take two 3-minute timed writings. Compute your speed and count errors.

Goal: 32 wam/3'/5e

G. 3-MINUTE TIMED WRITING

```
                    1              2              3              4
11      We have all seen instances of misunderstandings in our   12
                  5              6              7
12  personal ties and in our work lives.  To a much greater      23
           8          9           10            11
13  extent, we must be aware that such problems may arise when   35
         12             13           14
14  we deal with those from foreign cultures.                    44
         15             16           17           18
15      The quiet manner of the people and the customs in a      55
              19         20          21           22
16  country like Japan may be quite different from our way of    67
             23           24          25          26
17  life.  Even when English is the language being used, lazy    78
               27            28          29
18  speech patterns and slang may foul up the real message.      89
       30              31             32
19  Body language also plays a part.                             96
```

| | 1 | 2 | 3 | 4 | 5 | 6 | 7 | 8 | 9 | 10 | 11 | 12 |

DOCUMENT PROCESSING

LETTER 5
BLOCK STYLE

Date: 2 inches

Working Papers: 33

When possible, use a person's name in the salutation. The correct form is the courtesy title and the last name (Dear Ms. Varney:). If no name is available, use a title (Dear Credit Manager:) or Ladies and Gentlemen:.

Some frequently used business closings are: *Sincerely, Sincerely yours, Yours truly,* and *Very truly yours.*

This letter from Marcia D. Turini / Accounting Department is to be dated August 28, 19—. Send the letter to Mr. Mark D. O'Brien / Office Manager / Wester Abstract & Title Co. / 2407 Mayo Park Drive, SE / Rochester, MN 55904 / (Supply an appropriate salutation and closing lines.)

Please excuse the delay in replying to your letter of August 16. The delay was due to our company's move to our new location on August 21.

Your comments concerning Invoice 35847, dated August 11, are correct. The total amount, $279.58, should have been adjusted to reflect a 10 percent discount. We will credit your account in the amount of $27.96.

Thank you for calling this matter to our attention. We look forward to serving you even better in our new store.

T. FORMATTING TABLES TURNED SIDEWAYS

Paper turned sideways (called the *landscape* mode) is 8½ inches long and contains 51 lines vertically (8½ × 6). It is 11 inches wide, so each line contains 110 10-pitch spaces (11 × 10, with 55 as the center point) or 132 12-pitch spaces (11 × 12, with 66 as the center point). Use these measurements for centering the table vertically and horizontally.

To format Table 46, insert the paper sideways into the typewriter and reset left and right margins for ½ inch. Determine the vertical placement in the usual manner, except use 51 as the total lines available instead of 66. You can still use automatic centering to center the key line and plan your tab stops.

DOCUMENT PROCESSING

TABLE 46
RULED TABLE
FORMATTED SIDEWAYS

Leave 3 spaces between columns.

Center the table on one sheet of paper turned sideways.

Use blocked column headings.

LEHIGH FINANCIAL SERVICES

Schedule of Accounts Receivable by Age

October 31, 19—

Account Name	Balance	1–30 Days	31–60 Days	61–90 Days	91–120 Days
Chemical Rehab, Inc.	$ 320.00	$ 320.00			
Chesapeake International	68.00		$ 26.00	$ 17.00	$25.00
Crown Electric Utility	126.00			126.00	
First Fidelity	800.00	800.00			
Monarch Capital	400.00	400.00			
Providence Industries	1,175.32		1,050.32		
Salem Paper Company	116.50				116.50
Waste Management	905.25	905.25			
TOTALS	$3,911.07	$2,425.25	$1,076.32	$143.00	$141.50

C. ABBREVIATIONS

C. Study the rules at the right. Then key lines 9–12, making any necessary changes.

Rule: Always abbreviate *Mr.*, *Mrs.*, *Ms.*, and *Dr.* when they are used with personal names. In general, spell out all other titles used with personal names.

Ms. Mabel E. Jackson is our company's new treasurer.

Rule: Always abbreviate *Jr.*, *Sr.*, and *Esq.* when they follow personal names. Do not use a comma before *Jr.* or *Sr.*

Lilly Ontiveros, Esq., will probably appeal the case. John Jones Jr. is here.

9 The surgical procedure was introduced by Doctor Eric Salo.
10 Mister and Mrs. Tom Berutti serve as our faculty sponsors.
11 Jason E. Phillips Jr. is meeting with Prof. Abrams.
12 Francis Howard Senior is a member of another committee.

D. COMPOSING

D. Answer each question with a single word.

13 What is your favorite pet?
14 What kind of music do you prefer listening to?
15 Have you read a novel during the past year?
16 What is one state you think has pretty scenery?
17 What is your favorite day of the week?
18 In what month is your birthday?
19 What is your favorite season of the year?
20 Have you ever had to give a speech?

SKILLBUILDING

E. PROGRESSIVE PRACTICE: NUMBERS

Turn to the Progressive Practice: Numbers routine at the back of the book. Take six 30-second timed writings, starting at the point where you left off the last time.

F. SYMBOL PRACTICE

F. Key lines 21–24 twice each. Then take two 1-minute timed writings on lines 25–28.

```
21 sws sw2s s2s s@s s2s@s s2@s frf fr4f f4f f$f f4f$f f4$f $44
22 lol lo9l 19l 1(1 191(1 19(1 ded de3d d3d d#d d3d#d d3#d #33
23 ju7 ju7j j7j j&j j7j&j j7&j frf fr5f f5f f%f f5f%f f5%f 55%
24 ;p; ;p0; ;0; ;); ;0;); ;0); kik ki8k k8k k*k k8k*k k8k *** 
```

25 Dodd & Marcus collect our state's 6% sales tax ($6 for $100   12
26 in sales) at their #9 and #10 stores and then "send it on!"   24
27 Was he self-taught? His 14 + 3 = 18 answer suggested this;   36
28 he also computed $1.80 for 1 1/2 dozen eggs @ $1 per dozen.   48

| 1 | 2 | 3 | 4 | 5 | 6 | 7 | 8 | 9 | 10 | 11 | 12

In addition to the regular column headings, it may be desirable at times to use an additional heading that relates to two or more columns. This is called a *braced heading,* and it should be centered over the columns to which it applies. For example, in Table 42 below, the heading *Male Members* applies to both the *Number* and the *Percent* columns. The presence of a braced heading requires that the table be formatted in boxed style.

To format Table 42 below:
1. Determine the vertical placement, and key the title. (Table 42 occupies 15 lines.)

2. Determine the horizontal placement, and set the tabs.
3. Key the first horizontal rule; then go down 5 lines (thus leaving space for the braced heading) and center the column headings.
4. Roll the paper back 3 lines so that the braced heading *Male Members* will be a triple space above the column headings.
5. To center *Male Members* (12 characters) over *Number* + 6 + *Percent* (19 characters), indent *Male Members* 3 spaces from the start of *Number:* 19 − 12 = 7; 7 ÷ 3 = 3½ = 3.

DOCUMENT PROCESSING

TABLE 42
BOXED TABLE WITH BRACED HEADINGS

Spacing: Single

PHOENIX ECONOMICS CLUB

Year	Male Members		Female Members	
	Number	Percent	Number	Percent
1970	102	88.7	13	11.3
1975	112	82.4	24	17.6
1980	122	68.5	56	31.5
1985	149	65.1	80	34.9
1990	133	55.4	107	44.6

TABLE 43
BOXED TABLE WITH BRACED HEADING

Spacing: Single

Center a table number (for example, *Table 14*) a double space above the title in uppercase and lowercase letters and in plain (rather than bold) text.

Table 14
COMPOUND INTEREST
Accrued Annually

Year	Rate of 9%		
	Beginning Amount	Interest	Ending Amount
1	$50.00	$ 4.50	$54.50
2	54.50	4.91	59.41
3	59.41	5.35	64.76
4	64.76	5.83	70.59
5	70.59	6.35	76.94
TOTAL	....	$26.94	....

G. PERSONAL-BUSINESS LETTERS

Personal-business letters are written to conduct one's personal business affairs. Personal-business letters are keyed on plain paper rather than letterhead. Therefore, the writer's return address must be included in the letter. Since the writer of the letter also prepares the letter, reference initials are not used.

In the following letter, the return address is keyed directly beneath the writer's name in the closing lines. Another acceptable format is to key the inside address before the date at the top of the page.

DOCUMENT PROCESSING

LETTER 7
PERSONAL-BUSINESS
LETTER IN BLOCK STYLE

Date: 2 inches

Alternate style: Key the return address immediately above the date, starting 2 inches from the top of the page; for example,

1427 Laurel Drive
Albany, NY 12211
September 16, 19—

Reference initials are not used in letters you key for yourself.

↓ 2 inches

September 16, 19-- ↓ 1 inch   line 13

Mr. Clarence M. Hammar, Director
Family Social Services of Albany
4813 Dowling Road
Albany, NY 12205-4903

Dear Mr. Hammar:

The article in Sunday's issue of the <u>Albany Times</u> that told of the work of your agency impressed me very much. I was not aware of many of the community needs that your organization serves.

I am a second-year student at Franklin Business College. Although my college work and a part-time job keep me busy, I would like to spend some time each week as a volunteer with your agency.

Please let me know the steps I should take to get involved. I would particularly enjoy working with older people. However, I shall be happy to serve wherever you feel there is a need.

Sincerely, ↓ 4

(Miss) Tracy L. Ernsberger
1427 Laurel Drive
Albany, NY 12211

Personal-business letter in block style with (a) all lines beginning at left margin and (b) standard punctuation.

In addition to the horizontal lines of a ruled table, a *boxed* table has vertical ruled lines to separate the columns. Format the table as you would a ruled table, including the horizontal ruled lines. After proofreading, remove the paper from the machine and carefully draw in the vertical lines with a black pen and ruler. Center the vertical lines within the 6 blank spaces separating the columns. The lines divide the headings and columns but do not close in the sides of the table.

DOCUMENT PROCESSING

TABLE 40
BOXED TABLE

Center the column headings and center the vertical lines in the blank space between the columns.

Do not key the % sign in a column when the word *Percent* is used in the column heading.

COMPOSITION OF LAKESHORE WORK FORCE

Lower Harbor Branch Plant

February 1, 19--

Category	Male	Percent Male	Female	Percent Female
Factory	274	53	243	47
Office	21	25	62	75
Supervisory	22	55	18	45
Managerial	11	46	13	54

TABLE 41
BOXED TABLE

Center the column headings. You may abbreviate in tables when the entries would otherwise be too long.

Use periods across the width of a column to indicate no entry.

HOUSE SALES
Week of February 22, 19--

Address	Type	Price	Agent
2480 Ridge	3-bdrm. ranch	$ 94,500	Wilson
3600 Rice	lake cabin	38,900	Canale
1308 Birch	4-bdrm. bi-level	142,000	Prusi
18 Oak Lane	5-bdrm. 2-story	189,500	Grauck
7803 Candace	4-bdrm. 2-story	93,600	Hart
809 Waldo	3-bdrm. ranch	87,200	Bjork
TOTAL	. . . .	$645,700	. . . .

PERSONAL-BUSINESS LETTER IN BLOCK STYLE

Date: 2 inches

(handwritten annotations: Line 11 948 Boisseau Avenue RETURN ADDRESS, 12 Shreveport, LA 71103, 13 Nov. 2, 1994 DATE Line, 6 lines, Mr. Richard A. Alderton, Owner, The Garden Room Restaurant, 726 Bayou Drive, INSIDE ADDRESS, Shreveport, LA 71105, 2 lines, Dear Mr. Alderton: SALUTATION, 2 lines, BODY, 1 line)

This personal-business letter is from Wallace G. Helfinstein, who lives at 948 Boisseau Avenue in Shreveport, LA 71103. Use today's date, and supply an appropriate salutation and closing lines. The letter is to be sent to Mr. Richard A. Alderton, Owner / The Garden Room Restaurant / 726 Bayou Drive / Shreveport, LA 71105.

Thanks to you and hundreds of other Shreveport citizens, the fall Special Olympics events were highly successful. Our planning committee is very appreciative of the ways in which you helped.

We particularly wish to thank you for the use of your conference room for our committee's meetings. And the committee members thoroughly enjoyed the refreshments that you provided. Thank you for your kindness.

The smiles on the faces of our special friends who participated in the games are the rewards we seek. As chairperson for the planning committee, however, I want to extend special thanks to you for your generous contributions.

LETTER 9

PERSONAL-BUSINESS LETTER IN BLOCK STYLE

Date: 2 inches

(handwritten annotations: Sincerely, COMPLIMENTARY CLOSING, 4 lines, Mr. Wallace G. Helfinstein SIGNATURE, Mixed or standard punctuation, no ref. initials, no enclosure)

Revise Letter 8 as follows. Send the letter to Ms. Cynthia Spelgatti / 3526 Crofton Street / Shreveport, LA 71101. Replace the second paragraph with the following: *We particularly wish to thank you for the manner in which you handled the details for the awards ceremony. You made it very clear that all participants were indeed winners. Thank you for your kindness.*

---

30 LESSON

Letter Review

Margins: 1 inch • Tab: 5 spaces • Spacing: Single • Drills: 2 times • Format Guide: 7–9 • Working Papers: 37–40

Goals:
To key 32 wam/3'/5e; to format business and personal-business letters.

A. WARMUP

```
1     Hazel and/or Blake joined 5 others in 1980 to create a    12
2  quality firm.  After adding 6 or 7 people in 1993, they had  24
3  exactly 24 sales representatives; and it continued to grow.  36
   |  1  |  2  |  3  |  4  |  5  |  6  |  7  |  8  |  9  |  10  |  11  |  12
```

SKILLBUILDING

B. Use the shift lock to key a word or series of words in all-capital letters.

B. TECHNIQUE PRACTICE: SHIFT LOCK

```
4 RHONDA KORDICH was promoted on APRIL 1 to SENIOR SECRETARY.
5 The SOLD sign replaced the FOR SALE sign at 19 ELDER DRIVE.
6 The trip from LOUISVILLE to NASHVILLE was on INTERSTATE 65.
7 ADAMS-PAULIN, INC., is owned by Allen Adams and Hal Paulin.
8 The SPRING AUTO SHOW was held at LAKEVIEW ARENA on APRIL 8.
```

Q. CENTERED COLUMN HEADINGS

To center a short column heading over a column:

1. Determine the key line and set the tabs for the columns.
2. Subtract the number of spaces in the column heading from the number of spaces in the longest item in the column.
3. Divide the difference by 2 (drop any fraction).
4. Indent the column heading that number of spaces from the start of the column.

When a column heading is the longest item in a column, use the column heading as part of the key line. To center a column under a long column heading:

1. Determine the key line and set the tabs for the columns.
2. Key the column headings.
3. Subtract the number of spaces in the longest item in the column from the number of spaces in the column heading.
4. Divide the difference by 2 (drop any fraction).
5. Indent the column that number of spaces from the start of the column.
6. Clear the original tab for the column and set a new tab.

DOCUMENT PROCESSING

TABLE 38
TABLE WITH CENTERED COLUMN HEADINGS

Center the table vertically and horizontally. Center the column headings over the columns.

SALES QUOTAS

Second Quarter, 19--

Sales Manager	Region	Quota
Chan, Chew Wah	Eastern	$1,156,000
Getzen, Patti K.	Southern	1,114,000
Ludwig, Adele G.	North-Central	993,000
Oja, Gregory J.	Southwest	1,156,000
Upton, Gwen M.	Rocky Mountain	987,000
Woodbridge, Phillip J.	Western	1,134,000

TABLE 39
TABLE WITH CENTERED COLUMN HEADINGS

REGIONAL SALES COMPARISION

First Four Months

Month	Eastern	SouthEastern	Mid-Continent
January	$21,770	$14,883	$ 32,664
Febuary	122,819	19,274	14,560
March	15,114	16,932	32,497
April	10,001	11,933	450,476
Total	$97,025 59,641	$93,391 63,022	$193,133 120,197

C. DIAGNOSTIC PRACTICE: ALPHABET

Turn to the Diagnostic Practice: Alphabet routine at the back of this book. Take the Pretest and record your performance. Then, practice the drill lines for those reaches on which you made errors. Finally, repeat the Pretest and compare your performance.

D. 3-MINUTE TIMED WRITING

D. Spacing: double. Take two 3-minute timed writings. Compute your speed and count errors.

Goal: 32 wam/3'/5e

```
 9      There are good reasons why a young office worker will    12
10  want to demonstrate that he or she uses time well.  Some     23
11  cultures have quite different views; but in this country     35
12  one is expected to report to work on time, to be on time     46
13  for meetings, and to meet all deadlines.                     54
14      In order to do these things, an organized plan for       65
15  daily action should be developed.  Just as a pilot prepares  77
16  a flight plan, the efficient worker will start each day by   89
17  listing tasks in priority order.                             96
```
   | 1 | 2 | 3 | 4 | 5 | 6 | 7 | 8 | 9 | 10 | 11 | 12

DOCUMENT PROCESSING

LETTER 10
BLOCK STYLE

Date: 2 inches

Working Papers: 37

Key this business letter for Vincent J. Robare / President. Use the current date, and send the letter to Ms. Catherine A. Cox, Manager / City-Wide Insurance Agency / 2810 Canyon View Drive East / Flagstaff, AZ 86001. Supply an appropriate salutation and complimentary closing.

Thank you for seeing me at your office last Thursday. You provided the guidance I needed in order to review our firm's present insurance coverages. I appreciate your taking time to explain to me the many new options that are available.

It seems that there are several weaknesses that must be corrected. Therefore, I would like to request that your agent, Dale Starr, meet with our senior accountant and me at my office within the next ten days. We would like to review our property, liability, and employee group health insurance policies.

There is also the likelihood that group life insurance coverage for our employees will be added within the next six months. We are in the midst of contract negotiations, and this new coverage will be a topic for discussion in the near future. Perhaps Dale can present some basic plans to us that incorporate shared premium payments by both the employer and employees.

I appreciate your seeing me on such short notice last week. As a result of our discussion, I am confident that appropriate adjustments in our coverages can be made within a short period of time. The manner in which your agency continues to satisfy our insurance needs is sincerely appreciated.

TABLE 36
RULED TABLE

Center and key the title in all-capital letters and bold.

Reminders:
1. All horizontal rules extend to the edges of the table.
2. Single-space before a ruled line, and double-space after a ruled line.

Time and Place	Topic and Speaker
8 a.m.–9 a.m. Velvet Room	MicroTech Bytes Back Jorge Morales
9 a.m.–10 a.m. Salon I	A Model for Pricing Software Hans M. Allwang
10 a.m.–11 a.m. Salon II	Software Support Options Louise Summer-Ames
11 a.m.–12 noon Grand Ballroom	SDIG Business Meeting Terry Ledesma, President

TABLE 37
OPEN TABLE

The $ sign must align at the top and bottom of a column.

LEHIGH FINANCIAL SERVICES
Projected Operating Expenses

Expense	1995	1996	1997
Officers' Salaries	$ 6,300	$ 26,400	$ 36,000
Clerical Salaries	26,100	27,200	34,000
Advertising	30,300	49,900	70,400
Depreciation	21,900	28,700	26,600
Office Supplies	12,200	11,500	15,300
Payroll Taxes	10,700	14,600	13,900
Rent	10,400	12,000	12,600
Insurance	6,200	7,600	10,000
Telephone	9,200	8,000	8,900
Printing	4,300	3,600	5,500
Utilities	3,600	3,200	3,300
Hospitalization	2,000	2,800	3,100
Postage	2,000	2,200	3,100
Local Taxes	1,800	2,100	2,800
Dues and Licenses	2,000	1,200	2,100
TOTAL	$ 149,000	$ 201,000	$ 247,600

Use today's date and key this letter from Lloyd J. Mattila / Assistant Manager to Ms. Erica L. Yoder, Manager / New Image Salon / 2342 Como Avenue / St. Paul, MN 55108 / (Supply an appropriate salutation and closing lines.)

Rick Mariani has told me about the progress that has been made in converting your salon's office operation to a computer system. He is confident that the Model 738 will adequately serve your needs for the foreseeable future. Incidentally, Rick was very pleased about the compliments that you have given him about the conversion process.

While the 738 has an excellent performance record, you may want to consider the purchase of a long-term maintenance contract to take effect when the warranty period expires. Our records show that approximately 80 percent of our computer sales include this coverage.

Thank you for choosing HiTech for your computer needs. We look forward to working closely with you in satisfying your software needs and in providing orientation workshops for your office employees. Our involvement extends far beyond the date of purchase.

LETTER 12
PERSONAL-BUSINESS
LETTER IN BLOCK STYLE

Date: 2 inches

This personal-business letter is from Charlene H. Washington, who lives at 2406 25th Avenue, SE, Apt. 318, in Hillsboro, OR 97123-5632. Use today's date, and supply an appropriate salutation and closing lines. The letter is to be sent to Mrs. Doris R. Hall, Manager / CDs and More / 1817 Dierdorff Road, NW / Hillsboro, OR 97123-2781.

I was in your Dierdorff Road store last evening while shopping for a birthday gift for my son. After making my purchase, I returned home, thinking that I had placed my small purse in the package with the CD.

At 10 p.m. I received a phone call from your employee, Rae Ann Marshall, informing me that my purse had been found and was safely stored in your store's safe. She was calling from her home after returning from work. I was not even aware that my purse was missing.

Ms. Marshall went out of her way to relieve me of any anxieties I might have had. You are lucky to have her working for you. I shall look forward to having her serve me again the next time I am in your store.

N. Clear all tabs. Then set four new tabs every 10 spaces. Key lines 65–68, using the tab key to go across from column to column.

N. TECHNIQUE PRACTICE: TAB KEY

65 561	343	892	621	816
66 403	189	267	394	408
67 532	679	790	855	921
68 148	289	365	402	579

O. Take three 12-second timed writings on each line. The scale gives wam for a 12-second timed writing.

O. 12-SECOND SPRINTS

69 Tom, Sue, Ann, and Ralph went to see the Statue of Liberty.
70 Radio City Music Hall is located on Avenue of the Americas.
71 Route 80 East goes right into the George Washington Bridge.
72 The New York Stock Exchange is situated in lower Manhattan.

`1 | | | |5| | | |10| | |15| | |20| | |25| | |30| | |35| | |40| | |45| | |50| | |55| | |60`

P. Spacing: double.
Take two 5-minute timed writings. Compute your speed and count errors.

Goal: 47 wam/5′/5e

P. 5-MINUTE TIMED WRITING

73   Around the world, summer is considered the best time   12
74 for taking a vacation. Hot days, warm nights, and no kids   23
75 in school encourage many people to pack up and go. But   35
76 where you go and for how long varies quite a bit depending   46
77 on where you live.   50

78   In our country, one or two weeks for vacation time is   62
79 quite common. Some people and managers can expect to have   74
80 much more time off. As the trend for Americans to take   85
81 shorter trips several times a year increases, destinations   97
82 are more likely to be close to home. Organized trips are   108
83 popular too, and jaunts to theme parks and all-inclusive   120
84 resorts rank high for families and singles.   129

85   If two weeks off sounds too short, then perhaps you   140
86 should work in Italy, where a month off is typical. The   151
87 Italians quench their thirst for relaxation by visiting   163
88 one of the hundreds of beaches that dot their coastline.   174
89 The Japanese also enjoy vacations by the ocean, with the   186
90 most popular spots being company-owned centers. However,   197
91 if you like long vacations, don't get a job in Japan; the   209
92 average Japanese takes off only eight days a year. It may   221
93 seem short, but even a few days in the sun can make anyone   232
94 feel refreshed.   235

`| 1 | 2 | 3 | 4 | 5 | 6 | 7 | 8 | 9 | 10 | 11 | 12`

31 LESSON

One-Page Reports

Margins: 1 inch • Tab: 5 spaces • Spacing: Single • Drills: 2 times • Format Guide: 9

Goals:
To improve speed and accuracy; to format bold text; to format a one-page report.

A. WARMUP

```
1      Jake volunteered quickly for the tax group.  He organ-   12
2 ized 19 to 20 volunteers as well--do you believe this group   24
3 will soon "rescind" Amendments #36 and #48 on pages 7 & 25?   36
   |  1  |  2  |  3  |  4  |  5  |  6  |  7  |  8  |  9  |  10  |  11  |  12
```

LANGUAGE ARTS

B. Study the rules at the right. Then key lines 4–7, making any necessary changes.

B. CAPITAL LETTERS

Rule: Capitalize the first word of all sentences and the first word of an expression used as a sentence.

How come? We thought there would be a lengthy delay.

Rule: Capitalize every proper noun. A proper noun is the official name of a particular person, place, or thing.

Brady Wahlstrom plans to drive his Chevrolet to Miami.

```
4 really?  we had planned to go to the concert on the 14th.
5 both parties modified their positions on the cable issue.
6 wendy and nicholas bought the hotpoint range in flagstaff.
7 jung lee chaired one of the environmental committees.
```

SKILLBUILDING

PRETEST.
Take a 1-minute timed writing; compute your speed and count errors.

PRACTICE.
Speed Emphasis: If you made 2 or fewer errors on the Pretest, key each line twice.
Accuracy Emphasis: If you made 3 or more errors, key each group of lines (as though it were a paragraph) twice.

C. PRETEST: HORIZONTAL REACHES

```
8      She thinks the chief hired a loyal agent for the extra   12
9 ship.  He was alarmed by hints of terrorism.  The agent was   24
10 armed and received valued input daily from all his sources.   36
   |  1  |  2  |  3  |  4  |  5  |  6  |  7  |  8  |  9  |  10  |  11  |  12
```

D. PRACTICE: IN REACHES

```
11 oy foyer loyal buoys enjoy decoy coyly royal cloy ploy toys
12 ar argue armed cared alarm cedar sugar radar area earn hear
13 pu pumps punch purse spurt input spurn purge pull spur push
14 lu lucid lunch lured bluff value blunt fluid luck lush blue
```

E. PRACTICE: OUT REACHES

```
15 ge geese genes germs agent edges dodge hinge gear ages page
16 da daily dazed dance adapt sedan adage panda dash date soda
17 hi hints hiked hired chief think ethic aphid high ship chip
18 ra radar raise raved brain moral cobra extra race brag okra
```

I. TECHNIQUE PRACTICE: SPACE BAR

I. This paragraph is made up of very short words, requiring frequent use of the space bar. Take two 1-minute timed writings. Do not pause before or after striking the space bar.

36   I will stop by to see you at your office at about one.   12
37 We can check the order that was sent in by Kay, and then we   24
38 can plan on lunch at two. I will take you to that new deli   36
39 that just opened. When lunch is over, we can plan to go to   48
40 see that new pet shop that opened at the mall on Wednesday.   60

    | 1 | 2 | 3 | 4 | 5 | 6 | 7 | 8 | 9 | 10 | 11 | 12

J. NUMBER PRACTICE

J. Take two 1-minute timed writings. The last two digits of each number provide a cumulative word count to help you determine your wam speed.

41 2301 7402 6503 9804 1705 3106 4407 8208 9509 1610 2911 4412
42 9813 7214 8515 6116 2317 7518 8119 4220 3921 8422 1923 3824
43 6625 9526 1127 9328 4029 6530 9031 4232 6333 8834 7535 1236
44 3737 5038 2239 4940 9141 9342 4443 1244 9845 2646 8347 2048

K. TECHNIQUE PRACTICE: CONCENTRATION

K. Each of these sentences contains two words that are not used properly. Correct those words as you key each sentence twice.

45 The principle of the high school was quiet upset on Friday.
46 Please except the congratulations from the too individuals.
47 There house was on the rode that went near the new schools.
48 If the home team could beet them, it would be a great feet.

L. PROGRESSIVE PRACTICE: NUMBERS

Turn to the Progressive Practice: Numbers routine at the back of the book Take six 30-second timed writings, starting at the point where you left off the last time.

M. SUSTAINED PRACTICE: CAPITALIZATION

M. Take a 1-minute timed writing on the first paragraph to establish your base speed. Then take four 1-minute timed writings on the remaining paragraphs. As soon as you equal or exceed your base speed on one paragraph, advance to the next one.

49   An objective held by some people is to visit the fifty   12
50 states in our land. While they visit each one, the idea of   24
51 seeing each capital is appealing. Can you identify some of   36
52 the capital cities of our fifty states that are well known?   48

53   For example, the capital of Massachusetts has played a   12
54 major role in our American history. Boston is very closely   24
55 associated with the Revolutionary War and is recognized for   36
56 the role it played in critical events in our early history.   48

57   Many of the states in the South have well-known cities   12
58 that serve as capitals. In Alabama, the city of Montgomery   24
59 has played significant roles. The Confederate States began   36
60 there in 1861, and Rosa Parks attracted national headlines.   48

61   Some state capitals are not as well known. Would many   12
62 people be able to identify the capitals of Delaware, Maine,   24
63 South Dakota, Alaska, and Montana? The right answers would   36
64 be as follows: Dover, Augusta, Pierre, Juneau, and Helena.   48

    | 1 | 2 | 3 | 4 | 5 | 6 | 7 | 8 | 9 | 10 | 11 | 12

Repeat the Pretest (C) and compare performance.

G. This paragraph is made up of very short words, requiring the frequent use of the space bar. Key the paragraph twice. Do not pause before or after striking the space bar.

F. POSTTEST: HORIZONTAL REACHES

G. TECHNIQUE PRACTICE: SPACE BAR

19   We will all go to the race if I win the one I am going   12
20 to run today. Do you think I will be able to finish in the   24
21 front of the pack, or do you think there are lots of really   36
22 fast runners there who surely can finish ahead of me? It's   48
23 going to be a lot of fun, and I look forward to this event.   60

  | 1 | 2 | 3 | 4 | 5 | 6 | 7 | 8 | 9 | 10 | 11 | 12

H. PACED PRACTICE

Turn to the Paced Practice routine at the back of the book. Take four 2-minute timed writings, starting at the speed at which you left off the last time.

FORMATTING

Titles and side headings appear in bold.

I. BASIC PARTS OF A REPORT

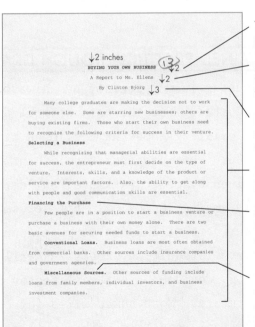

TITLE. Subject of the report; centered in bold print; keyed in all-capital letters.

SUBTITLE. Secondary or explanatory title; centered a double space (1 blank line) below the title, with first and principal words capitalized.

BYLINE. Name of the writer; centered a double space below the subject or, if no subtitle is used, a double space below the title.

BODY. Text of the report; separated from the heading(s) by a triple space (2 blank lines).

SIDE HEADING. Major subdivision of the report; keyed at the left margin in bold print with first and principal words capitalized; preceded and followed by a double space.

PARAGRAPH HEADING. Minor subdivision of the report; indented 5 spaces in bold, with first and principal words capitalized; followed by a period and 2 spaces.

J. ONE-PAGE REPORTS

Side Margins: 1 inch.
Top Margin: 2 inches; center the title.
Bottom Margin: 1 inch.
Tab Setting: 5 spaces (used for indenting paragraphs).

Spacing: One blank line between the title, subtitle, and byline. Two blank lines between the title block and the body. Change to double spacing before keying the body of the report.

PRETEST.
Take a 1-minute timed writing; compute your speed and count errors.

PRACTICE.
Speed Emphasis: If you made no more than 1 error on the Pretest, key each line twice.
Accuracy Emphasis: If you made 2 or more errors on the Pretest, key each group of lines (as though it were a paragraph) twice.

POSTTEST.
Repeat the Pretest (D) and compare performance.

H. Take a 1-minute timed writing on the first paragraph to establish your base speed. Then take four 1-minute timed writings on the remaining paragraphs. As soon as you equal or exceed your base speed on one paragraph, advance to the next one.

D. PRETEST: COMMON LETTER COMBINATIONS

```
 8      We were careful to pick forty capable persons to serve   12
 9 on the committee.  Some complex questions concerning upkeep   24
10 of the condos were to be part of the discussions.  A former   36
11 member made a motion to table the motion on building plans.   48
   |  1  |  2  |  3  |  4  |  5  |  6  |  7  |  8  |  9  |  10  |  11  |  12
```

E. PRACTICE: WORD BEGINNINGS

```
12 for forty forth format former forget forest forearm forbear
13 con condo conic contra confer convey concur concern condemn
14 per peril perky period permit person peruse perform persist
15 com combo comic combat commit common combed compose complex
```

F. PRACTICE: WORD ENDINGS

```
16 ing doing mixing living filing taping sending biking hiding
17 ble cable nimble fumble dabble bobble capable marble mumble
18 ion onion nation lotion motion option mention fusion legion
19 ful awful useful joyful earful lawful helpful sinful armful
```

G. POSTTEST: COMMON LETTER COMBINATIONS

H. SUSTAINED PRACTICE: ROUGH DRAFT

```
20      Housing in our society has always been a topic that is   12
21 hotly debated.  For the past several decades, the prices of   24
22 new and existing homes have climbed higher than the rate of   36
23 inflation.  What are some significant housing developments?   48
24      Driven by cost restraints, builders will be encouraged   12
25 to build smaller homes.  To off set smaller and fewer rooms, 24
26 house builders will offer as much open interior space as is   36
27 possible.  In addition, the lot sizes will also be smaller.   48
28 Technology will be a critical factor in all new houses       12
29 in the future.  Most homes will be wired for communications  24
30 and central electronic controls.  This will help home owners 36
31 to keep a standard style of living that's comfortable and secure. 48
32      Paying for housing has always been a concern.  One new  12
33 method used for financing new homes has been an adjustable-  24
34 rate mortgage.  However, there seems to be more interest in  36
35 getting a conventional mortgage in today's financial arena.  48
   |  1  |  2  |  3  |  4  |  5  |  6  |  7  |  8  |  9  |  10  |  11  |  12
```

REPORT 1

Top margin: 2 inches
Tab: 5 spaces
Spacing: Double

Key the title block and triple-space before changing to double spacing.

↓ 2 inches **THE FUTURE OF INFORMATION STORAGE** ↓2 *line 3*
Business Technology Conference ↓2
By Marianne Townsend ↓3 (10)

Much of what we save as files on computers today is stored on hard disks or diskettes. The future of information storage, however, clearly rests in the technology of compact disc storage or CD-ROM as it is often labeled. ↓2

Basic Features ↓2

A single compact disc can store about 700 megabytes of information. With this capability, a computer user can store an entire encyclopedia or dictionary, a vast assortment of graphic images and clip art pieces, as well as a considerable number of individual software packages. A CD-ROM drive will cost between $400 and $1,200. ↓2

Using CD-ROM ↓2

Using a CD-ROM disc will free up space on your hard disk, and it will give you immediate access to many software packages. Thus, you can have at your disposal an entire encyclopedia or call up an image from thousands of clip art pieces stored on the disc. However, the CD-ROM drive is presently more expensive and slower than other drives, and it is impossible to erase the CD-ROM. Also, because of the vast amount of storage on just one disc, the purchase price of a prerecorded disc may be high.

Rough-Draft Reports

LESSON 32

Margins: 1 inch • Tab: 5 spaces • Spacing: Single • Drills: 2 times • Format Guide: 9

Goals:
To key 33 wam/3'/5e; to use proofreaders' marks; to format a report from rough-draft copy.

A. WARMUP

1   The quiz will cover just pages 17-28, 39-40, and 65-70   12
2 from Quinn's article called, "Back Up Your Disk." Will any   24
3 extra pages be required for the summary that we must write?   36

| 1 | 2 | 3 | 4 | 5 | 6 | 7 | 8 | 9 | 10 | 11 | 12

Margins: 1 inch • Spacing: Single • Drills: 2 times • Format Guide: 67–71 • Working Papers: 187–188

Goals for Unit 20

Begin each day with approximately 15 minutes of skill-building, selecting activities from pages 220–223. In the remaining class time, complete as many production jobs from pages 224–231 as you can.

1. To improve accuracy and speed on alphabet and number keys.
2. To key 47 wam for 5 minutes with no more than 5 errors.
3. To improve proficiency in composing at the keyboard.
4. To format tables with centered column heads.
5. To format and key boxed tables, boxed tables with braced headings, and tables turned sideways.

A. WARMUP

```
1       Get them a requisition to purchase 18 items @ $105 and    12
2 23 items @ $96.  Just add the 7% sales tax for a total cost    24
3 of $4,384.86.  Be sure to check and verify those two sizes.    36
  |  1  |  2  |  3  |  4  |  5  |  6  |  7  |  8  |  9  |  10  |  11  |  12
```

LANGUAGE ARTS

B. Study the rules at the right. Then key lines 4–7, making necessary changes.

B. APOSTROPHES

Rule: If the addition of an extra syllable to a singular noun would make a word that is difficult to pronounce, add only the apostrophe to make it possessive.

Mrs. Sanders' advice to the strikers was well received.

Rule: To make a plural noun not ending in *s* possessive, place the apostrophe before the *s*.

Place all children's shoes in a display area by the aisle.

```
4 The article featured four of New Orleans's restaurants.
5 Jim Phillips' negotiating skills helped us get a contract.
6 Kathleen and Kris helped in designing the womens' lounge.
7 An announcement of the four alumnis' gifts was published.
```

C. COMPOSING

Compose the body of a letter to respond to Letter 54, Unit 18, p. 206, using the following suggestions for each paragraph:

Paragraph 1. Thank Mr. Hallam for his interest in becoming a distributor for English China, Ltd.

Paragraph 2. Explain that although much of our stock is stored in a warehouse and available only by direct order, our full product line must be displayed by our distributors. Also explain that in order for him to become a distributor, Mr. Hallam must provide us with a five-year business plan and a five-year marketing strategy.

Paragraph 3. Tell Mr. Hallam that once I receive these materials and have looked them over, I will call to arrange a meeting with him to discuss the remaining details.

LANGUAGE ARTS

B. These words are among the 500 most frequently misspelled words in business correspondence.

B. SPELLING

4 per provided international receipt commission present other
5 questions maintenance industrial service following position
6 management absence proposal corporate mortgage support well
7 approval recommendations facilities balance experience upon
8 premium currently because procedure addition paid directors

SKILLBUILDING

C. Take a 1-minute timed writing on the first paragraph to establish your base speed. Then take four 1-minute timed writings on the remaining paragraphs. As soon as you equal or exceed your base speed on one paragraph, advance to the next one.

C. SUSTAINED PRACTICE: SYLLABIC INTENSITY

9   When you have to give a talk and would like to impress   12
10 your audience, it is essential that you use graphics. Here   24
11 are a few suggestions to help you if you must use graphics.   36

12   Try to distribute your graphics evenly throughout your   12
13 talk. Highlight the important points as you present all of   24
14 your talk; be certain to spend enough time on these points.   36

15   Select only one graphic design for your graphics. The   12
16 single graphic design means that you select the layout only   24
17 once, thus conveying a sense of organization to your group.   36

| 1 | 2 | 3 | 4 | 5 | 6 | 7 | 8 | 9 | 10 | 11 | 12

D. Take two 1-minute timed writings. The last two digits of each number provide a cumulative word count to help you determine your wam speed.

D. NUMBER PRACTICE

18 6301 8402 9503 1104 7205 3806 4907 5508 6609 3210 9511 6712
19 9413 8314 6615 9316 4017 9118 1219 3720 8921 8422 3623 4824
20 5625 8226 4127 9028 3329 9430 4531 9232 9333 9834 7035 2036
21 8737 9838 5539 2440 8141 7642 6343 8244 1045 8246 7347 8848

E. Spacing: double.
Take two 3-minute timed writings. Compute your speed and count errors.

Goal: 33 wam/3'/5e

E. 3-MINUTE TIMED WRITING

22   Although you attend college so that you can find a job   12
23 upon graduation, there is a better than average chance that   24
24 you will not stay with that job for your entire career. If   36
25 you find yourself searching for a job, what is one quick   47
26 suggestion that you can make to help you expand your search   59
27 for that job?   62
28   An absolute must is that you organize your plan of   73
29 attack and focus on a final objective. Target a certain   84
30 company and find out before your interview as much as you   96
31 can about it.   99

| 1 | 2 | 3 | 4 | 5 | 6 | 7 | 8 | 9 | 10 | 11 | 12

REPORT 48
POWER OF ATTORNEY

Tabs: 1 inch; center
Spacing: Double

Be It Known that I, Dale D. Lindsey, have made ^and ,constituted, appointed and by these presents do make, appoint, (and constitute) Teresa R. Lindsey, my true and lawful attorney-in-fact, for me and in my name, place, and stead ^and on my behalf, to do and perform for me anything of any character which I might do or perform for myself if personally present and acting.

Should my ^said attorney ^-in-fact predecease me or otherwise be unable to perform all the matters and things here in set out to be done and perform ^ed, then, and in that event, and thereafter I do hereby constitute and appoint no one my true and lawful attorney-in-fact with full power and authority to do and perform in my name, ^and stead all matters and things herein authorized to be done and preformed by the said attorney-in-fact with all the power and authority here in given.

IN WITNESS WHEREOF, I have executed the fore going Power of Attorney, this twenty-sixth day of June, 19--.

_____

Signed and affirmed in the presence of

_____ and _____

REPORT 49
POWER OF ATTORNEY

Some software programs have a Thesaurus feature that enables you to look up selected words on screen and to choose a replacement word from those displayed.

Revise Report 48 making the following changes:

1. In paragraph 1, line 1, replace *Dale D. Lindsey* with *Joseph M. Mini.*
2. In paragraph 1, line 2, replace *appoint* with *designate.*
3. In paragraph 1, line 3, replace *Teresa R. Lindsey* with *Dawna B. Mini.*
4. In paragraph 1, line 4, replace *perform* with *execute.*
5. In paragraph 1, line 5, replace *perform* with *accomplish.*
6. In paragraph 2, line 7, replace *power* with *capacity.*
7. In paragraph 3, line 2, replace the date with *nineteenth day of February, 19--.*

F. PROOFREADERS' MARKS

The proofreaders' marks shown below are used to indicate changes or corrections to be made in a rough-draft document that is being revised for final copy. Study the chart to learn what each of the marks means.

Proofreaders' Mark	Draft	Final Copy
⌒ Omit space	data base	database
∽ Transpose	they all see	they see all
∧ Insert	she may not go	she may not go
☰ Capitalize	Maple street	Maple Street
✗ Delete	a final draft	a draft copy
↗ Move as shown	no (copy) machine	no machine
⁋ Paragraph	Most of the	Most of the

horizontal
∧ space
℔# delete horizontal space
•••••• stet leave as originally written before proofreader's marks

REPORT 2
ONE-PAGE REPORT

Top margin: 2 inches
Spacing: Double

REPORT 3

Revise Report 2 making these changes:
1. Add a byline with your name in the heading.
2. Delete the first sentence of the report.
3. Change the paragraph headings to read as follows: *Time as a Cultural Difference. Space as a Cultural Difference.*

INTERNATIONAL COMMUNICATIONS BOLD (14)
Cultural Differences L3 (10)

The marvel of technology has changed communications in that we are seeing an emphasis increased on the inter national dimension. Because of the ease with which we can communicate with other people from around the globe, it is becoming increasingly important that we learn about communications differences within a variety of cultures.

Cultural differences vary considerably around the world. The way we walk, smile, or use our hands can convey different meanings to particular cultures. A smile, for example, is used in our culture to convey friendliness; yet, it may be a sign of weakness in another culture.

BOLD **Views about time.** We look at time as an element that must be planned carefully; yet others may have a much more relaxed view of time To some, it is considered appropriate to BOLD be late because it shows that one is a busy person. ⁋ **Views About space.** We prefer from two to three feet between ourselves and those with whom we communicate. People from some cultures, however, prefer to stand closer when speaking.

Two common legal documents are a bill of sale and a power of attorney.

A *bill of sale* is an agreement by which one person agrees to sell a piece of personal property to another. A *power of attorney* gives one person the power to act as an agent, or proxy, for another.

Study the illustrations below; then key Report 47 and Report 48.

Note: Reports 47 through 49 are one-page legal documents; therefore, page numbers are not necessary. For a two-page legal document, the cumulative page count *(Page 1 of 2, Page 2 of 2)* is centered 1 inch from the bottom. The second page has a 1½-inch top margin.

Note: Key the title in all-capital letters and bold.

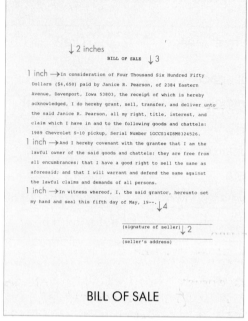

BILL OF SALE

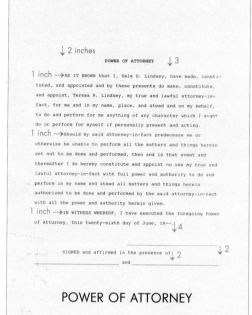

POWER OF ATTORNEY

DOCUMENT PROCESSING

REPORT 47
BILL OF SALE

Tabs: 1 inch; center
Spacing: Double

Note: Key the title in all-capital letters and bold.

Start the signature line at the center.

BILL OF SALE ↓3

In consideration of Four Thousand Six Hundred Fifty Dollars ($4,650) paid by Janice R. Pearson, of 2384 Eastern Avenue, Davenport, Iowa 52803, the receipt of which is hereby acknowledged, I do hereby grant, sell, transfer, and deliver unto the said Janice R. Pearson, all my right, title, interest, and claim which I have in and to the following goods and chattels: 1989 Chevrolet S-10 pickup, Serial Number 1GCCS14Z8M8324526.

And I hereby covenant with the grantee that I am the lawful owner of the said goods and chattels; that they are free from all encumbrances; that I have a good right to sell the same as aforesaid; and that I will warrant and defend the same against the lawful claims and demands of all persons.

In witness whereof, I, the said grantor, hereunto set my hand and seal this fifth day of May, 19—. ↓4

_____

(signature of seller) ↓2

_____

(seller's address)

33 LESSON

Enumerations and Outlines

Margins: 1 inch • Tab: 5 spaces • Spacing: Single • Drills: 2 times • Format Guide: 9—11

Goals:
To improve speed and accuracy; to improve proofreading and composing skills; to format enumerations and outlines.

A. WARMUP

1   David, Jake, and Zach have quite a few baseball cards. 12
2   They possess 258 from the 1970s and 346 from the 1980s, and 24
3   in the next months they can get more from different places. 36

| 1 | 2 | 3 | 4 | 5 | 6 | 7 | 8 | 9 | 10 | 11 | 12

LANGUAGE ARTS

B. Key the paragraph, correcting all errors.

B. PROOFREADING

4   What is it taht makes one person more succesful than
5   another when thier backgrounds, esperience, and education
6   are very similar? Many studies have been conducted in an
7   attempt to anser this particuler question, and the
8   findings almost always reveal that the differenses in
9   success are almost always related to personal intiative,
10 enthusiasm, and attitude. An individual with a postive
11 attitude and noticable enthusiasm has great potential for
12 success. These personnal characteristics will often play a
13 more important role than eduction or experience when
14 success is evalauted.

Margin wrong

C. Answer each question with a single word or a short phrase.

C. COMPOSING

15 What is your favorite day of the week? SATURDAY
16 What sport do you like to watch on television? FOOTBALL
17 What is the last name of your favorite female vocal artist? CAREY
18 How much money do you expect to pay for your next car? $5-$6000
19 What is the name of the largest state in the United States? Alaska
20 What is the name of the smallest state in the United States? Rhode Island
21 What is your favorite snack? Chocolate
22 Where would you like to spend your next vacation? California

---

SKILLBUILDING

D. PACED PRACTICE

Turn to the Paced Practice routine at the back of the book. Take four 2-minute timed writings, starting at the speed at which you left off the last time.

E. PROGRESSIVE PRACTICE: ALPHABET

Turn to the Progressive Practice: Alphabet routine at the back of the book. Take six 30-second timed writings, starting at the point where you left off the last time.

U. AUTHOR/YEAR CITATIONS

When preparing a report, you must document (or cite) any information that is taken from other sources. The author/year method of citation includes the following information in parentheses at the appropriate point within the text: the author's last name, the year of publication (followed by a comma), and the page number; for example (Smith, 1993, p. 52). If the author's name appears within the text, give only the year and page number in parentheses.

If a source has two authors, give both last names joined by *and.* If a source has three or more authors, give the last name of the first author followed by *et al.*

REPORT 45
TWO-PAGE REPORT
WITH AUTHOR/YEAR
CITATIONS

Spacing: Double

THE FEASIBILITY OF PURCHASING A DTP SYSTEM FOR BLAKE ASSOCIATES

This report will investigate some of the major uses and advantages of desktop publishing to determine if it is feasible to purchase a new DTP system for Blake Associates during the current fiscal year.

Uses of Desktop Publishing

The purchase of a new desktop publishing system would enable Blake Associates to produce its own company newsletter. Currently, our newsletter is drafted in the Communications Department and then sent to Quick Press for layout, design, and typesetting. According to Hirsch (1994), we would also be able to use desktop publishing to produce our annual report.

In addition to the purchase of a desktop publishing system, it would be in the best interests of Blake Associates to obtain a copy of the popular ArtCraft clip art package so that we could use desktop publishing in our advertising campaign. The clip art could also be used to promote our catalog products throughout the year. With desktop publishing, these promotion spots could be created with camera-ready perfection (Slade, 1993, p. 48).

Advantages of Purchasing a DTP System

On the basis of current figures, it is estimated that first-year savings in printing costs for Blake Associates would amount to a minimum of $9,450. Savings in the second year of operation should reach $15,000. According to Collins (1994), printing cost savings in the first five years of operation could approach 80 percent.

REPORT 46
REFERENCE LIST

Center and key the title "References" in all-capital letters and bold 2 inches from the top, and indent the turnover lines 5 spaces.

Collins, Wanda, "Taking a Journey With DTP," DTP Computing, May 1994, p. 28.

Hirsch, Mitchell, DTP Manual for Executives, Computer Press, Denver, 1994.

Slade, Beth, Desktop Publishing Comes of Age, Midwestern Book Company, Kansas City, 1993, p. 48.

F. INDENT

Indent is used to indent text from the left margin to the next tab setting. Indent sets a temporary left margin at this tab setting.

To set an indent for an enumeration (a numbered list), clear all tabs and set a left tab 4 spaces from the left margin. To key an enumeration, key the item number followed by a period. Turn on indent and key the text to be indented. At the end of the last line of a numbered item, turn off indent to return to the left margin to key the next item number.

DOCUMENT PROCESSING

REPORT 4
ENUMERATION

Top margin: 2 inches
Tab: 4 spaces

Turnover lines: the second and succeeding lines in an enumerated list.

G. ENUMERATIONS

Read the information in Report 4 before you key the assignment. Study the format so that you get a mental picture of the layout before keying it. Use Indent after keying the number and period so that turnover lines are indented.

ENUMERATIONS

1. An enumeration may be a series of numbered items, Although letters may be used. Numbers are keyed at the left margin and followed by a period and two spaces.

2. Turn over lines are indented 4 spaces from the left margin. Set a left tab 4 spaces from the left margin. Use the left indent after keying the number and period to guarantee that turnover lines are indented as they are in this enumeration.

3. If numbered items take one line or less, they are single spaced with no blank lines between them. However, if most items have more than one line (as they do in this enumeration), they are single spaced with a double spaced (one blank lines) between numbered items.

4. The periods following the introductory numbers should be aligned vertically. if the enumeration runs to ten or more items, a decimal tab should be set to align the periods for all numbers.

5. The title of an enumeration is keyed 2 inches from the top of the page. The title should be centered, boldface, and all caps. Side margins are 1 inch.

T. HEADERS AND FOOTERS

A header is information keyed at the top of the second and any succeeding pages of a document. Key the header 1 inch from the top of the page; then double-space.

A footer is information keyed at the bottom of pages a double space below the text. The last line of the footer should end approximately 1 inch from the bottom of the page. Determine the number of lines needed for the double space, the footer, and the bottom margin. Use the page-end indicator or make a light pencil mark at the left edge of your page that number of lines from the bottom to indicate where to stop keying the text.

DOCUMENT PROCESSING

REPORT 44
PROCEDURES MANUAL–
PAGE 5

To align the enumerated items, set tabs 5 spaces and 9 spaces from the left margin.

Paragraphs are indented 5 spaces.

Key a header for the information to appear at the top of the page. Key a footer to include *Training Program* at the bottom right of the page.

Employees' Manual   Kramer, Inc., Page 5

This procedures manual, therefore, is designed to assist managers who are responsible for developing training programs for all new employees hired in any of the five regional branches of Kramer, Inc. The following paragraphs outline the basic content of a training program.

Introduction

This section should explain the content of the manual and specific ways in which it may be used within the company. It should provide answers to the following questions:

1. Who is the training manual designed for, and what does it contain?
2. Where does the training manual fit within the training program?
3. How should the training manual be used?
   A. As self-paced instructional material?
   B. As classroom material?
   C. As a study guide for students?

Program Philosophy and Goals

The program philosophy and goals section reveals the nature of the training program. These statements provide the context for all courses within Kramer, Inc. This section should focus on two major areas:

1. Program Philosophy
   A. Why does this program exist, and who will benefit from it?
   B. What company needs are satisfied by this training program?
2. Goal Statements
   A. What tasks, competencies, and goals are satisfied by this program?
   B. What specific skills does this training program develop?

Training Program

REPORT 5
OUTLINE

Top margin: 2 inches
Tabs: 4, 7, 11, 15 spaces
Spacing: Single

The first tab in Report 5 is set as a decimal tab to align the periods following the roman numerals.

 Some software programs contain an outline feature that automatically formats different levels of heads.

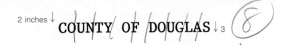

2 inches ↓ COUNTY OF DOUGLAS ↓3 ⑧

I. ADMINISTRATION ↓2

   A. Commissioner's Office
   B. Fiscal Services
   C. Planning and Evaluation ↓3

II. PLANNING AND ECONOMIC DEVELOPMENT ↓2

   A. Government Center
      1. Economic development and promotion policies
      2. Research development and information
      3. Current planning and zoning policies
   B. Special Services Division
   C. Technical Services Division ↓3

III. PUBLIC WORKS ↓2

   A. Emergency Services
   B. Garbage and Trash Disposal
   C. Land Development
   D. Water and Street Department

---

34 LESSON

One-Page Reports

Margins: 1 inch • Tab: 5 spaces • Spacing: Single • Drills: 2 times • Format Guide: 11

Goals:
To key 34 wam/3'/4e; to format reports from rough-draft copy.

A. WARMUP

1 Brazil, Mexico, and Pakistan qualified for the U.N. in   12
2 the 1940s along with 156 other countries. In the 1990s, we   24
3 saw another seven nations join. Might we see more by 2023?   36

  | 1 | 2 | 3 | 4 | 5 | 6 | 7 | 8 | 9 | 10 | 11 | 12

SKILLBUILDING

B. TECHNIQUE PRACTICE: RETURN KEY

B. Key each sentence on a separate line.

4 Where is my new diskette? You placed it on my office desk.
5 Why did you miss my meeting? I was working at the exhibit.
6 When do you expect to return? We will be back on Thursday.

7 Eleven computers are missing. They must be out for repair.
8 The sessions were canceled. The speaker could not make it.
9 My telephone is now working. We all have better equipment.

10 The business trip is scheduled. Will we fly to Pittsburgh?
11 We ordered new software. On what day will it be installed?
12 You have an interview tomorrow. What time will you return?

REPORT 43
MINUTES OF A MEETING

Key these minutes in report format. Use single spacing. Key the side headings in bold with a double space before and after.

Minutes of the Meeting
September 8, 19--

PERSON(N)EL COMMITTEE

Attendance of the Personnel Committee

A special meeting of the Personnel Committee was held in the office of Mr. Carpenter, who chaired the meeting. All members were present except Ron Farley, who was represented by Heather Zukowski. The meeting was called to order at 2 p.m.

Unfinished Business

Ms. Samuels distributed and reported on the survey of company personnel. A copy of the survey is attached to the minutes. The minutes of the last monthly meeting were read and approved.

New business

Mr. Carpenter discussed the need for plan(n)ing a campaign for letting job applicants know about position openings within the company. Richard Smiley Adams and Donna Newby will draft a promotion piece to be sent to the chronic(al).

Programs for the H R D Conference to be held in Fargo Bismarck were distributed to all members. Each committee member was asked to distribute these copies to all employees in his or her departments.

ADJOURN Adjournment

The meeting for October 9 was adjourned at 3:15 p.m. The next meeting has been scheduled in the Communications Center.

Respectfully submitted,

Blake Lanier, Secretary

S. PROCEDURES MANUAL

Organizations often prepare procedures manuals to identify the steps or methods to be followed to accomplish a particular task. These manuals are often formatted as unbound reports, but with single spacing. It is important that the pages be clearly labeled. The top of each page may include such items as the company name, a section title, and a page number. The bottom of each page may include the same items or may identify the content on that page (for example, *Policies*).

Employees' Manual   Kramer, Inc., Page 5

This procedures manual, therefore, is designed to assist managers who are responsible for developing training programs for all new employees hired in any of the five regional branches of Kramer, Inc. The following paragraphs outline the basic content of a training program.

Introduction

This section should explain the content of the manual and specific ways in which it may be used within the company. It should provide answers to the following questions:

1. Who is the training manual designed for, and what does it contain?
2. Where does the training manual fit within the training program?
3. How should the training manual be used?
   A. As self-paced instructional material?
   B. As classroom material?
   C. As a study guide for students?

Program Philosophy and Goals

The program philosophy and goals section reveals the nature of the training program. These statements provide the context for all courses within Kramer, Inc. This section should focus on two major areas:

1. Program Philosophy
   A. Why does this program exist, and who will benefit from it?

C. DIAGNOSTIC PRACTICE: NUMBERS

Turn to the Diagnostic Practice: Numbers routine at the back of this book. Take the Pretest and record your performance. Then, practice the drill lines for those reaches on which you made errors. Finally, repeat the Pretest and compare your performance.

D. 3-MINUTE TIMED WRITING

D. Spacing: double. Take two 3-minute timed writings. Compute your speed and count errors.

Goal: 34 wam/3'/4e

```
13      What does the future of computers hold for us?  Just        12
14  a few years ago we were amazed at the storage space of a         23
15  hard disk, the quickness of the dot-matrix printer, and the      35
16  beauty of a color screen.  Now, those hardware features          46
17  are thought to be old technology.                                53
18      In the future, we will be storing much of our data on        64
19  compact discs, our printing will most likely be produced by      76
20  a color laser printer, the images on our monitors will be        88
21  as clear as on a movie screen, and images will very likely      100
22  be animated.                                                    102
```

| 1 | 2 | 3 | 4 | 5 | 6 | 7 | 8 | 9 | 10 | 11 | 12 |

DOCUMENT PROCESSING

REPORT 6
ONE-PAGE REPORT

Top margin: 2 inches
Spacing: Double

AUTO INSURANCE COVERAGE
By Andrea Parker

All of us are required to carry automobile insurance on our cars, regardless of the state in which we live. The following paragraphs reveal coverages found in some insurance policies.

Medical Payments Coverage

This coverage will pay for all reasonable medical expenses incurred because of bodily injury caused by an accident. Coverage is available to the insured and his or her family.

Coverage for Damage to an automobile

This coverage is usually paid directly for loss to any covered automobile, minus any deductible in the policy. Part of this coverage may also include transportation expenses incurred while the automobile is being repaired.

Certain exclusions usually apply to auto coverage. Insurance companies will not pay for damages if the auto was used to carry persons for a fee. Nor will they pay for damage caused by wear and tear of the auto, freezing, or mechanical failure.

REPORT 42

MINUTES OF A MEETING

Tabs: 15 spaces; center

Key the name of the committee in all-capital letters and bold. Key the remaining heading lines in regular type with double spacing. Triple-space after the heading.

Begin closing lines at the center.

Key the side headings in all-capital letters and bold; then indent to begin the paragraphs.

---

2 inches ↓

PLANNING COMMITTEE
Minutes of the Meeting ↓2
March 15, 19-- ↓2
↓3

ATTENDANCE

The Planning Committee meeting was called to order at 3 p.m. on March 15, 19--, by Michael Nix, chairperson. Members present were Curtis Avery, T. L. Balenger, Shelly Karle, Michael Nix, and Lisa Spense. ↓3

OLD BUSINESS

The members of the committee reviewed bids submitted for the purchase of a laser printer. Shelly Karle will contact the two lowest bidders to obtain information on color capabilities. ↓3

NEW BUSINESS

The committee reviewed a proposal for a new plant in Redwood City. After much discussion, the committee agreed to contact the county clerk's office and ask for the Redwood City zoning ordinances. ↓2

A request for five microcomputers (with CD-ROM drives) in the Records Office was approved. ↓3

ADJOURNMENT

The meeting was adjourned at 4:30 p.m. The next meeting is scheduled for April 16 in the Boardroom. ↓2

Respectfully submitted, ↓4

T. L. Balenger, Secretary

Top margin: 2 inches
Spacing: Double

MAKING A DECISION

By Candace Benedict

Making a decision is often a difficult task, but it is one that is performed on a routine basis. The steps to decision making vary, but they can be summarized in four activities that are described in the following paragraphs.

Identify the Problem

The first step in the decision-making process is to identify that you do have a problem. Unless you can focus on the problem, you may never resolve it.

List All Possible Solutions

Once the problem has been identified, you need to identify all possible solutions to the problem. "Brainstorming" is an excellent technique that is used to identify various solutions.

Analyze All Possible Solutions

In this step, you must study carefully all the solutions and narrow your list of possible choices to two or three. Study the strengths and weaknesses of each of these solutions.

Choose the Best Solution

The final step is to select the best solution from those you identified as the final two or three. This step may take several days, depending on how much input you expect from others.

R. ITINERARIES

An itinerary is a proposed outline of a trip that provides a traveler with information such as flight and meeting times, travel dates, and room reservations. It may also include notes of special interest to the traveler.

Key dot leaders between the flush-left entries (such as the cities) and the flush-right entries (such as the flight numbers).

DOCUMENT PROCESSING

REPORT 41
ITINERARY

Tabs: 4 spaces; flush right
Spacing: as directed

↓ 2 inches **ATLANTA ITINERARY**

Paula Mc Keenan

July 23-24, 19-- ↓3

Tuesday, July 23 ↓2

Seattle/Denver .Delta 249
    4   Leave 2:15 p.m.; arrive 5:33 p.m.
spaces Seat 5C; one stop ↓2
→

Denver/Atlanta . . . . .Delta 108
        Leave 6:30 p.m.; arrive 11:15 p.m.
        Seat 8A; nonstop; dinner ↓3

July 24, Wednesday

N.A.B.R. Meeting . . . . Atlanta hilton
        General session, 9:30 a.m., Alexander Room
        Buyers' Forum, 10:15-11:30 a.m., Conference Room A
        Regional Meetings, 1:30 p.m., Parlors I, II, III & IV ↓3

Thursday, July 25

Atlanta/Seattle . . . . Delta 250
        Leave 9:30 a.m.; arrive 11:28 a.m.
        Seat 3a; non stop; snack ↓4

NOTES ↓2

1. A hotel limousine is available at Harts field to take you
    directly to the Atlanta Hilton, and back to the airport on Thursday.

2. A reservation has been made at the Atlanta Hilton
    and is guaranteed for late arrival (No. 513-38414-2370).

Enumerations and Bibliographies

Margins: 1 inch • Tab: 5 spaces • Spacing: Single • Drills: 2 times • Format Guide: 11

Goals:
To improve speed and accuracy; to improve skills in formatting from rough-draft copy and word-division skills; to format a report with an enumeration and a bibliography.

A. WARMUP

1   The quake in Brazil destroyed approximately 875 to 925   12
2 buildings. We are fortunate that 12,643 buildings had been   24
3 reinforced just 10 months prior; they haven't been damaged.   36

| 1 | 2 | 3 | 4 | 5 | 6 | 7 | 8 | 9 | 10 | 11 | 12 |

SKILLBUILDING

B. Take three 12-second timed writings on each line. The scale shows your wam speed for a 12-second timed writing.

B. 12-SECOND SPRINTS

4 We use the computer to prepare all of the work at our home.
5 All the players were ready to play their best on the court.
6 It will start to rain, and then our game might be canceled.
7 We must order all our stock by the second day of the month.

| | 5 | | 10 | | 15 | | 20 | | 25 | | 30 | | 35 | | 40 | | 45 | | 50 | | 55 | | 60 |

C. Take a 1-minute timed writing on the first paragraph to establish your base speed. Then take four 1-minute timed writings on the remaining paragraphs. As soon as you equal or exceed your base speed on one paragraph, advance to the next one.

C. SUSTAINED PRACTICE: ROUGH DRAFT

8   Ethics in business has always been very important. If   12
9 we are honest in our work and respect the ethical standards   24
10 of our company, we'll be creating a positive image for all.   36
11 A new challenge to ethical standards in the work place has   12
12 been more apparent in the past few years because of the use   24
13 of computers. How have computers challenged ethical codes?   36
14   One of the most severe ethical problems has to do with   12
15 the use of software. Every copy of software sold caries a   24
16 serial number, and it's given to the owner of the software.   36
17   Some people will take anothers software, however, and   12
18 copy it as their own. so doing violates ethical codes, and   24
19 people who so do are dishonest in using the software.   36

| 1 | 2 | 3 | 4 | 5 | 6 | 7 | 8 | 9 | 10 | 11 | 12 |

D. Set a tab in 5 spaces; then set tabs every 16 spaces. Tab in to key the first column. Key those words that can be divided with a hyphen to show where the word can be divided (for example, *forefront*).

D. WORD DIVISION

?Look up   Divide compound words?

20 taught	address	business	counterpart
21 finance	weren't	expressway	alarm
22 monthly	USAF	thanked	self-defense
23 can't	knowledge	TWA Name	afford

O. SYMBOL PRACTICE

73 Invoice #3212 to Klekburg & Baines requested the following:
74 (1) 9 disks @ $2.60 each, (2) 7 tapes @ $2 each, (3) 8 pens
75 @ $1.10 each, and (4) 18 records @ $6 each; the sum for the
76 bill is $154.20, with a 7% sales tax adding another $10.79.

P. DIAGNOSTIC PRACTICE: ALPHABET

Turn to the Diagnostic Practice: Alphabet routine at the back of this book. Take the Pretest and record your performance. Then practice the drill lines for those reaches on which you made errors. Finally, repeat the Pretest and compare your performance.

Q. Spacing: double.
Take two 5-minute timed writings. Compute your speed and count errors.

Goal: 46 wam/5'/5e

Q. 5-MINUTE TIMED WRITING

77   Many Americans are entering the nineties by embracing   12
78 simpler pleasures and homier values. They are thinking   23
79 hard about what really matters to them and have decided   34
80 that having time for family, friends, and relaxation is   45
81 more important than status symbols and corporate ladders.   57
82 All over the country folks are trying to find a quieter   68
83 life with deeper meaning.   74
84   Part of this zest for down-home values is based on   85
85 changes in our economy. In the past, families could get   96
86 by on one salary. The majority of U.S. families now rely   108
87 on two incomes to keep things running. That extra salary   119
88 no longer pays for vacations and fancy clothes but instead   131
89 is used for such things as mortgages, food, and gasoline   143
90 for the family car.   147
91   Maybe because people are working so hard for their   158
92 money, they have become more careful in how they spend it.   170
93 Renting a movie to watch at home has surpassed the desire   181
94 to see new releases in the theaters. Gourmet cooking is   193
95 being replaced by fast, healthy foods which can feed twice   205
96 the number of people for the same cost. All in all, people   217
97 are realizing that the value of life may not be in just   228
98 making money.   230

| 1 | 2 | 3 | 4 | 5 | 6 | 7 | 8 | 9 | 10 | 11 | 12 |

E. HANGING INDENT

To create a hanging indent (the first line is keyed at the margin; remaining lines are indented 5 spaces) as shown in Report 9 below, reset the left margin in 5 spaces. To key the first line of an entry, release the left margin and backspace 5 times.

DOCUMENT PROCESSING

REPORT 8
REPORT WITH ENUMERATION

Tabs: 5 and 9 spaces
Spacing: Double

Single-space the lines within a numbered item; double-space between numbered items.

Numbered items are indented 5 spaces, and turnover lines are indented 9 spaces.

Read Report 8 for the information it contains. Then carefully follow the instructions at the left, noting that a tab must be set at 5 spaces for the numbered items.

PREPARING A BIBLIOGRAPHY
By Bonnie Sparks

A bibliography is an alphabetic listing of sources and is placed at the end of a report. Follow these instructions:

1. Use the side margins of the report (usually 1 inch).

2. Center the title in bold print, all caps, 2 inches from the top. Triple-space after the title.

3. Arrange book entries in this sequence: author, title (underlined or in italics), publisher, place of publication, and date.

4. Arrange information for journal articles in this order: author, title of article (in quotation marks), title of journal (underlined or in italics), series number, volume number, issue number, date, and page number or numbers.

REPORT 9
BIBLIOGRAPHY

Tab: 5 spaces

Prepare Report 9 from the copy below using a hanging indent to automatically indent the turnover lines. Book and journal titles may be underlined or printed in italics if available.

BIBLIOGRAPHY

Book by one author

Blanchard, Christie, Experience a Successful Interview, Beringson Printing, New York, 1990.

Book by two authors

Dolfeld, Kyle B., and Lisa R. Simmons, Using an Interview to Get the Job, Masterson Books, Aptos, California, 1989.

Article by one author

Johnston, Karen C., "What to Do After the Interview," Journal of Communications, Vol. XVII, No. 6, May 1980, pp. 17-20.

Article by three or more authors (et al. means "and others")

Lymanski, James T., et al., "The Secrets to Interviewing: Style and Organization," HRD Journal, Vol. LXVII, No. 5, October 1992, pp. 58-61.

Article—no author

"Preparing for the Interview," Sales Marketing Journal, Vol. XXVII, No. 2, August 21, 1991, pp. 103-105.

Organization as author

Secretarial Association, The Job Interview and Your Success, Georgia College Press, Carrollton, Georgia, 1992.

J. NUMBER PRACTICE

J. Take two 1-minute timed writings. Note that the last two digits of each number provide a cumulative word count to help you determine your wam speed.

41 3201 4702 5603 8904 7005 1306 4407 2808 5909 6010 9211 4412
42 8913 2714 5815 6016 3217 5718 1819 2420 9321 4822 9123 8824
43 6625 5926 1127 3928 4029 5630 9031 3432 3633 8834 5635 2136
44 7337 5038 2239 9440 1941 3942 4443 2144 8945 6246 3847 2048

K. TECHNIQUE PRACTICE: TAB KEY

K. Clear all tabs. Then set four new tabs every 10 spaces. Key lines 45–48, using the tab key to go across from column to column.

45 straw	safer	dense	purer	trace
46 desks	after	truck	sadly	dance
47 named	roped	along	quite	pound
48 using	enemy	point	loyal	quiet

L. 12-SECOND SPRINTS

L. Take three 12-second timed writings on each line. The scale gives wam for a 12-second timed writing.

49 Invoice #561 was for $850.35; Invoice #421 was for $565.20.
50 *One-fifth or 1/5 equals 20%; two-fifths or 2/5 equals 40%.
51 Check these invoices: (1) #3419, (2) #4623, and (3) #3518.
52 Order #34 from Quinn & Son; Item #78 will be sold by N & B.

| | | | 5 | | | |10| | | |15| | |20| | | |25| | |30| | | |35| | |40| | | |45| | | |50| | |55| | |60

M. TECHNIQUE PRACTICE: CONCENTRATION

M. Insert the necessary vowels as you key these sentences twice.

53 Th- --ght m-n w-rk d-wn by th- b-g l-k- f-r th- r-ch w-d-w.
54 H- m-ght m-k- th- --rly tr--n -f h- c-n d- h-s w-rk by s-x.
55 Th- w-m-n -wns h-lf th- l-k- -nd h-lf th- l-nd by th- t-wn.
56 Y-- w-ll w-nt t- d- s-m- f-sh-ng wh-n y-- v-s-t th- -sl-nd.

N. SUSTAINED PRACTICE: SYLLABIC INTENSITY

N. Take a 1-minute timed writing on the first paragraph to establish your base speed. Then take four 1-minute timed writings on the remaining paragraphs. As soon as you equal or exceed your base speed on one paragraph, advance to the next one.

57   The cost of going to school after high school has been   12
58 increasing rapidly during these past few years. There have   24
59 been several studies that have shown how that cost has been   36
60 rising faster than the rate of inflation that we have seen.   48

61   The cost of higher education may depend on the type of   12
62 school that is being considered. For example, the cost for   24
63 a private school is substantially higher than the cost of a   36
64 public one. The reputation of the school is also a factor.   48

65   By analyzing these increases, it will be obvious where   12
66 the rapid growth is taking place. Tuition charges show the   24
67 big jumps, but housing and food are at about the same level   36
68 as inflation. Student activity fees have also skyrocketed.   48

69   Parents with new babies should carefully consider what   12
70 this means. If these increases continue, it is critical to   24
71 consider financial investments. Instead of putting savings   36
72 into regular accounts, different investments may be needed.   48

| 1 | 2 | 3 | 4 | 5 | 6 | 7 | 8 | 9 | 10 | 11 | 12

Simple Tables

LESSON 36

Margins: 1 inch • Tab: 5 spaces • Spacing: Single • Drills: 2 times • Format Guide: 11–13

Goals:
To key 35 wam/3'/4e; to format simple tables.

A. WARMUP

1   Have you read Jackie's article entitled "Civilized Exports" in yesterday's newspaper? It's on pages B34 and B67 and quotes your 1989-92 study of the Fortune 500 companies.

12 24 36

| 1 | 2 | 3 | 4 | 5 | 6 | 7 | 8 | 9 | 10 | 11 | 12 |

LANGUAGE ARTS

B. Study the rules at the right. Then key lines 4–7, making necessary changes.

B. NUMBERS

Rule: Key percentages in figures, and spell out the word *percent.*
Note: The percent sign (%) may be used in tables.

An accuracy rate of 97 percent was reported for the month.

Rule: When ages are used as significant statistics, key them in figures.

He was excited because he would be able to vote at age 18.

4 The quality-control group reports a 2.7% defect rate.
5 The absentee rate was lowered by twenty-three percent.
6 Pension eligibility was reduced to the age of 62.
7 Of the executive group, only one member is age fifty-two.

SKILLBUILDING

C. Set a tab in 5 spaces; then set tabs every 12 spaces. Tab to begin Column 1. Use the tab key to move from column to column.

D. Spacing: double. Take two 3-minute timed writings. Compute your speed and count errors.

Goal: 35 wam/3'/4e

C. TECHNIQUE PRACTICE: TAB KEY

8	A. Allen	B. Cable	D. Drake	E. Eaton	F. Frank
9	G. Grant	H. Henry	I. Ilanu	J. Kirby	L. Lopez
10	M. Mills	N. Nolan	O. Ortiz	P. Quinn	R. Rosen
11	S. Simon	T. Tyler	U. Vidah	W. Xerox	Y. Zulch

D. 3-MINUTE TIMED WRITING

12   There has surely been quite an increase in emphasis on international business in the past few years, but we should not forget that you do not have to leave this country in order to encounter cultures that are different from the one with which you may be most at ease. This is true no matter if you belong to a majority or to a minority group. Look around the room the next time you are in a meeting. You will be amazed at the diversity that is there. You should learn to be comfortable with those different from you.

12 24 35 47 59 71 82 94 105

| 1 | 2 | 3 | 4 | 5 | 6 | 7 | 8 | 9 | 10 | 11 | 12 |

D. PACED PRACTICE

Turn to the Paced Practice routine at the back of the book. Take four 2-minute timed writings, starting at the speed at which you left off the last time.

Turn to the Paced Practice routine at the back of the book.

PRETEST.
Take a 1-minute timed writing; compute your speed and count errors.

E. PRETEST: HORIZONTAL REACHES

```
13      Art enjoyed his royal blue race car.  He bragged about    12
14 how he learned to push for those spurts of speed which made    24
15 him win races.  The car had a lot of get-up-and-go.  He had    36
16 daily meetings with his mechanics when a race date was set.    48
   |  1  |  2  |  3  |  4  |  5  |  6  |  7  |  8  |  9  |  10  |  11  |  12
```

PRACTICE.
Speed Emphasis: If you made no more than 1 error on the Pretest, key each line twice.
Accuracy Emphasis: If you made 2 or more errors on the Pretest, key each group of lines (as though it were a paragraph) twice.

F. PRACTICE: IN REACHES

```
17 oy ahoy ploy toys loyal coyly royal enjoy decoy Lloyd annoy
18 ar fare arch mart march farms scars spear barns learn radar
19 pu pull push puts pulse spurt purge spuds pushy spurs pupil
20 lu luck blue lure lucid glued lumps value lulls bluff lunge
```

G. PRACTICE: OUT REACHES

```
21 ge gear gets ages getup raged geese lunge pages cagey forge
22 da dare date data dance adage dazed sedan daubs cedar daily
23 hi high hick hill hinge chief hires ethic hiked chili hitch
24 ra rate rare brag ranch brace ratio bravo rayon prawn races
```

POSTTEST.
Repeat the Pretest (E) and compare performance.

H. POSTTEST: HORIZONTAL REACHES

I. Take a 1-minute timed writing on the first paragraph to establish your base speed. Then take four 1-minute timed writings on the remaining paragraphs. As soon as you equal or exceed your base speed on one paragraph, advance to the next one.

I. SUSTAINED PRACTICE: NUMBERS

```
25      The division managers were reviewing the sales figures   12
26 for the last fiscal year.  They were anxious to review what   24
27 the sales figures of autos would be for each state.  The 10   36
28 states in the Southern region had impressive sales figures.   48

29      Thomas Hundley was the top salesperson in Alabama.  He   12
30 sold 70 autos in the past year.  Total revenue generated by   24
31 the sales was $870,100.  This was a great increase for Tom.   36
32 He will be recognized at the banquet in Birmingham in June.   48

33      Sales in Alabama were the highest for that region.  In   12
34 reviewing the sales data, there were 4,563 autos sold for a   24
35 total sales revenue of $56,718,090.  This represented a big   36
36 increase for the state over sales for just the year before.   48

37      The Southern region sold a total of 32,650 cars during   12
38 the past year.  This gave us a total of $405,957,950 in our   24
39 revenues for the year.  For the entire region, there was an   36
40 increase of 1,162 automobiles sold over the preceding year.   48
   |  1  |  2  |  3  |  4  |  5  |  6  |  7  |  8  |  9  |  10  |  11  |  12
```

E. BASIC PARTS OF A TABLE

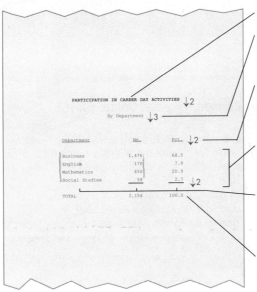

PARTICIPATION IN CAREER DAY ACTIVITIES ↓2

By Department ↓3

Department	No.	Pct. ↓2
Business	1,476	68.5
English	170	7.9
Mathematics	450	20.9
Social Studies	58	2.7 ↓2
TOTAL	2,154	100.0

TITLE. Center and key in all caps and in bold.

SUBTITLE (optional). Center a double space below the title, with the first and all principal words capitalized.

COLUMN HEADINGS. Align at the left for word columns and at the right for number columns; underline, and leave 2 blank lines before and 1 after.

BODY. Center horizontally, usually with 6 spaces between columns; may be either single-spaced or double-spaced.

COLUMN. Align columns of words at the left, column of whole numbers at the right, and columns of decimal numbers on the decimal point.

TOTAL LINE. Make the underline before the total line the length of the longest number in the column. Double-space before the total line.

F. TABLES

Follow these steps to format Tables 1–3:

1. Insert a sheet of scrap paper and clear all tab stops.
2. Horizontally center the key line—an imaginary line made up of the longest item in each column plus 6 spaces for each open area between columns.
3. Key the line and determine where tabs should be set. For text columns, position the carrier under the first character of the column and set a left tab. For number columns, position the carrier to the right of the last digit and set a right tab.
4. Determine the starting line to vertically center the table.
5. Insert a clean sheet of paper, space down to the correct starting line.
6. Center and key the title in all-capital letters and bold. Double-space and center and key the subtitle in upper- and lowercase normal type followed by a triple space.
7. Change line spacing if necessary, and tab to begin Column 1. Use the tab key to move from column to column.

DOCUMENT PROCESSING

TABLE 1
2-COLUMN TABLE

Spacing: Double
Set 2 left tabs.

Key Line:

ANNUAL REPORT ASSIGNMENTS ↓2

By Priority ↓3

Letter from the CEO	Walter Behrens
The Year in Review	Anne Smithson-Elliott
Financial Picture	Auditors
Spotlight on New Products	Alan C. Wingett
A Look Ahead	Barbara J. Arno

Spotlight on New Products123456Anne Smithson-Elliott

Margins: 1 inch • Spacing: Single • Drills: 2 times • Format Guide: 63–65

Goals for Unit 19

Begin each day with approximately 15 minutes of skill-building, selecting activities from pages 209–212. In the remaining class time, complete as many production jobs from pages 213–219 as you can.

1. To improve accuracy and speed on alphabet and number keys.
2. To key 46 wam for 5 minutes with no more than 5 errors.
3. To develop proficiency in spelling commonly misspelled words.
4. To format and key an itinerary.
5. To format and key the minutes of a meeting.
6. To format and key a procedures manual.
7. To format and key reports with side headings and author/year citations.
8. To format and key various types of legal documents.

A. WARMUP

1   Our accounts receivable clerk found Invoice #139 for a   12
2 total of $1,894.20 from Max Joy was past due. In addition,   24
3 Invoice #642 for $975 from Gunther Zak was not quite right.   36

| 1 | 2 | 3 | 4 | 5 | 6 | 7 | 8 | 9 | 10 | 11 | 12 |

LANGUAGE ARTS

B. APOSTROPHES

B. Study the rules at the right. Then key lines 4–7, making necessary changes.

Rule: To make a singular noun possessive, place the apostrophe before the s.

The company's assets had nearly doubled in two years.

Rule: To make a possessive from a singular noun that ends in an s sound, be guided by the way the word is pronounced. If a new syllable is formed by making the noun possessive, add an apostrophe and an s.

The jurors were all shaken by the witness's testimony.

4 Miss Hayward's new car had been stored in the warehouse.
5 A business firms' parking lot must meet zoning standards.
6 Minneapolis' downtown area has been transformed.
7 We helped select the new furniture for our boss' office.

C. SPELLING

C. These words are among the 500 most frequently misspelled words in business correspondence.

8 coverage schedules substantial ordinance scheduling counsel
9 termination instructions acquisition claimant allowed value
10 techniques capabilities requirement discussion emphasis out
11 participate various concern months provide notify establish
12 entered subsequent particularly communications studies some

TABLE 2
3-COLUMN TABLE

Spacing: Double
Set 3 left tabs.

TABLE 3
3-COLUMN TABLE

Spacing: Single
Set 3 left tabs.

SECTION 5: A LOOK AHEAD
Deadlines for First Drafts

New Products	Alan C. Wingett	October 15
The Economy	Chad Spencer	December 1
International Dimensions	Sherri Jordan	October 15
The Competition	Pedro Martin	November 15

SECTION 5C: INTERNATIONAL DIMENSIONS
Agent Locations

Canada	Pearson, Ltd.	Toronto, Canada
Central America	Escadrille	Panama City, Panama
South America	Desarrollo Minero	Salvador, Brazil
Europe	Der Widermaster	Bonn, Germany
Near East	Porat Industrial	Haifa, Israel
Far East	Ito-Yokado	Osaka, Japan

37 LESSON

Tables With Number Columns

Margins: 1 inch • Tab: 5 spaces • Spacing: Single • Drills: 2 times • Format Guide: 13

Goals:
To improve speed and accuracy; to format tables with number columns.

A. WARMUP

```
1     I'll fly Flight 1482 on 10/23/96.  It departs New York    12
2 City at 10:57 p.m. and arrives in Caracas, Venezuela, quite   24
3 late the next morning.  The Boeing jet is most comfortable.   36
```
| 1 | 2 | 3 | 4 | 5 | 6 | 7 | 8 | 9 | 10 | 11 | 12

LANGUAGE ARTS

Answer each question with a single word or a short phrase.

B. COMPOSING

4 What is your favorite color combination?
5 If you could take a "dream vacation," where would you go?
6 What two qualities do you look for in a friend?
7 What kinds of books do you like to read?
8 Approximately how many miles do you drive each week?
9 What personality traits do you admire?

MEMO TO: Nicole Rohlin / Reservations Manager / **FROM:** Ardella Eagle, Manager / **DATE:** January 9, 19— / **SUBJECT:** Season Rates

May 14 will be the last day for our special off-season rates. The new season rates have been established and will go into effect on June 1 and continue through October 31.

The daily rates for two–four persons will be as follows: luxury condominium, $130; beachfront cottage, $108; poolside apartment, $86; and apartment, $76. For more than four persons there will be an additional charge of $15 per person.

The weekly rates for two–four persons will be as follows: luxury condominium, $820; beachfront cottage, $693; poolside apartment, $555; and apartment, $492. For more than four persons there will be an additional charge of $80 per person.

Now that you have these new rates, we can have the brochures printed in time for our February campaign.

(Your Initials) / c: Accounts Receivable

LETTER 57
MODIFIED-BLOCK STYLE

Working Papers: 185

Subject:, In re:, or *Re:* usually precedes the actual subject but may be omitted in a subject line.

Word processing programs with a merge feature are used to create personalized form letters. With merge, you can create a single letter and merge variable information such as names and addresses to create individualized copies of the form letter.

Use the information in Memo 21 as you format the following letter. The opening lines are as follows: January 24, 19-- / Mr. and Mrs. Roy Krizan / 925 Sagewood Avenue / Casper, WY 82601 / Dear Mr. and Mrs. Krizan: / Re: New Season Rates

The season rates at Breezy Point Resort will be in effect from June 1 through October 31.

The weekly rates for two-four people will be $_____ for a luxury condominium, $_____ for a beachfront cottage, $_____ for a poolside apartment, and $_____ for an apartment.

The daily rates for two-four people will be $_____ for a luxury condominium, $_____ for a beachfront cottage, $_____ for a poolside apartment, and $_____ for an apartment.

Additional charges for more than four people are $_____ a day and $_____ a week per person.

Our reservations number is 314-555-1826. We shall look forward to your call.

Sincerely,

Nicole Rohlin
Reservations Manager

Remember your reference initials.

PRETEST.
Take a 1-minute timed writing; compute your speed and count errors.

PRACTICE.
Speed Emphasis: If you made 2 or fewer errors on the Pretest, key each line twice.
Accuracy Emphasis: If you made 3 or more errors, key each group of lines (as though it were a paragraph) twice.

POSTTEST.
Repeat the Pretest (C) and compare performance.

C. PRETEST: COMMON LETTER COMBINATIONS

10   At the conference last week, some person made a formal 12
11 motion that might be useful to us in the coming months. It 24
12 should enable us to easily comply with our building permit. 36

| 1 | 2 | 3 | 4 | 5 | 6 | 7 | 8 | 9 | 10 | 11 | 12

D. PRACTICE: WORD BEGINNINGS

13 for forget formal format forces forums forked forest formed
14 con concur confer conned convoy consul convey convex condor
15 per perils period perish permit person peruse perked pertly
16 com combat comedy coming commit common compel comply comets

E. PRACTICE: WORD ENDINGS

17 ing acting aiding boring buying ruling saving hiding dating
18 ble bubble dabble double enable feeble fumble tumble usable
19 ion action vision lesion nation bunion lotion motion legion
20 ful armful cupful earful eyeful joyful lawful useful woeful

F. POSTTEST: COMMON LETTER COMBINATIONS

DOCUMENT PROCESSING

TABLE 4
2-COLUMN TABLE WITH NUMBERS

Spacing: Double
Set 1 left and 1 right tab.

The underline must be the width of the longest item in the column.

NUMBER OF POLICIES WRITTEN

January 1–September 30

Automobile	10,076
Business liability	436
Homeowner's	4,385
Term life	1,452
Whole life	986
TOTAL	17,335

TABLE 5
3-COLUMN TABLE WITH NUMBERS

Spacing: Single
Set 1 left and 2 decimal tabs.

To set a decimal tab, position the carrier under the decimal point in the key line and set a dec tab at this point.

Double-space before the total line.

MIDCONTINENT STATE-PRIDE AWARD WINNERS

(Annual Sales in $000)

Ohio	6,305.7	39.56%
Indiana	4,206.5	26.39%
Minnesota	2,177.4	13.66%
Iowa	1,092.7	6.86%
Michigan	945.8	5.93%
Illinois	803.6	5.04%
Wisconsin	408.2	2.56%
TOTAL	15,939.9	100.00%

U. MULTIPLE ADDRESSES AND WRITERS

If a letter is addressed to two people at different addresses, key each name and address one under the other, with 1 blank line between them. If a letter is addressed to two people at the same address, list each name on a separate line of the same inside address.

If a letter is to be signed by two people, key each name and title one under the other, with 3 blank lines between them.

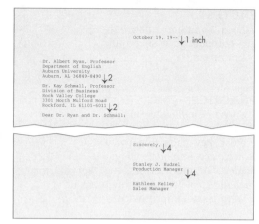

DOCUMENT PROCESSING

LETTER 56
MODIFIED-BLOCK STYLE
WITH INDENTED
PARAGRAPHS

Working Papers: 183

The format for the date (day, month, year, with no commas) is used by all U.S. military organizations as well as by business organizations, especially for international correspondence.

Paragraph indentions may be used with modified-block style letters but never with block-style letters.

Indent the display paragraph 5 spaces from both margins; then tab to indent the first line.

Remember your reference initials and the enclosure notation.

12 November 19--

Mr. Douglas R. Powers
City Manager
Municipal Building
406 Wall Street
Midland, TX 79701-3528

Ms. Joanne Starke
Director of Human Resources
City of Midland
404 Wall Street, Annex b #
Midland, TX 79701-3528

Dear Mr. Powers and Mrs. Starke: still

Yes, the city of Midland can join the ~~many~~ municipalities in Texas that have made long-term-care insurance available to their employees, retirees, and spouses at a reasonable cost. ¶ The federal government recently published these statistics:

Nearly 60% of those over age 65 will need some type of long-term care, and almost 43% are expected to spend some time in a nursing home.

To reconsider adopting ~~of~~ long-term-care coverage would be wise. We would be happy to meet with you further to describe the benefits and exclusions contained in the enclosed materials.

Yours Truly,

Howard J. Larscheid
Executive Director

B. T. Mays
MEIG Chief Administrator

TABLE 6
4-COLUMN TABLE WITH
NUMBERS

Spacing: Double
Set 2 left and 2 decimal tabs.

Leave 10 spaces between Columns 2 and 3 and 6 spaces between the other columns.

MIDCONTINENT THIRD-QUARTER SALES
As a Percentage of Sales Goal

Illinois	93.5	Minnesota	103.7
Indiana	113.7	Missouri	96.5
Iowa	100.0	Ohio	129.6
Michigan	85.6	Wisconsin	99.1

Tables With Blocked Column Headings

LESSON 38

Margins: 1 inch • Tab: 5 spaces • Spacing: Single • Drills: 2 times • Format Guide: 13–15

Goals:
To key 35 wam/3'/4e; to format tables with blocked column headings.

A. WARMUP

1   On our next job, we will increase our contributions to   12
2 a retirement plan from 18% to 20%; this should very quickly   24
3 bring the size of our blue-chip investments up to $375,469.   36

| 1 | 2 | 3 | 4 | 5 | 6 | 7 | 8 | 9 | 10 | 11 | 12

SKILLBUILDING

B. Take a 1-minute timed writing on the first paragraph to establish your base speed. Then take four 1-minute timed writings on the remaining paragraphs. As soon as you equal or exceed your base speed on one paragraph, advance to the next one.

B. SUSTAINED PRACTICE: NUMBERS

4   Michael learned through firsthand experience last week   12
5 that the cost of a week on the water can vary a great deal.   24
6 He says that a rowboat would be about right for his wallet.   36

7   His Uncle Al told him that when he was his age, he had   12
8 rented a small cabin for the huge sum of $105 for one week.   24
9 For $23 more, he rented a small boat and an outboard motor.   36

10   Then his uncle went on to say that when he rented that   12
11 same cabin last year, the fee had gone up to either $395 or   24
12 $410.   The boat and motor rentals now cost from $62 to $87.   36

13   Aunt Kate said that she and her husband will be paying   12
14 either $1,946 or $2,075 for one week's sailing on a 53-foot   24
15 yacht.   The boat has a 4-person crew and was built in 1982.   36

| 1 | 2 | 3 | 4 | 5 | 6 | 7 | 8 | 9 | 10 | 11 | 12

C. PACED PRACTICE

Turn to the Paced Practice routine at the back of the book. Take four 2-minute timed writings, starting at the speed at which you left off the last time.

Working Papers: 179

LETTER 54
BLOCK STYLE WITH
OPEN PUNCTUATION

No punctuation marks are used after the salutation and the complimentary closing when the open punctuation style is used.

Key a delivery notation on the line below the enclosure notation (if used) or on the line below the reference initials. A delivery notation comes before a copy notation.

urs
Enclosure
By Fax
c: Mr. M. R. Crews

September 4, 19--

Mr. Seane R. Tilden
English China, Ltd.
852 Sudbury Street N.
Sault ste. Marie, Ontario
CANADA R3B 2Z6
Dear Mr. Tilden

As the North American distributor of several fine English China patterns, you are very well known in the United States. I would like to have my store become an authorized retail outlet for your company. Please provide answers to these questions:

1. Is it true that only samples are stocked in your retail outlets and that all purchases are made by customers on an order basis? This is very appealing to me because of the virtual elimination of inventory costs?

2. What types of information and/or documentation should I send to your office for review?

3. What is the earliest likely date that I would become an authorized outlet?

I look forward to receiving answers to these questions so that I can become a distributor for your china as soon as possible.

Sincerely yours

D.M. Hallam, Owner

(Your Initials)
By Overnight Mail

LETTER 55
BLOCK STYLE WITH
RULED TABLE

Working Papers: 181

Refer to the Reference Section (page R-12) for the proper format for a ruled table. Leave 1 blank line before and after the table.

October 24, 19— / Mrs. Huong Quan / 12782 Highway 37 / Greeley, CO 80631-4591 / Dear Mrs. Quan:

Yes, individual pieces of Royal Sheldon and Belmore china may be replaced. Here is the information for the items about which you inquired:

Item	Pattern	Price
Dinner plate	Royal Sheldon	$80
Salad plate	Royal Sheldon	38
Cup	Belmore	42
Saucer	Belmore	32

As these pieces must be special-ordered, there likely will be a delay of about three or four weeks after the order is processed. Fifty percent of the purchase price will be due at the time the order is placed, and the balance will be due when the shipment arrives.

Thank you for contacting Hallam's about your china needs. I am enclosing brochures for both Royal Sheldon and Belmore that include prices.

Sincerely yours, / D. M. Hallam, Owner / (Your Initials) / Enclosures 2

D. Spacing: double. Take two 3-minute timed writings. Compute your speed and count errors.

Goal: 35 wam/3'/4e

D. 3-MINUTE TIMED WRITING

The United States plays a major role in world trade, both as a buyer and as a seller. We are now the largest importer of goods in the whole world and the second largest exporter. Thus it is quite important that all members of an organization learn as much as they can about each of the cultures with which they may be dealing. When we talk about culture, we simply mean the typical traits of a group of people. We need to learn how these people dress, think, talk, and carry out their business and private affairs.

FORMATTING

E. BLOCKED COLUMN HEADINGS

Blocked column headings align with their columns—at the left for word columns and at the right for number columns.

If a column heading is the longest item in a column, use it as part of the key line to horizontally center the table. Triple-space before and double-space after col-umn headings. Column headings are keyed in upper- and lowercase letters and underlined.

If a column heading is over a column with decimals, set a right tab rather than a decimal tab for the column to right align the column heading.

DOCUMENT PROCESSING

TABLE 7
3-COLUMN TABLE WITH BLOCKED COLUMN HEADINGS

Align columns that contain both words and numbers at the left.

EMPLOYEE UPDATE FILE

New Hires Since March 1

Employee Name	Soc. Sec. No.	Empl. Date
Chalupa, B. J.	246-72-8384	May 1
Dye, R. E.	382-43-8823	May 15
Grunkemeyer, R. L.	130-03-7255	August 15
Ma, P. F.	281-19-2877	July 10
Mundrake, J. A.	380-32-3476	June 9
Sanchez, E. T.	154-14-3228	August 25
Sormunen, R. A.	130-29-9931	June 18
Underwood, R. L.	222-38-0934	July 25
Zimpfer, M. A.	191-73-0221	August 10

TABLE 8
3-COLUMN TABLE WITH BLOCKED COLUMN HEADINGS

These changes require new tab settings.

Make the following changes to Table 7:
1. Ms. Sormunen uses a hyphenated last name: Sormunen-Jones.
2. Mr. Mundrake's social security number is 308-32-3476.

3. Ms. Ma was actually hired on February 27, so her name should be deleted from the table.
4. The following name should be added to the list in alphabetic order: R. T. Alli-son, 379-42-3715, August 31.

LETTER 53
MODIFIED-BLOCK STYLE
FOR WINDOW
ENVELOPE

Working Papers: 177

After formatting Letter 53, fold it for insertion into a window envelope.

Send this letter to Mr. James L. Alvarez / 417 Graham Street / Missoula, MT 59802-6341. Date the letter August 19, 19—.

Dear Mr. Alvarez:

Our firm will be conducting a one-day seminar on Friday, September 23, 19__, in Missoula on a topic that is relatively new. The topic is compaction grouting.

Detailed information for the seminar will be sent to you in about ten days, but you may want to reserve the date on your calendar now. As we expect that many members of the Missoula Builders Association will want to attend, the seminar fee will be only $100.

I, along with other members of our seminar team, shall look forward to seeing you in Missoula on September 23.

Yours truly,

Francis J. Fabereisen, P.E.
Consulting Engineer

PS: A social hour and dinner will follow the seminar.

If a postscript is added to a letter, it is keyed as the last item in the letter, preceded by 1 blank line. If the paragraphs in the letter are indented, the first line of the postscript should be indented as well.

FORMATTING

T. FOREIGN ADDRESSES

Key the name of a foreign country in all-capital letters on a separate line at the end of the address.

```
                              February 17, 19--



Ms. Monique LaCroix
747 Lacasse Street
Bordeaux, Gironde
FRANCE

Dear Ms. LaCroix:
```

TABLE 9

4-COLUMN TABLE WITH
BLOCKED COLUMN
HEADINGS

Spacing: Double
Tabs: 1 left and 3 right
tabs

A table feature in one word processing program enables you to enter a formula to automatically calculate column totals.

WAREHOUSING DEPARTMENT (11)

January Payroll Report (11)

Employee Name	Gross Pay	Deductions (10)	Net Pay
C. S. David	2,025.00	404.75	1,620.25
P. M. Gieselman (156)	1,984.10	396.82	1,587.28
J. T. Peralta	1,278.32	285.66 ~~273.66~~ (6)	992.66
D. J. Terrell	2,406.91	481.38	1,925.53
E. D. Wyllie	2,978.35	595.67	~~2~~382.68 (8)
Total	10,672.68 (9)	~~2,152.28~~ 2,164.28	8,508.40

---

39 LESSON

Tables With Two-Line Blocked Column Headings

Margins: 1 inch • Tab: 5 spaces • Spacing: Single • Drills: 2 times • Format Guide: 15

Goals:
To improve speed and accuracy; to format tables with two-line blocked column headings.

A. WARMUP

1 Four dozen of our taxi drivers had just quit because I 12
2 asked them to drive between 1:30 and 6:45 a.m. Their union 24
3 (Local #2798) hired Page & Lambert to overturn my decision. 36

| 1 | 2 | 3 | 4 | 5 | 6 | 7 | 8 | 9 | 10 | 11 | 12

LANGUAGE ARTS

B. These words are among the 500 most frequently misspelled words in business correspondence.

B. SPELLING

4 complete recent members enclosed determine development site
5 medical facility permanent library however purpose personal
6 electrical implementation representative discussed eligible
7 organization discuss expense minimum performance next areas
8 separate professional changes arrangements reason pay field

SKILLBUILDING

C. Take three 12-second timed writings on each line. The scale shows your wam speed for a 12-second timed writing.

C. 12-SECOND SPRINTS

9 Fritz saw many old jets at the air show held in the spring.
10 Jim kept Gil away because four dozen taxi drivers had quit.
11 They will take their rowboat when they go back to the lake.

12 They caught the last boat back to the mainland at the dock.
13 Fay's wipers quit just when Marv locked the zoo's gate box.
14 Did Mac Wiker prize the five or six big quarterly journals?

| | | | 5 | | | |10| | | |15| | |20| | | |25| | |30| | | |35| | | |40| | | |45| | | |50| | | |55| | | |60

Remember to leave a blank line between the heading entries when formatting memorandums. Also, there are 2 blank lines before the body in a memo.

Remember to use your reference initials when formatting memos.

MEMO TO: Harvey Valenti, Vice-President for Finance
FROM: Patsy Valenti-Jants, President
DATE: *(Current)*
SUBJECT: Policy for franchise allocation

Eight letters have been received the past three or four months from people who would like to consider opening a second Valenti Pizza Parlor in cities with a population under 100,000.

I have concluded that our present policy of awarding only one franchise in a city with a population under 100,000 should be reviewed. Your office can provide useful financial information to aid me in making the correct decision. Please provide me with sales and net profit figures for all Valenti parlors in the four-state area, along with population numbers for the cities in which they are located. I am asking Bill Lakomis to obtain the franchise policies of our top 5 or 6 pizza chain competitors.

FORMATTING

S. WINDOW ENVELOPES

No. 10 window envelopes are often used to eliminate the need for addressing envelopes. Letters are prepared so that the inside address shows through the window.

To format a letter for a window envelope, key the date 2 inches from the top of the page followed by a triple space (leaving 2 blank lines). Next, key the inside address followed by a triple space.

To fold a letter for a window envelope so that the inside address appears through the window:

1. Place the letter *face down,* and fold the bottom third of the letter up toward the top.
2. Fold the top third down so that the address shows.
3. Insert the letter into the envelope with the address facing the window and check to be sure it is visible.

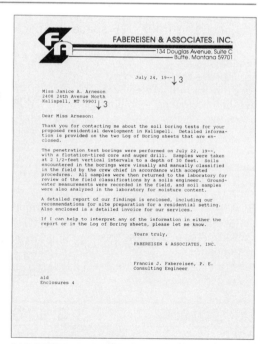

MODIFIED-BLOCK STYLE LETTER FOR WINDOW ENVELOPE

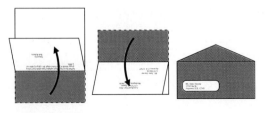

D. PROGRESSIVE PRACTICE: NUMBERS

Turn to the Progressive Practice: Numbers routine at the back of the book. Take six 30-second timed writings, starting at the point where you left off the last time.

E. TECHNIQUE PRACTICE: SHIFT KEY

E. All 26 capital letters are included in the passage. Keep your eyes on the copy, and try not to slow down for the capital letters.

```
15      Z. L. Ford from Eaton, Ohio, and Dr. B. I. Quincy from    12
16  Venice, Utah, attended the Miss America Pageant in Atlantic    24
17  City, New Jersey.  They met Helen X. Wood from South Dakota    36
18  and Gay Y. Kane from Puerto Rico, who is Miss Congeniality.    48
```
| 1 | 2 | 3 | 4 | 5 | 6 | 7 | 8 | 9 | 10 | 11 | 12 |

DOCUMENT PROCESSING

TABLE 10
3-COLUMN TABLE WITH 2-LINE BLOCKED COLUMN HEADING

Leave 2 blank lines between the table title and the first line of a two-line column heading. Underline and single-space each line. The bottom lines of all column headings should align horizontally.

FAX PHONE DIRECTORY

Marketing Representative	Company	Fax Phone
Wayne, Fran	Pinnacle West	415-555-3076
Allan, May	Herman Miller	207-555-1932
Murphy, P. J.	Northern Savings	943-3211
Harp, Dolores	U.S. Markets	802-555-7453
Dawkins, Amy	Western Digital	816-555-2222
Oglesby, Peter	General States	616-555-8654
Carmichael, Robert	Quaker & Southern	481-3287
Tanton, Clay	Sears Mobil	802-555-2961
Eaton, T. Susan	Fairchild Industries	719-555-0841
Latz-Wells, Ada	Healthco	314-555-8765
Shaorenzski, Mike	Circus Pacific	943-5768
Coffin, William	Central Air	802-555-3333
Boyer, Ellen	Smithfield	816-555-3429
Kuiper, Cheryl	Union Labs	733-8655
Hebert, Marilyn	Rubbermaid	831-3288
McKenna, P. O.	Guilford Mills	605-555-3838
May, Martin	RJR Nabisco	800-555-0888
Rodriguez, Robert	Nordstrom	314-555-2907

R. TWO-PAGE LETTERS

To format a two-page business letter:

1. Key the first page on letterhead stationery and the second page on plain paper that matches the letterhead.
2. Use a standard format for page 1 and leave at least a 1-inch bottom margin.
3. Key the page 2 heading (addressee's name, page number, and date) 1 inch from the top, blocked at the left margin and followed by a double space.

```
↓ 1 inch
Mr. Michael J. O'Keefe
Page 2
August 14, 19--↓ 2
since May 1, 19--. As you have lived at your present address for
eight months of the year, you are required to pay state income
taxes on two-thirds of your reported federal taxable income.
```

DOCUMENT PROCESSING

LETTER 52
TWO-PAGE LETTER IN MODIFIED-BLOCK STYLE WITH STANDARD PUNCTUATION

Working Papers: 173

Treat this comment as a display paragraph.

Page-ending guidelines:
1. Do not divide the last word on a page.
2. Leave at least 2 lines of a paragraph at the bottom of the first page and carry forward at least 2 lines of the paragraph to the next page.
3. Page 2 should contain at least 2 lines of the body of the letter.

August 16, 19— / Mr. Myron D. Maciewski / MDM Furniture and Carpet, Inc. / 4200 Havre Avenue / Great Falls, MT 59405-3287 / Dear Mr. Maciewski:

At your request I inspected the commercial building located at 407 Larch Street on August 15, 19—.

This is a one-story, wood-frame structure with a full basement. It is approximately four years old and has been used as a warehouse facility.

In addition, I reviewed the Franz Intertec report. (The report is enclosed for the record.) Of particular concern are their comments that relate to the fill material on which the building stands:

> Two soil borings were taken on the west side of the building. They revealed that the fill material is in a soft, loose condition.

They go on to say that the fill material is compressible under the weight of the building and the weight of the fill itself. This is a nice way of saying that the structure is going to settle.

The basement floor slab has a number of cracks, some patched, of varying size. I noticed a pattern that seemed to imply a settlement of the west wall area. Further investigation showed that the structure slopes from 1 1/2 to 2 inches toward the west wall. Further settling may require the use of a new procedure called compaction grouting to raise the west wall.

On the basis of a review of the Franz report and my inspection of the facility, I would make two recommendations should you wish to further consider the purchase of the building. First, have the compaction reports that are available in the City Buildings office reviewed by a soils engineer. Second, obtain an estimate from a contractor for compaction grouting.

If I can be of further help, please let me know.

Yours truly, / FABEREISEN & ASSOCIATES, INC. / Francis J. Fabereisen, P.E. / Consulting Engineer / (Your Initials) / Enclosure

TABLE 11
3-COLUMN TABLE WITH
2-LINE BLOCKED
COLUMN HEADING

Revise Table 10 as follows:
1. Delete the names of and information for Dolores Harp and Marilyn Hebert.
2. Double-space the body of the table.
3. Add the following name and information at the end of the table: Steven L.

Pierce, Allied Fertilizer, 919-555-4022.
4. Change Clay Tanton's telephone number to 617-555-4370.
5. Change Martin May's company and telephone number as follows: Neiman Industries, 601-555-8990.

TABLE 12
4-COLUMN TABLE WITH
2-LINE BLOCKED
COLUMN HEADING

Spacing: Double

ROI stands for *Return on Investment.*

STOCK PORTFOLIO ANALYSIS

For Year Ended June 30

Company	Percent of Total	Major Product	ROI %
Mellon Bank	29.3	Retail banking	23.1
Occidental Oil	21.7	Agribusiness	5.4
Stanley Works	15.6	Home improvement	8.6
Norfolk Southern	12.6	Rail shipments	12.5
Armstrong World	11.7	Floor coverings	7.4
Tyson Foods	9.1	Poultry products	9.5
TOTAL	100.0		66.5

(handwritten notes: underline for longest #3x, DS.)

Formatting Review

LESSON 40

Margins: 1 inch • Tab: 5 spaces • Spacing: Single • Drills: 2 times • Format Guide: 15–17 • Working Papers: 47

Goals:
To key 36 wam/3'/4e; to format a table, a report, and a letter.

A. WARMUP

1 Just five or six of my quarterly journals cost as much 12
2 as $45 a year; most cost me between $16 and $30. A sizable 24
3 number of them are free, but Parks Digest is $27.89 a year. 36

| 1 | 2 | 3 | 4 | 5 | 6 | 7 | 8 | 9 | 10 | 11 | 12 |

LANGUAGE ARTS

B. Compare this table with the body of Table 13 on the next page. Key a list of the errors, correcting them as you key.

B. PROOFREADING

Date	Resort	State	Price (Mil)
1989	Steamboat	Colorado	$110
1989	Stratton	Vermont	85
1990	Heavenly Valley	Colorado	80
1898	Brackenridge	California	65
1990	Snowshoe	West Virginia	20

DEEP LETTERHEAD. For a letterhead deeper than 2 inches, key the date ½ inch below the letterhead.

DISPLAY PARAGRAPHS. Indent 5 spaces from each margin. Double-space before and after.

COMPANY NAME IN CLOSING LINES. Key in all-capital letters a double space below the complimentary closing. Leave 3 blank lines between the company name and the writer's name.

LEFT-WEIGHTED STATIONERY. Move the left margin ½ inch to the right of the widest item in the left column of the letterhead.

DEEP-LETTERHEAD STATIONERY. Letter shown in block style with open punctuation.

LEFT-WEIGHTED STATIONERY. Letter shown in modified-block style with standard punctuation.

DOCUMENT PROCESSING

LETTER 50
BLOCK STYLE

Working Papers: 169

Format this letter for deep-letterhead stationery, and insert the company name in the closing lines as illustrated above.

Treat this quotation as a display paragraph. Indent 5 spaces from each margin.

(Current Date) / Mr. Adolph R. Thompson / 734 28th Avenue South / Grand Forks, ND 58201 / Dear Mr. Thompson:

Your letter in which you inquired about the opening of a second Valenti Pizza Parlor in Grand Forks arrived yesterday. My parents opened the doors of their first parlor almost 20 years ago. When they expanded to a franchise operation in 1985, they adopted the following as one of their guidelines:

Population size shall be the primary consideration in determining the number of parlors to be authorized in a particular city.

The specific application of this guideline has been to award only one Valenti Pizza Parlor franchise in a city with a population of less than 100,000. As you likely are aware, the population of Grand Forks is somewhat less than this.

I would like to keep your inquiry on file. If this policy should change at some future date, I shall let you know.

Sincerely yours, / VALENTI PIZZA PARLORS / Patsy Valenti-Jants / President / (Your Initials)

LETTER 51

Working Papers: 171

Format this letter for left-weighted stationery as illustrated above.

Revise Letter 50 as follows: Send the letter to Mr. and Mrs. Francis E. Lessar / 426 Second Street, SE / Rochester, MN 55904. Remember to change the salutation.

Change *Grand Forks* to *Rochester* in both the first and third paragraphs. Also, delete the company name in the closing lines.

C. DIAGNOSTIC PRACTICE: ALPHABET

Turn to the Diagnostic Practice: Alphabet routine at the back of the book. Take the Pretest and record your performance. Then, practice the drill lines for those reaches on which you made errors. Finally, repeat the Pretest and compare your performance.

D. Take two 1-minute timed writings. The last two digits of each number provide a cumulative word count to help you determine your wam speed.

D. NUMBER PRACTICE

11 1801 3802 3403 2904 3805 4606 1107 0208 3909 4810 8711 9112
12 3813 3914 3015 3416 1217 9918 0719 6820 0621 5622 2123 2024
13 3425 3026 2227 9828 5729 5930 3631 4032 2433 2934 0135 2636
14 7137 3438 6439 8340 2941 4942 1243 3444 0945 8746 6947 0348

E. Spacing: double. Take two 3-minute timed writings. Compute your speed and count errors.

Goal: 36 wam/3'/4e

E. 3-MINUTE TIMED WRITING

15   Everyone is aware that his or her actions must never 12
16 exceed the law. However, it is sometimes true that being 23
17 legally right does not justify our actions. All of us have 35
18 our own code of ethics, or rules of conduct that go beyond 47
19 legal rules and tell us how to act when the law is silent. 59
20   Ethical people should first ask themselves if what 70
21 they say and what they write are true and then ask if these 82
22 are in the best interests of their organization. They 93
23 should always try to achieve their own goals while acting 105
24 in an ethical manner. 109

| 1 | 2 | 3 | 4 | 5 | 6 | 7 | 8 | 9 | 10 | 11 | 12 |

DOCUMENT PROCESSING

TABLE 13
4-COLUMN TABLE

RECENT SKI RESORT PURCHASES
(1988–90)

Date	Resort	Location	Price (Mil)
1989	Steamboat	Colorado	$110
1989	Stratton	Vermont	85
1990	Heavenly Valley	California	80
1988	Breckenridge	Colorado	65
1990	Snowshoe	West Virginia	20

N. ALPHABET REVIEW: INFREQUENT-LETTER PRACTICE

J 73 Jovial Joe joked with Josh while they jogged in torn jeans. 12
K 74 Kevin Packard knew that Rick and Kelly liked baked chicken. 12
Q 75 Quincy quietly quoted the quip about the quartet's quarrel. 12
X 76 Max fixed those taxi exits for the six excited taxi owners. 12

| 1 | 2 | 3 | 4 | 5 | 6 | 7 | 8 | 9 | 10 | 11 | 12

O. DIAGNOSTIC PRACTICE: NUMBERS

Turn to the Diagnostic Practice: Numbers routine at the back of this book. Take the Pretest and record your performance. Then practice the drill lines for those reaches on which you made errors. Finally, repeat the Pretest and compare your performance.

P. Spacing: double.
Take two 5-minute timed writings. Compute your speed and count errors.

Goal: 45 wam/5'/5e

P. 5-MINUTE TIMED WRITING

77   It seems as if there are many people around today who   12
78 have put themselves into a stressful situation because they   24
79 have made a decision they feel is morally wrong. Whether   35
80 it is adjusting sales numbers, borrowing office supplies,   47
81 or stretching an expense account, they know deep down that   59
82 they have made unethical choices.   66

83   Many people contend that there is now a large gray   77
84 area between right and wrong, and they use it as an excuse   89
85 not to worry about being ethical. Business students must   100
86 question that logic. Much of the grayness can be taken out   112
87 of ethical dilemmas if one takes the time to sort things   124
88 through. It is easy to charge ahead without thinking and   135
89 then rationalize your behavior after the fact. But the   146
90 truth is that there is no right way to do a wrong thing.   158

91   More and more companies are trying to provide ethical   170
92 guidelines for their employees by clearly stating the type   181
93 of behavior they expect. If a company wishes to be viewed   193
94 as honest, unbiased, and moral, then it must encourage its   205
95 employees to be responsible for their actions and not to   216
96 engage in unethical or immoral behaviors.   225

| 1 | 2 | 3 | 4 | 5 | 6 | 7 | 8 | 9 | 10 | 11 | 12

INVESTING IN THE SKI RESORT INDUSTRY
By I. William Berry

REPORT 10

Spacing: Double

A review of industry and demographic data shows that Valdese Associates should not explore further the possible purchase of a ski resort either in the Northeast or in the Northwest.

Industry Trends

Neither past performance nor the outlook for the future provides any support for investing in a ski resort.

Past Performance. Most of the $7 billion U.S. ski resort industry lost money last year. Analysts attribute the poor economic showing to a combination of bad weather, a weak economy, uncontrolled costs, and overbuilding.

Future Outlook. Strict environmental controls are making it difficult for resorts to make the capital improvements that are needed to attract more business. In addition, the weak housing market and tax-law changes have weakened condominium sales, which formerly provided a major share of resort profits.

Demographic Data

By its nature, skiing tends to attract 25- to 35-year-olds in the middle- to upper-income brackets. But as the U.S. population ages and as a weak economy continues, the interest in skiing will probably dwindle, making the purchase of a ski resort a risky investment for Valdese Associates.

LETTER 13
BLOCK STYLE

Working Papers: 47

May 5, 19— / Mr. Hiro Matsushita / Director of Planning / Valdese Associates / 30 South Wacker Drive / Chicago, IL 60606-1233 / Dear Mr. Matsushita:

As you requested, I have studied the feasibility of Valdese Associates' investing in the U.S. ski resort industry. I reviewed industry and demographic data and spoke with several resort operators.

The enclosed report summarizes my initial reactions and may be used for your Investment Committee meeting in July. A more detailed report will be prepared in time for your annual planning meeting in August. I've also enclosed a table showing the recent selling prices of ski resorts. Incidentally, all resorts were purchased by Japanese concerns.

Please call me if you wish additional information for your July committee meeting or if you wish me to explore additional segments of the market for the August report.

Sincerely, / Malcolm J. Davis / Management Consultant / (Your Initials) / Enclosures

J. TECHNIQUE PRACTICE: RETURN KEY

J. Key each sentence on a separate line.

42 Cut the lawn. Wash the glasses. Vacuum the kitchen floor.
43 Paint the bedroom. Dust the furniture. Put up the shades.
44 Clean out the attic. Repair the window. Spade the garden.
45 Trim the bushes. Sweep the sidewalk. Replace the battery.
46 Clean out the cellar. Put up the wallpaper. Wash the car.

K. TECHNIQUE PRACTICE: CONCENTRATION

K. Insert the necessary capital letters as you key these sentences twice.

47 Diane and jim took the new jersey turnpike to philadelphia.
48 The chicago bears will play the buffalo bills on october 9.
49 When visiting san francisco, you can see fisherman's wharf.
50 Vicki and frank will take megan for a vacation to cape cod.
51 Take time to explore the piazza san marco in venice, italy.

L. 12-SECOND SPRINTS

L. Take three 12-second timed writings on each line. The scale gives wam for a 12-second timed writing.

52 Please send me 35 cases of part number 907864 by August 12.
53 The 1:30 game drew a crowd of 78,569 on Sunday, October 24.
54 I counted 29 or 30 cars in the lot at 4856 North 17 Avenue.
55 Models 74, 86, and 93 were out of stock for 15 to 20 weeks.
56 Order #459367 will likely be received within 18 or 20 days.

| | | | |5| | | |10| | |15| | |20| | |25| | |30| | |35| | |40| | |45| | |50| | |55| | |60

M. SUSTAINED PRACTICE: CAPITALIZATION

M. Take a 1-minute timed writing on the first paragraph to establish your base speed. Then take four 1-minute timed writings on the remaining paragraphs. As soon as you equal or exceed your base speed on one paragraph, advance to the next one.

57   The senior class from the area high school have worked 12
58 on raising funds for the class trip for the past two years. 24
59 The class members will be holding a meeting within the next 36
60 two weeks to make the final selection of their destination. 48

61   The meeting was scheduled for one day next week. Four 12
62 class members will give an overview of the choices for this 24
63 trip. It seems that New York and Boston will be the cities 36
64 that will receive the most support from many class members. 48

65   Many of the members of the class are in favor of going 12
66 to New York City because they are anxious to see the Statue 24
67 of Liberty and the Empire State Building. In addition, the 36
68 members of the class are hoping to see the midtown section. 48

69   The members of the class wanting to go see Boston have 12
70 a number of sites in mind. They are anxious to see the Old 24
71 North Church and the Bunker Hill Monument. Some want to go 36
72 visit Fenway Park, the home of the baseball Boston Red Sox. 48

| | 1 | 2 | 3 | 4 | 5 | 6 | 7 | 8 | 9 | 10 | 11 | 12

proofreader's marks – p.66

Progress Test on Part 2

TEST 2

TEST 2-A
3-MINUTE TIMED
WRITING

Spacing: Double

Working Papers: 51

When doing a tax return for a small business, the use 12
of Schedule C will be required. In the first stage, the 24
gross income is found. Once gross income is determined, a 35
careful check of all the deductions and expenses is made. 46
Analyzing all of these dollar amounts is very important 57
because it can reduce the net profit that will be carried 69
forward so that a person's taxable income is found. Using 81
a tax table or a tax rate schedule, a tax person can find 93
the amount of tax that is owed. To complete Schedule C 103
will require hours. 108

| 1 | 2 | 3 | 4 | 5 | 6 | 7 | 8 | 9 | 10 | 11 | 12

o manage own line lengths!

p.50

12

NOV. 23 1994

Inside Address

Dear Mr. Sheldrake!

BODY
Sin the space
Double Betw. par –

Sincerely yours,

Donald C. Williams
Account Executive

Enclosure

(Current Date) / Mr. Ralph Sheldrake, Director / Administrative Office Services / Seneca Pharmaceutical, Inc. / 62 Fontana Avenue / Nashville, TN 37204 / Dear Mr. Sheldrake:

Your inquiry about the training program that we have available for data-entry clerks has come to my attention. I believe that we have just the training package that you are looking for.

I am enclosing a copy of this instructional package to review on a ten-day trial basis without charge. When you have had an opportunity to review it, I am confident that you will be impressed with its capability to train your data-entry clerks.

In two weeks I will contact you to arrange a time when I can meet with you to answer any questions you may have about the program. At that time we can determine whether you would be interested in using this program on a full-time basis.

Sincerely yours, / Donald C. Williams / Account Executive / (Your Initials) /
Enclosure

D. PACED PRACTICE

Turn to the Paced Practice routine at the back of the book. Take four 2-minute timed writings, starting at the speed at which you left off the last time.

E. PRETEST: DISCRIMINATION PRACTICE

14   Did the new clerk join your golf team? John indicated 12
15 to me that Beverly invited her prior to last Wednesday. He 24
16 believes she must give you a verbal commitment at once. We 36
17 should convince her to join because she is a gifted golfer. 48

| 1 | 2 | 3 | 4 | 5 | 6 | 7 | 8 | 9 | 10 | 11 | 12 |

F. PRACTICE: LEFT HAND

18 vbv bevy verb bevel vibes breve viable braves verbal beaver
19 wew went week weans weigh weave wedges thawed weaker beware
20 ded dent need deals moved ceded heeded debate edging define
21 fgf guff gift flags foggy gaffe forget gifted guffaw fights

G. PRACTICE: RIGHT HAND

22 klk kale look kilts lakes knoll likely kettle kernel lacked
23 uyu buys your gummy dusty young unduly tryout uneasy jaunty
24 oio oils roil toils onion point oriole soiled ration joined
25 jhj jell heed eject wheat joked halved jalopy heckle jigsaw

H. POSTTEST: DISCRIMINATION PRACTICE

I. SUSTAINED PRACTICE: NUMBERS AND SYMBOLS

26   Retailers need to carefully consider the markup on any 12
27 items that are sold. They also have to be especially aware 24
28 of their inventory status on various products. Controlling 36
29 these factors can help ensure the success of the operation. 48

30   For example, purchasing items that cost $50 each and a 12
31 markup of 20% would give the retailer a markup of $10 for a 24
32 selling price of $60. On the other hand, if the markup was 36
33 30%, the selling price for an individual item would be $65. 48

34   The inventory on these items (#3410, #4223, and #5920) 12
35 has been depleted very rapidly. The supplier (Kell & Drew) 24
36 for these items is located in Cambridge. Place a new order 36
37 with them. In addition, order a supply of #6120 and #6430. 48

38   The new items (#6120 and #6430) must be priced at $20, 12
39 which would be a markup of 40%. Increase the markup to 50% 24
40 on those items (#3410, #4223, and #5920) being replenished. 36
41 Kell & Drew will be pleased with this new order for $1,600. 48

| 1 | 2 | 3 | 4 | 5 | 6 | 7 | 8 | 9 | 10 | 11 | 12 |

Spacing: Double

Working Papers: 55

Center horizontally and vertically.

GLOBE COMPUTER SUPPLIES, INC.
Sales of Computer Furniture

Item	Number	Percent
Workstation	370	26.2
Riser	334	23.7
Printer Stand	273	19.3
Storage Hutch	147	10.5
Mobile Micro Cart	132	9.3
PC Tilt & Swivel	88	6.2
Shelf Riser	68	4.8
TOTAL	1,412	100.0

Spacing: Double

Working Papers: 57

JOB SPECIFICATIONS
By Judith Durish

Personnel departments have the responsibility of working with department supervisors to determine the specifications or requirements for a given position. Two common criteria often found in job specifications are education and experience.

Education Requirements

Some education beyond the secondary level is becoming more and more common when job openings are advertised. This post-secondary education can be at a private business school, a two-year community college, or a four-year college.

Experience Requirements

There are two aspects of experience that may be required. One deals with time spent in the work force, and the other deals with specific skills used on the job.

Time in Work Force. There might be a requirement that an individual have a minimum number of years in a certain position to be considered for the advertised job.

Specific Skills on Job. It is possible that the job being advertised requires an individual who has some specific skills. For example, the applicant must know "Word Perfect."

Margins: 1 inch • Spacing: Single • Drills: 2 times • Format Guide: 59–63 • Working Papers: 169–186

Goals for Unit 18

Begin each day with approximately 15 minutes of skill-building, selecting activities from pages 198–201. In the remaining class time, complete as many production jobs from pages 202–208 as you can.

1. To improve accuracy and speed on alphabet and number keys.
2. To key 45 wam for 5 minutes with no more than 5 errors.
3. To improve proofreading skills.
4. To format and key correspondence from various types of input, including handwritten, rough-draft, and unarranged text.
5. To format and key correspondence making various changes for two-page letters, multiple addresses and writers, special letterheads, and window envelopes.
6. To format and key memorandums with different features.

A. WARMUP

```
1      Three law firms (Quentin & Brint, Zenith & Jevsen, and   12
2 Paxen & Krey) submitted statements to collect the following   24
3 amounts for the legal actions:  $872.50, $940.30, and $610.   36
   |  1  |  2  |  3  |  4  |  5  |  6  |  7  |  8  |  9  | 10 | 11 | 12
```

LANGUAGE ARTS

B. Study the rules at the right. Then key lines 4–7, making necessary changes.

B. COMMAS

Rule: Do not use commas to set off an expression that is *essential* to the completeness of a sentence.

Those workers who have seniority will have preference.

Rule: Use commas to set off the year when it follows the month and day.

They will meet on July 24, 1994, in Government Center.

```
4 The form was received after you left last evening.
5 All students, who are commuters, are invited to attend.
6 The December 31 1995 deadline will not be changed.
7 The book being published in April 1994 is on schedule.
```

C. Compare this paragraph with the last paragraph of the 5-minute timed writing on page 201. Key a list of the words that contain errors, correcting the errors as you key.

C. PROOFREADING

```
8      More and more companies are trying to provide ethacal
9 guide lines for their employees by clearly stating the type
10 of behavior they expect.  If a company wishes to be veiwed
11 as honest, unbiased, and morale, then it must encourage is
12 employees to be responsable for their actions and not to
13 engage in unethical or immorale behaviors.
```

SKILLBUILDING
Correspondence, Reports, and Employment Documents

OBJECTIVES

KEYBOARDING

To key 40 words a minute on a 5-minute timed writing with no more than 5 errors.

LANGUAGE ARTS

To improve language arts skills, including correct grammar and spelling and the correct use of punctuation marks, capitalization, and numbers.

To proofread documents and correct errors.

To develop keyboard composing skill.

DOCUMENT PROCESSING

To format memorandums and modified-block style letters.

To format one- and two-page unbound and bound reports with enumerations, footnotes, endnotes, bibliographies, and supplementary pages.

To prepare employment documents, including a resume, a letter of application, and a follow-up letter; and take an employment test.

© Andy Sacks/Tony Stone Worldwide

TABLE 35
FOUR-COLUMN RULED
TABLE

Spacing: Double

STEINBAUGH ASSOCIATES
NEW HIRES
June 15, 19--

Employee	SS Number	Division	Rank
Dansby, Julie	237-50-6713	Payroll	G-3
Helma, Thomas	312-78-9267	Finance	G-5
Isaac, Lewis	423-89-2313	Payroll	G-3
Richards, Donald	231-81-4876	Receiving	G-5
Ripley, Keith	237-67-3481	Office	G-5
Seijo, Rose	145-78-6612	Purchasing	G-8
Solomon, Albert	673-33-8923	Sales	G-9
Vasquez, Mary	567-24-7812	Mail	G-3

Leave 3 blank lines before and after a table with a title.

MEMO TO: Kurt Smith, Advertising Designer

FROM: Louise Grooms, Purchasing

DATE: June July 25, 19--

SUBJECT: New Copy for Two-Drawer Filing Cabinets

I have just written completed the copy for our three-dawer two-drawer filing cabinets for the 1994 catalog. I am sure the following copy table will meet all of the your specifications established by you.

TWO THREE-DRAWER FILING CABINETS--49" 42" HIGH

Color	Size	Style	Price
Black	Letter	E4-512-P	$163.00
Tropic Sand	Letter	E4-512-K	163.50
Putty	Legal Letter	E4-512-L	163.00
Light Gray	Letter	E4-512-Q	146.00 145.5
Tropic Sand	Legal	E4-512C-7	195.00
Black	Legal	E4-512C-8	195.50
Putty	Legal	E4-512-9	195.00
Light Grey	Letter Legal	E4-512C-X	187.00

If you have questions about this table as an insert, please let me know.

initials

LESSON 41

Memorandums

Margins: 1 inch • Tab: 5 spaces • Spacing: Single • Drills: 2 times • Format Guide: 17—19 • Working Papers: 59—62

Goals:
To improve speed and accuracy; to format interoffice memorandums.

A. WARMUP

1   A 14-page report was faxed to 26 new offices in all 13   12
2 zones in this region. Total costs for my project were very   24
3 high, $98,750; and there likely will be numerous questions.   36

   | 1 | 2 | 3 | 4 | 5 | 6 | 7 | 8 | 9 | 10 | 11 | 12

SKILLBUILDING

PRETEST.
Take a 1-minute timed writing; compute your speed and count errors.

PRACTICE.
Speed Emphasis: If you made 2 or fewer errors on the Pretest, key each line twice.
Accuracy Emphasis: If you made 3 or more errors, key each group of lines (as though it were a paragraph) twice.

POSTTEST.
Repeat the Pretest (B) and compare performance.

B. PRETEST: CLOSE REACHES

4   Did anybody try to stymie the enemy when he loaded his   12
5 weapon? Sad to say, all fifty of them had no choice but to   24
6 attempt to avoid more bloodshed by not making a loud noise.   36

   | 1 | 2 | 3 | 4 | 5 | 6 | 7 | 8 | 9 | 10 | 11 | 12

C. PRACTICE: ADJACENT KEYS

7 tr traded tragic sentry trace tries stray extra metro retry
8 po pocket poorly teapot point poise pound spoke vapor tempo
9 sa salads sanded mimosa sadly safer usage essay visas psalm
10 oi boiled noises choice oiled doing coins avoid broil spoil

D. PRACTICE: CONSECUTIVE FINGERS

11 my myself myrtle myopia myths myrrh enemy foamy roomy slimy
12 ft drafts soften thrift after often fifty lifts craft graft
13 ny anyone canyon colony nylon nymph vinyl agony corny funny
14 lo loaded blouse pueblo loans locks along color hello cello

E. POSTTEST: CLOSE REACHES

FORMATTING

F. INTEROFFICE MEMORANDUMS

An interoffice memorandum is usually sent from one person to another in the same organization. Plain paper, letterhead stationery, or special memo forms may be used. Follow these steps to format a memo on plain paper or letterhead stationery:

1. Margins: 1-inch side; 2-inch top.

2. Heading lines: bold; double spaced.

3. Tab: 10 spaces; left tab to align heading information.

4. Double-space the heading lines; triple-space to key the body.

5. Double-space and key your reference initials.

TABLE 34
BALANCE SHEET WITH
LEADERS

Center the table vertically.

Leave 2 spaces between money columns.

To keep your place when keying a financial statement, put a ruler or card under the line being keyed, and keep moving it as you go down the page.

BARKER-FOWLER ELECTRICAL REPAIR↓2

BALANCE SHEET↓2

October 31, 19--↓3

ASSETS↓2

Current Assets:
Cash	$ 9,475.03	
Change Fund	75.00	
Accounts Receivable	12,581.35	
Merchandise Inventory	8,523.00	
Prepaid Insurance	250.00	
Total Current Assets		$30,904.38

Equipment:
Repair Equipment	$12,350.00	
Office Equipment	6,230.50	
Total Equipment		18,580.50↓2

Total Assets		$49,484.88↓3

LIABILITIES↓2

Current Liabilities:
Accounts Payable	$ 435.74	
Sales Taxes Payable	315.00	
Federal Income Taxes Payable . . .	425.00	
FICA Taxes Payable	440.00	
State Income Taxes Payable	212.00	
Federal Unemployment Taxes Payable .	125.00	
State Unemployment Taxes Payable . .	90.00	
State Small Business Taxes Payable .	230.00	
Total Current Liabilities		$ 2,272.74

Long-Term Liabilities:
Three-Year Bank Note Payable		15,500.00

Total Liabilities		$17,772.74↓3

OWNERS' EQUITY↓2

Fred L. Barker, Capital	$15,856.07	
Lance J. Fowler, Capital	15,856.07	31,712.14

Total Liabilities and Owner's Equity		$49,484.88

MEMO 1

Tab: 10 spaces

Working Papers: 59

Key the bold headings: *MEMO TO:, FROM:, DATE:,* and *SUBJECT:*

Most memos are keyed with blocked paragraphs (no indentions) and 1 blank line between paragraphs.

The use of *MEMO TO:* eliminates the need to key the word *MEMORANDUM* at the top of the document. After keying the colon at the end of each bold heading, tab once to reach the point where the heading entries begin.

Key your initials for the reference initials.

↓ 2 inches ⎸ Tab

MEMO TO: Curtis Marlowe, Home Designs↓2   line 13

FROM:　　Doug Nestell, Sales Director↓2

DATE:　　October 18, 19--↓2

SUBJECT:　Timber Creek Site↓3

Some observations seem appropriate now that the laying of wiring and conduits for Phase I of the Timber Creek site is being finalized. It is my understanding that a high percentage of Timber Creek residents likely will be first-time home buyers.↓2

Cost will be an important criterion; but on the basis of our previous experience with this type of development, other factors should be considered. Our model homes should reflect today's informal life-style. The use of a great room rather than both a family room and a living room is one way to reduce costs. Also, since both the husband and wife in most homes will work outside the home, there should be two-car garages. We have also found that many people like the option of leaving certain areas unfinished; these can be finished later as the family grows and as finances permit.↓2

I shall be happy to meet with you to discuss these concerns.↓2

bjh

MEMO 2

Tab: 10 spaces

Working Papers: 61

With word processing software, you may be able to use different font styles and sizes and graphics to create distinctive memo headings.

MEMO TO:　Marian Dickenson, Sales Associate

FROM:　　Doug Nestell, Sales Director

DATE:　　October 18, 19—

SUBJECT:　Timber Creek Model Homes

The first model homes at the Timber Creek site will be ready for showing by January 1. On the basis of your sales performance during the past year, I would like to have you assume total marketing responsibility for the project.

This may well come as a complete surprise to you. For that reason, please delay your decision until November 1. You likely will want to think through the nature of this assignment and discuss implications with your family.

I know that you can do a fine job with this project; I hope your answer will be "Yes!"

(Your Initials)

S. FINANCIAL STATEMENTS WITH LEADERS

Financial statements are formatted almost like other tables. The exceptions are:

1. Leave 2 spaces between money columns.
2. Set right tabs for money columns.
3. Key dot leaders to end 2 spaces before the dollar sign in the first money column.
4. Indent individual items under major categories 3 spaces.
5. Key a double underline the width of the longest item in the column to indicate a table (financial) total.

T. DOUBLE UNDERLINE

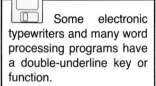

Some electronic typewriters and many word processing programs have a double-underline key or function.

A double underline is used to indicate a table total. To create the first line, turn underlining on and key the text to be underlined. Then use the reverse index key or other appropriate key to turn the paper up one-half line and key the second underline.

DOCUMENT

PROCESSING

TABLE 33
INCOME STATEMENT
WITH LEADERS

Center the financial statement vertically.

Leave 2 spaces between money columns.

Extend the underlines to cover the longest item in each column, including the $ sign.

BARKER-FOWLER ELECTRICAL REPAIR↓2

INCOME STATEMENT↓2

For the Month Ended October 31, 19--↓3

REVENUE FROM SALES
3→ Sales $23,670.25
    Less: Sales Returns $700.10
           Sales Discounts . . . 125.10   825.20
    Net Sales $22,845.05

COST OF GOODS SOLD   3,200.00

GROSS PROFIT ON SALES $19,645.05

OPERATING EXPENSES
    Advertising . . . . $ 1,376.40
    Delivery Service 431.20
    Insurance 150.50
    Payroll Taxes 1,075.00
    Rent 975.00
    Rental (Machine) 100.00
    Salary 10,400.00
    Supplies 375.60
    Utilities 478.31
    Miscellaneous 76.32
    3→ Total Expenses 15,438.33

NET INCOME BEFORE TAXES . . . . $ 4,206.72

Margins: 1 inch • Tab: 5 spaces • Spacing: Single • Drills: 2 times • Format Guide: 19 • Working Papers: 63–70

Goals:
To key 38 wam/3'/3e; to format interoffice memorandums.

A. WARMUP

1   All 32 graduates were given the 555-7469 number. They   12
2 were excited and amazed at how quickly they could get 1,108   24
3 research questions proofed. They just couldn't believe it!   36

| 1 | 2 | 3 | 4 | 5 | 6 | 7 | 8 | 9 | 10 | 11 | 12

LANGUAGE ARTS

B. COMMAS

B. Study the rules at the right. Then key lines 4–7, making necessary changes.

Rule: Use a comma to separate two independent clauses in a compound sentence when they are joined by *and, but, or,* or *nor.*

The bus was late, but he was able to get there on time.

Rule: Use commas to separate three or more items in a series when the last item is preceded by *and, or,* or *nor.*

The invoice, contract, and cashier's check were enclosed.

4 Joan works in Plainview but Joyce works in Gwinn.
5 Two men came to the house and they installed the furnace.
6 Promotions were received by Matt Pamela and Sissy.
7 The grapes plums and peaches were sent from California.

SKILLBUILDING

C. PACED PRACTICE

Turn to the Paced Practice routine at the back of the book. Take three 2-minute timed writings, starting at the speed at which you left off the last time.

D. Spacing: double. Take two 3-minute timed writings. Compute your speed and count errors.

Goal: 38 wam/3'/3e

D. 3-MINUTE TIMED WRITING

8   The profit motive is the one main force that drives   11
9 the economy of this country. Strong arguments are voiced   23
10 which support the belief that all of the profits should be   35
11 used either to expand business growth or to pay those who   46
12 own the stock.   49
13   In the past few decades, most business firms seem to   61
14 be judged more and more by the extent to which profit   72
15 dollars are used to satisfy citizens' needs. An example   83
16 would be the providing of quality day-care centers for   94
17 parents who work. Also, there are more and more concerns   106
18 about the environment and consumer needs.   114

| 1 | 2 | 3 | 4 | 5 | 6 | 7 | 8 | 9 | 10 | 11 | 12

LETTER 48
BLOCK-STYLE LETTER
WITH THREE-COLUMN
TABLE

Working Papers: 165

Leave 1 blank line before and after a table with column headings but no title.

August 1, 19— / Mr. Alex Horton / Vice President for Sales / Bower & Lyons, Inc. / 5623 McCormick Boulevard / Chicago, IL 60659-2317 / Dear Mr. Horton:

Thank you for your letter of July 24 in which you inquired about our company's distributing your new fax machines in Florida.

Listed below are the cities, the number of units in each city and its surrounding area, and our fax representative in that city.

City	Units	Representative
Bradenton	10	Rufus Spencer
Fort Lauderdale	120	Alan Omoto
Miami	115	Virginia L. O'Rourke
Tampa	104	Lewis Garcia

I will be glad to meet with you to discuss the contractual arrangements for our distributing and selling your fax equipment. Please call me at your convenience to establish a date for our meeting.

Sincerely yours, / Louise Atkinson / Vice President / *Your Initials* / c: Jack Martin

LETTER 49
MODIFIED-BLOCK STYLE
LETTER WITH FOUR-
COLUMN TABLE

Working Papers: 167

Leave 3 blank lines before and after a table with a title.

March 15, 19— / Mr. Robert Karns, Editor / Office Systems Publications, Inc. / 31 St. James Street / Boston, MA 02116-0326 / Dear Mr. Karns:

I have just compiled the information you requested about our office employees last week. Listed below is the data on our employees' ages and gender for your article.

THE J. THOMPSON COMPANY
Employee Age Distribution and Gender

Age	Male	Female	Total
20–39	31	159	190
40–59	52	64	116
60–65	30	38	68
TOTAL	113	261	374

I hope this information will assist you with your writing.

Sincerely yours, / Jason Smith / Research Director / *Your Initials*

E. ATTACHMENT NOTATION

Attachment (rather than *Enclosure*) is keyed below the reference initials when material is physically attached (stapled or clipped) to a memorandum.

Example:

(Your Initials)
Attachment

DOCUMENT PROCESSING

MEMO 3

Tab: 10 spaces

Working Papers: 63

Single Space / Block (handwritten)

MEMO TO: Randy Garner, President
FROM: Doug Nestell, Sales Director
DATE: October 20, 19--
SUBJECT: Marketing of Timber Creek site

The Timber Creek project continues to be a high-priority venture for the company. Curtis Marlowe and his staff assure me that the the models under construction have been designed to attract first-time homes buyers, with respect to both features and cost. You will be pleased to learn that Marian Dickenson has agreed to assume total marketing responsibility for the project. She has informed me that a tentative plan for media exposure will be ready for our review within ten days. She will likely have some quite imaginative strategies in her plan.

I am confident that the quality reputation of Garner Homes, Inc., will be further enhanced by the Timber Creek project. A schedule of progress reports for the next year is attached.

As you know, it is vitally important that we keep the Timber Creek project on schedule. Garner Homes has built up a great reputation of being able to deliver on time. This reputation has given us a distinct advantage over our competition and we don't want to lose that advantage now.

jlk

Attachment

Use your own reference initials.

MEMO 4

Tab: 10 spaces

Working Papers: 65

Revise Memo 3. Marcie DeWitt, not Marian Dickenson, will assume total marketing responsibility for the project and will have a tentative plan ready for review within 14 days. Make the necessary changes in the second paragraph.

R. RULED TABLES

A ruled table has horizontal rules (lines) that divide the parts of the table. To format a ruled table:

1. Center the table vertically and horizontally.
2. Determine the tab settings.
3. Center and key the title in all-capital letters and bold, double-space, center and key the subtitle, and then single-space.
4. Key a horizontal rule, extending it to the edges of the table.
5. Double-space and key the column headings. Do not underline column headings in a ruled table.
6. Single-space and key the horizontal rule below the column headings.
7. Double-space and key the table body.
8. Single-space after the last line of the body and key the horizontal rule.
9. Double-space and key the total information (if any); then single-space and key the horizontal rule.

DOCUMENT PROCESSING

TABLE 31
THREE-COLUMN RULED TABLE

Align the $ signs at the top and bottom of the column.

CANDIDATES FOR PROMOTION↓2

January 1, 19--↓1

Candidate's Name	New Position Title	Salary ↓2 ↓1
		↓2
D'Hadilla, Tariocha	Engineer I	$ 47,000
Kolberg, Amy	Accountant II	43,200
Solomon, David	Laboratory Technician	29,100
Tracy, James	Auditor	45,000
Wolter, Karl	Sales Representative	38,000 ↓1
		↓2
TOTAL		$202,300 ↓1

TABLE 32
FOUR-COLUMN RULED TABLE

Spacing: Double

Center a table number a double space above the title, and key it in uppercase and lowercase.

Unlike the $ sign, the % sign is used with every number if the word *Percent* does not appear in the column heading.

Table 5

SALARY INCREASES BY LEVEL

Level	Old Salary	New Salary	Increase
T-1	$16,500	$17,500	6.06%
T-2	17,000	18,250	7.35%
T-3	18,500	20,225	9.32%
T-4	19,575	21,000	7.28%
T-5	24,000	26,500	10.42%
T-6	25,700	27,700	7.78%
T-7	28,000	30,000	7.14%
T-8	30,000	32,500	8.33%

Tab: 10 spaces

Working Papers: 67

The use of nicknames and the omission of middle initials and courtesy titles reflect the informal nature of memos as compared with letters.

MEMO TO: Gayle Allenstein
FROM: Hank Swanson, Personnel Director
DATE: October 20, 19--
SUBJECT: Promotion to Department Head

You will be pleased to learn that on November 1, you will be promoted to the position of Head of the Housewares Department. This is a reflection of the confidence we have in you on the basis of your performance at Layton's Department Store over the past 18 months.

The Housewares Department plays a key role in achieving the objectives of our anchor store in downtown Lowell. There is a need for someone with broad experience in the retail field who can provide leadership in this department.

Gayle, I am confident that as Head of the Housewares Department, you will fit in well as a member of the Layton management team. Congratulations!

Remember to key your own reference initials.

MEMO 6

Working Papers: 69

Revise Memo 5. There are some new changes in the November 1 personnel assignments. Gayle Allenstein is now being assigned to head the Home Appliance Department rather than the Housewares Department. Make the necessary revisions in Memo 5 to Gayle.

Modified-Block Style Letters

Margins: 1 inch • Tab: 5 spaces • Spacing: Single • Drills: 2 times • Format Guide: 19–21 • Working Papers: 71–76

Goals:
To improve speed and accuracy; to format modified-block style letters.

A. WARMUP

1 Jack Jacobson said he acquired G & H Imports from Troy 12
2 Frazier in November of 1993. The exact price was $685,240. 24
3 Mr. Jacobson now owns seven (7) retail outlets in the mall. 36

| 1 | 2 | 3 | 4 | 5 | 6 | 7 | 8 | 9 | 10 | 11 | 12

TABLE 28
THREE-COLUMN TABLE
WITH COLUMN
HEADINGS

Spacing: Single

Set a right tab for a heading over a column that contains decimals.

Do not key the % sign in a column when the word *Percent* or a % sign is used in the column heading.

Columns that contain both text and numbers (as in Column 1) are aligned at the left.

SALES VOLUME FOR SELECTED CATEGORIES
March 30, 19—

Model	Sales Volume	Percent of Sales
AC-101	$ 14,360	2.19
AD-222	132,158	20.18
BA-110	66,400	10.14
BE-215	215,340	32.87
CB-200	16,980	2.59
CQ-415	89,470	13.66
DF-316	109,365	16.70
DJ-400	10,945	1.67
TOTAL	$655,018	100.00

TABLE 29
THREE-COLUMN TABLE
WITH COLUMN
HEADINGS

Spacing: Double

VINSON INC. CORPORATE OFFICES
~~June 30~~, July 1, 19--

Name	Company Title	Office
James L. Reade	Chairman of the Board	2106
~~Lousie~~ Lucy Sauce	President	2109
Anthony Koo	Senior Vice President	2104
~~Betty L.~~ Elizabeth Green	Senior Vice President	2102 22
William A. Smith	Vice President	2207 22
Jason T. Fox	Vice President	2209
Mary L. Lox	Comptroller	2113
Lawrence Bass	Secretary	2101

TABLE 30
THREE-COLUMN TABLE
WITH COLUMN
HEADINGS

Spacing: Double

MAGAZINE SUBSCRIPTION RENEWALS
APRIL 15, 19--

DEPARTMENT	MAGAZINE	EMPLOYEE
ACCOUNTING	ISSUES IN ACCOUNTING	LEE BROWN
CORPORATE	FORTUNE	JILL LOGAN
MARKETING	JOURNAL OF MARKETING	ALEY MAY
SALES	BUSINESS WEEK	SUSAN MARCH

B. PROOFREADING

4 The Suncourt was designed specially for the small family.
5 The modest monthly association fees will free you from such
6 chores as lawn mowing and exterior maintainance of the
7 property. This extra liesure time will enable the two of
8 you to enjoy the swimming pool, tennis courts and other
9 health club facilities funded by the association fees.

C. SUSTAINED PRACTICE: PUNCTUATION

C. Take a 1-minute timed writing on the first paragraph to establish your base speed. Then take four 1-minute timed writings on the remaining paragraphs. As soon as you equal or exceed your base speed on one paragraph, advance to the next one.

10 Many young people rent their own apartments after they	12
11 complete their education and secure their first jobs. Some	24
12 acquire a feeling of contentment that lasts for many years.	36
13 After living in rented apartments for a few years, the	12
14 people wish for greater independence. The thought of one's	24
15 becoming a first-time homeowner begins to suddenly develop.	36
16 The possibilities are numerous; four familiar types of	12
17 homes are co-operative apartments, condominiums, one-family	24
18 houses, and townhomes that vary greatly in style and price.	36
19 First-time owners' choices are based on these factors:	12
20 space (square footage), "sweat equity" required, negotiated	24
21 cost, and appearance and quality of the whole neighborhood.	36

| 1 | 2 | 3 | 4 | 5 | 6 | 7 | 8 | 9 | 10 | 11 | 12

D. BUSINESS LETTERS IN MODIFIED-BLOCK STYLE

The modified-block style is one of the most commonly used formats for business letters.

1. Use 1-inch side margins.
2. Set a tab at the center of the page.
3. Key the date 2 inches from the top of the page at the tab setting.
4. Key the inside address 1 inch below the date at the left margin.
5. Double-space before and after the salutation.
6. Single-space the body of the letter, but double-space between paragraphs. Paragraphs may be indented, but the preferred style is blocked.
7. Double-space after the body of the letter and key the complimentary closing at the center tab.
8. Space down 4 lines and key the writer's identification at the center.
9. Double-space and key your reference initials at the left margin.

Many word processing programs have a date code that inserts the current date with just one or two keystrokes.

MODIFIED-BLOCK STYLE. The date, complimentary closing, signature, and writer's identification begin at the center of the page.

Underlined column headings are used to identify the information in the columns. Blocked column headings are used most often because they are quick and easy to format. When formatting tables, set a left tab to align word columns and their headings at the left and set a right tab to align number columns and their headings at the right.

If a column heading is the longest item in a column, use the column heading to determine the key line.

DOCUMENT PROCESSING

TABLE 26
FOUR-COLUMN TABLE
WITH COLUMN
HEADINGS

Spacing: Double

The $ sign is not repeated after the first entry in a column of figures.

SALES BONUSES

September 30, 19--

Representative	Region	Manager	Bonus
Bassetto, Sally	Central	Lukens	$11,525
Chan, Xin-Ben	Southern	Wilson	975
Curtis, Bruce	Western	Whittemore	12,500
Daniels, May	Eastern	Zhang	1,675
Ferns, George	Central	Lukens	2,750
Legoff, May	Northern	Everson	875
Rosaen, Nellie	Southern	Wilson	1,375
Silverman, Rod	Eastern	Zhang	12,655

TABLE 27
THREE-COLUMN TABLE
WITH COLUMN
HEADINGS

Spacing: Double

AUTOMOBILE DEALERS

Company Name	Address	Manager
Beacon Sales, Inc.	5014 Grand River	John F. Lipson
Brooks Imported Cars	1285 Lansing Road	Elsie Stone
Buege Buick, Inc.	3625 Pennsylvania	Alex Larson
Capitol Cadillac	5901 Pennsylvania	Joseph Lewis
Dodge Sales	6131 Saginaw	Jose Ortego
Larson Sales	345 East Mount Hope	May Lewis
Story Oldsmobile	3133 Michigan	Louis Fox
Toyota Sales	134 Grand River	Paul Atkins
White's Ford, Inc.	535 South Cedar	Peter Davis
Wilson Imports	4212 North Larch	Alex Jones

LETTER 15
MODIFIED-BLOCK STYLE

Tab: Center

Working Papers: 71

Save this letter for use in Lesson 44 where you will learn how to fold a letter for a large envelope.

↓ 2 inches *(Current Date)* ↓ 1 inch

Mr. and Mrs. Charles Kolb-Norman
2308 Hannegan Road
Bellingham, Wa 98225

Dear Mr. and Mrs. Kolb-Norman:

Delores Matlon, who hosted the open house at our Ridgeway model last Saturday, has referred your unanswered questions to me. We are pleased that you are interested in a Garner home.

The usual down payment is 20 per cent of the total selling price, but some lending agencies require a smaller amount in certain situations. Garner Homes is not itself involved in the financing of its homes, but we work closely with the financial institutions shown on the enclosed list.

Yes, the lot that you prefer can accommodate a walk-out basement. Delores will be in touch with you soon. We can have your new ridgeway ready for occupancy within 90 days.

Sincerely,

Douglas A. Nestell
Sales Director

(Your Initials)
Enclosure

LETTER 16
MODIFIED-BLOCK STYLE

Tab: Center

Working Papers: 73

Save this letter for use in Lesson 44 where you will learn how to fold a letter for a small envelope.

Stacey Covell and her daughter are buying a home. Use the current date as you format a letter to Ms. Covell / 4304 Keller Lane / Mount Vernon, WA 98273-4156 / Dear Ms. Covell:

We at Garner Homes feel that your selection of a Suncourt townhome is just the right choice for you. Marian Dickenson informs me that she particularly enjoyed working with you over the past few months.

The Suncourt was designed especially for the small family. The modest monthly association fee will free you from such chores as lawn mowing and exterior maintenance of the property. This extra leisure time will enable the two of you to enjoy the swimming pool, tennis courts, and other health club facilities also funded by the association fees.

All townhomes and one-family units at the Timber Creek site are unconditionally guaranteed for the first year of occupancy. If you have any questions or concerns, please let us know. Thank you, Ms. Covell, for selecting a Suncourt townhome.

Sincerely, / Douglas A. Nestell / Sales Director / *(Your Initials)*

M. Take three 1-minute timed writings on each line. Try not to slow down for the capital letters.

M. TECHNIQUE PRACTICE: SHIFT KEY

56 Ray, Bob, and John went to Harrisburg on Tuesday, April 20. 12
57 The Pittsburgh Pirates were playing the Chicago Cubs today. 12
58 Sue took Flight 261 for Miami and Fort Lauderdale on May 6. 12
59 Tom Crane's new address is 15 Lincoln Road in Boise, Idaho. 12

| 1 | 2 | 3 | 4 | 5 | 6 | 7 | 8 | 9 | 10 | 11 | 12 |

N. Change every plural noun to a singular noun.

N. TECHNIQUE PRACTICE: CONCENTRATION

60   The employees read the letters from the annoyed customers
61 and gave the letters to the managers in charge of the sections
62 to handle. The managers will respond to the questions raised
63 by the customers. Hopefully, the answers will be acceptable.

O. PACED PRACTICE

Turn to the Paced Practice routine at the back of the book. Take three 2-minute timed writings, starting at the speed at which you left off the last time.

P. Spacing: double.
Take two 5-minute timed writings. Compute your speed and count errors.

Goal: 44 wam/5'/5e

P. 5-MINUTE TIMED WRITING

64   A recent study, directed by a psychology professor, 11
65 created a method to measure and evaluate the pace of life. 23
66 Researchers observed how fast pedestrians walked on the 35
67 downtown streets, how long it took postal clerks to fill 46
68 out requests, and the number of people wearing watches. 57
69 Of the six countries studied, only Japan beat the United 69
70 States regarding the fast pace of public life. 78
71   Here at home, Boston was shown to be the fastest city, 90
72 followed by New York and then Salt Lake City. The question 102
73 that these facts raise is, why? Why are some cities more 114
74 hectic than others? No one has the entire answer, but one 125
75 theory suggests that fast cities attract people who enjoy 137
76 living life in the fast lane and repel people who despise 149
77 the fast pace. 152
78   Where you live may affect your health. Smoking, a 163
79 major risk factor for heart disease, shows the very same 174
80 regional pattern. Smoking is often linked to stress, and 186
81 living in a time-pressured environment may cause people to 198
82 smoke. So the very next time you are about to rush out the 210
83 door, slow down and don't follow a crazy schedule. 220

| 1 | 2 | 3 | 4 | 5 | 6 | 7 | 8 | 9 | 10 | 11 | 12 |

LETTER 17
MODIFIED-BLOCK STYLE

Tab: Center
Date: Current

Working Papers: 75

Mr. and Mrs. Matthew A. Longstreet are newly retired and have just purchased a Parkview model townhome at Garner's Gillette site in Bellingham. The real estate agent involved was Maria Quintero (not Marian Dickenson). Revise Letter 16 as necessary. The Longstreets live at 3705 41st Street / Bellingham, WA 98226.

LESSON 44 — Envelopes

Margins: 1 inch • Tab: 5 spaces • Spacing: Single • Drills: 2 times • Format Guide: 21 • Working Papers: 79–84

Goals:
To key 38 wam/3'/3e; to format modified-block style letters; to format large and small envelopes.

A. WARMUP

1 "Do you know the glass factory has produced as many as   12
2 762 dozen large jars in one day?" Mavis asked. At 35 cents   24
3 per jar, I can acquire my boss's needs for exactly $981.40.   36

| 1 | 2 | 3 | 4 | 5 | 6 | 7 | 8 | 9 | 10 | 11 | 12

SKILLBUILDING

B. DIAGNOSTIC PRACTICE: ALPHABET

Turn to the Diagnostic Practice: Alphabet routine at the back of this book. Take the Pretest and record your performance. Then practice the drill lines for those reaches on which you made errors. Finally, repeat the Pretest and compare your performance.

C. Spacing: double.
Take two 3-minute timed writings. Compute your speed and count errors.

Goal: 38 wam/3'/3e

C. 3-MINUTE TIMED WRITING

4   There surely is some truth to the notion that those   11
5 with high-level jobs are exposed to more stress factors   23
6 than those who have fairly routine jobs. And yet many top   34
7 executives seem to work and live in a tranquil state, while   46
8 others with quite routine jobs live in a heightened state   58
9 of anxiety.   60
10   Why is this so? While there is no one easy answer,   72
11 there seem to be two major reasons. The first is that   83
12 some people manage stress by being highly organized in both   95
13 their personal and work lives. A second factor is that   106
14 these people have a daily exercise routine.   114

| 1 | 2 | 3 | 4 | 5 | 6 | 7 | 8 | 9 | 10 | 11 | 12

I. PROGRESSIVE PRACTICE: ALPHABET

Turn to the Progressive Practice: Alphabet routine at the back of the book. Take six 30-second timed writings, starting at the point where you left off the last time.

J. Take three 12-second timed writings on each line. The scale gives wam for a 12-second timed writing.

J. 12-SECOND SPRINTS

36 Vince knew that Maxine just passed her formal biology quiz.
37 Felix might hit your jackpot even with the bad quiz answer.
38 Jack Bowman was very excited when my quilt got first prize.
39 Kyle mixed seven quarts of frozen grape juice with sherbet.

| | | |5| | | |10| | | |15| | | 20| | | |25| | | |30| | | |35| | | |40| | | |45| | | |50| | | |55| | | |60

K. Tab: center.
The opening lines of a letter require the quick operation of the Return key. Key these opening lines 3 times as quickly as possible.

K. TECHNIQUE PRACTICE: LETTER OPENING

(Current Date) ↓ 1 inch

Ms. Victoria R. Cull
Human Resources Administrator
Crane Financial Services
87 Lincoln Boulevard
Topeka, KS 66603-3161

Dear Ms. Cull:

L. Take a 1-minute timed writing on the first paragraph to establish your base speed. Then take four 1-minute timed writings on the remaining paragraphs. As soon as you equal or exceed your base speed on one paragraph, advance to the next one.

L. SUSTAINED PRACTICE: SYLLABIC INTENSITY

40   Many routine factory jobs and tasks are often not done   12
41 by people. Machines now perform some work that was done by   24
42 members of the labor force. What happens to these persons?   36
43 More and more firms are taking steps to solve this problem.   48

44   Perhaps you think that this brings about a shortage of   12
45 jobs for those who are laid off. This does not necessarily   24
46 happen because jobs are increasing in many new areas. Many   36
47 new jobs which call for different skills have been created.   48

48   In order to take advantage of these new emerging jobs,   12
49 young people must continue their education after completing   24
50 high school. People with specialized skills can always see   36
51 opportunities for using new skills in a different location.   48

52   History has continually repeated itself with regard to   12
53 this phenomenon. Just review what happened with the intro-   24
54 duction of the automobile to workers who were involved with   36
55 horses. New inventions can invariably require new workers.   48

| 1 | 2 | 3 | 4 | 5 | 6 | 7 | 8 | 9 | 10 | 11 | 12

D. ENVELOPES

Two-letter state abbreviations are keyed in all-capital letters with no periods.

Nothing should be keyed below the city, state, and ZIP Code line on an envelope.

A standard large envelope is 9½ by 4⅛ inches. A standard small envelope is 6½ by 3⅝ inches. Although either of the address formats shown below is acceptable, the format shown for the large envelope

(all-capital letters and no punctuation) is recommended by the U.S. Postal Service for mail that will be sorted by an electronic scanning device.

In business, standard large envelopes are referred to as No. 10 envelopes, and standard small envelopes are referred to as No. 6¾ envelopes.

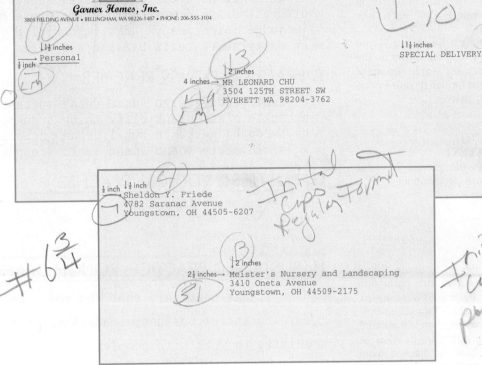

1. **RETURN ADDRESS.** Business envelopes usually have a return address printed in the upper left corner. If it is necessary to key a return address, begin the address ½ inch from both the top and left edges of the envelope. Single-space and block the lines at the left. Do not use the personal title *Mr.* Other titles may be used.

2. **ON-ARRIVAL DIRECTIONS.** Any on-arrival directions, such as *Personal, Confidential, Please Forward,* or *Hold for Arrival,* should be keyed 1½ inches from the top and ½ inch from the left edge of an envelope and underlined.

3. **ADDRESS.** On a large envelope, begin the name and address 2 inches from the top and 4 inches from the left edge

of an envelope. On a small envelope, begin the address 2 inches from the top and 2½ inches from the left edge. Single-space and block all lines at the left. Be sure the city, state, and ZIP Code are on the same line. Use the two-letter state abbreviation and 1 space before the ZIP Code.

When keying foreign addresses, key the country in all-capital letters as the last line of the address.

4. **DELIVERY NOTATIONS.** Key delivery instructions such as *special delivery* or *registered* in all-capital letters 1½ inches from the top of the envelope and ending approximately ½ inch from the right edge.

PRACTICE.
  Speed Emphasis: If you made no more than 1 error on the Pretest, key each line twice.
  Accuracy Emphasis: If you made 2 or more errors on the Pretest, key each group of lines (as though it were a paragraph) twice.

POSTTEST.
Repeat the Pretest (D) and compare performance.

H. Take a 1-minute timed writing on the first paragraph to establish your base speed. Then take four 1-minute timed writings on the remaining paragraphs. As soon as you equal or exceed your base speed on one paragraph, advance to the next one.

D. PRETEST: VERTICAL REACHES

```
 8       Just what does Dr. Carlson think is the basic cause of   12
 9  Justin's scalp problem?  A patch of hair at the back of his   24
10  neck can be treated with a new drug.  I dread that it might   36
11  leave quite a bad scar, but Dr. Carlson thinks it will not.   48
```
| 1 | 2 | 3 | 4 | 5 | 6 | 7 | 8 | 9 | 10 | 11 | 12 |

E. PRACTICE: UP REACHES

```
12  at atlas atone attic batch gates sweat wheat atom bath what
13  dr draft drank dryer drain drama dread dream drag drew drug
14  ju judge juice jumpy junks juror julep jumbo judo jump just
15  es essay nests tests bless dress acres makes uses best rest
```

F. PRACTICE: DOWN REACHES

```
16  ca cable caddy cargo scare decay yucca pecan cage calm case
17  nk ankle blank crank blink think trunk brink bank junk sink
18  ba bacon badge basin tubal urban scuba basic baby back base
19  sc scale scalp scene scent scold scoop scope scan scar disc
```

G. POSTTEST: VERTICAL REACHES

H. SUSTAINED PRACTICE: ROUGH DRAFT

```
20       It has been said that the most important tool required   12
21  for successful business leadership in the future will be an   24
22  ability to work with people.  A leader must be able to push   36
23  workers to be creative and to put forth their best efforts.   48
24  A leader must acknowledge the fact that people are the        12
25  most important resource in any enterprise.  Workers must be   24
26  made to feel part of the team.  It is essential for leaders   36
27  to encourage employees to contribute suggestions and ideas   48
28       Leaders need to maximize output with limited resources   12
29  and carefully monitor the allocation of resource.  This is   24
30  especially critical when the economy is sluggish.  A leader   36
31  is often judged by reviewing the loss and profit statement.   48
32       Successful leaders at every level know that no one has   12
33  all the answers.  However, they also understand that having   24
34  employees who work will together and who share common goals   36
35  and objectives might increase the productivity of any unit.   48
```
| 1 | 2 | 3 | 4 | 5 | 6 | 7 | 8 | 9 | 10 | 11 | 12 |

E. FOLDING LETTERS

To fold a letter for a large envelope:

1. Place the letter *face up* and fold up the bottom third.
2. Fold the top third down to ½ inch from the bottom edge.
3. Insert the last crease into the envelope first, with the flap facing up.

To fold a letter for a small envelope:

1. Place the letter *face up* and fold up the bottom half to ½ inch from the top edge.
2. Fold the right third over to the left.
3. Fold the left third over to ½ inch from the right edge.
4. Insert the last crease into the envelope first, with the flap facing up.

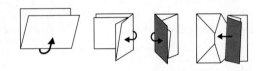

DOCUMENT PROCESSING

LETTER 18
PERSONAL-BUSINESS
LETTER IN MODIFIED-
BLOCK STYLE

Tab: Center
Date: 2 inches

Use November 2, 19—, as the date as you format this personal-business letter to be sent to the Sales Manager at Meister's Nursery and Landscaping / 3410 Oneta Avenue / Youngstown, OH 44509-2175. The letter is from Sheldon Y. Friede / 4782 Saranac Avenue / Youngstown, OH 44505-6207.

Dear Sales Manager:

On April 15 my wife and I purchased eight trees from you: four silver maples at your branch in Warren and four Japanese red maples at your branch in Niles.

After about three months one silver maple and one red maple had died. I telephoned both the Warren and Niles branches several times, but no one returned my messages.

As these trees were expensive, I fully expect that you will replace them next spring. I shall look forward to hearing from you.

Sincerely yours,

81-85 *LESSONS*

Margins: 1 inch • Spacing: Single • Drills: 2 times • Format Guide: 55—59 • Working Papers: 165—167

Goals for Unit 17

Begin each day with approximately 15 minutes of skill-building, selecting activities from pages 187–190. In the remaining class time, complete as many production jobs from pages 191–197 as you can.

1. To improve accuracy and speed on alphabet and number keys.
2. To key 44 wam for 5 minutes with no more than 5 errors.
3. To improve proficiency in composing at the keyboard.
4. To format short and long column heads in tables.
5. To format and key ruled tables and financial statements.
6. To format and key correspondence with tables.

A. WARMUP

1 Joe quickly boarded Flight #578 to Phoenix on July 20.   12
2 He spent $9.75 on snacks and magazines. On his return trip   24
3 on Flight #641, he spent $43.50 to have two gifts for home.   36

| 1 | 2 | 3 | 4 | 5 | 6 | 7 | 8 | 9 | 10 | 11 | 12 |

LANGUAGE ARTS

B. Study the rules at the right. Then key lines 4–7, making necessary changes.

B. COMMAS

Rule: When a dependent clause *precedes* the independent clause, separate the clauses with a comma.

If the quota is reached, a sizable bonus will be paid.

Rule: Use commas to set off a nonessential expression (that is, a word, phrase, or clause that may be omitted without changing the basic meaning of the sentence).

Our new goals, you must admit, are quite reasonable.

4 As you know, if it rains the art show will be held indoors.
5 When the shipment arrives Susan will prepare the display.
6 Our group wants Cory, the current senator, to be a candidate.
7 Michelle who was recently promoted puts in very long days.

C. COMPOSING

Compose the body of a memo to respond to Memo 12, Unit 13, p. 149, using the following suggestions for each paragraph:

Paragraph 1. Confirm that you have discussed the price and terms of the Marx Software with James Clayton and that the site license for the accounting software will cost around $550.

Paragraph 2. Indicate that Bonnie Chandler will be attending the three-day orientation in place of Mable Youngblood because of a previous meeting Mable had scheduled during that week.

Paragraph 3. Close with a positive paragraph that shows how very much interested you are in receiving the software.

LETTER 19
MODIFIED-BLOCK STYLE

Tab: Center

Working Papers: 81

Use today's date as you format this letter to be sent to Mr. Wayne B. Saatzer / 3427 Stromquist Avenue / Lowell, MA 01852-6905 / Dear Mr. Saatzer:

Yesterday we received your letter in which you inquired about employment in our Security Division. Your timing was good, as we do have a position open at the present time.

In order to be considered an official applicant for the position of security officer, you must appear in person at our Personnel Department located on the fourth floor of our downtown Layton store. An Application for Employment form must be completed by you at that time.

When you become an official applicant for a position at Layton's Department Store, you will be kept informed about the status of your application. The interview process for finalists will be completed within two weeks, and our decisions will be made one week later. You will hear from us soon.

Yours truly, / Holly Jean Lainsbury / Personnel Department / *(Your Initials)*

LETTER 20
MODIFIED-BLOCK STYLE

Tab: Center
Date: Current

Working Papers: 83

Ms. Lorna J. Jordan has inquired about employment as a buyer in the Purchasing Department at Layton's Department Store. Ms. Jordan lives at 637 Melrose Avenue, Apt. 209 / Lowell, MA 01854. Layton's does have one buyer's position open at this time; revise Letter 19 as needed.

LESSON 45 Letters and Memorandums With Copies

Margins: 1 inch • Tab: 5 spaces • Spacing: Single • Drills: 2 times • Format Guide: 21–23 • Working Papers: 87–88

Goals:
To improve speed and accuracy; to format interoffice memorandums and a modified-block style letter; to format copy notations.

A. WARMUP

```
1      The Baxter/Kaczmarek Company distributes 10 dishwasher   12
2 detergent brands; and our jovial washers can't quite decide   24
3 which of three selling for $2.47, $3.59, and $3.68 is best.    36
   |  1  |  2  |  3  |  4  |  5  |  6  |  7  |  8  |  9  |  10  |  11  |  12
```

LANGUAGE ARTS

B. Answer each question with a complete sentence.

B. COMPOSING

4 What is your closest friend's best quality and why is this important to you?

5 How much would you spend on dinner in a nice restaurant and what would you order?

6 What is your career goal and how do you hope to achieve it?

7 Why is it important to have a balanced diet?

8 What one trait is most valued in an employee and why is it important?

9 If you could live anywhere in the world, where would you reside and why?

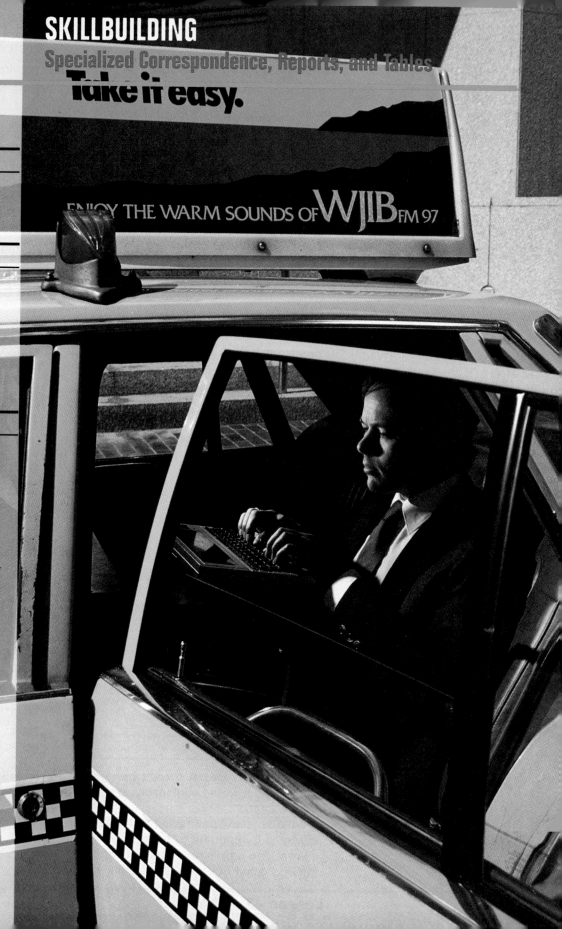

5

OBJECTIVES

KEYBOARDING

To key 47 words a minute on a 5-minute timed writing with no more than 5 errors.

LANGUAGE ARTS

To improve language arts skills.

To improve proficiency in composing at the keyboard.

To proofread and correct errors.

DOCUMENT PROCESSING

To format three- and four-column ruled tables with long and short column headings.

To format correspondence with displays and enumerations for various styles of stationery and window envelopes and to create form letters.

To format specialized reports such as minutes of meetings, itineraries, procedures manuals, and legal documents and to format author/year citations.

To format boxed tables and boxed tables with braced headings.

SKILLBUILDING
Specialized Correspondence, Reports, and Tables

Take it easy.

ENJOY THE WARM SOUNDS OF WJIB FM 97

C. SPELLING

10 address courses accounting return successful request review
11 maximum security either council project already using while
12 reference amount therefore supervisor university commitment
13 recommendation effective authorized adequate correspondence
14 forward district increased regarding included lease follows

SKILLBUILDING

D. 12-SECOND SPRINTS

D. Take three 12-second timed writings on each line. The scale shows your wam speed for a 12-second timed writing.

V 15 Vivian was very vexed when Dave waved a flag at five doves.
X 16 Tex and Max were vexed at lax tax codes enforcement by Rex.
Y 17 Cowboys yodeled as they swayed back and forth by the dairy.

| | | | 5 | | | |10| | | |15| | | |20| | | |25| | | |30| | | |35| | | |40| | | |45| | | |50| | | |55| | | |60

E. PROGRESSIVE PRACTICE: ALPHABET

Turn to the Progressive Practice: Alphabet routine at the back of the book. Take six 30-second timed writings, starting at the point where you left off the last time.

FORMATTING

F. COPY NOTATIONS

It is good business practice to make file copies of all documents you prepare. You may want to print additional originals (if you can store documents) or make photocopies. You may also need copies to send to people other than the addressee of the original document.

A copy notation is keyed on a document to indicate that someone else is receiving a copy of that document.

1. The copy notation is keyed on the line below the reference initials or below the attachment or enclosure notation.
2. At the left margin, key a lowercase *c* followed by a colon and two spaces and the name of the person receiving the copy.
3. If more than one person is receiving a copy, list the names, single spaced, one beneath the other.

Word processing systems enable multiple copies of documents to be printed, reducing or eliminating the need for photocopying.

```
                              Sincerely yours,


                              Douglas A. Nestell
                              Sales Director

        jlp
        c:  Paula Marini
```

Working Papers: 43

Center the table horizontally and vertically.

SUNSHINE HOUSEHOLD PRODUCTS, INC.
Third-Quarter Sales for New England Region

District	Sales	Quota	Percent of Quota
Boston	$1,380,000	$1,500,000	92.0
Concord	975,800	950,000	102.7
Hartford	1,115,000	1,000,000	111.5
Portland	860,000	800,000	107.5
Providence	1,150,000	1,200,000	95.8
TOTAL	$5,480,800	$5,450,000	100.6

Spacing: Double

Working Papers: 45

Depreciation Expenses

With the new legislation regarding tax reform, there has now been a change in calculating our depreciation expenses on any assets put in service after January 1, 1987. This new system, which is called the "Modified Accelerated Cost Recovery System," must be understood in order to comply with Internal Revenue Service directives.

To compute the MACRS deduction, multiply the unadjusted basis of the asset by a percentage taken from the MACRS tables. These tables are available in our corporate tax department. First, determine the number of years it will take to fully depreciate or recover the cost or other basis of the asset. Then, referring to the table, follow the column with the correct number of years to determine the rate for depreciation in each year of the life of the asset. This system enables us to recover a greater portion of the cost of our assets in the beginning years of their being in service, compared with taking a straight-line depreciation, which spreads the cost evenly throughout the life of the asset.

Section 179 Expense Deduction It is possible to deduct up to $10,000 of certain property in the year of acquisition instead of recovering that amount under MACRS. This deduction will only be taken with the approval of our Director of Accounting.

November 5, 19--

LETTER 21
MODIFIED-BLOCK STYLE
Tabs: 4 spaces; center
Working Papers: 87

Mr. Sheldon Y. Friede
4782 Saranac Avenue
Youngstown, OH 44505-6207

Dear Mr. Friede:

This is in response to your recent letter:

Each numbered item in a letter or a memo is treated as a separate paragraph, arranged with the number at the left margin and turnover lines indented 4 spaces.

Indent turnover lines 4 spaces.

1. Your low trees will be replaced without cost next spring. The new trees will match the others in both size and color. A copy of our warranty policy is enclosed for your review.

2. The survival rate for trees cannot be perfect; however, we are indeed sorry that you have had to have this temporary setback.

3. The communication breakdown with our two branch offices should not have occurred. We will take steps to ensure that this will not happen in the future. You can be confident that the appearance of your yard will be restored as soon as conditions are right next spring.

                                    Yours truly,

                                    Margie Hooverman, co-owner

(Your Initials)
Enclosure
c: Mr. George Lambrecht, co-owner
    Mr. Randy Shequen, Warren Branch
    Ms. Glenda Bizzano, Niles Branch

MEMO 7

Working Papers: 89

The word RE is sometimes used in place of the word SUBJECT in a memo or a letter.

The three enumerated entries should be treated as separate paragraphs.

Attachments 2 is the appropriate entry when two items are attached.

MEMO TO: Randy Shequen / Manager, Warren Branch / **FROM:** Margie Hooverman, Co-owner / **DATE:** November 6, 19— / **RE:** Communication Breakdown

Because of a letter (copy attached) I received from Mr. Sheldon Y. Friede, the following actions have been taken: 1. I have sent a letter of apology to Mr. Friede; a copy is also attached. 2. The replacement project has been scheduled on our master calendar for next May. Glenda Bizzano and you will provide the replacement trees from your branch outlets. 3. A meeting has been scheduled in my office with you, Glenda, and George Lambrecht for the purpose of reviewing our present policies so that communication breakdowns like this do not happen in the future.

Randy, let's view this as an opportunity for both you and Glenda to improve communication procedures at your branches.

Your Initials / Attachments 2 / c: Mr. George Lambrecht, Co-owner

MEMO 8

Working Papers: 91

Revise Memo 7 to send to Glenda Bizzano / Manager, Niles Branch. Search carefully for the necessary changes.

Progress Test on Part 4

If you are to be a success in the world of work, you   12
must possess the ability to get along with others. Men and   24
women of all ages, experience, and education have found   35
this ability a key requirement for success in jobs in which   47
people work side by side. Those who lack the know-how they   59
need for getting along with others will not win advancement   71
nearly as quickly as do those who may have less knowledge   82
and skill but more ability in getting along with others.   94
You have to ask yourself what the knack of getting along   105
with others is and what you hope to do to achieve it.   116

Getting along with others is somewhat hard to define,   128
but it is expressing yourself in a manner that shows you   139
recognize and respect how others feel. No one can be sweet   151
all the time, but no one ever has to be rough or mean. No   163
one should insult or bully others or ignore their feelings   175
and expect those people to become friends or to provide   186
help up the ladder of success. The maxim about treating   197
others the way you wish them to treat you is a good formula   210
that you can use for business.   215

| 1 | 2 | 3 | 4 | 5 | 6 | 7 | 8 | 9 | 10 | 11 | 12 |

TEST 4-B
LETTER 47
MODIFIED-BLOCK
LETTER WITH INDENTED
PARAGRAPHS

Working Papers: 41

(*Current Date*) / Mr. Joseph Alholm, Jr. / Regional Manager / Sunshine Household Products, Inc. / 158 Prince Street / Boston, MA 02113 / Dear Joe: / Subject: Sales in New England Region

Although Sunshine Household was removed from the umbrella of Capital Products last year, I have been getting sales figures for each of the districts.

Enclosed is the sales data concerning the New England Region. This information is absolutely essential to you as you make long-range plans and strategies. While I no longer have responsibility for Sunshine products, I am pleased to note the New England Region met its sales quota.

I am also pleased that the Portland office is having such a banner year. It would be good if some of the excitement from that office would touch the Boston crew; you might want to see what the problem is in Boston.

Sincerely yours, / Jack Canton / Vice President of Marketing / (*Your Initials*) / Enclosure

Two-Page Reports

Margins: 1 inch • Tab: 5 spaces • Spacing: Single • Drills: 2 times • Format Guide: 23

Goals:
To study the use of semicolons; to key 39 wam/3'/3e; to use proofreaders' marks; to format a two-page unbound report.

A. WARMUP

```
1     A crazy dog ran in Lanes 1, 2, and 3; and then it took    12
2  a quick jump over the extra lanes labeled 4, 5, and 6.  The   24
3  "feat" was accomplished on 07/08/90 near seats 201 and 203.   36
   |  1  |  2  |  3  |  4  |  5  |  6  |  7  |  8  |  9  |  10  |  11  |  12
```

LANGUAGE ARTS

B. Study the rules at the right. Then key lines 4–7, making necessary changes.

B. SEMICOLONS

Rule: Use a semicolon to separate two independent clauses that are not joined by *and, but, or, or nor.*

Cindy will be here before next Saturday; Julie will not.

Rule: If either of the independent clauses in a compound sentence contains a comma, separate the clauses with a semicolon rather than a comma.

If you wish, the job is yours; but there will not be a wage increase.

```
4 Brian applied for a promotion, Scott did not.
5 Kim held the pieces, and Michael attached the hinges.
6 Lee will bring a fax machine, I will return it Tuesday.
7 As usual, Sean is the captain, but Jan is the substitute.
```

C. PROOFREADERS' MARKS

The most frequently used proofreaders' marks were introduced on page 66, Lesson 32. Additional proofreaders' marks are presented at the right. Study all the marks carefully before keying Report 12, page 103.

Proofreaders' Mark		Draft	Final Copy
SS	Single-space	SS ⌈first line / second line⌋	first line / second line
ds	Double-space	ds ⌈first line / second line⌋	first line / / second line
V or ∧	Insert punctuation	if hes not∧	if he's not,
#	Insert space	allready to	all ready to
new/old	Change word	and ~~if~~ you ∧when	and when you
...	Don't delete	a ~~true~~ story	a true story
⌡	Delete and close up	co/operation	cooperation
/	Use lowercase letter	our Ｐresident	our president
◯	Spell out	the only ①	the only one
⌉	Move right	⌐Please send	Please send
⌐	Move left	⌐ May I	May I

REPORT 39
BOOK MANUSCRIPT

Left margin: 1½ inches
Spacing: Double

Begin page numbering with *page 62*.

Every year that goes by reveals that computers are becoming increasingly more popular in the nation's business offices. These computers are used by managers, supervisors, office personnel, and others who manipulate data on a day-to-day basis. Using computers has become a way of life for all of these people, and their daily routines have changed dramatically because of computers.

Among those people who use computers as tools to help them perform office activities at a faster pace and with more accuracy, most reveal that they use a computer for one of five basic functions: word processing, spreadsheet, database, communications, and programming. Also mentioned as very popular uses of computers are graphics and desktop publishing.

In a recent survey on how people use computers in an office, the greatest percentage of respondents (29 percent) indicated that word processing is the package they use most often. Following closely in second place was spreadsheet software, with 23 percent of the respondents indicating an interest in this package. The third most frequent response was database, with 19 percent of all respondents indicating this choice. These results and other findings are revealed in Table 5, page 63.

Leave 3 blank lines (2 double spaces) before and after a table that contains a title within a report.

Table 5

BUSINESS COMPUTER USAGE

(Most Popular Software Packages)

Type of Package	Percent
Word Processing	29
Spreadsheet	23
Database	19
Communications	9
Programming	7
Graphics	6
Desktop Publishing	5
Other	2
TOTAL	100

Do not split a block of text (for example, a table) between two pages. If all of the block will not fit on one page, key the entire block on the next page.

It is likely that in the future computers will be used even more heavily in the business office than they are today. The greatest usage will likely come from people who conduct the majority of their business on a computer or use peripheral equipment (such as a modem or fax machine) to communicate their ideas to others across the nation and around the globe.

D. 3-MINUTE TIMED WRITING

D. Spacing: double.
Take two 3-minute timed writings. Compute your speed and count errors.

Goal: 39 wam/3'/3e

```
 8      Software has changed to a great extent the way we take   12
 9   care of business in the office.  There was a time not that   24
10   long ago when pens and pencils were used to record all of    35
11   our daily business transactions.  Today all such work is     47
12   quickly done by a spreadsheet on our computers.  For many     58
13   years, we also used those same pens and pencils to organize   70
14   our thoughts on tablets.  Next came the typewriter to speed   82
15   up the process, and today we use word processing to create    94
16   output tenfold.  Software packages will continue to help     106
17   increase the work we produce on the job each and every day.  117

     |  1  |  2  |  3  |  4  |  5  |  6  |  7  |  8  |  9  |  10  |  11  |  12
```

E. TWO-PAGE REPORTS

The second and any additional pages of a report are formatted as follows:

1. Side margins: 1 inch
2. Top margin: 1 inch
3. Page number: keyed at the right margin, 1 inch from the top of the page.
4. Body: begins a double space below the page number and is double spaced.

5. Bottom margin: 1 inch
   To leave a 1-inch bottom margin, use the page-end indicator to show the number of lines or inches to be left in the bottom margin or make a light pencil mark on the left edge of the page about 1½ inches from the bottom to warn you that you are reaching the end of the page.

F. WIDOW/ORPHAN

Widow/orphan protection is a special word processing feature which automatically breaks pages correctly.

The last line of a paragraph by itself at the top of a new page is called a *widow*; the first line of a paragraph by itself at the bottom of a page is called an *orphan*. To avoid widows and orphans, always key at least two lines of a paragraph at the top or bottom of a page. If only one line of a new paragraph will fit at the bottom of a page, begin the paragraph on the next page (leaving slightly more than a 1-inch bottom margin). If only one line of a paragraph will be carried to the top of a new page, either key that line at the bottom of the previous page (leaving slightly less than a 1-inch margin) or carry an additional line from the bottom of the previous page to the top of the new page.

U. BOOK MANUSCRIPTS

Follow these steps when formatting the individual pages for a book manuscript:
1. Key the manuscript in standard "bound report" format (1½-inch left margin; 1-inch right margin).
2. Position the page number at the top right corner of every page.

DOCUMENT PROCESSING

REPORT 38
BOOK MANUSCRIPT

Left margin: 1½ inches
Spacing: Double

Note: The portion of book manuscript at the right begins with *page 142*.

142

Storing information in an office can take many forms. Information must be stored so that it can be found quickly when it is needed. Most information today is stored either on paper, on magnetic disks, or on laser disks.

Paper Storage

Most of the written or printed information that was created in the past two decades is still being stored on paper. In fact, some authorities estimate that we currently have over a trillion pages of information stored on paper.[1] Today, most paper documents are stored by one of four methods.

1. Vertical filing is the most common method for paper storage. In this method, all paper is stored in stacked drawers.
2. In lateral filing, papers face the sides of the cabinet.
3. In open-shelf filing, everything is stacked vertically so that you can see everything that is stored on the shelf.
4. In rotary filing, a document can be accessed by turning or rotating the "cabinet" until it is in front of you.

Magnetic Storage

Magnetic storage is in common use today, and its most popular forms are the floppy disk, the hard disk, and CD-ROM. Some floppy disks can hold as much as 400 pages of information, and about six floppy disks can store about one file drawer of paper. A hard disk can store many more pages than a floppy disk. Today's hard disks can store over 100,000 pages, or about 40 file drawers of paper documents.

Laser Storage

Optical disk storage (CD-ROM) can hold yet more information than either the floppy disk or the hard disk. An optical disk is written and read by lasers. One laser optical disk is capable of storing over 6.8 gigabytes of information.[2] As prices continue to come down, optical disks could eventually replace magnetic storage.

---

[1]Sharon Lund O'Neil, Office Information Systems, 3d ed., Glencoe Division, Macmillan/McGraw-Hill School Publishing Company, Westerville, Ohio, 1990, p. 197.

[2]Ibid., p. 201.

REPORT 12
TWO-PAGE REPORT

Spacing: Double

Determine where to end your first page in order to leave a 1-inch bottom margin.

Many word processing programs have an automatic page-numbering feature that enables the user to select the desired position of the page number.

JUDGING A COMPUTER SYSTEM
By Marilyn Clark

Judging the effectiveness of a computer system has taken on a new dimension in the past few years, if for no particular reason other than the wide range of computer systems from which the user can select. It is important, therefore, that we investigate the criteria that should be considered in making this important decision.

Criterion 1: Speed

This is probably the most obvious criterion considered when one purchases a computer system. The value of a computer is directly related to its speed, and a computer's speed is often measured in megahertz (MHz). A MHz is equivalent to one million cycles per second, and many of today's microcomputers run in the range of 30 to 40 MHz.

Criterion 2: Flexibility

This second criterion is especially important because of the rapid turnover of hardware and software in the computer industry. The flexibility of a computer system is important for two general reasons:

To **accommodate** a **variety** of **programs.** Hundreds and possibly thousands of software packages are available today to meet the needs of computer users. The computer you purchase must be able to accommodate this variety of software and be flexible enough to change with the increasing sophistication of software packages. To **Permit Expandability.** Because of the substantial investment you make in a computer, you do not want to commit your resources to a computer that cannot be expanded to handle (1) newer, more powerful operating systems; (2) "memory-hungry" software packages; (3) network interfaces; and (4) additional users.

Criterion 3: Convenience

A 3d consideration is convenience. Is it easy to learn how to operate your computer? Does the manufacturer stand by its warranty, and is it difficult to obtain repairs? How convenient is it to buy parts for your computer (such as memory boards and drives) if you want to expand your system? these questions need to be answered, and the answers should be weighed carefully before you purchase a new computer system.

Margins: 1¾ inches
Spacing: Double

Remember to add the author's name and page number on the continuing page.

DISCOUNT SERVICES FOR USPA MEMBERS
By Brenda K. Allen

As an employee of USPA, you are eligible for a wide range of discount services available to all employees and their dependents. These consumer savings provide you with tremendous buying power for a wide variety of items and services, from automobiles to jewelry to travel plans. Here are some examples of the quality merchandise and services that are available from USPA.

Auto Pricing and Purchase

You can order the most sophisticated auto information guide on the market. It will give you information on suggested retail prices, vehicle specifications, safety equipment, and factory option packages.

When you are ready to make your purchase, a team of company experts will work with you to ensure that you are getting the best possible price through a network of nationwide dealers.

Extended Services

A wide range of services will appeal to you, especially when you are ready to travel by auto.

Emergency Road Service. You can enjoy the security of emergency road service through the USPA Road and Travel Plan. This comprehensive plan also includes discounts on hotels and motels.

Car Rental Discounts. Special rates from four of the largest auto rental agencies make this service extremely popular with our employees.

Travel Service. As a USPA traveler, you can take advantage of our exclusive discounts and bonuses on cruises and tours. Our travel plan provides daily and weekend trips to over 100 destinations. Take advantage now of this wonderful opportunity to let USPA serve all your travel needs.

Revise Report 12 making the following changes:

1. Change the title to **JUDGING COMPUTER EFFECTIVENESS.**
2. Use your name in the byline.
3. Change the side headings to the following:
   Computer Operating Speed
   System Flexibility
   Overall Convenience
4. Transpose the two paragraphs that begin with paragraph headings (Paragraphs 4 and 5).
5. Delete the final enumerated item under the **Expandability** heading.
6. Replace the final question in the **Convenience** section with the following: *How far would you have to travel to secure replacement parts (if needed), or how many days would you have to wait if you ordered them from the dealer?*

Bound Reports

LESSON 47

Margins: 1 inch • Tab: 5 spaces • Spacing: Single • Drills: 2 times • Format Guide: 25

Goals:
To improve speed and accuracy; to format a two-page bound report.

A. WARMUP

1 Buzz & Jackie moved to Texas on 8/15/94 and were quite   12
2 glad to learn that their computers (Carton 2-A) and printer   24
3 (Carton 7-F) arrived by truck yesterday (8/30/94) at 6 p.m.   36

| 1 | 2 | 3 | 4 | 5 | 6 | 7 | 8 | 9 | 10 | 11 | 12 |

LANGUAGE ARTS

B. These words are among the 500 most frequently misspelled words in business correspondence.

B. SPELLING

4 assistance compliance initial limited corporation technical
5 operating sufficient operation incorporated writing current
6 advise together prepared recommend appreciated cannot based
7 benefit disability analysis probably projects before annual
8 issue attention location association participation proposed

---

SKILLBUILDING

PRETEST.
Take a 1-minute timed writing; compute your speed and count errors.

C. PRETEST: ALTERNATE- AND ONE-HAND WORDS

9 I will defer the amendment that will attract a minimum   12
10 of a million visitors eastward to the island since it might   24
11 create a problem. Did their auditors turn down my request?   36

| 1 | 2 | 3 | 4 | 5 | 6 | 7 | 8 | 9 | 10 | 11 | 12 |

T. MAGAZINE ARTICLES

Magazine Article Page Heading

Read the instructions for preparing a magazine article in the report that follows before you begin the report. Include the author's name with the page number in the continuing pages of the report (see the illustration at the left). Key the author's name, two hyphens, and the page number. Double-space and continue keying the report.

DOCUMENT PROCESSING

REPORT 36
MAGAZINE ARTICLE

Margins: 1¾ inches
Spacing: Double
Tab: 5 spaces, 9 spaces

↓ 2 inches
FORMATTING A MAGAZINE ARTICLE ↓2
By Jeremy N. Shroeder ↓3

To format a magazine article, which is classified as a report, you follow many of the formatting rules for preparing reports. However, a few differences need to be pointed out. The information in this article identifies the formatting rules that are common to many magazines.

One measure of the success of an article is the writer's ability to prepare a document that is pleasing to the eye of the editor. These guidelines will help you prepare a quality document for a magazine.

Formatting Rules

To prepare a quality manuscript, you must make your article look professional. Here are a few suggestions:

1. Use a 5-inch line for the article.
2. Except on page 1, key the author's name and the page number at the top right on all pages of the article.
3. Follow the style required by the magazine to which you are sending your article.
4. If enumerations are used, indent the first line 5 spaces. Turnover lines indent 9 spaces. Double-space the enumerations.

Formatting Continuing Pages

Use the same line length you used on page 1 of the article. Key the heading (author's last name, two hyphens, and the page number) 1 inch from the top edge at the right margin. Leave one blank line (a double space) after the page heading.

Speed Emphasis: If you made 2 or fewer errors on the Pretest, key each line twice.

Accuracy Emphasis: If you made 3 or more errors, key each group of lines (as though it were a paragraph) twice.

POSTTEST.

Repeat the Pretest (C) and compare performance.

D. PRACTICE: ALTERNATE HANDS

12 visible signs amendment visual height turndown suspend maps
13 element amend endowment signal handle ornament auditor half
14 figment usual authentic emblem island clemency dormant snap
15 problem chair shamrocks profit thrown blandish penalty form

E. PRACTICE: ONE HAND

16 trade poplin greater pumpkin eastward plumply barrage holly
17 exact kimono created minikin cassette opinion seaweed union
18 defer unhook reserve minimum attracts million scatter plump
19 serve uphill exceeds killjoy carefree homonym terrace onion

F. POSTTEST: ALTERNATE- AND ONE-HAND WORDS

G. PACED PRACTICE

Turn to the Paced Practice routine at the back of the book. Take four 2-minute timed writings, starting at the speed at which you left off the last time.

FORMATTING

H. BOUND REPORTS

A left bound report requires a wider left margin for binding. To format a bound report, reset the left margin to 1½ inches. Leave the right margin at 1 inch.

DOCUMENT PROCESSING

REPORT 14
TWO-PAGE BOUND REPORT

Left Margin: 1½ inches
Right Margin: 1 inch
Spacing: Double

Key the title, side headings, and paragraph headings in bold.

Documents created with word processing programs can be reformatted without having to be rekeyed.

MANAGING YOUR TIME
The Key to Success in an Office

Using your time more efficiently in an office will help you get more work done in less time. Wasted time cannot be recovered; therefore, the suggestions given in this report will help you better manage your time.

Plan Your Work Each Day

Take a few minutes at the beginning of each workday to plan your day's activities. Decide which tasks you need to finish first and which tasks can be completed at a later time.

Obtaining Necessary Materials. Gather all necessary supplies and materials that you will need to accomplish the tasks you have decided must be completed first. Have all your paper, pens and pencils, folders, and correspondence at your desk and within easy reach if you need to use them.

Completing Individual Tasks. Regardless of the work in which you are involved, it is usually better to finish one task before beginning another. However, if your supervisor assigns you a priority task that must be accomplished immediately, the original task may have to be completed at a later

(Continued on next page.)

the

SS
1. Come in ^shade, texture, and weight you want?
2. Meet laser printer requirements?
3. Fit your budget?
4. Suit the (audience) intended?
5. Convey your intended message?[3]

ds
If you have positive response^ to each of these question^s, you are on your way to selecting the paper that is appropriate for you.

ds
[1]Elizabeth Adler, "Paper," Publish, (Sept). 1991, p. 76.
[2]Carmen Reynolds, "Today's paper standards," Communications Technology, March 1993, p. 42.
ds
[3]Adler, p. 83.

FORMATTING

S. NEWS RELEASES

To format a news release:

1. Use 1-inch side margins and a 2-inch top margin.
2. Double-space the body, and indent paragraphs 5 spaces.
3. Key *NEWS RELEASE* in all-capital letters and bold at the left margin.
4. Begin the identifying information at the top margin, flush right.
5. Center the title of the news release in all-capital letters with bold print.
6. Key a date line—city, state, abbreviated date, and a dash—before the first sentence.

DOCUMENT PROCESSING

REPORT 35
NEWS RELEASE

Spacing: Double

Tabs: 5 spaces, flush right

↓ 2 inches

NEWS RELEASE

From Jeanette Bullard
Nevada Systems Association
2483 Carter Drive
Reno, NV 89509
Release April 17, 19-- ↓2
↓3

NSA SPONSORS SYSTEMS MEETING ↓3

Reno, NV, Apr. 15--The Nevada System^s Association hosted the annual National Systems Association convention in Reno from (Apr.) 13 through (Apr.) 15. More than 800 computer systems person^nel attended the meeting, which attracted representatives from as far away as Puerto Rico and Toronto.

Next year's meeting will be held April 10-1^3 in Columbus, Ohio. The them^e for the meeting will be "Communication^s technology in ^# the ^Next decade."
At this^ year's meeting, computer manufacturers revel^a^ed some of their latest advances in laser printing technology. Color printers purchased for ~~business~~ office use ~~can compete with~~ now provide previously found (quality) only in high-volume operations such as printing and publishing.

REPORT 16
ONE-PAGE UNBOUND
REPORT WITH
FOOTNOTES

Spacing: Double

Note: As you key each super-script in the body of a report, estimate the number of lines needed for the corresponding footnote. Then place a light pencil mark in the left margin at the point where you should stop keying the text in order to leave enough room at the bottom of the page for the footnotes and the 1-inch bottom margin.

SHOPPING FOR A HOME

Center on writing line

(Part I)

Buying a home is a process that many of us will go through in our life time. If we are like many other prospective buyers, we will experience this decision three or four major times in our working years. A home is typically the largest purchase we will make, and it deserves therefore our careful attention.

Considered by many as the most important criteria in shopping for a home is its site.[1] The site should be on land that is well drained and free from from flooding that can cause extensive damage. Check the area local city zoning plan to determine if you have chosen a site that is free from flooding and highwater levels that can cause extensive damage.

You should also check to see if the ground is stable. Ground that shifts considerably can cause cracks in foundations and walls.

You should also consider the quality of construction when shopping for a home. Slight cracks and signs of settling are not a major concern. Kramer and Reynolds state that "larger cracks may indicate unstable ground or poor construction techniques and this is an extremely a very serious concern"[2] If you are looking for a home with a basement, check for any water leaks along the basement walls or along the ground level of the exterior walls.

_____

[1]"Building a Home for Tomorrow," Homes & Gardens, Apr. 27, 1992, pp. 17-24.

[2]David L. Kramer and Leslie T. Reynolds, Strategies for Building a Home Better, Bandana Books, St. Louis, MO, 1992, p. 214.

N. Insert the necessary capital letters as you key these sentences twice.

N. TECHNIQUE PRACTICE: CONCENTRATION

66 Pat met mr. and mrs. hajducky when they flew to sacramento.
67 American flight 110 to nova scotia made a stop in hartford.
68 Lynn and john left for paradise island on saturday, july 6.
69 see the new york mets game at shea stadium with bob carlin.

O. Clear all tabs. Then set four new tabs every 10 spaces. Key lines 70–73, using the tab key to go across from column to column.

O. TECHNIQUE PRACTICE: TAB KEY

70 coins	await	eagle	berry	dairy
71 horse	fruit	jelly	gable	igloo
72 major	unite	offer	ledge	night
73 roast	phase	toast	valve	strap

P. PACED PRACTICE

Turn to the Paced Practice routine at the back of the book. Take four 2-minute timed writings, starting at the speed at which you left off the last time.

Q. Spacing: double. Take two 5-minute timed writings. Compute your speed and count errors.

Goal: 43 wam/5'/5e

Q. 5-MINUTE TIMED WRITING

74   The paradox of time is that people rarely think they   12
75 have enough when in fact all of us have the same amount.   23
76 Time goes by faster and faster; days blur; seasons tumble   35
77 after seasons. It seems as if the faster we go, the faster   47
78 time goes. Most people compensate for this by trying to do   59
79 things quickly, by cramming more into the same space.   69
80   We walk faster, talk faster. In our cars, otherwise   81
81 calm people become Type A personalities, impatient at the   93
82 slightest delay. This furious pace can be seen by visiting   105
83 any big city. Pedestrians hurry down the street checking   116
84 their watches. Shoppers zip in and out of stores clutching   128
85 their bags. It almost seems as if one must rush about when   140
86 visiting a big city just to keep up.   148
87   Our perception of how fast time passes also depends on   160
88 what we are doing: it is one thing while we are on a trip,   172
89 another if our fingers are caught in a car door. In our   183
90 busy lives, it often appears impossible to try to find a   194
91 quiet moment for ourselves, but we must learn to give time   206
92 to time, to plan for a day and for a decade.   215

REPORT 17
TWO-PAGE UNBOUND REPORT WITH FOOTNOTES

Spacing: Double

Revise Report 16 making the following changes:
1. Change the page reference in footnote 1 to *p. 19*.

2. Add the following paragraphs and references to the end of page 2 of the report:

The walls, ceiling, and floors (if you have a basement) need to be checked for proper insulation. "Both the depth and 'R' factor need to be checked for proper levels."[3] In addition, cross braces should have been used between the beams supporting a floor.

Finally, a thorough check should be made of the heating, cooling, and electrical systems in the home. "These features are often overlooked by prospective home owners; nevertheless, they are as critical as any others to be examined."[4]

[3]"Home Construction in the 90's," Family Living, October 9, 1992, p. 75.
[4]Randall Evans and Marie Alexander, Home Facilities Planning, Bradshaw Publishing, Salt Lake City, Utah, 1992, p. 164.

49 LESSON

Endnotes

Margins: 1 inch • Tab: 5 spaces • Spacing: Single • Drills: 2 times • Format Guide: 27–29

Goals:
To increase speed and accuracy; to format a report with endnotes.

A. WARMUP

```
1       Jack paid for six games and quit; as he walked to Room   12
2  389, he realized that he had scored 76 points more than Bev   24
3  (on Game #5) and 40 points more than Jeffrey (on Game #12).   36
   |  1  |  2  |  3  |  4  |  5  |  6  |  7  |  8  |  9  | 10  | 11  | 12
```

SKILLBUILDING

B. Take three 12-second timed writings on each line. The scale shows your wam speed for a 12-second timed writing.

B. 12-SECOND SPRINTS

```
4 You must try to key as fast as you can on these four lines.
5 The screens were very clear, and the print was easy to see.
6 We will not be able to print the copy until later on today.
7 The disk will not store any of the data if it is not clean.
   | | | |5| | | |10| | | |15| | | |20| | | |25| | | |30| | | |35| | | |40| | | |45| | | |50| | | |55| | | |60
```

J. This paragraph is made up of very short words, requiring frequent use of the space bar. Key the paragraph twice. Do not pause before or after striking the space bar.

J. TECHNIQUE PRACTICE: SPACE BAR

41   If I can see you at one or two, I can get to my job by   12
42 six and not be late. I will try to take a cab or walk to a   24
43 bus stop for a ride. My boss wants me to be on time for my   36
44 shift. If I work for six hours, I will have my time in for   48
45 the week. I will then see if I can join all of you at one.   60

| 1 | 2 | 3 | 4 | 5 | 6 | 7 | 8 | 9 | 10 | 11 | 12

K. Take two 1-minute timed writings. The last two digits of each number provide a cumulative word count to help you determine your wam speed.

K. NUMBER PRACTICE

46 3801 4702 1803 9304 6305 8006 2807 3308 5909 6110 9011 1212
47 4813 1914 7915 5316 8117 2418 7619 3720 9421 5922 7023 2324
48 8825 4126 6827 3128 9629 7530 5331 2632 1733 8834 6235 4036
49 2737 8538 5539 1140 3941 4642 9943 6744 7345 8146 3947 5248

L. DIAGNOSTIC PRACTICE: NUMBERS

Turn to the Diagnostic Practice: Numbers routine at the back of this book. Take the Pretest and record your performance. Then practice the drill lines for those reaches on which you made errors. Finally, repeat the Pretest and compare your performance.

M. Take a 1-minute timed writing on the first paragraph to establish your base speed. Then take four 1-minute timed writings on the remaining paragraphs. As soon as you equal or exceed your base speed on one paragraph, advance to the next one.

M. SUSTAINED PRACTICE: ROUGH DRAFT

50   When you begin a new job, a few things can help ensure   12
51 success. The first deals with getting along with others in   24
52 the workplace. Maintaining a good rapport with supervisors   36
53 and coworkers should always be a prime goal of new workers.   48
54   Listen~ing~ carefully to instructions and endeav~oring~ to   12
55 ~complete~ ~~finish~~ assigned tasks accurately are quite important. It   24
56 is ~essential~ ~~necessary~~ that a new worker understand what must be done   36
57 and then finish ~~the~~ ~that~ task in an efficient, accurate manner.   48
58   Another useful tip is being a ~dependable~ ~~cooperative~~ worker. When   12
59 a ~new~ worker maintains a ~good~ ~~fine~~ attendance pattern, its just   24
60 like a good credit ~rating~. Do not be late for work, and be   36
61 very certain that ~your~ absences from work are at a minimum.   48
62   It's ~vital~ ~~essential~~ for ~one~ ~~you~~ to become part of the team quickly.   12
63 Learn to cooperate with ~other~ workers in ~the~ ~~your~~ office, and ask   24
64 question~s~ when ~u~nsure of some thing. In order for a unit or   36
65 department to suc~c~eed, everyone should be working together.   48

| 1 | 2 | 3 | 4 | 5 | 6 | 7 | 8 | 9 | 10 | 11 | 12

C. SUSTAINED PRACTICE: ROUGH DRAFT

8 An entrepreneur can be defined as an innovative person 12

9 who assumes the risks of starting a business to develop new 24

10 products or ideas. Such people have high levels of energy. 36

11 What is it we know about entrepreneurs that makes them 12

12 different from the average small-business owners? Many times, 24

13 a new idea, a few dollars, and drive are what they require. 36

14 Also, the entrepreneur normally begins starts as a sole owner 12

15 but soon changes to a corp. so that much more capital can 24

16 be found for expanding the venture business as soon quickly as possible. 36

17 It should be noted that entrepreneurs are not always the 12

18 same as inventors. entrepreneurs may invent a product, but 24

19 they also have the needed skills to market it with success. 36

| 1 | 2 | 3 | 4 | 5 | 6 | 7 | 8 | 9 | 10 | 11 | 12

D. DIAGNOSTIC PRACTICE: NUMBERS

Turn to the Diagnostic Practice: Numbers routine at the back of this book. Take the Pretest and record your performance. Then practice the drill lines for those reaches on which you made errors. Finally, repeat the Pretest and compare your performance.

FORMATTING

E. ENDNOTES

Like footnotes, endnotes indicate sources of facts or ideas in a report. However, endnotes are placed on a separate page at the end of the report. To format endnotes, follow these steps:

1. Center and key the title **NOTES** in all-capital letters and bold 2 inches from the top of the page; then triple-space.
2. Indent the first line of the reference 5 spaces. Key the reference number (not a superscript) followed by a period and 2 spaces. Then, key the endnotes single-spaced with a double space between notes.
3. Center and key the page number 1 inch from the bottom of the page.

Some word processing programs have an endnote feature that automatically inserts endnotes on a separate page. If notes are added or deleted within the report, the endnotes are automatically renumbered.

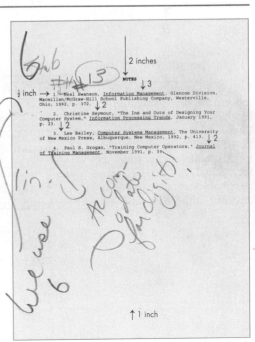

PRETEST.
Take a 1-minute timed writing; compute your speed and count errors.

D. PRETEST: ALTERNATE- AND ONE-HAND WORDS

13   The usual visitors to the rocky island are from either   12
14 the city of Lakeland or Honolulu. They like to visit hilly   24
15 areas and taste the giant fruit. The eight signs that girl   36
16 made gave us an extra boost and some added revenue as well.   48

  | 1 | 2 | 3 | 4 | 5 | 6 | 7 | 8 | 9 | 10 | 11 | 12

PRACTICE.
Speed Emphasis: If you made no more than 1 error on the Pretest, key each line twice.
Accuracy Emphasis: If you made 2 or more errors on the Pretest, key each group of lines (as though it were a paragraph) twice.

E. PRACTICE: ALTERNATE-HAND WORDS

17 also angle field bushel ancient emblem panel sight fish big
18 both blame fight formal element handle proxy signs girl and
19 city chair giant island visitor profit right their laid cut
20 down eight laugh theory chaotic visual shape usual work she

F. PRACTICE: ONE-HAND WORDS

21 acts hilly award uphill average poplin refer jolly adds him
22 area jumpy based homily baggage you'll serve union beat ink
23 case onion brave limply greater kimono taste plump draw oil
24 gave pupil extra unhook wastage unholy wages imply star you

POSTTEST.
Repeat the Pretest (D) and compare performance.

G. POSTTEST: ALTERNATE- AND ONE-HAND WORDS

H. Take three 12-second timed writings on each line. The scale gives your wam speed for a 12-second timed writing.

H. 12-SECOND SPRINTS

25 Check #187 was for $2,056.50 and Check #98 was for $190.20.
26 Carlson & Son won't buy #4; H & N won't buy #5; but I will.
27 "One-tenth or 1/10 equals 10%; one-half or 1/2 equals 50%."
28 Pay these expenses: (1) travel, (2) food, and (3) lodging.

  | | | | 5 | | | | |10| | | |15| | | |20| | | |25| | | |30| | | |35| | | |40| | | |45| | | |50| | | |55| | | |60

I. Take a 1-minute timed writing on the first paragraph to establish your base speed. Then take four 1-minute timed writings on the remaining paragraphs. As soon as you equal or exceed your base speed on one paragraph, advance to the next one.

I. SUSTAINED PRACTICE: SYLLABIC INTENSITY

29   As we have learned more and more about the benefits of   12
30 exercise, large numbers of people have gotten involved in a   24
31 broad range of sports. They want their workouts to be fun.   36

32   There are those who become puzzled after they discover   12
33 that they perform much better when they are practicing than   24
34 when competing. They can't keep their minds on their game.   36

35   Some of these discouraged athletes have sought counsel   12
36 from sports psychologists. They tell these special experts   24
37 that they handicap themselves because of these self-doubts.   36

38   Just as when working with professional athletes, there   12
39 is a basic challenge for the sports psychologist: What can   24
40 I do to rebuild confidence and refine concentration skills?   36

  | 1 | 2 | 3 | 4 | 5 | 6 | 7 | 8 | 9 | 10 | 11 | 12

DESIGNING A COMPUTER SYSTEM

Designing a computer system involves a variety of different operations such as word processing, data processing, communications, printing, and other office-related functions. Because of computers, these areas can be integrated into a very powerful computer system.

Designing the System

One of the first steps is to determine what information is going to be computerized and what personnel will need these resources.[1] This decision should involve all departments in the planning stage of system design. If necessary, you may have to invite input from those departments which are going to be closely involved in computer use after the system has been designed.

There may also be a need to acquire the systems design experience of outside experts—people whose careers consist primarily of planning and developing computer systems for management.[2]

Selecting Hardware and Software

Bailey believes that "the selection of software precedes any hardware choices. Too many people, however, select the hardware first and then try to match their software with the computer."[3] After the software has been selected, a decision must be made as to whether hardware should be purchased or leased. Although many firms decide to purchase their own hardware, others have taken the route of time-sharing or remote processing whereby the costs of processing data can be shared with other users.

Training Operators

Many firms neglect this important phase of designing a computer system. It is not enough to offer a one-week training course in an applications package and then expect proficiency from a worker. Training must occur over time to help those who will be using computers every day on the job.

NOTES

1. Neal Swanson, Information Management, Glencoe Division, Macmillan/McGraw-Hill School Publishing Company, Westerville, Ohio, 1992, p. 372.

2. Christine L. Seymour, "The Ins and Outs of Designing Your Computer System," Information Processing Trends, January 1991, p. 23.

3. Lee Bailey, Computer Systems Management, The University of New Mexico Press, Albuquerque, New Mexico, 1992, p. 413.

Begin the Notes on a separate page.

Endnotes are arranged in numeric order, following the order of reference numbers in the report (not in alphabetic order as in a bibliography). The first line is indented 5 spaces; turnover lines start at the left margin.

76-80 LESSONS

Margins: 1 inch • Spacing: Single • Drills: 2 times • Format Guide: 51–55

Goals for Unit 16

Begin each day with approximately 15 minutes of skill-building, selecting activities from pages 173–176. In the remaining class time, complete as many production jobs from pages 177–183 as you can.

1. To improve accuracy and speed on alphabet and number keys.
2. To key 43 wam for 5 minutes with no more than 5 errors.
3. To develop proficiency in spelling commonly misspelled words.
4. To improve proficiency in formatting footnotes in a report.
5. To gain proficiency in formatting a display in a report.
6. To format a news release, magazine articles, and book manuscripts.
7. To format and key various types of reports with different features.

A. WARMUP

```
1       Request 18 items @ $74 and another 21 items @ $53.  If    12
2  you add the 6% sales tax, the total purchase will amount to    24
3  $2,591.70.  Just analyze the invoice before making payment.    36
     |  1  |  2  |  3  |  4  |  5  |  6  |  7  |  8  |  9  |  10  |  11  |  12
```

LANGUAGE ARTS

B. Study the rules at the right. Then key lines 4–7, making necessary changes.

B. UNDERLINE/PERIOD

Rule: Underline titles of complete published works, and use quotation marks around titles that represent only a part of a complete published work.

One of the required books was entitled <u>Family Finance</u>.

Rule: Use a period to end a sentence that is a polite request, suggestion, or command if you expect the reader to respond by *acting* rather than by giving a yes-or-no answer.

Will you please send your check for $142.38 before May 1.

```
4  I read the article entitled A Right Price for Your House.
5  The article was in Friday's issue of the Washington Post.
6  May I have a copy of the proposal before the meeting?
7  Will you please inform me if I can be of any further help.
```

C. These words are among the 500 most frequently misspelled words in business correspondence.

C. SPELLING

```
8  practice continue regular entitled course resolution assist
9  weeks preparation purposes referred communication potential
10 environmental specifications original contractor associated
11 principal systems client excellent estimated administration
12 responsibility mentioned utilized materials criteria campus
```

Revise Report 18 and add the following paragraph (as well as the accompanying endnote) as the final paragraph and the final endnote in the report.

Finally, it should be recognized that training is an ongoing responsibility. As technology, software, hardware, and procedures change, training must occur regularly and on a continuing basis.[4]

4. Paula Blair, <u>Administrative Management</u>, Southern Publishing Company, Atlanta, Georgia, 1992, p. 420.

LESSON 50

Special Report Pages

Margins: 1 inch • Tab: 5 spaces • Spacing: Single • Drills: 2 times • Format Guide: 29

Goals:
To key 39 wam/3'/3e; to format a table of contents; to format a title page.

A. WARMUP

```
1      Jo made $8.74 (9% profit) on six dozen jewelry pieces,    12
2  but I quickly found that Al would have to sell $53.20 worth   24
3  of oranges so May could buy 16 boxes of Mother's Day cards.  36
```
| 1 | 2 | 3 | 4 | 5 | 6 | 7 | 8 | 9 | 10 | 11 | 12 |

LANGUAGE ARTS

B. Compare this paragraph with the first paragraph of Report 18 on page 111. Then key a list of the words that contain errors, correcting the errors as you key.

B. PROOFREADING

```
4      Desining a computer system involves a varaity of
5  diferent operations such as word processing, processing
6  data, comunications, printing, and other office-related
7  functions.  because of computers these areas can be made
8  into a powerful computer.
```

SKILLBUILDING

C. Spacing: double.
Take two 3-minute timed writings. Compute your speed and count errors.

Goal: 39 wam/3'/3e

C. 3-MINUTE TIMED WRITING

```
9       In just a short period of time, computers have changed   12
10  the way goods and services are now produced.  We often think  24
11  of the computer as a means by which we can work with just     36
12  numbers or words.  There are quite a few other ways in which  48
13  the computer can also be used.  In the production of goods,   60
14  however, firms are more apt to use robotics.  Robotics is     72
15  the use of computer-driven machines to do the work formerly   84
16  done by humans.  A robot can be used to do such tasks as      95
17  weld, sew, mark, and select on an assembly line.  It is      106
18  amazing what businesses expect from their computers now.     117
```
| 1 | 2 | 3 | 4 | 5 | 6 | 7 | 8 | 9 | 10 | 11 | 12 |

MEMO TO: Dolly Carpenter, Rehearsals Coordinator
FROM: Sam Steele, Executive Director
DATE: March 1, 19--
SUBJECT: Summer Cabaret Pops Concert

We are pleased that you will be our rehearsals coordinator for this summer's Cabaret Pops concerts. The five biweekly concerts will run from June 13 through August 8.

As the concert schedule is much lighter during the summer months, I am quite confident that you will be able to use the Orchestra Hall stage for all rehearsals. This is the preference of Edo Dorati, who will be the conductor for this year's Cabaret Pops concerts.

I look forward to seeing you on June 1.

Remember your reference initials.

LETTER 46
PERSONAL-BUSINESS
LETTER IN MODIFIED-
BLOCK STYLE WITH
INDENTED PARAGRAPHS

Date the letter October 2, 19—. This letter is also going to Ms. Gorski. It is from Margot Ault / 13894 Combs Ferry Road / Lexington, KY 40509.

Dear Theresa:

Thank you for inviting me to attend your book group's discussion of my new novel, <u>Wilderness Passages</u>. This was my first opportunity to discuss the book with a group this large, all of whom had already read it.

I am returning the honorarium check for $100. Please apply the amount to your college scholarship fund.

It was wonderful to see so many of my old friends again. Thank you for this special evening.

Sincerely,

Enclosure

If a report title or subtitle must be divided between 2 lines, try to have the second line shorter than the first, resulting in an inverted pyramid.

Many word processing programs have an option that enables you to vertically center a page of text when it is printed.

D. TITLE PAGE

Reports should have a title page, which at the very least, shows the report title, the writer's name and identification, and the date. The title (and subtitle, if any) are keyed on the top part of the page; the writer's name and identification are keyed in the center of the page; and the date is keyed on the lower part of the page.

To format a title page, follow these steps:

1. Center and key the report title in all-capital letters and bold 2 inches from the top of the page.
2. Double-space and center and key the subtitle (if there is one) in upper- and lowercase letters and regular type.
3. Space down 15 lines and center and key the words *Prepared by;* then double-space.
4. Center and key the writer's name, title, and company information on separate lines, single-spaced.
5. Space down 15 lines and center and key the date.

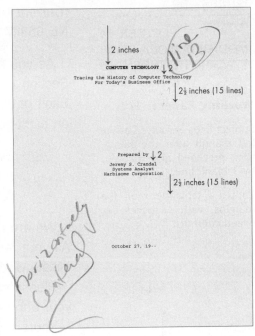

E. TABLE OF CONTENTS

A table of contents (see page 114) is usually supplied with a report. The table of contents identifies the major sections of a report and the page numbers where they can be found.

1. Use the same margins that were used for the report.
2. Align roman numerals at the period.
3. Center and key the title 2 inches from the top of the page in all-capital letters and bold followed by a triple space.

4. Follow an outline format—key the major headings in all-capital letters; triple-space before and double-space after them.
5. Key subheadings in upper- and lowercase letters and single spacing.
6. Align page numbers flush right and key them with dot leaders—a series of periods that help guide the reader's eye across the page to the page number on the same line.

F. DOT LEADERS

Dot leaders (rows of periods) are used to lead the eye across the page. To format dot leaders, follow these steps:

1. Key the first line in the first column and space once.
2. Note whether the print-point indicator is on an odd or even number. If it is on an odd number, begin all remaining lines of leaders on an odd number. If it

is on an even number, begin the leaders on an even number.
3. Key the leaders with or without spaces between the periods (. . . or ....), ending at least one space before the right column.
4. Key the remaining entries, beginning each row of dot leaders on an odd or even number to be sure they align.

LETTER 44
MODIFIED-BLOCK STYLE
WITH INDENTED
PARAGRAPHS

Working Papers: 37

Subject lines are keyed at the left margin after the salutation, preceded and followed by 1 blank line.

Center a table between the margins, with 6 spaces between columns.

(Current Date) / Mrs. Katie Holister / 11426 Prairie View Road / Kearney, NE 68847 / Dear Mrs. Holister: / Subject: Site for New Elementary School

As you are aware, your 160-acre farm, located in the northeast quarter of Section 25 in Tyro Township, is a part of Independent School District 17. Each of our three elementary schools occupies two acres and is adjoined by an eight-acre park. The schools and their adjoining parks are:

Evelyn Moen Elementary School	Maple Grove Park
Percy Miller Elementary School	T. J. Blomgren Park
Spring Creek Elementary School	Spring Creek Park

We are now in the early planning stages for a fourth elementary school. As your farm is centrally located, the District 17 Board has directed me to initiate discussions with you for the purchase of eight acres of land.

Please call me at your convenience to arrange a meeting with you and/or your attorney and me. I look forward to our discussions.

Yours truly, / Irvin J. Hagg / Superintendent of Schools / *(Your Initials)* / c: District 17 Board

LETTER 45
PERSONAL-BUSINESS
LETTER IN BLOCK STYLE

March 21, 19--

Dr. Arif Gureshi
8726 E. Ridge Drive
Morehead, KY 40351-7268

Dear dr. Gureshi:

Your book *The Middle East In The Year 2000* has been getting excellent reviews. The citizens of Morehead are highly pleased that a respected member of one of our local colleges is receiving much national attention. Our book discussion group here in Morehead, composed of members of AAUW (American Association of University Women), has selected your book for discussion at our May meeting. We would like you to be a participant; your attendance at that meeting would be a real highlight.

I shall call you next week. Our members are hoping that you will be able to attend and that an date can be mutually arranged.
acceptable

ds Sincerely,

Theresa A. Gorski
2901 Garfield Court
Morehead, KY 40351-2687

REPORT 20
TITLE PAGE

Center each line horizontally.
Follow the spacing indicated
on page 113.

THE SECRETARY IN TODAY'S AUTOMATED OFFICE

*Maintaining Traditional Skills While
Developing High-Tech Competence*

*Prepared by
Phyllis G. Browe
Systems Analyst
The Western Office Group*

December 9, 19___

REPORT 21
TABLE OF CONTENTS

Tabs: Decimal, 3 spaces;
left, 7, 11; right, right margin

Use dot leaders (rows of periods) to lead the eye across the
page.

Press tab before keying the
roman numerals.

Some word pro-
cessing programs have a
dot leader tab that when
set automatically inserts
leaders when the tab key is
pressed.

↓ 2 inches **CONTENTS**
↓ 3

I.	THE EARLY YEARS OF TECHNOLOGY	1 ↓2
	A. Vacuum Tubes	3
	B. Transistors.	4
	C. Integrated Circuits.	4 ↓3
II.	HARDWARE DEVELOPMENTS.	5 ↓2
	A. Computer Terminals	6
	B. Monitors and Keyboards	8
	C. Modems	9
	D. Scanners	10
	E. Printers	11 ↓3
III.	SOFTWARE DEVELOPMENTS	13 ↓3
IV.	THE FUTURE OF TECHNOLOGY	17 ↓2
	A. Artificial Intelligence.	20
	B. Parallel Processing.	22

As you know, my wife Tana is a member of the local AAUW chapter. She, Dwight, and I will look forward to being at the Federated Women's Club building at 7:30 p.m. on May 17.

Sincerely, / Arif Gureshi / 8726 East Ridge Drive / Morehead, KY 40351-7268 / c: Mr. Dwight Friesen

MEMO 17

If necessary, refer to the Reference Section to review proper format for memos (page R-4) and tables (page R-12).

Center the table between the margins, with 6 spaces between columns.

MEMO TO: Larry Hackworth, Manager
FROM: Rosa Bailey-Judd, Recreation Coordinator
DATE: Current
SUBJECT: Fitness Room

The new Fitness Room will be ready for use in about one month. Your leadership in bringing this about is sincerely appreciated. After extensive investigation (much reading and several interviews), I likely will be requesting approval soon to purchase the following equipment:

Number	Type
4	exercise bicycles
2	treadmills
2	rowing machines
1	muscle-toning machine

Three other types of equipment were seriously considered, but those listed above enable users to reach objectives without excessive cost and duplication.

Thanks again for your full support and cooperation with this project.

FORMATTING

U. SUBJECT LINES

A subject line indicates what a letter is about. It is keyed below the salutation at the left margin, preceded and followed by 1 blank line. (The term *Re* or *In re* may be used in place of *Subject*.)

Mrs. Melanie Stewart
511 Whitley Drive
Gahanna, OH 43230

Dear Mrs. Stewart:

Subject: Kindergarten Preregistration

Kindergarten preregistration for the coming school year is being held on Wednesday, May 15 from 9 a.m. to 1 p.m.

On that day, you are welcome to tour the facility. Staff members will be available to answer questions and to tell you about the various programs that are available.

Resumes

LESSON 51

Margins: 1 inch • Tab: 5 spaces • Spacing: Single • Drills: 2 times • Format Guide: 29

Goals:
To improve speed and accuracy; to format a resume.

A. WARMUP

1   The mixture (fresh water and lemon) quickly gave Jacob   12
2 Dolze a chance to prove that his 6/25/90 statement was true   24
3 and that the mixture sells for $1.37/ounce and $1.48/ounce.   36

  | 1 | 2 | 3 | 4 | 5 | 6 | 7 | 8 | 9 | 10 | 11 | 12

SKILLBUILDING

PRETEST.
Take a 1-minute timed writing; compute your speed and count errors.

PRACTICE.
Speed Emphasis: If you made 2 or fewer errors on the Pretest, key each line twice.
Accuracy Emphasis: If you made 3 or more errors, key each group of lines (as though it were a paragraph) twice.

POSTTEST.
Repeat the Pretest (B) and compare performance.

B. PRETEST: VERTICAL REACHES

4   He knew about the rival races away from home and today   12
5 ordered Gilbert to skip the seventh race. The race at Cole   24
6 may be one that Gilbert may want to enter at an early date.   36

  | 1 | 2 | 3 | 4 | 5 | 6 | 7 | 8 | 9 | 10 | 11 | 12

C. PRACTICE: UP REACHES

7 aw aware flaws drawn crawl hawks sawed awful flaw bawl draw
8 se seven reset seams sedan loses eases serve used seed dose
9 ki skids kings kinks skill kitty kites kilts kits kids kick
10 rd board horde wards sword award beard third cord hard lard

D. PRACTICE: DOWN REACHES

11 ac races pacer backs ached acute laced facts each acre lace
12 kn knave knack knife knows knoll knots knelt knew knee knit
13 ab about abide label above abode sable abbey drab able cabs
14 va evade avail value vapor divan rival naval vain vale vane

E. POSTTEST: VERTICAL REACHES

FORMATTING

F. RESUMES

When you apply for a job, you may be asked to submit a resume. The purpose of a resume is to convey your qualifications for the position you are seeking. In addition to personal information (name, address, telephone number), your resume should also include a summary of your educational background and special training, previous work experience, and any activities or accomplishments that relate to the position for which you are applying. A resume may also include your career goal and references. References should consist of at least three people who can

(Continued on next page.)

(Current Date)

Leave 5 blank lines here

Mr. Timothy E. Kerfeld
1260 Glenmar (St.), APT. 4
ds Wilburton, Ok 74578
Dear Tim:

As we agreed, your fiance's ring is being ~~shipped~~ sent today by (National Express) overnight. It will be delivered to you in person tomorrow morning.

You were wise to include both Jodi and your self in the selection of the diamond. Though the dollar amount represents a significant investment, the sentimental aspect should also be considered. Jodi will treasure the ring because the two of you were involved in the selection (all the more).

I was impressed with the way in which both of you had ~~taught~~ educated yourselves about the various criteria for diamond selection. Many people seem to ~~think~~ believe that size alone (represented by carat weight) determines the value of a diamond. Your knowledge that cut, color, and clarity are also important factors enabled you to make a wise choice. Thank you for choosing Dorsheim's for this important purchase. We look forward to helping you and Jodi with your ~~fine~~ jewelry and gift selections in the future.

Sincerely,

3 blank lines here

Beth E. Dryden, G.G.

(Your Initials)

March 28, 19— / Ms. Theresa A. Gorski / 2901 Garfield Court / Morehead, KY 40351-2687 / Dear Ms. Gorski:

I am looking forward to being a guest at your AAUW book group meeting on May 17.

Since I spoke to you on the phone earlier this week, there has been a new development. My editor, Mr. Dwight Friesen, will be in Morehead that day to conduct a seminar at Culver College. As he will be staying overnight, I would like to bring him along. He is truly one of our country's experts on the cultures of Middle Eastern countries.

(Continued on next page.)

tell a prospective employer what kind of worker you are. Always obtain permission from these people you want to use as references *before* using their names.

Often, your resume creates the first impression you make on a prospective employer; be sure it is free of errors.

A variety of styles is acceptable for formatting a resume (see Illustrations 1 and 2 below). Choose a style (or design one) that is attractive and that enables you to get all the needed information on one or two pages.

List all items in reverse chronological order (most recent first).

If work experience is your strongest asset, list it first.

You may also list the names and addresses of at least three specific references. Be sure to obtain permission before using someone's name as a reference.

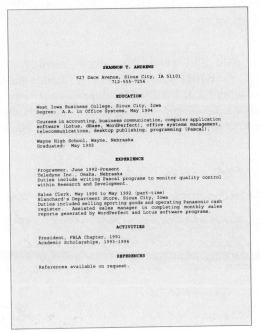

Illustration 1

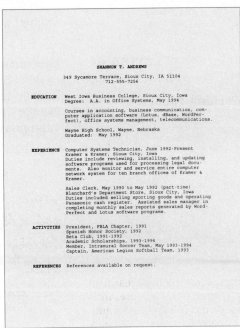

Illustration 2

DOCUMENT PROCESSING

REPORT 22
RESUME

Prepare the resume on the next page so that it is similar to Illustration 1. Follow these steps:

1. Use a 2-inch top margin.
2. Center and key the name in bold; then double-space.
3. Center and key the address and telephone number on separate lines, followed by a triple space.
4. Clear all tabs and set a left tab 12 spaces from the left margin.
5. Key the word *Education* in all-capital letters and bold at the left margin.
6. Indent and key the name and address of the school and any degrees earned.
7. Double-space, indent, and key the course information. Double-space, indent again, and complete the Education information.
8. Triple-space before beginning each new section.

(Continued on next page.)

During the next few months we will be equipping a new gymnasium. The dimensions of the gym are shown on the enclosed sketch. There will be exercise bicycles, treadmills, and rowing machines. In addition, we would like to install a muscle-toning machine that includes features such as the following: leg press, chest press, shoulder press, arm pull, leg pull, arm lift, leg lift, and sit-up board.

Do you have a sales representative serving this area who could meet with me within a week or ten days? As an alternative, perhaps you have some brochures, including prices, that could be sent to me.

Sincerely yours, / Rosa Bailey-Judd / Recreation Coordinator / *(Your Initials)* / Enclosure

LETTER 41
BLOCK STYLE

Working Papers: 31

Use today's date and send this letter to Mr. Kent R. Raudenbush / Choice Athletic Equipment Co. / 5800 Moreland Avenue / Athens, GA 30601-4279. Use an appropriate salutation and complimentary closing. This letter is also from Rosa Bailey-Judd / Recreation Coordinator. Use your own reference initials, key an enclosure notation, and send a copy to Mr. Larry Hackworth, Manager.

Thank you for being so kind when I visited your showroom last week. Having Joe present to actually demonstrate the use of each muscle-toning device was very helpful. I really feel that I am now aware of the special features of your equipment.

Please send me a quotation that includes the cost of your equipment, delivery and installation charges, and taxes. A specification sheet is enclosed.

Please provide this information quickly, as we hope to make a selection within ten days.

FORMATTING

T. MODIFIED-BLOCK STYLE WITH INDENTED PARAGRAPHS

Paragraphs in the body of a modified-block style letter may be indented (usually 5 spaces) or blocked at the left margin. However, paragraphs in a block-style letter are never indented.

Mr. Daniel Vlasuk
8 Hillside Avenue
Peabody, MA 01869

Dear Mr. Vlasuk:

It is likely that the new warehouse will be built at the intersection of Maple Ridge Avenue and 44th Street. This area has been surveyed and construction plans have been drawn up.

We are now in the process of obtaining the necessary building permits from the city. As soon as the city approves the plans and issues these permits, construction will begin. We expect that to be some time in March.

↓ 2 inches
SHANNON T. ANDREWS ↓2

349 Sycamore Terrace, Sioux City, IA 51104
712-555-7256 ↓3

EDUCATION	West Iowa Business College, Sioux City, Iowa Degree: A.A. in Office Systems, May 1994 ↓2
	Courses in accounting, business communication, computer application software (Lotus, dBase, WordPerfect), systems management, telecommunications. ↓2
	Wayne High School, Wayne, Nebraska Graduated: May 1992 ↓3
EXPERIENCE	Computer Systems Technician, June 1992-Present Kramer & Kramer, Sioux City, Iowa Duties include reviewing, installing, and updating software programs used for processing legal documents. Also monitor and service entire computer network system for ten branch offices of Kramer & Kramer. ↓2
	Sales Clerk, May 1990 to May 1992 (part-time) Blanchard's Department Store, Sioux City, Iowa Duties included selling sporting goods and operating Panasonic cash register. Assisted sales manager in completing monthly sales reports generated by WordPerfect and Lotus software programs. ↓3
ACTIVITIES	President, FBLA Chapter, 1991 Spanish Honor Society, 1992 Beta Club, 1991-1992 Academic Scholarships, 1993-1994 Member, Intramural Soccer Team, May 1993-1994 Captain, American Legion Softball Team, 1993 ↓3
REFERENCES	References available on request.

REPORT 23
RESUME

Revise Report 22 making the following changes:

1. Change the address to: *927 Dace Avenue, Sioux City, IA 51101.*
2. Change the side headings to centered heads. Triple-space before and double-space after the headings.
3. Add *desktop publishing* and *programming (Pascal)* to the Education section.
4. Replace the first work experience with: *Programmer, June 1992–Present / Teledyne Inc., Omaha, Nebraska / Duties include writing Pascal programs to monitor quality control within Research and Development.*
5. Delete the Spanish Honor Society, Beta Club, Softball Team, and Soccer Team entries in the Activities section.

LETTER 39
BLOCK STYLE

Working Papers: 27

Use March 2, 19—, as the date for this letter to Ms. Maureen Testa / 372 Central Park West, Apt. 812 / New York, NY 10025-4690. Use an appropriate salutation.

We are ~~pleased~~ _delighted_ that you will be with us for ④ Cabaret Pops concerts this year. Your appearance in Next in Order on Broadway, which earned you a Tony Award nomination, has won you thousands of new fans in the Philadelphia area. They are looking forward to seeing you at Orchestra hall.

ss

As your agent and I discussed on the telephone, the four concerts have been scheduled on the following dates for 8 p.m.:

Cole Porter Revisited	June 13
Big Bands of the Forties	June 27
A Century of Irving Berlin	July 11
Blues, Blues, Blues	July 25

Center the table between the margins, with 6 spaces between columns.

Our Cabaret Pops Series continues to be a popular summer offering. While most of our patrons are serious classical music devotees, they also enjoy the ~~lighter~~ diversion offered by our pops concerts.

Sincerely yours,

Samantha A. Steele, Executive Director
Philadelphia Orchestral Association

rak.P23

A word processing file reference number is often used in combination with the reference initials. The P23 indicates that this letter is stored on disk P as document 23.

LETTER 40
BLOCK STYLE

Working Papers: 29

(Current Date) / Master Gyms, Inc. / 4201 Castine Court / Raleigh, NC 27613-5981 / Ladies and Gentlemen:

We have 494 apartments here at Fountain Ridge. As the Recreation Coordinator for the complex, I have concerns not only about the leisure-time activities of our residents but also about the health and physical fitness of the more than 1,100 people who call Fountain Ridge home.

Our recreation facilities are excellent. In addition to our two outdoor tennis courts and swimming pool, we also have the following indoor facilities: two racquetball courts, swimming pool, whirlpool bath, sauna, steam room, and two billiard tables. However, we have no workout equipment.

(Continued on next page.)

Letters of Application

Margins: 1 inch • Tab: 5 spaces • Spacing: Single • Drills: 2 times • Format Guide: 29–31

Goals:
To key 39 wam/5'/5e; to format a letter of application.

A. WARMUP

```
1      Do not jeopardize an equal tax by having Mack vote too    12
2 swiftly on 11/23/92.  Last year my precinct (the 46th) tied   24
3 when voting on Resolutions 50 & 78--it was a fierce battle!   36
```

| 1 | 2 | 3 | 4 | 5 | 6 | 7 | 8 | 9 | 10 | 11 | 12 |

LANGUAGE ARTS

B. PROOFREADING

B. Compare this paragraph with the fourth paragraph of Report 18, page 111. Then key a list of the words that contain errors, correcting the errors as you key.

```
4      Bailey believed that "a selection of software precedes
5 the hardware choices.  Two many people, however, select the
6 hardware first and then try to match the software with the
7 computer."3  After the software has been chosen, a decision
8 must be made as to weather hardware should be purchased or
9 leased.  Although most firms decide to purchase there own
10 hardware, others have taken the route of time-sharing or
11 remote processing whereby the cost of proccessing data will be
12 shared with other people.
```

SKILLBUILDING

C. TECHNIQUE PRACTICE: TAB KEY

C. Set tabs every 15 spaces. Use the tab key to go from column to column. Key lines 13–18 once.

```
13 aisle      above      blank      begin      candy
14 canal      cycle      drain      eagle      fifth
15 given      hoist      ivory      jewel      knack
16 large      money      notch      ounce      patch
17 quick      ready      stand      troop      under
18 video      waist      excel      youth      zebra
```

D. TECHNIQUE PRACTICE: CONCENTRATION

Change every singular noun to a plural noun.

```
19      If the man, woman, and child want to vacate the old
20 apartment, the manager must issue the permit to make the
21 transfer legal.  The tenant must approve the plan before
22 the vacancy or listing can be printed in the newspaper.
```

Change every plural noun to a singular noun.

```
23      The managers asked your assistants to key the letters and
24 reports that the officers had dictated earlier.  When the jobs
25 had been completed, the secretaries consulted your assistants.
26 Your assistants discovered the errors and had the jobs redone.
```

Change all first-person pronouns to the second person and vice versa; for example, change *I* to *you* and change *you* to *I* or *me*.

```
27      You must give me your recipe for success in your career
28 if I intend to follow you.  If I become a broker also, you
29 can help me by giving me some leads and other contacts; you
30 could also have me subcontract a few of your small accounts.
```

MEMO 15

This memo from Sam Steele, Executive Director, is for Edo Dorati, Cabaret Pops Conductor. Use the current date and Irving Berlin Concert *as the subject.*

Before beginning to format Memo 15, review the proofreaders' marks on page R-13 in the Reference Section.

Our Patron Advisory Program Committee recommends inits ~~their~~ # attached letter that the Irving Berlin concert begin with some pre-World War I hits, followed by songs from the '20s and '30s. Favorites from this era are hit songs from Music Box Revue, Puttin' on the Ritz, and Follow the Fleet. ¶After the intermission the committee suggests songs from the '40s and '50s, hits from Annie get your Gun, Call Me Madam, Easter Parade and

A planning meeting has been scheduled for you, Dolly Carpenter (the Rehearsals Coordinator), and me on March 9 at 10 a.m. at Orchestra Hall. I shall look forward to seeing you then.

Key your own initials for the reference initials. **ds**

dal

Attachment

c: Dolly Carpenter

MEMO 16

MEMO TO: Frank Janowicz / Ticket Manager / **FROM:** Sam Steele / Executive Director / **DATE:** March 1, 19— / **SUBJECT:** Ticket Sales Campaign

We tentatively have scheduled 114 concerts for Orchestra Hall for the calendar year beginning September 1, 19—. The attached list shows the new season ticket prices for the main floor, mezzanine, balcony, and gallery.

These prices are grouped in 11 different concert categories which reflect the varied classical tastes of our patrons. These groupings also consider preferences for day of the week, time of day, and season of the year.

A reminder: The paragraphs in memorandums are always blocked.

Please see me at 3 p.m. on March 10 so that we can review our ticket sales campaign. Last year's season ticket holders have had ample time to renew their subscriptions; we must now concentrate on attracting new season subscribers. I shall look forward to reviewing your plans on the 10th. *(Your Initials)* / Attachment

FORMATTING

S. TABLES IN OTHER DOCUMENTS

To format a table that is part of a letter, memorandum, or report:

1. Leave 1 blank line above and below a table without a title (regardless of whether the table has column headings) and 3 blank lines above and below a table with a title.
2. Single-space the body of the table.
3. Keep the table within the margins of the document. If necessary, the normal 6 spaces between columns may be reduced to a minimum of 2 spaces.
4. Never split a table between two pages. If it will not fit at the bottom of the page on which it is first mentioned, place it at the top of the next page.

31   Applying for a job is likely to be one of the most   11
32 critical steps in your career. This is the one chance you   23
33 have to impress a prospective employer, and it is very true   35
34 that first impressions are lasting ones. Without a doubt,   47
35 at this time you want to look your very best and put forth   58
36 the strongest case you can for yourself.   67
37   Be sure that the clothes you choose for your interview   79
38 are free of lint and wrinkles and that they typify clothes   90
39 worn by those who now work for the company. When you talk   102
40 with the interviewer, you should use language that sends   114
41 your message clearly, succinctly, and accurately. When you   126
42 are asked a question, answer it completely, but don't give   137
43 excessive answers to any of the questions you are asked.   149
44 Recognize that you should ask a question or two at the end   161
45 of the interview. Often the interviewer might want to know   173
46 if you have done any background research on the company and   185
47 would like to ask any questions about its operations.   195

| 1 | 2 | 3 | 4 | 5 | 6 | 7 | 8 | 9 | 10 | 11 | 12 |

FORMATTING

F. LETTERS OF APPLICATION

A letter of application is sent along with a resume to a prospective employer. Together, the letter and the resume serve to introduce a person to the organization.

The letter of application should be no longer than one page and should include: (1) the job you are applying for and how you learned of the job, (2) the highlights of your enclosed resume, and (3) a request for an interview.

DOCUMENT PROCESSING

LETTER 22
MODIFIED-BLOCK STYLE

Whenever possible, it is best to address the letter to a *person* rather than to a *title* when applying for a job.

March 15, 19— / Ms. Kay Brewer, Personnel Director / Blanchard Computer Systems / 2189 Dace Avenue / Sioux City, IA 51107 / Dear Ms. Brewer:

Please consider me as an applicant for the position of data records operator advertised in the March 13 edition of the Sioux City Press.

In May I will graduate with an A.A. degree in Office Systems from West Iowa Business College. As indicated in my resume, which is enclosed, I have completed courses in Lotus, dBase, WordPerfect, and office systems. These courses are ideally suited for the position at Blanchard because these software packages are used in all of your Sioux City offices.

The position with your company is very appealing to me. If you wish to interview me for this position, please call me at 712-555-7256.

Sincerely, / Shannon T. Andrews / 349 Sycamore Terrace / Sioux City, IA 51104 / Enclosure

O. DIAGNOSTIC PRACTICE: ALPHABET

Turn to the Diagnostic Practice: Alphabet routine at the back of this book. Take the Pretest and record your performance. Then practice the drill lines for those reaches on which you made errors. Finally, repeat the Pretest and compare your performance.

P. Clear all tabs. Then set four new tabs every 10 spaces. Key lines 73–76, using the tab key to go from column to column.

P. TECHNIQUE PRACTICE: TAB KEY

73 171	292	383	464	595
74 626	737	828	909	210
75 387	910	621	745	973
76 517	620	864	389	402

Q. PACED PRACTICE

Turn to the Paced Practice routine at the back of the book. Take three 2-minute timed writings, starting at the speed at which you left off the last time.

R. Spacing: double. Take two 5-minute timed writings. Compute your speed and count errors.

Goal: 42 wam/5'/5e

R. 5-MINUTE TIMED WRITING

```
77      Foreign companies and the folks who manage them are        11
78 buying slices of American business and expanding them from      23
79 coast to coast.  The result is more and more U.S. workers        35
80 who will have to learn what it is like to have a boss from       47
81 another part of the world.                                       52
82      Once an American agrees to work for a foreign company,      64
83 he or she is faced with the job of adjusting to its unique       76
84 style.  Take the task of making decisions.  American bosses      88
85 tend to move quickly on things.  They are not afraid of          99
86 acting on their own or making a mistake.  Foreign bosses,       111
87 on the other hand, take a long time to analyze the facts        122
88 and tend to make more decisions in a group.                     131
89      There may also be different ideas about how long the       142
90 workday should last.  For the Japanese, long hours are the      154
91 norm; it is rare for them to leave their jobs before ten        166
92 at night.  Americans who are used to heading home early         177
93 may be viewed as lazy.  A final tip for those anxious to        188
94 succeed with a foreign boss:  buckle down and learn the         199
95 language spoken in the home office and use it often.            210
```

| 1 | 2 | 3 | 4 | 5 | 6 | 7 | 8 | 9 | 10 | 11 | 12 |

August 10, 19-- / Personnel Director / Arlington Communications / 2403 Sunset Lane / Arlington, TX 76015-3148 / Dear Personnel Director: / I have always been interested in working for ^Arlington Communications you and was encouraged to apply for a position in your company. after completing my cooperative program worklast May

The two part‑time jobs I held during the summer months at your company convinced me that arlington comunications ^m ^is a leader in the field and a place where I could make a ^definite contribution. My strengths have always been in the ^communication arts, as you can see on the ^enclosed resume, which reveals ^lists a number of courses in English, and ^,and communication technology speech.

If you would like to interview me ^for any possible openings this summer or fall, ^please call me at (214‑)555‑2340. I look forward to hearing from you.

Sincerely yours, / Kenneth R. Talbot / 6892 Center ^ville Road / Garland, TX 75041-9285 / Enclosure

---

53 LESSON

Employment Tests

Margins: 1 inch • Tab: 5 spaces • Spacing: Single • Drills: 2 times • Format Guide: 31

Goals:
To improve speed and accuracy; to key an employment test.

A. WARMUP

1   About 10 to 18 excited jackals squeezed through a gate   12
2 to freedom. Their pelts are worth less than $23 (top-grade   24
3 pelt); on May 7, 1995, we were able to get from $36 to $46.   36

| 1 | 2 | 3 | 4 | 5 | 6 | 7 | 8 | 9 | 10 | 11 | 12

B. These words are among the 500 most frequently misspelled words in business correspondence.

B. SPELLING

4 means entry valve officer industry similar expenses patient
5 quality provisions judgment academic cooperation previously
6 foreign construction especially secretary indicated closing
7 manufacturing assessment continuing monitoring registration
8 accordance products presently policies implemented capacity

C. Take three 12-second timed writings on each line. The scale gives your wam speed for a 12-second timed writing.

C. 12-SECOND SPRINTS

9 We all had fun in the sun when we spent a day at the beach.
10 Mary will be able to buy a new desk when this one gets old.
11 Take time each day to do those things that are fun for you.
12 This is the first time we have had to stop and look around.

| | | | 5 | | | 10 | | | 15 | | | 20 | | | 25 | | | 30 | | | 35 | | | 40 | | | 45 | | | 50 | | | 55 | | | 60

J. NUMBER PRACTICE

J. Take two 1-minute timed writings. The last two digits of each number provide a cumulative word count to help you determine your wam speed.

41 3301 5502 6603 8804 2205 4406 9907 7708 1109 2110 3111 4112
42 5613 6714 2015 3816 9117 9018 3719 5220 1921 7922 5923 2024
43 8225 6026 4127 8728 4229 7930 2131 6432 5833 2834 3035 9736
44 1437 3638 1239 8240 5441 9142 3443 7844 6845 4046 9547 8248

K. 12-SECOND SPRINTS

K. Take three 12-second timed writings on each line. The scale gives your wam speed for a 12-second timed writing.

45 I need seats 10, 29, 38, 47, and 56 for today's first game.
46 Flight 29 leaves at 10:47, while Flight 38 leaves at 10:56.
47 We had 2,945 employees in 1988 and 1,036 employees in 1978.
48 He mailed out 10, 29, 38, 47, and 56 packages in five days.

| | | |5| | | |10| | |15| | |20| | |25| | | |30| | |35| | | |40| | |45| | | |50| | |55| | | |60

L. TECHNIQUE PRACTICE: RETURN KEY

L. Key each sentence once on a separate line.

49 Call the client. Answer the letter. Prepare the mailings.
50 Fax the response. Ship the package. Forward the estimate.
51 Copy the document. Collate the handout. Add the receipts.
52 Deposit the cash. Reconcile the checks. Post the account.

M. TECHNIQUE PRACTICE: CONCENTRATION

M. Change every plural noun to a singular noun.

53   The managers asked the secretaries to key the letters and
54 reports that the officers had dictated earlier. When the jobs
55 had been completed, the secretaries consulted your assistants.
56 Your assistants discovered the errors and had the jobs redone.

N. SUSTAINED PRACTICE: ALTERNATE-HAND WORDS

N. Take a 1-minute timed writing on the first paragraph to establish your base speed. Then take four 1-minute timed writings on the remaining paragraphs. As soon as you equal or exceed your base speed on one paragraph, advance to the next one.

57   The chairman of that civic club also has to make a new   12
58 amendment to change the shape of the map for downtown. The   24
59 rich visitor owns eight of the giant lots that are visible.   36
60 The town did not permit the antique-shop owner to relocate.   48

61   The problem with the audit is that the city will blame   12
62 our firm. Some may not wait for us to make a profit on the   24
63 deal. If that is the case, we shall refuse to participate.   36
64 A panel is hard at work to correct the major discrepancies.   48

65   I once lived in the downtown section of Knoxville. My   12
66 best neighbor there was a guy named Michael Bono. The only   24
67 problem with him was that he tended to act like an elitist.   36
68 He spent lots of time in his home with some of his friends.   48

69   Phil and Edward had wasted a million pumpkins by scat-   12
70 tering the vegetables along the street in Sweetwater, Ohio.   24
71 Everyone was quite aggravated by the great waste of effort.   36
72 This was especially true of his closest friends and family.   48

| | 1 | 2 | 3 | 4 | 5 | 6 | 7 | 8 | 9 | 10 | 11 | 12

D. PROGRESSIVE PRACTICE: NUMBERS

Turn to the Progressive Practice: Numbers routine at the back of the book. Take six 30-second timed writings, starting at the point where you left off the last time.

E. PROOFREADING SKILLS

An interview may also consist of taking an employment test to determine the background knowledge and level of skill you possess in certain areas. Proofreading and language arts are two skills that are considered essential for office employees.

The remaining exercises in this lesson are designed to test your ability to find and correct mistakes in spelling, punctuation, and grammar. Proofread each of the exercises carefully before you key it in final form with all errors corrected. Format the letter in block style. Provide any missing information that is required to complete each of the jobs.

DOCUMENT PROCESSING

EMPLOYMENT TEST A
APPLICATION
LETTER 24

November 14, 19-- / Mr. Margin T. Hegman / 182 Bonanza Avenue / Anchorage, AK 99502 / Dear Mr. Hegman:

We are delighted that you will be with us for our business conference on Febuary 15th. Your presentation on "CD-ROM: the future of multi-media presentations," is timely and will be well recieved by our audience. By the way, You can expect from 100 to 150 participants in your session that will be held from 1:00 p.m. to 2:45 p.m. in Conference Room 2.

Also enclosed with this letter is a parking permit that will allow you to park free of charge at the hotel Alexander. Just place the permit in your wind shield, and the parking lot attendant will let you enter without charge. The permit is good for all 3 days of the Conference should you choose to attend some of our other sessions conferences while you are in San Francisco.

Please complete and return to me the speaker equipment form with this letter that is enclosed. We have most any equipment you might need for your presentation; but in the event that you have some unique request, we want to be sure all your equipment needs will be met.

Please be sure to call me at 415-555-3874 if there are any questions you have concerning the conference. We look forward to seeing you in February March. / Sincerely, / Jane R. Kelley / conference chair / Enc.

SKILLBUILDING

PRETEST.
Take a 1-minute timed writing; compute your speed and count errors.

PRACTICE.
Speed Emphasis: If you made no more than 1 error on the Pretest, key each line twice.
Accuracy Emphasis: If you made 2 or more errors on the Pretest, key each group of lines (as though it were a paragraph) twice.

POSTTEST.
Repeat the Pretest (D) and compare performance.

H. Take two 1-minute timed writings on each line as you concentrate on infrequently used letters.

I. Take a 1-minute timed writing on the first paragraph to establish your base speed. Then take four 1-minute timed writings on the remaining paragraphs. As soon as you equal or exceed your base speed on one paragraph, advance to the next one.

D. PRETEST: CLOSE REACHES

13   Old Uncle Evert lived northeast of the swamp, opposite 12
14 a dirty old shop. Last week we asked him to agree to allow 24
15 Aunt Gretel to purchase a jeweled sword for her next birth- 36
16 day. He fooled us all by getting her a new topaz necklace. 48

| 1 | 2 | 3 | 4 | 5 | 6 | 7 | 8 | 9 | 10 | 11 | 12 |

E. PRACTICE: ADJACENT KEYS

17 as asked asset based basis class least visas ease fast mass
18 op opera roped topaz adopt scope troop shops open hope drop
19 we weary wedge weigh towed jewel fewer dwell wear weed week
20 rt birth dirty earth heart north alert worth dart port tort

F. PRACTICE: CONSECUTIVE FINGERS

21 sw swamp swift swoop sweet swear swank swirl swap sway swim
22 un uncle under undue unfit bunch begun funny unit aunt junk
23 gr grade grace angry agree group gross gripe grow gram grab
24 ol older olive solid extol spool fools stole bolt cold cool

G. POSTTEST: CLOSE REACHES

H. ALPHABET REVIEW: INFREQUENT-LETTER PRACTICE

J 25 Jill Jenkins adjusted her jogging jacket and jumped across. 12
K 26 Kaye Kane packed stacks of bricks in the back of the truck. 12
Q 27 Quentin Quamm was quite quiet but quickly requested equity. 12
X 28 Rex Truex got excited as he expertly fixed those six taxis. 12

| 1 | 2 | 3 | 4 | 5 | 6 | 7 | 8 | 9 | 10 | 11 | 12 |

I. SUSTAINED PRACTICE: NUMBERS

29   A committee was appointed in order to begin making the 12
30 plans for our annual meeting. It was made up of 12 members 24
31 from the Hills Region, 10 from Valley, and 8 from Stanhope. 36

32   The members in charge of exhibits are hoping to invite 12
33 34 exhibitors to utilize 50 booths in Convention Hall at 87 24
34 Midway. Last year we had 26 exhibitors at this conference. 36

35   The members in charge of the luncheon are hoping for a 12
36 total of 350 persons for lunch at $17.50 each. Last year a 24
37 ticket cost $16.40 for all those who attended the luncheon. 36

38   Attendance at last year's meeting was 1,230. The goal 12
39 for this year is to have 1,410 people. This will enable us 24
40 to project an increase of 180 people, a 14.63 percent rise. 36

| 1 | 2 | 3 | 4 | 5 | 6 | 7 | 8 | 9 | 10 | 11 | 12 |

The following page from a company report contains several errors in punctuation, spelling, and grammar that must be identified and corrected.

Double-space the report, use standard margins for an unbound report, number the page as *Page 3,* and correct the errors.

Income Stock Fund. The Income Stock Funds' objective is curent income with the prospect of increasing dividend income, and the potential for capital appreciation.

The first six month's of the fiscal year produced a total return of 25.4% including a dividend income distribution, of $.38 per share. Electric utilties petroleum and drugs is the largest holdings in the portfolio. Net assets of the fund has grown to $225.7 million from $104.5 million on September 1.

Income fund. The Income Fund's investment objective are maxamum current income without undue risk to principle. Consitant with this objective, the fund held 68.3% in mortgage securities 12,8% in corporite bonds, and 19.9% in high yield electric utility comon stocks.

The fund also has a portion invested in high yeild common stocks which have yeilds almost as high as bonds, and offer the potential for increasing dividends overtime. These comon stocks react quickly to changes in interest rate levels, and genrally have the highest price volatilety in the fund's portfolio.

Money Market Fund. The money Market Fund's investment objective is maximum curent yield without undue risk to principle. There are no deviation from this policy in order to achieve aditional yield. During the past six months the yield advantage increased from 25 basis points to 29 basis points. Net assits of the fund have grown to $1,375.5 milion from $927.5 milion on September 30.

Prepare the following table with double spacing. Arrange the items in the "Expense" column alphabetically. Supply missing information where necessary. Check totals for accuracy.

STATEMENT OF EXPENSES
June 30, 19--

Expense	Income Stock	Income Fund	Money Market
Management Fees	$923,928	$232,687	
Postage	43,369	19,921	130,472
Legal Fees	1,968	1,968	1,968
Audit Fees	13,715	13,715	13,715
Registration Fees	35,427	11,823	66,121
Miscellaneous	10,871		29,513
TOTAL EXPENSES	1,290,278	288,743	2,780,431

Margins: 1 inch • Spacing: Single • Drills: 2 times • Format Guide: 47–51 • Working Papers: 27–38

Goals for Unit 15

Begin each day with approximately 15 minutes of skill-building, selecting activities from pages 162–165. In the remaining class time, complete as many production jobs from pages 166–172 as you can.

1. To improve accuracy and speed on alphabet and number keys.
2. To key 42 wam for 5 minutes with no more than 5 errors.
3. To improve proofreading skills.
4. To format tables within correspondence.
5. To format correspondence in modified-block style with indented paragraphs.
6. To format subject lines in various types of correspondence.
7. To format and key correspondence from various sources, especially handwritten and rough-draft copy.

A. WARMUP

1 Invoice #1874 for $1,862 was for Brad Quigley; Invoice 12
2 #1967 for $864 was for Alexis Jenik; Invoice #2042 for $350 24
3 was for Dominick Zaccaro. These amounts were all past due. 36

| 1 | 2 | 3 | 4 | 5 | 6 | 7 | 8 | 9 | 10 | 11 | 12

LANGUAGE ARTS

B. Study the rules at the right. Then key lines 4–7, making necessary changes.

B. SEMICOLON/HYPHEN

Rule: Use a semicolon to separate items in a series if any of the items already contain commas.

The cities selected are Boise, ID; Memphis, TN; and Buffalo, NY.

Rule: Hyphenate a compound adjective (two or more words that function as a unit to describe a noun) that comes *before* a noun. **Exception:** If the first word is an adverb ending in *ly*, do not hyphenate.

Mr. Montgomery has made some cost-effective decisions.

4 The meetings will be held on Monday, April 5, Monday, April 12, and Monday, April 19.
5 Other cities considered were Provo, Utah, St. Cloud, Minnesota, and Greensboro, North Carolina.
6 A decision was made to purchase three high speed printers.
7 The group was challenged to develop a long range plan.

C. Compare this paragraph with the first paragraph of the 5-minute timed writing on page 165. Key a list of the words that contain errors, correcting the errors as you key.

C. PROOFREADING

8 Foriegn companies and the folks who manager them are
9 buying slices of American busness and expanding them from
10 coast to coast. The result is more U.S. workers
11 that will have to live what it is like to have a boss from
12 another part of the country.

Follow-Up Letters

Margins: 1 inch • Tab: 5 spaces • Spacing: Single • Drills: 2 times • Format Guide: 31

Goals:
To key 39 wam/5'/5e; to format a follow-up letter.

A. WARMUP

```
 1     Jack Fox placed 15 big quartz vases in the top drawer,   12
 2   and on 4/26/93 he paid $58.70 for a new vase (at a 10% dis-  24
 3   count).  When must he buy another vase for the 8/3/93 show?  36
     |  1  |  2  |  3  |  4  |  5  |  6  |  7  |  8  |  9  |  10  |  11  |  12
```

LANGUAGE ARTS

B. Study the rules at the right. Then key lines 4–7, making necessary changes.

B. CAPITAL LETTERS

Rule: Capitalize the names of specific course titles. However, do not capitalize the names of subjects or areas of study (except for any proper nouns or adjectives in such names).

Both students enrolled in College Algebra 105, even though they are majoring in history.

Rule: Capitalize a noun followed by a number or letter that indicates sequence. Do not capitalize the nouns *line, note, page, paragraph,* and *size.*

They will leave for Ottawa at 7:25 p.m. on Flight 68.

```
 4   She was advised to enroll in a College Algebra course.
 5   Many students were interested in a French Literature course.
 6   The logical place for table 7 is at the top of page 16.
 7   The $125.07 amount for invoice 94-683 is due on Monday.
```

SKILLBUILDING

C. Take a 1-minute timed writing on the first paragraph to establish your base speed. Then take four 1-minute timed writings on the remaining paragraphs. As soon as you equal or exceed your base speed on one paragraph, advance to the next one.

C. SUSTAINED PRACTICE: ROUGH DRAFT

```
 8     Early word processing software was heralded as a major   12
 9   breakthrough in technology.  Up to that time, any revisions  24
10   required total rekeying of the copy to free it from errors.  36
11     Word processing helped office workers save all their     12
12   work they had keyed for use at a later time.  All documents  24
13   could now be stored on a disk and called up sometime later.  36
14   The next characteristic of most software word processing    12
15   came with the advent of spellcheckers that would check for  24
16   speling errors we might have made in the work we prepared.   36
17     More current developments in wordprocessing included an   12
18   abilty to work with graphics and text simultaneous.  The    24
19   software now has some very nice desktop publishing features.  36
     |  1  |  2  |  3  |  4  |  5  |  6  |  7  |  8  |  9  |  10  |  11  |  12
```

W. ENDNOTES

Like footnotes, endnotes indicate sources of facts or ideas in a report. However, endnotes are placed on a separate page at the end of the report. To format endnotes, follow these steps:

1. Center and key the title **NOTES** in all-capital letters and bold 2 inches from the top of the page; then triple space.
2. Indent the first line of the reference 5 spaces. Key the reference number (not a superscript) followed by a period and 2 spaces. Then, key the endnotes single-spaced with a double space between notes.
3. Center and key the page number 1 inch from the bottom of the page.

> Some word processing programs have an endnote feature that automatically inserts endnotes on a separate page. If notes are added or deleted within the report, the endnotes are automatically renumbered.

REPORT 32
UNBOUND REPORT
WITH ENDNOTES

Revise Report 30, making the following changes.

1. Replace all occurrences of *Training* with *Training/Development.*
2. Move the last paragraph including the *Conference* side heading to immediately below the introductory paragraph.
3. Replace the last sentence in the introductory paragraph with *The most popular techniques used will be discussed in this report.*
4. Insert endnote number 1 at the end of the second paragraph and endnote number 2 at the end of the third paragraph (see below for the endnote text). Format the endnotes on a separate page with the heading **NOTES** centered 2 inches from the top of the page.

NOTES

1. Sandra Lattimer, "Spilling the Beans," Academic Journal, June 1994, p. 4.

2. "Stop Talking and Listen," Education Life, October 1995, p. 38.

Take two 5-minute timed writings. Compute your speed and count errors.

Goal: 39 wam/5'/5e

```
20      Dozens of suggestions have been given for what to do      12
21  at an interview.  Here are just a few guidelines to help      23
22  you during this important phase of your career.              33
23      It is critical that you are not late for an interview;   45
24  in fact, try to give yourself a little extra time for car    56
25  trouble or traffic delays.  Be sure to introduce yourself    68
26  when you arrive at the interview and tell that person why    79
27  you are there.  When you are asked in for the interview,     91
28  extend your hand if the interviewer offers to shake hands.  103
29  During the interview, maintain good eye contact; pay close  115
30  attention to what is being said, and be a good listener.    126
31  When you are asked a question, speak loudly and clearly.    138
32  Be conscious of the rate you are speaking and the volume of 150
33  your voice.  Point out your strengths, not your weaknesses. 162
34  Finally, at the end of the interview you should express an  174
35  interest in the job and in the company.  Before you leave,  186
36  find out when a hiring decision will be made.               195
```

| 1 | 2 | 3 | 4 | 5 | 6 | 7 | 8 | 9 | 10 | 11 | 12 |

FORMATTING

E. FOLLOW-UP LETTERS

As soon as possible after your interview (preferably the next day), you should send a follow-up letter to the person who conducted your interview.

In the letter, thank the person for the interview, highlight your particular strengths, and restate your interest in working for that organization.

DOCUMENT PROCESSING

LETTER 25
BLOCK STYLE

April 7, 19-- / Ms. Kay Brewer / Blanchard Computer Systems / 2189 Dace Avenue / Sioux City, IA 51107 / Dear Ms. Brewer:

Thanks you for the opportunity of interviewing with Blanchard computer Systems (yesterday). ¶The interview gave me a very positive feeling about the company, and the positive description you shared me with convinced me that blanchard is in deed at the top of the list. of the companies I have visited It appears to me that my strengths in software computer application soft ware and office systems would blend in well with your company profile.

I look forward to hearing you from soon regarding you decision on this position.

Sincerely, / Shannon T. Andrews / 349 Sycamore Terrace / Sioux City, IA 51104

REPORT 31
TWO-PAGE UNBOUND
REPORT WITH
FOOTNOTES

Spacing: Double

Report titles and side headings are keyed in bold.

Report titles and side headings are keyed in bold.

LEADERSHIP SKILLS NEEDED IN BUSINESS
By Sally Rodriguez

Leadership skills are needed now more than ever in business and industry if our nation is to maintain a leading role in the business world of tomorrow. With the advent of a common European community without boundaries, the Japanese influence throughout the world, and the development of a common North American business community, we must have leaders with vision and the appropriate skills for meeting the challenges of the new century.

Each of the skills that a successful leader needs will be discussed in the succeeding pages of this report.

Leadership

Leadership has been defined in a variety of ways. One of many is "the behavior of an individual when he (or she) is directing the activities of a group toward a shared goal."[1]

A successful leader is one who is committed to ideas—ideas for future products and services, for improving the firm's market position, and for the well-being of his or her employees. A leader possesses a value system that is ethically and morally sound. In addition, a leader has a set of beliefs that is a basis for his or her decisions affecting the firm, employees, and society.

Skills That a Leader Needs

A good leader must have the prerequisite skills if he or she is to be effective in business. Quible[2] lists such skills as characteristics. They are "getting others to cooperate, delegating responsibilities, understanding subordinates, and using fairness." However, Quible discusses human relations, teaching, coaching, and communications as special skills a leader should possess. These skills are often acquired on the job with the assistance of other leaders within the firm.

---

[1]Judith R. Gordon, A Diagnostic Approach to Organizational Behavior, 2d ed., Allyn and Bacon, Inc., Boston, 1987, p. 393.

[2]Zane K. Quible, Administrative Office Management: An Introduction, 4th ed., Prentice-Hall, Englewood Cliffs, N.J., 1988, pp. 212–216.

LETTER 26
MODIFIED-BLOCK STYLE

September 12, 19-- / Ms. Carole Rothchild / Personnel Director / Arlington Communications / 2403 Sunset Lane / Arlington, TX 76015-3148 / Dear Ms. Rothchild:

It was a real pleasure meeting with you yesterday and learning of the wonderful career opportunities at Arlington Communications. I enjoyed meeting all the people, especially those working in the Publications Division.

I believe my experience and job skills match nicely with those you are seeking for a desktop publishing individual, and this position is exactly what I have been looking for.

Please let me hear from you when you have made your decision on this position. I am very much interested in joining the professional staff at Arlington Communications.

Sincerely yours, / Kenneth R. Talbot / 6829 Centerville Road / Garland, TX 75041-9285

Integrated Employment Project

LESSON 55

Margins: 1 inch • Tab: 5 spaces • Spacing: Single • Drills: 2 times • Format Guide: 33

Goals:
To improve speed and accuracy; to reinforce employment skills.

A. WARMUP

1 Thomas Barrows of Phoenix, Arizona (602-555-8175), ran   12
2 just as quickly as he could as he competed in the Jergens &   24
3 Vance 15-kilometer race on Friday--1st prize was $493 cash!   36

| 1 | 2 | 3 | 4 | 5 | 6 | 7 | 8 | 9 | 10 | 11 | 12 |

LANGUAGE ARTS

B. COMPOSING

B. Answer each question with a sentence or two.

4 Why do you need to prepare yourself for an interview?
5 Why is it important to get good grades in school?
6 What section do you prefer to read in the newspaper and why?
7 How can good communication skills help you achieve your goals?
8 What are the three most important environmental issues today?
9 What advantages do you see in studying a foreign language?
10 Why are ethics important in business?
11 How can you improve your confidence in speaking before a group?

T. TWO-PAGE REPORTS

The second and any additional pages of a report are formatted as follows:

1. Side margins: 1 inch
2. Top margin: 1 inch
3. Page number: keyed at the right margin, 1 inch from the top of the page.
4. Body: begins a double space below the page number and is double-spaced.

5. Bottom margin: 1 inch

To leave a 1-inch bottom margin, determine the number of lines to be keyed on the page or the number of lines or inches to be left in the bottom margin, or use the page-end indicator to show the number of lines or inches to be left in the bottom margin.

U. WIDOW/ORPHAN

A special word processing feature is widow/orphan protection, which automatically breaks pages correctly.

The last line of a paragraph by itself at the top of a new page is called a *widow;* the first line of a paragraph by itself at the bottom of a page is called an *orphan.* To avoid widows and orphans, always key at least two lines of a paragraph at the top or bottom of a page. If only one line of a new paragraph will fit at the bottom of a page, begin the paragraph on the next page (leaving slightly more than a 1-inch bottom margin). If only one line of a paragraph will be carried to the top of a new page, either key that line at the bottom of the previous page (leaving slightly less than a 1-inch margin) or carry an additional line from the bottom of the previous page to the top of the new page.

V. REPORTS WITH FOOTNOTES

Some word processing programs have a footnote feature that automatically inserts footnotes at the end of a page. If notes are added or deleted, the program automatically reformats the page.

Footnote references indicate the sources of facts or ideas in a report. A superscript (raised) number is keyed after the fact or idea in the body of the report. The footnote reference is keyed at the bottom of the same page, separated from the text by a single space and a 2-inch underline. Footnotes are keyed a double space below the underline, single-spaced, and the first line is indented 5 spaces. The footnote includes the superscript number and the reference. Double-space between footnotes.

When the last page of a multipage report contains a footnote, the divider line and footnotes are keyed at the bottom of the page—not below the last line of text.

Note: As you key each superscript in the body of a report, estimate the number of lines needed for the corresponding footnote. Then place a light pencil mark in the left margin at the point where you should stop keying the text in order to leave enough room at the bottom of the page for the footnotes and the 1-inch margin.

C. PACED PRACTICE

Turn to the Paced Practice routine at the back of the book. Take four 2-minute timed writings, starting at the speed at which you left off the last time.

D. DIAGNOSTIC PRACTICE: NUMBERS

Turn to the Diagnostic Practice: Numbers routine at the back of this book. Take the Pretest and record your performance. Then practice the drill lines for those reaches on which you made errors. Finally, repeat the Pretest and compare your performance.

DOCUMENT PROCESSING

In this unit you learned how to prepare a resume, an application letter, and a follow-up letter—all of which are frequently used by job applicants.

You will now use all of these skills in preparing the documents necessary to apply for the job described in the newspaper ad appearing below.

REPORT 25
RESUME

Prepare a resume for yourself as though you are applying for the job appearing in the ad in the next column. Use actual data in the resume. Assume that you have just graduated from a postsecondary program. Include school-related activities, courses you will have completed, and any part-time or full-time work experience you may have acquired. Make the resume as realistic as possible, and provide as much information as you can about your background.

LETTER 27
APPLICATION LETTER

Prepare an application letter to apply for the position described in the ad at the right. Date your letter March 10. Emphasize the skills you have acquired during your years in school and while working in any part-time or full-time positions. Use Letters 22 and 23 (pages 119 and 120) as guides for your letter.

LETTER 28
FOLLOW-UP LETTER

Assume that your interview was held on March 25 and that you would very much like to work for Tri-State Publishing. It is now the day after your interview. Prepare a follow-up letter expressing your positive thoughts about working for Tri-State. Use Letters 25 and 26 (pages 124 and 125) as guides for your letter.

COMPUTER APPLICATIONS SPECIALIST

Tri-State Publishing, a New York City based publisher specializing in trade and industrial titles, has an immediate opening for a Computer Applications Specialist whose primary responsibilities include word processing and desktop publishing.

This is an entry-level position within the Public Relations Department in our Philadelphia office. Applicant must have had training in WordPerfect and desktop publishing (preferably PageMaker or Ventura). Knowledge of computer operating systems is also helpful.

Excellent company benefits available that include a comprehensive medical and dental program, disability insurance, and a company credit union.

If interested, send a letter of application and resume to:

Mr. David E. Frantelli
Personnel Department
Tri-State Publishing
9350 Andover Road
Philadelphia, PA 19114

Tri-State is an Equal Opportunity Employer

*Reports 1–29 appear in Lessons 1–60.

Spacing: Double

The title of a report is keyed in uppercase and bold. The by-line is keyed a double space below the title in normal type and followed by a triple space. The body is double-spaced.

Side headings and paragraph headings are keyed in upper- and lowercase and bold. Double-space before and after side headings.

See pages R-7 and R-8 in the Reference Section for formatting an unbound report.

↓ 2 inches

EMPLOYEE TRAINING PROGRAMS ↓₂

By *(Your Name)* ↓₃

There are various training techniques used in business and industry to update employees' skills and/or to ~~assist them in~~ help employees acquiring new skills. Some of the various techniques used in training will be discussed in this report.

On-the-Job Training and Lectures

On-the-job training and lectures are the ~~three~~ two most frequently used methods of training.

On-the-job. Training On-the-job training permits individuals to train at the workplace, thus saving time and money. This method lets the trainer use the workstation in place of a classroom.

Lectures. Lectures are often used because they are low-cost methods of instruction. Lectures usually are one-way communication techniques with little interaction on the part of the learner. They are often ineffective when used to introducing employees to new techniques and orientation them to new programs of work.

Conference

In this ~~the conference~~ method ~~of instruction,~~ small groups of employees are taught by a conference director. This method of instruction results in considerable give-and-take between the director and participants.

LESSON 56

Skillbuilding and Correspondence Review

Margins: 1 inch • Tab: 5 spaces • Spacing: Single • Drills: 2 times • Format Guide: 33 • Working Papers: 95–98

Goals:
To key 40 wam/5'/5e; to review correspondence formats.

A. WARMUP

1   Val bought two tickets for the concert at $19.75. The   12
2   next day the price was $24.30. He was amazed at that quick   24
3   jump in price of 23.0%. His three tickets cost him $63.80.   36

| 1 | 2 | 3 | 4 | 5 | 6 | 7 | 8 | 9 | 10 | 11 | 12

LANGUAGE ARTS

B. Study the rules at the right. Then key lines 4–7, making necessary changes.

B. GRAMMAR

Rule: A verb must agree with its subject in number and person.

Your purchase order for 12 printers was received on May 4.

Rule: The following words are always singular and take singular verbs: *each, neither, either, much,* and pronouns ending in *-body, -thing,* and *-one.*

Neither of them is responsible for the depreciation error.

4   The deliveries by the farmer was according to schedule.
5   The manager, along with four trainers, are going tomorrow.
6   Everybody in the adjoining offices were happy for her.
7   Either of them are qualified for the receptionist job.

SKILLBUILDING

C. Take three 12-second timed writings on each line. The scale gives your wam speed for a 12-second timed writing.

C. 12-SECOND SPRINTS

J 8   Judge Jones justly joined Judge Jettig on a major judgment.
Q 9   Quentin quietly and quickly quoted that eloquent quotation.
X 10 Alex took extra time to execute the exercise on a tax exam.
Z 11 Buzz was amazed at the size of the dozen zebras at the zoo.

| | | | 5 | | | | 10 | | | | 15 | | | 20 | | | | 25 | | | | 30 | | | | 35 | | | | 40 | | | | 45 | | | | 50 | | | | 55 | | | | 60

D. Take two 1-minute timed writings. The last two digits of each number provide a cumulative word count to help you determine your wam speed.

D. NUMBER PRACTICE

12   3601 4802 5903 1104 2705 8306 9407 5508 6609 2310 9511 7612
13   4913 3814 6615 3916 4017 1918 2119 7320 9821 4822 6323 8424
14   6525 7226 1427 9028 3329 4930 5431 2832 3933 7834 9135 2036
15   7837 8938 5539 4240 1841 6742 3643 2844 1045 2846 3747 8848

E. DIAGNOSTIC PRACTICE: ALPHABET

Turn to the Diagnostic Practice: Alphabet routine at the back of this book. Take the Pretest and record your performance. Then practice the drill lines for those reaches on which you made errors. Finally, repeat the Pretest and compare your performance.

TABLE 23

Spacing: Single

A $700 LOAN COMPOUNDED ANNUALLY FOR SEVEN YEARS AT 7 PERCENT

Yr	Interest	Value
1	$00.00	$ 700.00
2	49.00	749.00
3	52.43	801.43
4	56.10	857.53
5	60.03	917.56
6	64.23	981.79
7	68.72	1,050.51
8	78.68	1,129.19

FORMATTING

S. DOT LEADERS

Dot leaders (rows of periods) are used to lead the eye across the page. To format dot leaders, follow these steps:

1. Key the first line in the first column and space once.
2. Note whether the print-point indicator is on an odd or even number. If it is on an odd number, begin all remaining leaders on an odd number. If it is on an even number, begin the leaders on an even number.
3. Key the leaders with or without spaces between the periods, ending at least one space before the right column.
4. Key the remaining entries, beginning each row of dot leaders on an odd or even number to be sure they align.

DOCUMENT PROCESSING

TABLE 24

Spacing: Single

PURCHASING MANAGERS ASSOCIATION
Executive Board

President. . . . . Mark Mabrita
Dell Corporation

Vice President . . . . Chris Weston
Collingswood & Sanders

Recording Secretary. . . . . Inge Klopping
Central Wholesale Pharmaceuticals, Inc.

Corresponding Secretary. . . . . Paul Lunt
Westhampton Office Supplies

Treasurer. . . . . Ethel Jones-Tyler
Dunn Metallic Industries

Historian. . . . . Dorothy J. Windsor
Dell Corporation

Newsletter Editor. . . . . William H. Hart
L & M Transfer Company

F. Spacing: double. Take two 5-minute timed writings. Compute your speed and count errors.

Goal: 40 wam/5'/5e

```
16        Is your life a little crazy?  Do you find yourself        11
17  always feeling nervous or anxious?  At the end of the day       23
18  are your shoulder muscles tight and sore?  If the answer        34
19  to these questions is yes, then perhaps you are suffering       46
20  from an ailment that affects thousands each day:  stress.       57
21        The complex lives we lead often play havoc with our       69
22  good intentions to just relax and take things slowly.  At       80
23  times we feel quite stressed out and unable to function        92
24  as we would like.  Demands from work, family, and friends      103
25  might pull us in many directions.                              110
26        There are easily a dozen ways to manage stress.  From    122
27  a physical standpoint, it is essential to learn to relax       133
28  your body.  When nervous, most people take fast, shallow       145
29  breaths causing their heart rate to increase.  Try taking      156
30  slow, deep breaths instead and you will soon sense your        168
31  breathing pattern return to its normal state.                 177
32        In our hectic lives, it is too easy to let stress get    189
33  the best of you.  Remember, all you have to do is relax.       200
    |  1  |  2  |  3  |  4  |  5  |  6  |  7  |  8  |  9  |  10  |  11  |  12
```

DOCUMENT PROCESSING

LETTER 29
BLOCK STYLE

Working Papers: 95

(Current Date) / Ms. Wilma Newman, Director / Fremont Cooperative Nursery School / 121 Lincoln Highway / Fremont, NE 68025 / Dear Ms. Newman:

Thank you for your recent inquiry about having an article published in our magazine Only for Children. We are very pleased with the reception that this publication has received throughout Nebraska and some of the surrounding states. Consider the following points:

1. Our editor for that publication, Valerie Ritter, has final responsibility for accepting materials for publication. Send your article directly to her for consideration.

2. The magazine is published bimonthly; if your article is accepted for publication, you will receive a $100 payment.

Again, thank you for your interest in having an article published in one of our publications. I'm sure that Ms. Ritter will look forward to hearing from you.

Sincerely yours, / (Ms.) Maridel B. Ash / Editorial Director / (Your Initials)

TABLE 20

Spacing: Double

Center the table vertically and horizontally.

Set a right tab for number columns and their column headings and a left tab for word columns and their column headings.

AIR MILEAGE

Selected Cities

Origination	Destination	Miles	Airline
Los Angeles	Las Vegas	234	Northwest
Chicago	New York	733	United
Detroit	Cincinnati	229	Delta
Cleveland	Houston	1,091	Continental
Dallas	San Francisco	1,465	American

TABLE 21

Spacing: Double

Center the table vertically and horizontally.

Set a left tab for Column 1 and right tabs for Columns 2 and 3.

Review:
1. The underline is the full column width.
2. *TOTAL* is keyed at the first tab stop.
3. The $ sign in the bottom line must align with the $ sign above it.

THIRD FOUR-QUARTER SALES] Center

Ending September 30, 19--

MONTH	Sales Quota	Actual Sales
July	$ 335,400	$ 350,610
August	Leave 6 Spaces 370,760	246,230
September	386,824	425,110
TOTAL	$1,094,154	[$1,121951

TABLE 22

Spacing: Double

Center the table vertically and horizontally.

Set right tabs for Columns 2, 3, and 4.

LONGACRE PUBLISHING COMPANY
Staff, Texts Sold, and Sales Volume, 19--

Division	Staff	Texts	Sales Volume
Adult	54	20	$ 1,250,300
Elementary	110	75	5,369,765
Secondary	106	62	4,125,377
College	101	73	5,671,356
TOTAL	371	230	$16,416,798

LETTER 30
BLOCK STYLE

Working Papers: 97

(Today's date) / Ms. Victoria F. Eng / 85 Holly Drive / Chadron, NE 69337 / Dear Ms. Eng:

Thank you very much for your inquiry about Allwood Publications. It is a pleasure to respond.

We have six magazines. Their names, the names of their editors, and their cost per year are on the enclosed table. All are subscription magazines—that is, they are not sold at newsstands.

If you would like any other details, please let me know. In the mean-time, I will share a copy of your letter with Stephanie Pasquini, Sales Coordinator.

Sincerely yours, / Louis C. Hass / Editorial Assistant / (Your Initials) / Enclosure / c: Stephanie Pasquini

LESSON 57

Skillbuilding and Correspondence Review

Margins: 1 inch • Tab: 5 spaces • Spacing: Single • Drills: 2 times • Format Guide: 33–35

Goals:
To improve speed and accuracy; to review correspondence formats.

A. WARMUP

```
1      Invoice #13765 for $8,924 was for extra work needed to   12
2 install the computer network.  The size of the computer lab   24
3 totals 720 square feet.  It is just right for many classes.   36
   | 1 | 2 | 3 | 4 | 5 | 6 | 7 | 8 | 9 | 10 | 11 | 12
```

LANGUAGE ARTS

B. These words are among the 500 most frequently misspelled words in business correspondence.

B. SPELLING

```
4 executive distribution specific carried extension requested
5 recommended access alternative programs budget could issued
6 indicated family until objectives calendar could these your
7 fiscal past possibility administrative students accommodate
8 transportation employee's categories summary offered estate
```

SKILLBUILDING

PRETEST.
Take a 1-minute timed writing; compute your speed and count errors.

C. PRETEST: DISCRIMINATION PRACTICE

```
9       Polly alerted an astute older gentleman to wear proper   12
10 colored suits to the opera.  If one is of medium build, the   24
11 suits will look better and one can project his best manner.   36
   | 1 | 2 | 3 | 4 | 5 | 6 | 7 | 8 | 9 | 10 | 11 | 12
```

Unit 12   **Lesson 57**   **129**

Q. HORIZONTAL CENTERING

Horizontally centered text has equal white spaces to the left and right of it.

To center text using automatic centering, use the appropriate code or command keys to move the carrier to the center of the line (42 for 10-pitch type; 51 for 12-pitch type). Then key the text to be centered and press Return.

R. VERTICAL CENTERING

The concept of vertical centering is similar to that of horizontal centering. Vertically centered text has equal space above and below it. Text should appear to be framed on a sheet of paper with equal side margins and equal top and bottom margins.

To center text vertically:

1. Count the number of lines (including blank ones) that the text will fill.
2. Subtract that number from the number of lines on the page. Standard paper is 11 inches long; standard line-spacing is 6 lines per inch. Therefore, there are 66 lines on a page ($11 \times 6 = 66$).
3. Divide the remainder by 2 and drop any fraction and add 1 to find the line number on which to begin keying.

Example: To center 12 double-spaced lines on a full sheet, you will need 23 lines (12 keyed + 11 blank = 23; $66 - 23 = 43 \div 2 = 21.5$). Begin keying on line 22.

DOCUMENT PROCESSING

TABLE 19*

*Tables 1–18 appear in Lessons 1–60.

Spacing: Double

Center the table horizontally and vertically.

Review:

1. The key line consists of the longest item in each column plus 6 spaces between the columns.
2. Column headings for this table are blocked at the left.
3. For additional review of tabulation, see page R-12 in the Reference Section.

SOFTWARE DEMONSTRATION LOCATIONS ↓2

Demonstrations Start at 10:30 a.m. ↓3

Date	Location	Hotel
May 1	San Francisco	Hilton
June 10	Dallas	Crowne Plaza
July 17	Scottsdale	Mountain Shadows
August 1	Detroit	Westin
September 15	New York	Marriott Marquis

Key Line: September 15123456San Francisco123456Mountain Shadows

Speed Emphasis: If you made 2 or fewer errors on the Pretest, key each line twice.

Accuracy Emphasis: If you made 3 or more errors, key each group of lines (as though it were a paragraph) twice.

D. PRACTICE: LEFT HAND

12 rtr trip trot sport train alert courts assert tragic truest
13 asa mass salt usage cased cease astute dashed masked castle
14 sds used said winds bands seeds godson woodsy shreds wields
15 rer rear rest overt rerun older before entire surest better

E. PRACTICE: RIGHT HAND

16 mnm menu numb hymns unmet manly mental namely manner number
17 pop post coop opera pools opens polite proper police oppose
18 olo tool loon solos color lower locker oldest lowest frolic
19 iui unit quit fruit suits built medium guided helium podium

POSTTEST.
Repeat the Pretest (C) and compare performance.

F. POSTTEST: DISCRIMINATION PRACTICE

DOCUMENT PROCESSING

MEMO 9

This memorandum dated today is from Maridel Ash, Editorial Director, to Valerie Ritter, Editor of *Only for Children*. The subject is Potential Article.

I recently received a letter from Wilma Newman, of the Fremont Cooperative Nursery School. She expressed an interest in having an article published in Only for Children. *I have asked her to communicate directly with you regarding this possibility. Attached, you will find a copy of her letter to me and my response to her.*

If you have any questions about my response to her, please get in touch with me. I hope she contacts you, since we are always looking for appropriate articles.

By the way, please plan to attend an important meeting of all editors on Thursday, October 10, at 10 a.m. in H-110. We will review publication schedules for next year.

MEMO 10

This memorandum dated today is from Maridel Ash to Raymond Cozza in Sales/ Marketing about Achievement Awards in Sales/Marketing.

I was delighted to receive the information regarding sales/marketing revenue generated for the month of March by individuals reporting to you. To see Nancy Ostrowski as the top employee, with over $30,000 of revenue for the month, was a special delight. I know how much you have worked with Nancy in getting her to this point. Congratulations on helping her achieve this milestone.

We will be sponsoring a recognition luncheon for the employees who have achieved the best sales figures for March. Please invite Nancy, Joseph Simon, Kimberley Harris, David Klein, and Kathleen Lake to join us for this luncheon on April 14 at 12 noon at the Brookside Inn on Country Park Road.

N. ALPHABET REVIEW: INFREQUENT-LETTER PRACTICE

N. Take two 1-minute timed writings on each line as you concentrate on infrequently used letters.

Y 60 You and your young friend may buy a yellow yacht in a year. 12
Z 61 I was amazed at the size of a dozen lazy zebras at the zoo. 12
Q 62 She quickly qualified for equal quarterly quotas of quills. 12
X 63 Lex expects those extra deluxe taxis in exactly six months. 12

| 1 | 2 | 3 | 4 | 5 | 6 | 7 | 8 | 9 | 10 | 11 | 12

O. 12-SECOND SPRINTS

O. Take three 12-second timed writings on each line. The scale gives your wam speed for a 12-second timed writing.

64 A queen received prized onyx and ruby jewels from the king.
65 V. Peh felt lazy and quit working on the jumbled tax forms.
66 Sixty equals only five dozen, but we promised Jackie eight.
67 Bill Gavin was quite amazed about the extra copy for jokes.

| | | | 5 | | | |10| | | |15| | | |20| | | |25| | | |30| | | |35| | | |40| | | |45| | | |50| | | |55| | | |60

P. 5-MINUTE TIMED WRITING

P. Spacing: double.
Take two 5-minute timed writings. Compute your speed and count errors.

Goal: 41 wam/5'/5e

68   Human resource experts all over the country face tough   12
69 challenges in today's market. They are trying to match the   24
70 best people to the vacancies to be filled. How can job   35
71 seekers increase their chances of landing the job that they   47
72 want? One of the key traits an interviewer looks for is   59
73 enthusiasm. What do you think are some of the ways that a   70
74 person can show an upbeat attitude?   78
75   One way is to take a close look at your resume and   89
76 cover letter. When writing to a firm, it is helpful to   100
77 use strong action verbs. Tell how well organized you are   112
78 or what you have accomplished. This can make you appear   123
79 dynamic and might help to bring your resume to the top of   135
80 the stack.   137
81   A second idea is to take the time to practice your   148
82 communication skills. An applicant who quietly mumbles   159
83 his or her name when meeting someone new is not making a   171
84 good first impression. A firm handshake, good eye contact,   183
85 and a melodic pitch to the voice will all help give off the   195
86 aura of a happy, vibrant person who can do the job.   205

| 1 | 2 | 3 | 4 | 5 | 6 | 7 | 8 | 9 | 10 | 11 | 12

Ms. Valerie Ritter, Editor
Only for Children
Allwood Publishing Company

115 Grand Street

Omaha, NE 61803-0073

Dear ~~Editor:~~ Ms. Ritter:

I received a letter from Ms. ~~Maridel~~ Ash, Editorial Director for Allwood Publishing, telling me to contact you if I was interested in having an article published. in Only for Children

¶For the past 6 years, I have been ~~supervising~~ directing the Fremont Cooperative Nursey School. I have 12 staff members helping me with an average of about 100 ~~students~~ children in each quarter. About 3 years ago, we began a unique program of community involvement with the children in our program. Everyone in the town has been extremely supportive of the program.

Enclosed is an article that ~~explains~~ describes this program. I believe it would be of interest to the readers of ~~the~~ your magazine. Please let me know if you can use it in a future issue of the magazine.

Sincerely, yours

Wilma Newman

121 Lincoln Highway

Fremont, NE 68025

Reminder: Place the return address after the signature in a personal-business letter.

Skillbuilding and Report Review

LESSON 58

Margins: 1 inch • Tab: 5 spaces • Spacing: Single • Drills: 2 times • Format Guide: 35—37

Goals:
To key 40 wam/5'/5e; to review report formats.

A. WARMUP

1   Tickets #180-219 were issued to Granth & Bextley. The   12
2 cost for those 40 tickets came to $376. The 15 tickets for   24
3 Jomass & Olizetti for $141 were delivered to Quince Murphy.   36

| 1 | 2 | 3 | 4 | 5 | 6 | 7 | 8 | 9 | 10 | 11 | 12 |

I. TECHNIQUE PRACTICE: LETTER OPENING

I. Tab: center.
The opening lines of a letter require the quick operation of the Return key. Key these opening lines 3 times as quickly as possible.

↓ 2 inches
(Current Date) ↓ 1 inch

→TAB

Mr. Roger Allgor
Personnel Manager
Farview Travel Services
51 East Longview Boulevard
Wichita, KS 67202 ↓2

Dear Mr. Allgor:

J. TECHNIQUE PRACTICE: LETTER CLOSING

J. Tab: center.
The closing lines of a letter require the quick operation of the Return and tab keys. Key these closing lines 3 times as quickly as possible.

→TAB   Sincerely yours, ↓4

→TAB   Melanie B. Kaplan
→TAB   Director of Sales ↓2

urs
Enclosure

K. TECHNIQUE PRACTICE: SHIFT KEY

K. Take two 1-minute timed writings on each line. Try not to slow down for the capital letters.

41 Sue and Alan took Marsha to the Washington Monument in May. 12
42 On Al's trip to Nova Scotia, he stopped in Portland, Maine. 12
43 Cedar Rapids and Des Moines are the largest cities in Iowa. 12
44 Marie moved to 16 North Hollywood Boulevard in Los Angeles. 12

| 1 | 2 | 3 | 4 | 5 | 6 | 7 | 8 | 9 | 10 | 11 | 12

L. TECHNIQUE PRACTICE: CONCENTRATION

L. Key this paragraph once, concentrating on each letter keyed. Then take three 1-minute timed writings, trying to increase your speed each time.

45   El uso de la bicicleta es muy popular en Barranquilla. 12
46 Cuando el tiempo es bueno a toda la gente joven le gusta ir 24
47 a pasear en bicicletas. Me gusta ir a montar en bicicleta. 36

| 1 | 2 | 3 | 4 | 5 | 6 | 7 | 8 | 9 | 10 | 11 | 12

M. SUSTAINED PRACTICE: CAPITALIZATION

M. Take a 1-minute timed writing on the first paragraph to establish your base speed. Then take four 1-minute timed writings on the remaining paragraphs. As soon as you equal or exceed your base speed on one paragraph, advance to the next one.

48   Many people like to plan summer trips by auto in order 12
49 that they will see many sites. We all like discussing many 24
50 things we have seen or special places that we have visited. 36

51   If you know anyone who has driven to Florida, you will 12
52 most likely hear about the time spent at Walt Disney World. 24
53 This is one of the top tourist attractions in this country. 36

54   Anyone who has spent some time in Virginia would share 12
55 some comments about a trip to Virginia Beach, Williamsburg, 24
56 or Busch Gardens. Memories of Richmond may also be shared. 36

57   A trip to Boston will be fondly remembered. Following 12
58 the Freedom Trail is exciting. Seeing the Old North Church 24
59 and the Bunker Hill Monument can make history come to life. 36

| 1 | 2 | 3 | 4 | 5 | 6 | 7 | 8 | 9 | 10 | 11 | 12

B. Compare this paragraph with the last paragraph of the timed writing that follows. Key a list of errors, correcting the errors as you key.

B. PROOFREADING

4   Poeple in other counties do have sharply varied ways
5 of doing things. Each american businessperson who studies
6 these customs quickly learns their value when she or he
7 visits faraway nations on busness.

C. PACED PRACTICE

Turn to the Paced Practice routine at the back of the book. Take four 2-minute timed writings, starting at the speed at which you left off the last time.

D. Spacing: double.
Take two 5-minute timed writings. Compute your speed and count errors.

Goal: 40 wam/5'/5e

D. 5-MINUTE TIMED WRITING

8   This globe of ours is full of many exotic places where   12
9 travelers can visit. However, one should realize that even   24
10 though it is fun to go to these places, these spots are not   36
11 just for tourists. Business is becoming a global endeavor.   48
12 Each savvy businessperson knows that to be a success in   59
13 today's market, one must know about the world.   68
14   Asia is a region where cultural norms are very unlike   80
15 those in the United States. Doing business in Asia means   92
16 more than just hopping on a plane, meeting a few clients,   103
17 and closing the deal. For example, in Japan, clean socks   115
18 with no holes in the toes are crucial, since shoes come off   127
19 each time you visit someone's home or dine on straw mats   138
20 in a restaurant. And in China, a highly valued trait is   150
21 that of always being sure to be on time.   158
22   People in other countries do have sharply varied ways   170
23 of doing things. Each American businessperson who studies   181
24 these customs quickly learns their value when he or she   193
25 visits faraway nations on business.   200

| 1 | 2 | 3 | 4 | 5 | 6 | 7 | 8 | 9 | 10 | 11 | 12 |

REPORT 26
TWO-PAGE UNBOUND REPORT WITH FOOTNOTES

Spacing: Double

WOMEN AND CHILD CARE
By *(Your Name)*

A number of factors have had a tremendous impact on the role of women in the labor market and in our society. This report will first discuss some of the factors that have impacted the role of women in society and then will explore some of the issues dealing with child care.

(Continued on next page.)

PRETEST.
Take a 1-minute timed writing; compute your speed and count errors.

PRACTICE.
Speed Emphasis: If you made no more than 1 error on the Pretest, key each line twice.
Accuracy Emphasis: If you made 2 or more errors, key each group of lines (as though it were a paragraph) twice.

POSTTEST.
Repeat the Pretest (D) and compare performance.

D. PRETEST: COMMON LETTER COMBINATIONS

14   The insurance agents began to input the weekly renewal   12
15 data into the computer. They quickly decided which amounts   24
16 had to be increased by adding yearly totals to the formula.   36

| 1 | 2 | 3 | 4 | 5 | 6 | 7 | 8 | 9 | 10 | 11 | 12 |

E. PRACTICE: WORD BEGINNINGS

17 re- react ready refer relax remit renew repel really reveal
18 in- incur index infer input inset inert inept inches insert
19 be- befit began being below beach beams bears beauty beside
20 de- deals debit debug decay deeds delay denim decent delude

F. PRACTICE: WORD ENDINGS

21 -ly apply daily early hilly lowly madly truly simply weekly
22 -ed acted added based cited dated hired sized opened showed
23 -nt agent count event front giant meant plant amount fluent
24 -al canal decal equal fatal ideal local usual actual visual

G. POSTTEST: COMMON LETTER COMBINATIONS

H. SUSTAINED PRACTICE: ROUGH DRAFT

25   The interest in our global economy is growing by leaps   12
26 and bounds. Many of our politicians and leaders realize it   24
27 is essential that we keep abreast of all that is happening.   36
28 Economists are very busy studying this growing development.   48
29 For example, the rapid movement to a comon market for   12
30 the twelve european countries must be watched closely. The   24
31 import and export markets from this union will be critical.   36
32 The consumer market from this union will surpass our own.   48
33   When reveiwing all the changes taking place in Eastern   12
34 Europe there is also the realization that a national global economy   24
35 is pending. Again, this can change many things in the U.S.A. United States   36
36 The interest in free market trade in this area is exiting.   48
37   One of the major reasons behind all these developements   12
38 is the rapid fast growth of technology. It is now very easy for   24
39 businesses to share information and data across many miles.   36
40 Conducting business with distant clients has become common   48

| 1 | 2 | 3 | 4 | 5 | 6 | 7 | 8 | 9 | 10 | 11 | 12 |

Changing Role of Women

During the past 30 years, a major revolution has been taking place regarding the role of women in our society. A major factor has been the continuing increase in the number of women in the labor force.[1] This increased participation in the labor force on the part of women is due to several factors. First, women have been getting more and more education for careers. Second, more and more women are in the position of being a single parent. The need for income is critical. Even in those situations where there are two parents, the increased cost of living and continuing inflation have made it necessary for the family to have a second income.

Opportunities for women in the labor force have grown tremendously in the past several years. While the number of women attaining top-management positions is still relatively small, the number of women in middle-management and supervisory positions has shown continued growth. According to recent statistics, close to six million women were employed as executives, administrators, and managers in the different employment categories.[2]

Child-Care Issues

Of course, as women increase their participation in the labor force, many questions are raised regarding the child care available to them. This issue has been debated by Congress and is of concern to many business organizations. Recent statistics show that in the past 15 years, the number of 3- to 5-year-olds enrolled in nursery schools has increased by more than 150 percent.[3] At the same time, more and more business organizations have begun their own child-care facilities to meet the needs of their employees. The number of church-related nursery schools has also increased. Many states are now regulating child care by establishing standards to be met by typical nursery schools.

----

[1]Ruth A. Lupo, "Women in the Labor Force," U.S. Labor Bulletin, December 1992, p. 78.

[2]Thomas G. Laskert, Becoming Managers/Supervisors, American Management Association, New York, 1991, p. 241.

[3]Margaret Hajducky, "Child Care Issues," Working Women, October 1992, p. 37.

Some word processing software enables the user to convert endnotes to footnotes and footnotes to endnotes with a single command.

REPORT 27
TWO-PAGE UNBOUND
REPORT WITH
ENDNOTES

Revise Report 26 by making the following changes: delete the two side headings; omit the third paragraph; change the footnotes to endnotes.

Margins: 1 inch • Spacing: Single • Drills: 2 times • Format Guide: 43—47

Goals for Unit 14

Begin each day with approximately 15 minutes of skill-building, selecting activities from pages 151–154. In the remaining class time, complete as many production jobs from pages 155–161 as you can.

1. To improve accuracy and speed on alphabet and number keys.
2. To key 41 wam for 5 minutes with no more than 5 errors.
3. To improve proficiency in composing at the keyboard.
4. To gain proficiency in formatting tables.
5. To format and key unbound reports.
6. To format and key endnotes and footnotes.

A. WARMUP

1   Customers with bad debts (Zak & Juster, Power & Baxen,   12
2 and Quinn & Haven) had the following amounts due: $185.90,   24
3 $247.38, and $1,356. We asked our attorney to take action.   36

| 1 | 2 | 3 | 4 | 5 | 6 | 7 | 8 | 9 | 10 | 11 | 12 |

LANGUAGE ARTS

B. Study the rules at the right. Then key lines 4–7, making necessary changes.

B. ABBREVIATIONS

Rule: Spell out compass points used as ordinary nouns and adjectives or when included in street names. **Exception:** Abbreviate compass points without periods when they are used *following* a street name.

That lot is two blocks east of North Winnebago Drive.

Rule: Abbreviate units of measure when they occur frequently, as in technical or scientific work, on forms, and in tables. Do not use periods.

The 4- by 6- by 10-ft sizes are the most popular.

4 The shipping address is 4500 E. Country Club Road.
5 Ship the order to 3208 36th Street, Northeast, in Biloxi.
6 New quotations are $3.47 a gal and 95 cents a qt.
7 The 9 3/4-in by 2-ft 6-in tablet contains 292.5 sq in.

C. Answer each question with a short paragraph.

C. COMPOSING

8 What section do you prefer to read in the newspaper and why?
9 How can good communication skills help you achieve your goals?
10 What are the three most important environmental issues today?
11 What advantages do you see in studying a foreign language?
12 Why are ethics important in business?
13 How can you improve your confidence in speaking before a group?

Skillbuilding and Table Review

Margins: 1 inch • Tab: 5 spaces • Spacing: Single • Drills: 2 times • Format Guide: 37

Goals:
To improve speed and accuracy; to review table formats.

A. WARMUP

1　　　　Three of our employees (Zeeker, Quigley, & Justex) are　12
2　to be paid for the overtime.　Their social security numbers　24
3　are as follows:　154-28-0277, 147-28-5881, and 156-34-5998.　36

| 1 | 2 | 3 | 4 | 5 | 6 | 7 | 8 | 9 | 10 | 11 | 12

LANGUAGE ARTS

B. Answer each question with a sentence or two.

B. COMPOSING

4 Why do people procrastinate?
5 How do you judge the value of a friendship?
6 Why is punctuality important?
7 What qualifications should a teacher possess?
8 How do you make a decision?
9 How can you improve your listening skills?
10 Why do magic tricks fascinate most people?

SKILLBUILDING

C. Set four tabs every 10 spaces. Key lines 11–14, pressing the tab key to move from column to column.

C. TECHNIQUE PRACTICE: TAB KEY

11 Aurora	Urbana	Geneva	Moline	Illinois
12 Laurel	Towson	Avenel	Elkton	Maryland
13 Elmira	Oswego	Albany	Selden	New York
14 Vienna	McLean	Dublin	Reston	Virginia

PRETEST.
Take a 1-minute timed writing; compute your speed and count errors.

D. PRETEST: HORIZONTAL REACHES

15　　　　The legal facts gave our lawyers a sense that we could　12
16　be ready to wrap up this case quickly.　When a written copy　24
17　of our testimony is given us, we shall be extremely joyous.　36

| 1 | 2 | 3 | 4 | 5 | 6 | 7 | 8 | 9 | 10 | 11 | 12

PRACTICE.
Speed Emphasis: If you made 2 or fewer errors on the Pretest, key each line twice.
Accuracy Emphasis: If you made 3 or more errors, key each group of lines (as though it were a paragraph) twice.

E. PRACTICE: IN REACHES

18 wr wrap wren wreak wrist wrote writer unwrap writhe wreaths
19 ou pout ours ounce cough fouls output detour ousted coupons
20 ad adds dead adult ready blade advice fading admits adheres
21 py pyre copy pygmy pylon happy pyrene choppy pyrite pyramid

F. PRACTICE: OUT REACHES

22 yo yoga your youth yodel yowls yogurt joyous yonder younger
23 fa fact farm faith sofas fakes faulty unfair famous defames
24 up upon soup upset group upper upturn supply uplift upsurge
25 ga gate gave cigar gains legal gazing legacy gawked garbage

POSTTEST.
Repeat the Pretest (D) and compare performance.

G. POSTTEST: HORIZONTAL REACHES

MEMO 13
(Continued)

I am sure that ~~each and all of you~~ everyone will want to congratulate ~~him~~ Keith on his ~~program~~ promotion.

urs
c: Personnel

MEMO 14

MEMO TO: Annette O'Brien, Human Resources
FROM: Juan Garcia, Vice President
DATE: (Current)
SUBJECT: Performance Appraisals

I have felt for a long time that we must revise our policies for appraising workers both for retention and for promotion. I must say now that I agree with you that the supervisors need training in this aspect of supervision. Most of them were promoted because they could perform the jobs they supervise and not because of any insight into the principles of supervision.

Will you please outline a course in employee evaluation to present to Mr. Houston for approval. I would prefer either a one-day workshop or two half-day workshops. Please let me have an initial draft by next Friday.

Thanks for your help.

TABLE 16

ALLWOOD PUBLISHING COMPANY
Marketing Leaders for March

Employee	Revenue
Nancy Ostrowski	$32,400
Joseph Simon	29,900
Kimberley Harris	28,600
David Klein	27,800
Kathleen Lake	26,400

TABLE 17

ALLWOOD PUBLISHING COMPANY

Departmental Employees

Department *Put in alphabetic order*	Supervisor	Number of Employees
Personnel	Agnes Rossi	10
Accounting	Chinnapa Jayachandran	14
Editorial	~~Grace Whitford~~ Maridel Ash	21
Sales/Marketing	Raymond Cozza	~~17~~ 16
Techical/Design	John Imperato	15

TABLE 18

ALLWOOD PUBLISHING COMPANY

Magazines Published

Title	Editor	Current Orders	Price per Year
News of the World	Jesse Young	15,239	$22.50
Only for Children	Valerie Ritter	17,355	13.95
Recent Happenings	Wayne Lee Frost	11,463	15.80
Sports Events	Joseph Giannini	23,148	21.95
Women's Issues	Edith Hoxie	10,642	12.50
World of Cars	Thomas Preston	14,650	18.95

MEMO 12*

*Memos 1–11 appear in Lessons 1–60.

Tab: 1 inch

MEMO TO: Shirley Atwood, Purchasing Manager

FROM: Clinton Jones, Accounting Manager

DATE: *(Current)*

SUBJECT: Purchase of Marx Software ↓₃

Remember to bold the guide words, double-spacing between each line. Triple-space after the subject line to begin the body, and block the paragraphs.

Please order the Marx Software for use in the Accounting Department. We have tested it and its configuration appears to meet the needs of our staff.

Mable Youngblood and Marvin Knots will attend the three-day orientation program established by the Marx Company. Mable and Marvin were selected because they will be the principal managers of the unit in which the software is to be installed.

It is my understanding that James Clayton, the local representative of Marx, has discussed the price and terms of the sale with you. Is this so?

urs
c: Jason Black, President

MEMO 13

MEMO TO: All Departments

FROM: Allison Baker, Vice President

DATE: October 14, 19--

SUBJECT: New Vice President

I am happy to ~~tell you~~ announce that Mr. Keith MacPhee was appointed as our new vice president for Finance starting ~~February 20~~ March 1.

Keith, as you know, has had a very successful careers with us during the past 15 years. He was originally employed as an accountant in the Accounting department where he was instrumental in establishing our system-wide programs in Accounting.

(Continued on next page.)

Skillbuilding and Employment Documents Review

Margins: 1 inch • Tab: 5 spaces • Spacing: Single • Drills: 2 times • Format Guide: 37–39

Goals:
To key 40 wam/5'/5e; to review formats for employment documents.

A. WARMUP

1   Get 10 items @ $87, 15 items @ $92, and 9 items @ $96.   12
2   The entire bill is $3,114. After checking the invoice with   24
3   extra care, ship the order to P. J. Quincy in Greenlee, AZ.   36

| 1 | 2 | 3 | 4 | 5 | 6 | 7 | 8 | 9 | 10 | 11 | 12

SKILLBUILDING

B. DIAGNOSTIC PRACTICE: NUMBERS

Turn to the Diagnostic Practice: Numbers routine at the back of this book. Take the Pretest and record your performance. Then practice the drill lines for those reaches on which you made errors. Finally, repeat the Pretest and compare your performance.

C. Spacing: Double
Take two 5-minute timed writings. Compute your speed and count errors.

Goal: 40 wam/5'/5e

C. 5-MINUTE TIMED WRITING

4   Time is elastic; it can be stretched to include the   11
5   activities you enjoy doing as well as the tasks you are   23
6   obliged to do. How do people with crazy schedules find the   35
7   time for all they do? The secret is quite simple: they   46
8   don't find the time for their interests; they make it.   57

9   For example, did you ever notice how much time you   68
10   spend waiting in the supermarket checkout line or at the   80
11   doctor's office? Even though it is only ten minutes here   91
12   or five minutes there, when you add it all up, it can be   103
13   substantial. You could use the extra minutes to read a new   115
14   book or magazine.   118

15   Successful time managers also know that it is critical   130
16   to break a task down into small pieces. Say you wanted to   142
17   learn French. Few people could set aside the time required   154
18   to devote to the project. But what if you tried to learn   165
19   just ten new words each day? It might take you longer, but   177
20   in the end you would surely master a new language. Making   189
21   dreams come true is what time management is all about.   200

| 1 | 2 | 3 | 4 | 5 | 6 | 7 | 8 | 9 | 10 | 11 | 12

LETTER 38
MODIFIED-BLOCK STYLE

Working Papers: 25

Modified-block style: The date line, complimentary closing, and writer's identification begin at center. Paragraphs are blocked.

See page R-13 in the Reference Section for proofreaders' marks.

Addison & Moore

2701 WILSHIRE BOULEVARD • LOS ANGELES, CA 90057-1076 • 213-555-2200

↓ 2 inches
May ~~April~~ 3, 19-- ↓ 1 inch

Mr. Michael Mc Ginty
Starr & Morgan Company
One DuPont Circle
Washington, DC 20036-2133

Dear Mr. McGinty:

It was a pleasure to see you again at our sales conference last week. Your winning ~~our~~ the "Golden Apple" Award for the most sales for the ~~month~~ year was well deserved.

We comend you for obtaining the Westerminster Account. None of our companys sales representatives have ever been able to do accomplish this feate. Just the idean of a new account at over $500,000 is mind-boggling to say the least. How did you do it? Did you:

1. # Spend considerable time with the President, Mr. Arch Davis, or the Director of Purchasing, Ms. Betsy Matin?

2. COnduct a series of "hands-on" workshops for the employees and managers?

3. Develop a special marketing campaign for Westminster it selft or use a regular campaign model?

Please ~~Can you~~ let me know what your strategies were for this sale. I am sure that our representatives ~~should~~ would profit from your excellent work.

Sincerely yours, ↓ 4

Robert Miley
President ↓ 2

urs
c: R. Olson, Director of Sales

Numbered items are treated as separate paragraphs, with the number at the left margin and turnover lines indented 4 spaces.

A copy notation (c:) is keyed below the reference initials (or below an enclosure notation, if used).

(Current Date) / Ms. Anna B. Krajewski / Personnel Department / Compu-Serve Systems / 1531 Roosevelt Avenue / Peoria, IL 61603 / Dear Ms. Krajewski:

I saw your advertisement in Friday's edition of the Peoria Express, and I am interested in being considered for the position of assistant network administrator. Enclosed is a copy of my resume, which gives details of my education and work experience.

During the past two years, my work at Bentley & Simon has required me to use the computer on a regular basis. In addition, my course work at Iron Hills gave me skills that I could easily transfer to the position you advertised.

I will be happy to come for an interview at your convenience. Please call me any day after 5 p.m. at 309-555-8407.

Sincerely yours, / Joseph B. Hawkins / *Pick up address from below.* / Enclosure

REPORT 28
RESUME

JOSEPH B. HAWKINS

151 Greenwich Street, Peoria, IL 61603

309-555-8407

OBJECTIVE	To obtain a position with computer operations responsibilities in an automated office.
EDUCATION	Iron Hills Junior College, Peoria, Illinois A.A. in Automated Office Technology, May 1992
	Hoover High School, Peoria, Illinois Academic Curriculum; Graduated: June 1990
EXPERIENCE	Bentley & Simon, Peoria, Illinois Position: Data Entry Clerk June 1990-Present Responsibilities: Entering legal time spent into computer accounts of clients; generating monthly computer statements to clients.
	Caselli Florist Shop, Peoria, Illinois Position: Clerk June 1988-June 1990 Responsibilities: Assisted in taking orders at front desk. Handled telephone orders.
ACTIVITIES	Iron Hills: Student Government Delegate; Intramural Basketball; Office Automation Club
	Hoover H.S.: Varsity Basketball and Baseball; Class Treasurer; Key Club
REFERENCES	Furnished on request

Q. WORD-DIVISION REVIEW

Q. It is preferable not to divide a word at the end of a line. If it is necessary, though, follow these rules.

Many word processing programs have a hyphenation feature that will *(a)* divide words too long to fit on a line or *(b)* highlight words so that a hyphen can be inserted at the appropriate point.

1. Do not divide words pronounced as one syllable *(brought, trimmed),* contractions *(wouldn't, hasn't),* or abbreviations *(NASA, f.o.b.).*

2. Divide words only between syllables. Whenever you are unsure of where a syllable ends, consult a dictionary.

3. Leave at least three characters (the last will be a hyphen) on the upper line, and carry at least three characters (the last may be a punctuation mark) to the next line *(re- tain* and *broad- en;* but not *a- lert* or *seed- y).*

4. Divide compound words either at the hyphen *(self- contained)* or where the two words join to make a solid compound *(second- hand,* not *secondhand,* and *winter- green,* not *win- tergreen).*

R. Select the words in each line that can be divided, and key them with a hyphen to show where the division should be (Example: *try- ing).*

R. TECHNIQUE PRACTICE: WORD DIVISION

105	trying	rhyme	didn't
106	USAF	roadway	loudly
107	strayed	blamed	stepsister
108	wasn't	receive	lonesome
109	scholarship	extreme	caution
110	knowledge	crossing	self-evident

S. Key the paragraph dividing words as necessary at the end of lines to keep the right margin as even as possible.

S. TECHNIQUE PRACTICE: WORD DIVISION

The main attractions for the children in a municipal recreation league are the supervised sports activities. The neighborhood youngsters sign up for either basketball camp or swimming relays. Last year our recreation league was run by Al Biggerstaff. He was assisted in basketball by Anne Smith and in swimming by Marc Jaderstrom. Nearly a hundred children participated.

T. INDENT

Indent is used to indent text from the left margin to the next tab setting. Indent sets a temporary left margin at this tab setting.

To set an indent for an enumeration (a numbered list), clear all tabs and set a left tab 4 spaces from the left margin. To key an enumeration, key the item number followed by a period. Turn on indent and key the text to be indented. At the end of the last line of a numbered item, turn off indent to return to the left margin to key the next item number.

Progress Test on Part 3

TEST 3-A
5-MINUTE TIMED
WRITING

Spacing: Double

Working Papers: 101

         Most people file their income tax forms around the   11
middle of April. They have a choice as to whether they use   23
the standard deduction or itemize their deductions. The   35
wise taxpayer will use the method that is in his or her   46
best interest. When it is time to complete your income tax   58
forms, it may be quite beneficial if Schedule A is used   69
to compute your deductions. The amount saved by using this   81
form can be quite large. There are several sections on the   93
form. The first one deals with health expenses, which   104
might be deductible depending on the income you earned.   116
Some taxes and certain types of interest may also be used.   128
There are other sections that cover gifts, theft and other   139
types of losses, moving expenses, job expenses, and other   151
types of expenses. The major job of completing this   162
schedule is in keeping all the needed records through the   173
course of the year, but the benefits may be quite large.   185
One may be very well rewarded for the extra amount of time   197
that this may take.   200

| 1 | 2 | 3 | 4 | 5 | 6 | 7 | 8 | 9 | 10 | 11 | 12 |

TEST 3-B
LETTER 33
MODIFIED-BLOCK STYLE

Working Papers: 103

Use the current date.

The correct salutation is *Dear Mr. Beilow:*

Treat each item in the enumeration as a separate paragraph.

Please send the following letter to Mr. Robert D. Beilow, Director of Athletics, Mountainview Community College, 157 Valley Road, Winslow, AZ 86047.

As you are aware, the eight conferences of the quad states have now agreed to sponsor a basketball tournament to determine a champion from the quad states of Arizona, Colorado, New Mexico, and Utah.

1. The tournament will be held on the campus of Farmington Community College in Farmington, New Mexico, on March 19–21.

2. Each school must make its own travel arrangements. Lodging and meals will be available at Farmington. (Details are enclosed.)

3. On the basis of advertising and ticket revenues, each school participating in the tournament will receive some compensation.

Please call me if you have any questions about this invitation.

Sincerely, / Carline J. Wuoka / Administrator / *(Your Initials)* / Enclosure

LETTER 35
BLOCK STYLE

Working Papers: 21

Names of published works should be underlined.

June 3, 19— / Hampton Associates, Inc. / 830 Market Street / San Francisco, CA 94102-1925 / Ladies and Gentlemen:

I recently read an article in <u>Business Week</u> concerning how computer buyers can make standards happen. It was a very interesting article.

It indicates that if customers demand standard products when they purchase computers, participate in standard-setting groups, and band together with other customers, they will do better in the long run.

Have you had customer groups assist you or provide you with information on the adoption of more computer standards, such as in the areas of industrywide interfaces, a mix and match of computer gear and programs, and building the best system for each application utilized?

I would appreciate any data that you might furnish for me with relationship to customers and your firm working together to set past or future standards.

Sincerely yours, / Alice Karns / Vice President / *(Your Initials)*

LETTER 36
PERSONAL-BUSINESS
LETTER IN BLOCK STYLE

Personal-business letter in block style: All lines begin at the left margin. The return address is keyed under the writer's name. Reference initials are not used.

October 1, 19— / Dr. James L. Rowe / 2345 South Main Street / Bowling Green, OH 43402 / Dear Jim:

Thank you for your letter of September 25 in which you inquired about my trip to New York City.

I plan to leave on October 15 for a two-week business/vacation trip to the city. While at Columbia University, I will be conducting a workshop on the utilization of voice-activated equipment.

My work at Columbia will be completed on October 22, after which I plan to attend a number of plays, visit the Metropolitan Museum of Art, and take one of the sightseeing tours of the city.

If you would care to join me on October 22, please let me know. I would be most happy to make reservations at the hotel for you and to purchase theater tickets. Why don't you consider joining me in the "Big Apple."

Sincerely, / Bryan Goldberg / 320 South Summit Street / Toledo, OH 43604

LETTER 37
PERSONAL-BUSINESS
LETTER IN BLOCK STYLE

March 11, 19— / Mr. Sam Lukens / 1367 Lockland Road / Atlanta, GA 30316 / Dear Sam:

Did you receive my letter of March 1? I wrote you concerning my article on word processing.

As you know, I have had some problems in writing the article as a result of my changing software. I was so thoroughly knowledgeable about Apex that when I changed to Mars, I became somewhat confused. I need your help with the descriptions for some of the function keys.

Perhaps you have received my letter, and your answer is in the mail. If not, please call me at 602-555-6241.

Sincerely, / Lillian Smith / 1816 Vernon Avenue / Scottsdale, AZ 85257

BASKETBALL TOURNAMENT
By Charlotte Luna

On March 19, 19--, an exciting new competition will be inaugurated when the eight conference winners in the basketball programs in the community colleges of the quad states of (AZ), (CO), (NM), and (UT) meet in farmington, (NM).

NEW AGREEMENT

According to the agreement reached by the athletic directors from community colleges in the quad states, the eight league conferences in the (4) states will send their conference champion winner to a basketball tournament during the third week end of March to determine the quad states champion.[1]

Financial Benefits

The revenues raised generated from advertising and ticket sales will be returned distributed to the participa̶n̶t̶s̶ ting schools after the appropriate expenses have been deducted. The share of revenues earned will be based on the record achievement of the teams at the tournament.[2] Thus the tournament champion will collect the biggest share of revenues.

---

[1] ~~Thomas Foley~~ Pat Muranka, "Basketball Tournament Becomes a Reality," Quad States Community College Newsletter, July 1992, p. 12.

[2] Ibid.

Use the current date and send this memo to Marvin Palomaki, Athletic Director from Debra Marchant, Tournament Manager, concerning the Quad States Tournament.

The participating colleges in the quad states tournament have been sent the packet of information and forms. As this is my first experience in coordinating the activities for an event like this, I am very appreciative of everything that you have done to help me.

Housing arrangements have been made at the Manson Inn, and all meals will be provided at the Farmington Community College dining hall. The contracts for the officials (including referees) have all been received. All media personnel are being kept informed of the developments.

Please look over the attached list; have I overlooked anything?

(Your Initials) / Attachment

Human Relations Consultants, Inc.
150 STATE STREET, TRENTON, NJ 08608-200348   PHONE 609-555-3339

↓ 2 inches

April 3, 19-- ↓ 1 inch

*Letters 1–33 appear in Lessons 1–60.

Block style: All lines begin at the left margin.

Always respect a woman's preference in selecting *Miss, Mrs.,* or *Ms.* If her preference is unknown, use the title *Ms.*

Standard punctuation consists of a colon after the salutation and a comma after the complimentary closing.

Ms. Janice Jackson, President
Weston & Weston, Inc.
3667 Highland Avenue
Jersey City, NJ 07304-1034 ↓ 2

Dear Ms. Jackson:

Thank you for your letter of March 28 in which you asked me to address your local Rotary Club. I am happy to accept your invitation to speak on human relations in business.

Human relations development is a very current topic in the business world today. Businesses, more than ever, want to hire employees who can work to better serve customers and the firm. As you know, I have just completed a two-year study of human relations in business. It is interesting to note that the study indicates that more than 95 percent of all businessmen and businesswomen still believe that any employee with this ability is a major asset to the firm.

Enclosed is a copy of my article "Human Relations--Today and Tomorrow." If you feel this article would be of interest to the members of your club, I would be happy to have copies available.

I plan to arrive at the Holiday Inn Center by 11:30 a.m. as you have requested. It will be a pleasure to see you again.

Sincerely yours, ↓ 4

To indicate that an item is enclosed with a letter, key the word *Enclosure* a single space below the reference initials of a business letter.

James F. Rainey
Human Relations Consultant ↓ 2

urs
Enclosure

4

SKILLBUILDING
Correspondence, Reports, and Tables

OBJECTIVES

KEYBOARDING

To key 43 words a minute on a 5-minute timed writing with no more than 5 errors.

LANGUAGE ARTS

To improve language arts skills.

To proofread and correct errors.

To develop keyboard composing skill.

DOCUMENT PROCESSING

To review the formatting of correspondence, reports, and tables. To format business letters with tables, indented paragraphs, subject lines, and copy notations.

To format bound and unbound reports with side headings, enumerations, endnotes, footnotes; book manuscripts; a news release; and magazine articles.

To format open tables.

M. Key each sentence on a separate line.

M. TECHNIQUE PRACTICE: RETURN KEY

79 Move the desk. Hook up the computer. Hang the photograph.
80 File the invoices. Lower the chairs. Sharpen the pencils.
81 Adjust the new vertical blinds. Update the client records.
82 Empty the baskets. Polish the credenza. Remove the files.

N. DIAGNOSTIC PRACTICE: ALPHABET

Turn to the Diagnostic Practice: Alphabet routine at the back of this book. Take the Pretest and record your performance. Then practice the drill lines for those reaches on which you made errors. Finally, repeat the Pretest and compare your performance.

O. Take two 1-minute timed writings on each line as you concentrate on infrequently used letters.

O. ALPHABET REVIEW: INFREQUENT-LETTER PRACTICE

Y 83 Rory may try to fly to Yonkers if they buy the shiny plane. 12
Z 84 Zeke was amazed at the huge size of the dozen crazy prizes. 12
K 85 Kevin knew Kirk kicked a rock that struck a flock of ducks. 12
J 86 Jo jubilantly jumped with joy just as Jim joined the major. 12

| 1 | 2 | 3 | 4 | 5 | 6 | 7 | 8 | 9 | 10 | 11 | 12

P. Spacing: double.
Take two 5-minute timed writings. Compute your speed and count errors.

Goal: 40 wam/5'/5e

P. 5-MINUTE TIMED WRITING

87   A place for everything and everything in its place. 12
88 This old adage makes sense for today's businessperson who 23
89 is concerned with both neatness and efficiency on the job. 35
90 Whether you do your work at a desk in an office or in a 47
91 spare room in your home, these three guidelines may help 58
92 you be more organized: adequacy, closeness, and grouping. 70
93   Adequacy means sufficient for a specific requirement. 82
94 Quite simply, when your desk no longer holds your work, you 94
95 must add to your space or reduce the amount of work on your 106
96 desk. The next tip, closeness, means keeping those things 118
97 you use most often nearby. For example, current projects 129
98 should be on wall shelves or in top drawers where they can 141
99 most easily be reached. 146
100   And finally, it is helpful to group the things you 157
101 need according to their use. Books, records, forms, and 168
102 other supplies for each project should all be kept in just 180
103 one place. Use these tips to organize your space, and you 192
104 will present a sharp, professional image. 200

| 1 | 2 | 3 | 4 | 5 | 6 | 7 | 8 | 9 | 10 | 11 | 12

61-65 LESSONS

Margins: 1 inch • Spacing: Single • Drills: 2 times • Format Guide: 41–43 • Working Papers: 19–26

Goals for Unit 13

Begin each day with approximately 15 minutes of skill-building, selecting activities from pages 141–144. In the remaining class time, complete as many production jobs from pages 145–150 as you can.

1. To improve accuracy and speed on alphabet, number, and symbol keys.
2. To key 40 wam for 5 minutes with no more than 5 errors.
3. To develop proficiency in spelling commonly misspelled words.
4. To format and key various forms of correspondence—business letters, personal-business letters, and memorandums.

A. WARMUP

```
1        Pam inquired about Flight #670 to Zurich for April 21.    12
2 She found that the cost was $853 for a two-way ticket.  She     24
3 discovered that Flight #97 would be an extra $50 on June 4.      36
   |  1  |  2  |  3  |  4  |  5  |  6  |  7  |  8  |  9  |  10  |  11  |  12
```

LANGUAGE ARTS

B. Study the rules at the right. Then key lines 4–7, making necessary changes.

B. ABBREVIATIONS

Rule: Abbreviations made up of single initials in all-capital letters usually require no periods and no internal spaces. **Exceptions:** geographic names and academic degrees

The FIFO inventory valuation method is being used.

Rule: Abbreviations made up of single initials in small letters require a period after each initial but no space after each internal period. **Exceptions:** rpm, mpg, mph

The shipment of tires was to be made f.o.b. destination.

```
4 The N.F.C. and A.F.C. champions met in the Super Bowl.
5 Kamran was proud to receive his BS degree in the U.S.A.
6 The eom statement has an error in the amount of $79.42.
7 An m.p.g. average is affected by speed, roads, and weather.
```

C. These words are among the 500 most frequently misspelled words in business correspondence.

C. SPELLING

```
8 operations health individual considered expenditures vendor
9 beginning internal pursuant president union written develop
10 hours enclosing situation function including standard shown
11 engineering payable suggested participants providing orders
12 toward nays total without paragraph meetings different vice
```

H. PRETEST.
Take a 1-minute timed writing; compute your speed and count errors.

H. PRETEST: NUMBER AND SYMBOL REVIEW

47   Hall & Smith's catalog listed #489 (personal computer) 12
48 and #267 (disk) at a 15% discount. One-fourth (1/4) of all 24
49 of their items were on sale at 9:30 a.m. Ms. "Tillie" Yang 36
50 said the $7.50 tray sold well. However, the $9.65 did too. 48

| 1 | 2 | 3 | 4 | 5 | 6 | 7 | 8 | 9 | 10 | 11 | 12 |

I. PRACTICE.
1. Key lines 51–60 once.
2. Check the Pretest (H) for those keys on which you made errors, and key the corresponding lines 2 more times.

I. PRACTICE: NUMBERS

51 00 ;p0 000 0 pod, 00 pie, 00 par, 00 pale, 00 push, 00 past
52 11 aq1 111 1 ask, 11 add, 11 art, 11 quit, 11 zero, 11 zest
53 22 sw2 222 2 sew, 22 six, 22 was, 22 wise, 22 axes, 22 exam
54 33 de3 333 3 den, 33 dew, 33 end, 33 edge, 33 cede, 33 code
55 44 fr4 444 4 for, 44 far, 44 red, 44 rave, 44 very, 44 five

56 55 fr5 555 5 tar, 55 tag, 55 get, 55 gear, 55 boat, 55 verb
57 66 jy6 666 6 joy, 66 jog, 66 yet, 66 year, 66 nary, 66 navy
58 77 ju7 777 7 jug, 77 jib, 77 urn, 77 unto, 77 must, 77 mush
59 88 ki8 888 8 kit, 88 key, 88 icy, 88 inky, 88 kilt, 88 kite
60 99 lo9 999 9 lot, 99 log, 99 old, 99 oils, 99 loot, 99 oleo

J. PRACTICE.
1. Key lines 61–66 once.
2. Check the Pretest (H) for those keys on which you made errors, and key the corresponding lines 2 more times.

J. PRACTICE: SYMBOLS

61 % ft5% 18% 25% - ;--;- Smith-Brown's interest rate was 18%.
62 " ;'"' ;"' "A" / ;//;/ "Ed" and/or "Bo" got it for 1/5 off.
63 $ fr4$ $18 $35 : ;:::;: Ken sold shares for $45 at 9:30 a.m.
64 (lo9(1(1 (1( );p0); () Ike (the favorite) moved quickly.
65 & ju7& j&j &j& ; ;:;:;: Mo & Joe's sold it; but Al's didn't.
66 # de3# #82 #20 ' ;'';' Jay's #67 and #33 were like Marie's.

K. POSTTEST.
Repeat the Pretest (H) and compare performance.

K. POSTTEST: NUMBER AND SYMBOL REVIEW

L.
Take a 1-minute timed writing on the first paragraph to establish your base speed. Then take four 1-minute timed writings on the remaining paragraphs. As soon as you equal or exceed your base speed on one paragraph, advance to the next one.

L. SUSTAINED PRACTICE: SYLLABIC INTENSITY

67   The thought of owning a business can make a person get 12
68 very excited. To be your own boss and to call the shots is 24
69 a worthy aim. Think of your answers to some big questions. 36

70   What are your knowledge and background of this product 12
71 or service that you will provide? Are you prepared to make 24
72 a detailed, credible business plan for the first two years? 36

73   How is your product or service different from those in 12
74 your marketing area? Why would a client come to you rather 24
75 than support one of the other vendors located in your area? 36

76   Are your resources and credit adequate to help provide 12
77 the financial support necessary for the early stages? Have 24
78 you got a clear understanding of all the financial aspects? 36

| 1 | 2 | 3 | 4 | 5 | 6 | 7 | 8 | 9 | 10 | 11 | 12 |

D. 12-SECOND SPRINTS

D. Take three 12-second timed writings on each line. The scale gives your wam speed for a 12-second timed writing.

13 Rick made the dog sleighs for the six girls and their pals.
14 They paid a helpful neighbor to sit with their eight girls.
15 Pam did not cut the oak but let the men cut the fir for us.
16 The six forms she got from my firm may do for that problem.

| | | |5| | | |10| | |15| | |20| | | |25| | | |30| | | |35| | | |40| | | |45| | | |50| | | |55| | | |60

E. PRETEST: ALPHABET REVIEW

E. PRETEST.
Take a 1-minute timed writing; compute your speed and count errors.

17   The skill of listening is just as important as are the   12
18 skills of speaking and writing. Quite often we hear an em-   24
19 ployer say that workers are not paying attention to what is   36
20 being said. Listening is expected of everybody and prized.   48

| | 1 | 2 | 3 | 4 | 5 | 6 | 7 | 8 | 9 | 10 | 11 | 12 |

F. PRACTICE: ALPHABET KEYS

F. PRACTICE.
1. Key lines 21–46 (A–Z) once.
2. Check the Pretest (E) for those keys on which you made errors, and key the corresponding lines 2 more times.

21 A Alan also last easy vain bacon canoe attest ballad author
22 B Beth baby able best bibb derby limbo budget burger bronze
23 C Chip coco cold care fact crazy civic carpet octave scopes
24 D Dave date adds drop dent adore diner redeem hidden worded

25 E Ella ease else eyed epic treat check esteem elated talked
26 F Faye fold fair cuff fort beefs draft friend grafts finder
27 G Glen good gold ages page vigor begun grates legion jargon
28 H Hope hash high huge such north laugh thrust though chided

29 I Iris into inch tile fill music pinch picnic impart deceit
30 J John junk just join jowl bijou banjo jabber junior hijack
31 K Kate cork kind seek hawk kitty knack kinder shrink awaken
32 L Lane look alas late lime elate skill locale collar bleach

33 M Mary mate maid main amen moody smile memory motion muffin
34 N Nate note neon wind fend longs mints noodle nation inland
35 O Opal oleo tool code fold opens order mascot report casino
36 P Paul pork pine spot tips props soupy dipped purple upbeat

37 Q Quip quiz quad quit quay quaff equal square piqued squirm
38 R Rose rage roar rare rate resin orbit arrear droves drench
39 S Sara suit sale easy skis sable ashes attest tassel assort
40 T Tony toot unto tile test stair trash fitted ratify stayed

41 U Ural undo unit used upon truth union assume scours adjust
42 V Vera vail veto vest wave value vivid evenly avowed lavish
43 W Wilt were avow crow gnaw swept waits awards winked wigwag
44 X Xeno exit jinx oxen axle sixty taxed coaxed exiled exceed

45 Y Yale yawl yard eyed stay dimly yeast choppy yearly yellow
46 Z Zeke zest zero zone cozy pizza tizzy dozing zapped sneeze

G. POSTTEST.
Repeat the Pretest (E) and compare performance.

G. POSTTEST: ALPHABET REVIEW

Pick up any newspaper or turn on any news program on   12
TV, and it seems you will hear yet another story about an   23
oil tanker that has spilled its cargo or a landfill that   35
has reached its limit. As more and more people are paying   46
heed to the environmental concerns, more and more companies   58
are following suit by setting environmental goals.   68

What are the reasons so many firms have a new stance   80
on these issues? First, and foremost, there appear to be   92
more simultaneous threats to our world than in any other   103
moment in time. Our government believes that four out of   115
ten Americans live in places where the air is not healthy   127
to breathe. Other issues include ozone depletion, acid   138
rain, the fouling of thousands of rivers and lakes by raw   149
sewage and toxic wastes, destruction of rain forests, and   161
the greenhouse effect.   166

A second reason for the growing concern over these   177
issues in corporate America is a response to heightened   188
public awareness of the problems. Nine out of ten people   200
say they would be willing to make a special effort to buy   211
products that show concern for protecting the air, land,   223
and water. Membership in environmental groups is soaring.   235
There are now tens of thousands of conservation groups;   246
each town seems to have two or three doing anything from   257
trying to save a trout stream to stopping a shopping mall   269
from being built.   273

In the last two decades, more than a dozen major laws   285
have been passed. As a result, overall pollution levels   296
have dropped. New regulations now focus on management and   308
recordkeeping roles and have fewer quantitative, absolute   319
standards to which firms must adhere. While much has been   331
accomplished, strong maintenance is key to keeping our air,   343
water, and land clean in years ahead.   350

| 1 | 2 | 3 | 4 | 5 | 6 | 7 | 8 | 9 | 10 | 11 | 12 |

Diagnostic Practice: Alphabet

The Diagnostic Practice: Alphabet program is designed to diagnose and then correct your keystroking errors. You may use this program at any time throughout the course after you complete Lesson 9.

Directions
1. Key the Pretest/Posttest passage once, proofread it, and identify errors.
2. Note your results—the number of errors you made on each key and your total number of errors. For example, if you keyed *rhe* for *the,* that would count as 1 error on the letter *t.*
3. For any letter on which you made 2 or more errors, select the corresponding drill lines and key them twice. If you made only 1 error, key the drill once.
4. If you made no errors on the Pretest/Posttest passage, turn to the practice on troublesome pairs on page SB-3 and key each line once. This section provides intensive practice on those pairs of keys which are most commonly confused.
5. Finally, rekey the Pretest/Posttest, and compare your performance with your Pretest.

PRETEST/POSTTEST

Jacob and Zeke Koufax quietly enjoyed jazz music on my new jukebox. My six or seven pieces of exquisite equipment helped both create lovely music by Richard Wagner; I picked five very quaint waltzes from Gregg Ward's jazz recordings.

PRACTICE: INDIVIDUAL REACHES

```
aa Isaac badge carry dared eager faced gains habit dials AA
aa jaunt kayak label mamma Nancy oasis paint Qatar rapid AA
aa safer taken guard vague waves exact yacht Zaire Aaron AA

bb about ebbed ebony rugby fiber elbow amber unbar oboes BB
bb arbor cubic oxbow maybe abate abbot debit libel album BB
bb embed obeys urban tubes Sybil above lobby webby bribe BB

cc acted occur recap icing ulcer emcee uncle ocean force CC
cc scale itchy bucks excel Joyce acute yucca decal micro CC
cc mulch McCoy incur octet birch scrub latch couch cycle CC

dd admit daddy edict Magda ideal older index oddly order DD
dd outdo udder crowd Floyd adapt added Edith Idaho folds DD
dd under modem sword misdo fudge rowdy Lydia adept buddy DD

ee aegis beach cents dense eerie fence germs hence piece EE
ee jewel keyed leads media nerve poems penny reach seize EE
ee teach guest verse Wendy Xerox years zesty aerie begin EE
```

As human beings, our perception of time has grown out 12
of a natural series of rhythms which are linked to daily, 23
monthly, and yearly cycles. No matter how much we live by 35
our wristwatches, our bodies and our lives will always be 47
somewhat influenced by an internal clock. What is of even 59
greater interest, though, are the many uses and perceptions 71
of time based on individuals and their cultures. 81

Rhythm and tempo are ways we relate to time and are 92
discerning features of a culture. In some cultures, folks 104
move very slowly; in others, moving quickly is the norm. 115
Mixing the two types may create feelings of discomfort. 127
People may have trouble relating to each other because they 139
are not in synchrony. To be synchronized is to subtly move 151
in union with another person; it is vital to a strong and 162
lengthy partnership. 167

In general, Americans move at a fast tempo, although 178
there are regional departures. In meetings, they tend to 190
be impatient and want to "get down to business" right away. 202
They have been taught that it is best to come to the point 214
quickly and avoid vagueness. Because American business 225
works in a short time frame, prompt results are often of 236
more interest than the building of long-term relationships. 249

Time is also the basic organizing system for all of 260
life's events. Time is used for setting priorities. For 272
example, lead time varies quite a bit from one culture to 283
the next. When you conduct business with people of other 295
cultures, it is crucial to know just how much lead time is 307
required for each event. For instance, numerous corporate 318
executives have their time scheduled for months in advance. 330
Last-minute requests by phone are viewed as poor planning 342
and could even be perceived as an insult. 350

| 1 | 2 | 3 | 4 | 5 | 6 | 7 | 8 | 9 | 10 | 11 | 12

```
ff after defer offer jiffy gulfs infer often dwarf cuffs FF
ff awful afoul refer affix edify Wolfe infra aloof scarf FF
ff bluff afoot defer daffy fifty sulfa softy surfs stuff FF

gg again edges egged soggy igloo Elgin angel ogled Marge GG
gg outgo auger pygmy agaze Edgar Egypt buggy light bulge GG
gg singe doggy organ fugle agree hedge began baggy Niger GG

hh ahead abhor chili Nehru ghost Elihu khaki Lhasa unhat HH
hh aloha phony myrrh shale Ethan while yahoo choir jehad HH
hh ghoul Khmer Delhi Ohara photo rhino shake think while HH

ii aired bides cider dices eight fifth vigil highs radii II
ii jiffy kinds lives mired niece oiled piped rigid siren II
ii tired build visit wider exist yield aimed binds cigar II

jj major eject fjord Ouija enjoy Cajun Fijis Benjy bijou JJ
jj banjo jabot jacks jaded jails Japan jaunt jazzy jeans JJ
jj jeeps jeers jelly jerks jibed jiffy jilts joint joker JJ

kk Akron locks vodka peeks mikes sulky links okras larks KK
kk skins Yukon hawks tykes makes socks seeks hiker sulks KK
kk tanks Tokyo jerky pesky nukes gawks maker ducks cheek KK

ll alarm blame clank idled elope flame glows Chloe Iliak LL
ll ankle Lloyd inlet olive plane burly sleet atlas Tulsa LL
ll yowls axles nylon alone blunt claim idler elite flute LL

mm among adman demit pigmy times calms comma unman omits MM
mm armor smell umber axmen lymph gizmo amass admit demon MM
mm dogma imply films mommy omits armed smear bumpy axman MM

nn ankle Abner envoy gnome Johns input knife kilns hymns NN
nn Donna onion apnea Arnes snore undid owned cynic angle NN
nn entry gnash inset knoll nanny onset barns sneer unfit NN

oo aorta bolts coats dolls peony fouls goofs hoped iotas OO
oo jolts kooky loins moral noise poled Roger soaks total OO
oo quote voter would Saxon yo-yo zones bombs colts doles OO

pp apple epoch flips alpha ample input droop puppy sharp PP
pp spunk soups expel typed April Epsom slips helps empty PP
pp unpin optic peppy corps spite upset types apply creep PP

qq Iraqi equal pique roque squad tuque aquae equip toque QQ
qq squab squat squam quail qualm quart queen quell query QQ
qq quest quick quiet quill quilt quirk quota quote quoth QQ

rr array bring crave drive erode freak grain three irate RR
rr kraft inrun orate Barry tramp urges livre wrote lyric RR
rr Ezars armor broth crown drawl erect freer grade throw RR
```

As the lifestyles of most people continue to become 11
more and more complex, employers keep looking for ways to 23
help their employees manage their stress. Companies are 34
starting to view the health of their employees as an issue 46
that should be shared by both parties. Employer interest 58
in wellness programs is being driven by an assortment of 69
factors which include: rising health-care costs, an aging 81
work force, and a growing knowledge base about the effects 93
that lifestyle choices may have on one's health. 103

There are a wide range of conditions found in work 114
settings which place workers at risk of health breakdowns. 126
The most often quoted events include: a stressful work 137
atmosphere, tense work relationships, feeling a lack of 148
control over tasks at work, and having conflicts about how 160
much time can be spent with family or on leisure projects. 172

Firms are responding to these concerns by starting 183
on-site wellness programs. Staffed by trained experts, 194
these programs teach people how to stop smoking, reduce 206
their cholesterol, or control their blood pressure. To go 217
one step further, some firms are opening fitness centers 229
which not only teach the benefits of exercise but also give 240
people the chance to use the centers on a daily basis 252
during lunch or at any other times. 259

While stressed employees are embracing these benefits 271
with zealous energy, there is dispute among experts about 283
whether the data on wellness programs supports them. Fans 294
claim that these programs reduce the number of days workers 306
call in sick, increase levels of output, and reduce health- 318
care costs. Most users agree that it takes at least two 330
years for a company to show cost savings from these 341
programs and to improve the morale of employees. 350

| 1 | 2 | 3 | 4 | 5 | 6 | 7 | 8 | 9 | 10 | 11 | 12

```
ss ashen bombs specs binds bares leafs bangs sighs issue SS
ss necks mills teams turns solos stops stirs dress diets SS
ss usury Slavs stows abyss asked stabs cords mares beefs SS

tt attic debts pacts width Ethel often eight itchy alter TT
tt until motto optic earth stops petty couth newts extra TT
tt myths Aztec atone doubt facts veldt ether sight Italy TT

uu audio bumps cured dumps deuce fuels gulps huffy opium UU
uu junta kudos lulls mumps nudge outdo purer ruler super UU
uu tulip revue exult yucca azure auger burns curve duels UU

vv avows event ivory elves envoy overt larva mauve savvy VV
vv avant every rivet Elvis anvil coves curvy divvy avert VV
vv evict given valve ovens serve paves evade wives hover VV

ww awash bwana dwarf brews Gwenn schwa kiwis Elwin unwed WW
ww owner Irwin sweet twins byway awake dwell pewee tower WW
ww Erwin swims twirl awful dwelt Dewey owlet swamp twine WW

xx axiom exile fixed Bronx toxin Sioux Exxon pyxie axman XX
xx exert fixes Leonx oxbow beaux calyx maxim exact sixth XX
xx proxy taxes excel mixed boxer axing Texas sixty epoxy XX

yy maybe bylaw cynic dying eying unify gypsy hypos Benjy YY
yy Tokyo hilly rummy Ronny loyal pygmy diary Syria types YY
yy buyer vying Wyatt epoxy crazy kayak Byram cycle bawdy YY

zz Azure Czech adzes bezel dizzy Franz froze Liszt ritzy ZZ
zz abuzz tizzy hazed czars maize Ginza oozes blitz fuzzy ZZ
zz jazzy mazes mezzo sized woozy Hertz fizzy Hazel Gomez ZZ
```

PRACTICE: TROUBLESOME PAIRS

```
A/S Sal said he asked Sara Ash for a sample of the raisins.
B/V Beverly believes Bob behaved very bravely in Beaverton.
C/D Clyde and Dick decided they could decode an old decree.

E/W We wondered whether Andrew waited for Walter and Wendy.
F/G Griffin goofed in figuring their gifted golfer's score.
H/J Joseph joshed with Judith when John jogged to Johnetta.

I/O A novice violinist spoiled Orville Olin's piccolo solo.
K/L Kelly, unlike Blake, liked to walk as quickly as Karla.
M/N Many women managed to move among the mounds of masonry.

O/P A pollster polled a population in Phoenix by telephone.
Q/A Quincy acquired one quality quartz ring at the banquet.
R/T Three skaters traded their tartan trench coats to Bart.

U/Y Buy your supply of gifts during your busy July journey.
X/C The exemptions exceed the expert's wildest expectation.
Z/A Eliza gazed as four lazy zebra zigzagged near a gazebo.
```

The impact of computer technology and the related use of video display terminals are changing the work settings of America, and their use will continue to grow in future years. For instance, did you know that the number of video display terminals in use in offices has increased more than fifty times over the past twenty years?

Video display terminals are comprised of a display screen, a keyboard, and a central processing unit. The display screen is the output device that shows what the computer is working on. Display screens can be monochrome, which means they have green, white, or orange strokes on a black background, or they can be in color. Most of the new screens swivel, tilt, and lift, which allow the user to select the best angle based on height and viewing choice.

The keyboard is the input device that allows the user to send data to the brain of the computer. Keyboards are often used for data entry and inquiry. The keyboard is similar in most ways to a standard typewriter keyboard but has extra keys and functions. The keyboard should come apart from the screen and be adjustable to ensure proper position, angle, and comfort of the user. A work surface that is lower than normal may be required to keep a user's arms and hands in a more relaxed position.

The central processing unit is often thought to be the brain of the computer. It is the center of action for all of the computer processing and can perform calculations and organize the flow of data into and out of the system. This type of computer operates at a high voltage, but the power supplies that generate the voltage produce just a small bit of current. All data processing equipment must meet tough safety standards in this regard.

| 1 | 2 | 3 | 4 | 5 | 6 | 7 | 8 | 9 | 10 | 11 | 12 |

Diagnostic Practice: Numbers

The Diagnostic Practice: Numbers program is designed to diagnose and then correct your keystroking errors. You may use this program at any time throughout the course after you complete Lesson 14.

Directions

1. Key the Pretest/Posttest passage once, proofread it, and identify errors.
2. Note your results—the number of errors you made on each key and your total number of errors. For example, if you keyed *24* for *25,* that would count as 1 error on the number *5.*
3. For any number on which you made 2 or more errors, select the corresponding drill lines and key them twice. If you made only 1 error, key the drill once.
4. If you made no errors on the Pretest/Posttest passage, key the drills that contain all numbers on page SB-5.
5. Finally, rekey the Pretest/Posttest, and compare your performance with your Pretest.

PRETEST/POSTTEST

My inventory records dated December 31, 1994, revealed we had 458 pints, 2,069 quarts, and 4,774 gallons of paint. We had 2,053 brushes, 568 scrapers, 12,063 wallpaper rolls, 897 knives, 5,692 mixers, 480 ladders, and 371 step stools.

PRACTICE: INDIVIDUAL REACHES

1 aq aq1 aq1qa 111 ants 101 aunts 131 apples 171 animals a1
They got 11 answers correct for the 11 questions in BE 121.
Those 11 adults loaded the 711 animals between 1 and 2 p.m.
All 111 agreed that 21 of those 31 are worthy of the honor.

2 sw sw2 sw2ws 222 sets 242 steps 226 salads 252 saddles s2
The 272 summer tourists saw the 22 soldiers and 32 sailors.
Your September 2 date was all right for 292 of 322 persons.
The 22 surgeons said 221 of those 225 operations went well.

3 de de3 de3ed 333 dots 303 drops 313 demons 393 dollars d3
Bus 333 departed at 3 p.m. with the 43 dentists and 5 boys.
She left 33 dolls and 73 decoys at 353 West Addison Street.
The 13 doctors helped some of the 33 druggists in Room 336.

4 fr fr4 fr4rf 444 fans 844 farms 444 fishes 644 fiddles f4
My 44 friends bought 84 farms and sold over 144 franchises.
She sold 44 fish and 440 beef dinners for $9.40 per dinner.
The '54 Ford had only 40,434 fairly smooth miles by July 4.

As we move into a decade where most people have high
career expectations but low company loyalty, more and more
firms are feeling the pinch when a high-level executive
suddenly quits on them. Smart entrepreneurs are filling in
the gap by providing a unique twist on an old service--the
temporary agency. In the past, temporary agencies were
used when a department had a large mailing to be sent out,
a huge file project to be finished, or some other clerical
task that required a fast response. Today, firms can find
the same premise applied not just to support jobs but to
top-management functions as well.

The interim management firm works just like an agency
in that a short-term need is defined by a firm, the agency
is called with the specifics, and a qualified person is
sent over right away. The difference here is in the high
level of jobs being filled. Interim management firms work
with retired presidents, executives who have been outplaced
and have not yet located the right job, or someone who lost
his or her job in a merger and has decided not to return to
regular corporate life.

There are now highly skilled people who are interested
only in interim work. Others are more than willing to lend
their expertise for the nine to twelve months it may take
them to land another job. Still others accept interim work
in the hope that it will lead to a regular job, which it
sometimes does. There are many benefits to hiring interim
managers. They do the work they are hired to do rather
than telling what they think should be done. They also
have years of hands-on experience in a specialty, so a firm
may get more talent than they pay for. An interim manager
could be the best choice when a company needs help fast.

| 1 | 2 | 3 | 4 | 5 | 6 | 7 | 8 | 9 | 10 | 11 | 12 |

5 fr fr5 fr5rf 555 furs 655 foxes 555 flares 455 fingers f5
They now own 155 restaurants, 45 food stores, and 55 farms.
They ordered 45, 55, 65, and 57 yards of that new material.
Flight 855 flew over Farmington at 5:50 p.m. on December 5.

6 jy jy6 jy6yj 666 jets 266 jeeps 666 jewels 866 jaguars j6
Purchase orders numbered 6667 and 6668 were sent yesterday.
Those 66 jazz players played for 46 juveniles in Room 6966.
The 6 judges reviewed the 66 journals on November 16 or 26.

7 ju ju7 ju7uj 777 jays 377 jokes 777 joists 577 juniors j7
The 17 jets carried 977 jocular passengers above 77 cities.
Those 277 jumping beans went to 77 junior scouts on May 17.
The 7 jockeys rode 77 jumpy horses between March 17 and 27.

8 ki ki8 ki8ik 888 keys 488 kites 888 knives 788 kittens k8
My 8 kennels housed 83 dogs, 28 kids, and 88 other animals.
The 18 kind ladies tied 88 knots in the 880 pieces of rope.
The 8 men saw 88 kelp bass, 38 kingfish, and 98 king crabs.

9 lo lo9 lo9ol 999 lads 599 larks 999 ladies 699 leaders 19
All 999 leaves fell from the 9 large oaks at 389 Largemont.
The 99 linemen put 399 large rolls of tape on for 19 games.
Those 99 lawyers put 899 legal-size sheets in the 19 limos.

0 ;p ;p0 ;p0p; 100 pens 900 pages 200 pandas 800 pencils ;0
There were 1,000 people who lived in the 300 private homes.
The 10 party stores are open from 1:00 p.m. until 9:00 p.m.
They edited 500 pages in 1 book and 1,000 pages in 2 books.

All numbers   a1a s2s d3d f4f f5f j6j j7j k8k 191 ;0; Add 5 and 9 and 16.
Those 67 jumpsuits were shipped to 238 Birch on October 14.
Invoices numbered 294 and 307 are to be paid by November 5.
Flight 674 is scheduled to leave from Gate 18 at 11:35 a.m.

All numbers   a1a s2s d3d f4f f5f j6j j7j k8k 191 ;0; Add 6 and 8 and 29.
That 349-page script called for 18 actors and 20 actresses.
The check for $50 was sent to 705 Garfield Street, not 507.
The 14 researchers asked the 469 Californians 23 questions.

All numbers   a1a s2s d3d f4f f5f j6j j7j k8k 191 ;0; Add 3 and 4 and 70.
They built 1,200 houses on the 345-acre site by the canyon.
Her research showed that gold was at 397 in September 1994.
For $868 extra, they bought 27 new books and 62 used books.

All numbers   a1a s2s d3d f4f f5f j6j j7j k8k 191 ;0; Add 5 and 7 and 68.
A bank auditor arrived on May 26, 1994, and left on May 30.
The 4 owners open the stores from 9:30 a.m. until 6:00 p.m.
After 1,374 miles on the bus, she must then drive 185 more.

Each of us has a physical boundary, our bodies, that 12
separates us from our actual environment. We also have a 23
nonphysical boundary that is harder to define but is just 35
as real. It is called personal space and it is that space to 47
which a person lays claim and will defend against perceived 59
threats. Each person has around him a "bubble" of space 70
which expands and contracts depending on relationships to 82
others, emotional state, cultural background, and the event 94
taking place. Most of us do not realize that this space is 106
created by all of the senses, which is how we know that 117
someone is standing too close even if our eyes are closed. 129

Each of us learns thousands of spatial cues as we are 140
growing up, and we know their meaning in the context of our 152
own culture. These cues release innate responses in us; as 164
we travel around the world and see how space is handled, we 176
encounter amazing variations. The important thing to keep 188
in mind is that folks from other cultures use their senses 200
and organize their space differently. Both these facts 211
reflect cultural differences in perception and in how life 223
is structured. 226

For instance, it is quite common in many parts of the 238
world for people to crowd around and to shove each other. 249
This occurs in contact cultures. In noncontact cultures 261
people are taught not to touch others. When we describe a 273
foreigner as aggressive or pushy, it may mean his or her 284
handling of space is different from ours. Spatial changes 296
give tone to communication, accent it, and at times mean 307
more than the spoken word. The conversational distance 318
between strangers shows the value of the dynamics of space 330
interaction. If a person gets too close, our reaction is 342
immediate and automatic: we move away. 350

| 1 | 2 | 3 | 4 | 5 | 6 | 7 | 8 | 9 | 10 | 11 | 12

Progressive Practice: Alphabet

This skillbuilding routine contains a series of 30-second timed writings that range from 16 wam to 100 wam. The first time you use these timed writings, select a passage that is 2 words a minute higher than your current speed. Take five 30-second timed writings on the passage, trying to complete it within 30 seconds with no errors. When you have achieved your goal, note your results. Then, move on to the next passage and repeat the procedure.

16 wam An author is the creator of a document.

18 wam Access means to call up data out of storage.

20 wam A byte represents one character to your computer.

22 wam To store means to insert data in memory for later use.

24 wam Soft copy is text that is displayed on your display screen.

26 wam Memory is that part of the word processor that stores information.

28 wam A menu is a list of choices to guide the operator through a function.

30 wam A sheet feeder is a device that will insert sheets of paper into a printer.

32 wam Boilerplate copy is a reusable passage that is stored until needed in a program.

34 wam Downtime is the length of time that equipment is not usable because of a malfunction.

36 wam To execute means to perform some action specified by an operator or by a computer program.

38 wam Output is the result of a word processing operation. It is in either printed or magnetic form.

40 wam Format refers to the physical features which affect the appearance and arrangement of your document.

42 wam A font is a set of type of one size or style which includes all letters, numbers, and punctuation marks.

Americans have always had a commitment to the inherent value of hard work dating back to the early colonial days when work was considered a vocation and a duty. True to their heritage, people in the United States still work hard, putting in extra time at their daily jobs and taking second or even third jobs at night.

Why are people working so hard? Besides the popular work ethic, there are two main reasons. The most obvious reason people work is to pay their bills. Quite simply, the more things cost, the more money we must make to keep our standards of living the same. The second reason is more unique to our culture. In the United States, work is a major indicator of self-worth. More than in any other country, folks in America tend to believe that what they do is who they are.

Sharp observers note three basic types of workers: those who work to live, those who live to work, and those who value both their work and personal lives. The first type work because they have financial pressures they feel they must meet. Satisfaction comes from their families, friends, and outside interests. In exchange for a job well done, they want to be treated with fairness and respect.

Another type of worker lives to work. These people, more than the other types, define their identity in terms of their work. Their definition of success requires a big salary and a fair amount of prestige and power. The final type of workers look for greater balance between their work and their personal lives. These workers value meaningful work that enhances their own development. If a job does not provide challenge, variety, and flexibility, they might move on. They often indicate that they feel little loyalty to the organization.

44 wam	Ergonomics is the science of adapting working conditions or equipment to meet most physical needs of workers.
46 wam	Home position is the starting position of a document; it is typically the upper left corner of the display screen.
48 wam	An electronic typewriter is a word processor which has only limited functions; it may or may not have a visual display.
50 wam	An optical scanner is a device that can read text and enter it into a word processor without the need to rekeyboard the data.
52 wam	Hardware refers to the physical equipment used, such as the central processing unit, display screen, keyboard, printer, or drive.
54 wam	A peripheral device is any piece of equipment that will extend the capabilities of a computer system but is not necessary for its operation.
56 wam	A split screen displays two or more different images at the same time; it can, for example, display two different pages of a legal document.
58 wam	A daisy wheel is a printing element that is made of plastic or metal and is used on different printers. Each character is at the end of a spoke.
60 wam	A cursor is a special character, often a blinking box or an underscore, which shows where the next keyed character will appear on the display screen.
62 wam	The hot zone is the area before the right margin, typically five to ten characters wide, where words may have to be divided or transferred to another line.
64 wam	Turnaround time is the length of time needed for a document to be keyboarded, edited, proofread, corrected if required, printed, and returned to the executive.
66 wam	A local area network is a system that uses cable or another means to allow high-speed communication among various kinds of electronic equipment within a small area.
68 wam	To search and replace means to direct the word processor to locate a character, word, or group of words wherever it occurs in the document and replace it with newer text.

Reviewing the seven previous Paced Practice exercises, it can be concluded that specific work habits or traits can play a major role in determining the success of a worker at a given job or task. Most managers would be quick to agree on the importance of these traits. These habits would most likely be on any performance appraisal forms you might see.

Of course, while these work habits are critical to the success of an individual on the job, there is also the need for specific competencies and abilities for a given job. A new worker must size up the needed blend of these traits in addition to those required competencies. As will be noted, a worker needs many various skills to be a success at work.

A major part of office activity is deciding what kinds of equipment will best meet company objectives. One should analyze every system, checking for easy and flexible usage. The next step is then defining the requirements of each job in terms of volume of work, space needed, and how each cost fits into the overall budget. Organize types of functions, above all.

A complete itemized checklist of every task identifies various functions performed by each employee. This type of data can be obtained through questionnaires, interviews, or observation techniques. Some subjects covered are document creation, employee interaction, scheduling, typing, filing, and telephoning. Technology must then be selected to match job needs.

70 wam   Indexing is the ability of a word processor to accumulate a list of words that appear in a document, including the page numbers, and then to print it out in alphabetic order.

72 wam   The control key is a special key that does not print, but when used with some other key will enable you to complete a special function such as checking spelling or changing fonts.

74 wam   A facsimile is an exact copy of a document. It is also the process by which images, such as typed letters, signatures, and graphs, are scanned, transmitted, and then reprinted on paper.

76 wam   Compatibility refers to the ability of one machine to share information with another machine or to communicate with the other machine. It can be accomplished by using hardware or software.

78 wam   Indexing refers to determining the captions or titles under which a document would most likely be found. The term also encompasses cross-referencing each document under any other possible title.

80 wam   Wraparound is the ability of a word processor to move words from one line to another line and from one page to the next page as a result of inserting and deleting text or changing side-margin widths.

82 wam   The office is a place in which administrative functions are performed for a company or some other types of businesses. The most common duties include filing, document processing, and scheduling meetings.

84 wam   List processing is an ability of the word processor to keep lists of data that can be upgraded and sorted in alphabetic or numeric order. A list can also be added to any document that is stored in the computer.

86 wam   A computer is an electronic device; it accepts data that is input and then processes the data and produces output. The computer performs its work by using one or more stored programs which provide the instructions.

88 wam   The configuration is the components which make up your word processing system. Most systems include a keyboard that is used for entering data, a central processing unit, at least one disk drive, a screen, and a printer.

68 wam   Enthusiasm is still another work trait that is eagerly
sought by most employers. Being enthusiastic means that an
employee has lots of positive energy. This is reflected in
actions toward the work as well as toward the employer. It
has been noted that enthusiasm can be catching. If workers
have enthusiasm, they can reach for gold.

It might pay to examine your level of enthusiasm for a
given job or project. Analyze whether you help to build up
people or whether you aid in giving coworkers a negative or
pessimistic attitude. There will always be quite a few job
opportunities for workers who are known to possess a wealth
of enthusiasm for the work they are given.

70 wam   Understanding is another work habit or trait that is a
requirement to be an excellent worker. In this society the
likelihood of working with people who have many differences
is quite probable. It is essential to have workers who can
understand and accept those differences that are evident in
the employees who are in the unit or the division.

On the job it is imperative that a worker realize that
employees will have different aptitudes and abilities. The
chances are also great that differences in race, ethnicity,
religion, work ethic, cultural background, and attitude can
be found. With so many possible differences, it is obvious
that a greater degree of understanding is needed.

90 wam   A keypad meter is a device used to monitor usage of the office copier. It can be either a key or a coded card which, when inserted into your copier, unlocks the machine for use and keeps track of the number of copies made.

92 wam   An open office is a modern approach to office planning that combines modular furniture with an open layout. The larger offices separate workers by removable partitions instead of permanent walls, which provide greater flexibility.

94 wam   To scroll means to show a large block of text by rolling it either horizontally or vertically past your display screen. As the text disappears from the top section of the monitor, new text appears at the bottom section of the monitor.

96 wam   Justification is a form of printing that inserts additional space between words or characters to force each line to the same length; it can be called right justification, since it forces all the lines to end at the same point at the right.

98 wam   A stop code is a command that makes a printer halt while it is printing to permit an operator to insert text, change the font style, or change the kind of paper in the printer. To resume printing, the operator must use a special key or command.

100 wam   A computerized message system is a class of electronic mail that enables any operator to key a message on any computer terminal and have the message stored for later retrieval by the recipient who can then display the message on his or her terminal.

62 wam

Another trait or work habit essential for success on a job is accuracy. Accurate workers are in much demand. The worker who tallies numbers checks them very carefully to be certain there are no errors. When reviewing documents, the accurate worker has excellent proofreading skills to locate all errors.

Since accuracy is required on all jobs, it is critical to possess this trait. An accurate worker is usually quite thorough in all work that is undertaken or completed. If a worker checks all work which is done and analyzes all steps taken, it is likely that a high level of accuracy should be attained.

64 wam

Efficiency is another work habit that is much admired. This means that a worker is quick to complete an assignment and to begin work on the next job. Efficient workers think about saving steps and time when working. For example, one should plan to make one trip to the copier versus going for each individual job.

Being efficient means having all the right tools to do the right job. An efficient worker is able to zip along on required jobs, concentrating on doing the job right. Being efficient also means having all needed supplies for the job within reach. This means that a worker can produce more in a little less time.

66 wam

Cooperation is another desired work habit. This means that an employee is thinking of all the team members when a decision is made. A person who cooperates is willing to do something for the benefit of the entire group. As a member of a work unit or team, it is absolutely essential that you take extra steps to cooperate.

Cooperation may mean being a good sport if you have to do something you would rather not do. It could also mean a worker helps to correct a major error made by someone else. If a worker has the interests of the organization at heart, it should be a little easier to make a quick decision to be cooperative in most endeavors.

Progressive Practice: Numbers

This skillbuilding routine contains a series of 30-second timed writings that range from 16 wam to 70 wam. The first time you use these timed writings, select a passage that is 4 to 6 words a minute *lower* than your current alphabetic speed. (The reason for selecting a lower speed goal is that sentences with numbers are more difficult to key.) Take five 30-second timed writings on the passage, trying to complete it within 30 seconds with no errors. When you have achieved your goal, move on to the next passage and repeat the procedure.

16 wam   There were now 21 children in Room 211.

18 wam   Fewer than 12 of the 121 boxes have arrived.

20 wam   Maybe 2 of the 21 applicants met all 12 criteria.

22 wam   There were 34 letters addressed to 434 West Cranbrook.

24 wam   Jan reported that there were 434 freshmen and 43 transfers.

26 wam   The principal assigned 3 of those 4 students to Room 343 at noon.

28 wam   Only 1 or 2 of the 34 latest invoices were more than 1 page in length.

30 wam   They met 11 of the 12 players who received awards from 3 of the 4 coaches.

32 wam   Those 5 vans carried 46 passengers on the first trip and 65 on the next 3 trips.

34 wam   We first saw 3 and then 4 beautiful eagles on Route 65 at 5 a.m. on Monday, June 12.

36 wam   The 6 companies produced 51 of the 62 records that received awards for 3 of 4 categories.

38 wam   The 12 trucks hauled the 87 cows and 65 horses to the farm, which was about 21 miles northeast.

40 wam   She moved from 87 Bayview Drive to 657 Cole Street and then 3 blocks south to 412 Gulbranson Avenue.

42 wam   My 7 or 8 buyers ordered 7 dozen in sizes 5 and 6 after the 14 to 32 percent discounts had been granted.

44 wam   There were 34 women and 121 men waiting in line at the gate for the 65 to 87 tickets to the Cape Cod concert.

Going to work has always been a major part of being an adult. Of course, many adolescents also have jobs that can keep them extremely busy. The work one does or the job one holds is a critical factor in determining many other things about the way a person is able to live.

Various work habits are as crucial to one's success as the actual job skills and knowledge that one brings to that job. If one is dependable, organized, accurate, efficient, cooperative, enthusiastic, and understanding, one should be quickly recognized by most supervisors.

Being dependable is a desirable trait to have. When a worker says that something will be done by a specific time, it is quite assuring to a manager to know that a dependable worker is assigned to it. Workers who are dependable learn to utilize their time to achieve maximum results.

This trait can also be evident with workers who have a good record for attendance. If a firm is to be productive, it is essential to have workers on the job. Of course, the dependable employee not only is on the job, but also is the worker who can be counted on to be there on time.

Organization is another trait that can be described as necessary to exhibiting good work habits. To be organized, a worker should have a sense of being able to plan the work that is to be done and then to work that plan. It is quite common to notice that competent workers are well organized.

If an office worker is organized, requests are handled promptly, correspondence is answered quickly, and paperwork does not accumulate on the desk. In addition, an organized office worker returns all telephone calls without delay and makes a list of things to be accomplished on a daily basis.

46 wam   Steve had listed 5 or 6 items on Purchase Order 241 when he saw that Purchase Requisition 87 contained 3 or 4 more.

48 wam   The item numbered 278 will sell for about 90 percent of the value of the 16 items that have a code number shown as 435.

50 wam   The manager stated that 98 of the 750 randomly selected new valves had about 264 defects, far in excess of the usual 31 norm.

52 wam   Half of the 625 volunteers received about 90 percent of the charity pledges. Approximately 83 of the 147 agencies will get funds.

54 wam   Merico hired 94 part-time workers to help the 378 full-time employees during that 62-day period when sales go up by 150 percent or more.

56 wam   Kaye only hit 1 for 4 in the first 29 games after an 8-game streak in which she batted 3 for 4. She then hit at a .570 average for 3 games.

58 wam   The mailman delivered 98 letters during the week to 734 Oak Street and also delivered 52 letters to 610 Pioneer Road as he returned on Route 58.

60 wam   Pat said that about 1 of 5 of the 379 swimmers had a chance of being among the top 20. The finest 6 of those 48 divers will receive about 16 awards.

62 wam   It rained from 3 to 6 inches, and 18 of the 21 farmers were fearful that 4 to 7 inches more would flood about 950 acres along 3 miles of the new Route 78.

64 wam   The 7 sacks weighed 48 pounds, more than the 30 pounds that I had thought. All 24 think the 92-pound bag is at least 6 or 9 or 15 pounds beyond what it weighs.

66 wam   They ordered 7 of those 8 options for 54 of the 63 vehicles last month. They now own over 120 dump trucks for use in 9 of the 15 regions in the new 20-county area.

68 wam   Andrew was 8 or 9 years old when they moved to 632 Glendale Street from the 1700 block of Horseshoe Lane about 45 miles directly southwest of Boca Raton, Florida 33434.

70 wam   Claire had read 575 pages in the 760-page book by March 30; David had read only 468 pages. Claire has read 29 of those optional books since October 9, and David has read 18.

50 wam

We all want to work in a pleasant environment where we are surrounded with jovial people who never make a mistake. The realities of the real world tell us, however, that this likely will not happen; the use of corrective action may be required.

For the very reason that this trait is so difficult to cultivate, all of us should strive to improve the manner in which we accept constructive criticism. By recognizing the positive intent of supervisors, each of us will accrue extra benefits.

52 wam

The worker and the firm might be compared in some ways with a child and the family unit. Just as a child at times disagrees with a parent, the worker might question policies of the organization. In both cases, policies must exist for conflict resolution.

One option for a vexed child is to run away from home; an employee may type a letter of resignation. A far better option in both situations is the discussion of differences. The child remains loyal to family, and an employee remains loyal to the company.

54 wam

The person who aspires to a role in management must be equal to the challenge. Individuals who have supervisory responsibilities must make fine judgments as decisions are formed that affect the entire organization. The challenge of managing is trying and lonely.

While other labels are sometimes used to explain basic management functions, the concepts remain the same. The four main functions are involved with planning, organizing, actuating, and controlling of such components as personnel, production, and sales of products.

Paced Practice

The Paced Practice skillbuilding routine builds speed and accuracy in short, easy steps, using individualized goals and immediate feedback. You may use this program at any time after completing Lesson 9.

This section contains a series of 2-minute timed writings for speeds ranging from 12 wam to 74 wam. The first time you use these timed writings, select a passage that is 2 wam higher than your current keyboarding speed. Use this two-stage practice pattern to achieve each speed goal—first concentrate on speed, and then work on accuracy.

If you are not using the correlated software, have someone call out each 1/4-minute interval as you key. Strive to be at the appropriate point in the passage marked by a small superior number at each 1/4-minute interval.

SPEED GOAL. Take three 2-minute timed writings on the same passage until you can complete it in 2 minutes without regard to errors.

When you have achieved your speed goal, work on accuracy.

ACCURACY GOAL. To key accurately, you need to slow down—just a bit. Therefore, to reach your accuracy goal, drop back 2 wam to the previous passage. Take three 2-minute timed writings on this passage until you can complete it in 2 minutes with no more than 2 errors.

For example, if you achieved a speed goal of 54 wam, you should then work on an accuracy goal of 52 wam. When you have achieved 52 wam for accuracy, you would then move up 4 wam (for example, to the 56-wam passage) and work for speed again.

12 wam

What is the meaning of work? Why do most people work? The concept of work and careers is of interest to you.

14 wam

When doing something that is required, you think of it as working.

When doing something that you want to do, you think of it as fun.

16 wam

We often do not consider the amount of time and effort spent doing a task.

If we did, we would realize that many people work hard even while playing.

18 wam

For example, people sweat, strain, or even suffer from discomfort when playing sports.

People do this for fun. If they were required to do this, they might not be willing.

42 wam

Newly employed workers are quite often judged by their skills in informal verbal situations. A simple exchange of greetings when being introduced to a client is an example that illustrates one situation.

A new employee might have a very good idea at a small-group meeting. However, unless that idea can be verbalized to other members in a clear, concise manner, members will not develop proper appreciation.

44 wam

Many supervisors state that they want their workers to use what they refer to as common sense. Common sense tells a person to answer the phone, to open the mail, and to lock the door at the end of the working day.

It is easy to see that this trait equates with the use of sound judgment. The prize employee should desire to capitalize on each new experience that will help him or her to use better judgment when making decisions.

46 wam

Every person should set as a goal the proper balancing of the principal components in one's life. Few people will disagree with the conviction that the family is the most important of the four main ingredients in human life.

Experts in the career education field are quick to say that family must be joined with leisure time, vocation, and citizenship in order to encompass one's full "career." The right balance results in satisfaction and success.

48 wam

As we become an information society, there is an ever-increasing awareness of office costs. Such costs are labor intensive, and those who must justify them are increasingly concerned about workers' use of time management principles.

Researchers in the time management area have developed several techniques for examining office tasks and analyzing routines. The realization that "time is money" is only the beginning and must be followed with an educational program.

20 wam

Spending time on a job is work. For most people, work is something that they do to stay alive.

Today, work means more than staying alive. People expect different rewards from their careers.

22 wam

Work can be interesting, and more and more workers are now saying that their work should be interesting.

Sure, there are many boring jobs, and every job always has some less exciting and more routine features.

24 wam

Today there are many different types of jobs from which you may choose. They range from the routine to the exotic.

If you begin your planning early, you can work at different types of jobs and learn from the experience of each one.

26 wam

Workers tend to identify with their careers, and their careers in a real sense give them a sense of importance and belonging.

People's jobs also help determine how they spend their spare time, who their friends are, and sometimes even where they live.

28 wam

Work can take place in school, in a factory or office, at home, or outside; it can be done for money or experience or even voluntarily.

It should be quite clear that work can be any activity that involves a type of responsibility. The same thing can be said about a job.

30 wam

A career relates to work that is done for pay. But it means more than a particular job; it is the pattern of work done throughout your lifetime.

A career suggests looking ahead, planning, and setting goals and reaching them. The well-planned career becomes a part of the individual's life.

Whichever career path is selected,[1] the degree of pride shown in one's work[2] has to be at a high level. Others will[3] judge you by how well you do your work.[4]

Your self-image is affected by what[1] you believe others think of you as well[2] as by what you think of yourself. The[3] quality of your efforts impacts on both.[4]

If a matter is important to a supervisor or to a firm,[1] it should be important to[2] the employee too. The competent person can[3] be relied on to prioritize and execute.[4]

The higher your job-satisfaction level, the greater is[1] the likelihood that you will[2] be pleased with all aspects of your life.[3] Positive attitudes will bring rewards.[4]

Whenever people work together, attention[1] must be given to the human relations factor.[2] A quality organization will concern itself[3] with interpersonal skills needed by workers.[4]

Respect, courtesy, and patience are examples[1] of just a few of the words that combine[2] to bring about positive human relationships in[3] the office as well as in other situations.[4]

The alarm didn't go off. The bus was late.[1] The baby-sitter was sick. The car wouldn't[2] start. And for some, the list of excuses goes on.[3] Be thankful that this list is not yours.[4]

You will keep the tardy times to a minimum[1] by planning and anticipating. And you will realize[2] that those who jump the gun by quitting work[3] early at the end of the day have a bad habit.[4]

Some people take forever to become acquainted[1] with the office routines. Some must have every task[2] explained along with a list of things to be done.[3] Some go ahead and search for new things to do.[4]

Initiative is a trait that managers look for[1] in people who are promoted while on the job.[2] A prized promotion with a nice pay raise can[3] be the reward for demonstrating that a person has new ideas.[4]